LEADERS
WHO CHANGED THE
WORLD

LEADERS
WHO CHANGED THE
WORLD

by Gordon Kerr

Futura

A *Futura* Book

First published by Futura in 2009

Copyright © Omnipress 2009

ISBN: 978-0-7088-0162-8

Produced by Omnipress Ltd, United Kingdom

Printed in INDIA

Futura
An imprint of Little, Brown Book Group
100 Victoria Embankment
London EC4Y 0DY

Photo credits: Getty Images

CONTENTS

III: THE ENLIGHTENED WORLD

IV: THE NINETEENTH CENTURY

V: THE MODERN WORLD

INTRODUCTION

MOST OF US are happy just to get through life as best we can, filling the space from birth to death with little of importance for anyone but ourselves, our family and friends. There is a rare breed, however, that needs more than that from life. They take the initiative, grasp the nettle, seize the day – they are risk-takers, challengers of the mundane and the humdrum and they make a difference with their lives. Quite simply, they are leaders.

Leadership is a special quality. It is something that cannot really be learned in school or college. Rather, it is innate; you are born with it. How else can one explain the peculiar drive that powers the extraordinary human beings in *Leaders Who Changed the World*? How else to explain the motivation of conquerors such as Alexander the Great, Genghis Khan or Napoleon? They were born leaders, people who inspired others to do extraordinary things. Throughout history, people have had no hesitation in giving up their lives and following people such as these, sometimes travelling thousands of miles and being away from their home and loved ones for many years, unstintingly prepared even to make the ultimate sacrifice for their leaders, if necessary, by laying down their lives for them in battle.

Many, of course, come from generations of leaders. Winston Churchill, Britain's inspirational, cigar-smoking Prime Minister during World War II, for instance, was descended from the great English soldier and statesman, John Churchill, 1st Duke of Marlborough who played a leading part in crushing the Duke of Monmouth's rebellion against James II in 1685. Hannibal, the astonishing Carthaginian general, who led his men and elephants from Spain into Italy where they became a thorn in the flesh of Rome for thirteen years, had a famous general for a father. The South African Zulu chief, Shaka Zulu, the Angolan warrior queen, Nzinga Mbande, Mongol Emperor, Genghis Khan – all came from illustrious families in their societies, where their forbears had been kings and queens and conquerors.

Some, of course, came from nowhere. Margaret Thatcher, above all, perfectly demonstrates the notion that leaders are born, not created. Born Margaret Hilda Roberts in the English backwater of Grantham, her father was a humble grocer, although he was also a Conservative councillor. She studied chemistry, but her leadership qualities soon began to take over and she single-mindedly led Britain for eleven, often contentious, years. Horatio Nelson, one of Britain's most courageous and ingenious naval commanders, was the son of a vicar; Joseph Stalin's father was a cobbler who also happened to be a drunkard; Israeli Prime Minister Golda Meir's father was a carpenter; Nazi leader, Adolf Hitler's father was a customs official; and gang-leader Al Capone's father, like Margaret Thatcher's, was a grocer. These were people of humble origins who rose above their colleagues and associates to lead their army, party or country.

How leadership is used, of course, varies from person to person. Sometimes it is twisted and used for nefarious aims. Adolf Hitler, who rose no higher than the rank of corporal in the German army because his superiors did not believe that he possessed the requisite leadership qualities, used his charismatic personality to mesmerise an entire nation into perpetrating the most heinous of deeds. The Nazi death camps bear witness to that. Mao Zedong, Chinese Communist leader, took Hitler's personality cult and refined it until he was synonymous with his country. And in a sense, he created China in his own image, implementing sweeping changes as and when he wanted. His call for a Cultural Revolution in the mid-1960s, demonstrates the phenomenal hold that one person can have over a nation of hundreds of millions. His Red Guards rampaged unquestioningly through China for years, killing and destroying, erasing thousands of years of Chinese culture and ruining the lives of anyone deemed to be 'counter-revolutionary'.

On the other hand, leadership can, of course, be used for good. Nelson Mandela and Mahatma Gandhi provide us with the best examples. Both were freedom-fighters, fully engaged in the struggle for self-determination and democracy for their respective peoples. But they fought without weapons. Mandela used the eloquence of his oratory and the certain knowledge that he was on the side of right, to bring down the evil regime of apartheid in South Africa. Gandhi brought his extraordinary concept of *satyagraha* – non-violent protest – to his battle for Indian independence. Amazingly, with only very few exceptions, he inculcated it into the minds of his fellow Indians, so that a whole nation was involved in this type of protest. Personally, too, he made huge sacrifices. He would fast for days as a protest, acts that took a terrible toll on his body and his health, but, eventually, he occupied so much of the moral high ground that the British had no option in 1949 but to give India the independence for which Gandhi had been fighting for more than thirty years.

Like Gandhi and Mandela, many leaders have emerged when their country called on them. Movements have to be led by someone and when that someone is as extraordinary as North Vietnamese leader Ho Chi Minh, then success is assured. 'Uncle Ho' as he was affectionately known, was a stick-thin little man with a paucity of military experience, but who led his nation to victory against the might of two of the world's great powers – France and the United States. The achievements of his army number amongst some of the great military exploits of the 20th or indeed any century. The Ho Chi Minh Trail, the 600-mile-long complex of roads, bicycle paths, rivers and footpaths, has been described as one of the greatest military engineering accomplishments of the 20th century and it took a leader of astonishing quality and organisational skills to facilitate the building of such a thing without equipment and technology.

Some military leaders in history, of course, have neither fought for independence for their country nor defended themselves against enemies. They were simply rapacious conquerors who saw an opportunity for wealth and advancement and grabbed it. Alexander the Great, Genghis Khan and Tamerlane invaded countries because they could. They built vast empires and spent almost their entire lives fighting and conquering. Napoleon Bonaparte was a military genius who for years defeated every army sent against him. He would always say, 'Give me lucky generals', when asked whether skill, training or intelligence lay behind his success. It was his leadership, though, that really made the difference and the admirable audacity of a man who would lead a huge army in an invasion of the vast territory that was Russia. A step too far, of course – as it would also prove for Adolf Hitler almost 150 years later – but the astonishing thing is that he convinced his people that it was possible. And perhaps that is the defining element in the leader's make-up – the ability to convince followers that they can achieve the impossible.

The ultimate leaders who change the world, however, are probably not those who change the borders of countries – such as Napoleon and the other great conquering emperors – or devise the systems by which nations are ruled – such as Joseph Stalin. Rather, the ultimate leaders must be those that change the way we think and believe. The lives of Jesus Christ, Buddha and Muhammad are blurred by myth and legend that has grown around them in the centuries since the times in which they are believed to have lived. Their beliefs and the religions that have grown around them, however, survive even now and influence the daily lives of the majority of the people on earth. They provide us with astonishing examples of leadership that reverberates through the centuries.

Ultimately, we all leave our mark on the world in small ways. The men and women in this book have left their mark on the world in big and extraordinary ways that inspire us and make us believe that anything is possible. They truly are leaders who changed the world.

I
THE ANCIENT WORLD

PLATO

THE GREAT GREEK philosopher, Plato, was born into a good, well-respected family either in Athens or on the nearby island of Aegina around 428 BCE. His father, Ariston, claimed to be descended from Codrus, the last king of Athens and Melanthus, king of Messenia. His mother, Perictione, was related to the early Greek lawmaker and statesman, Solon, who is often credited with being the founder of Athenian democracy. She was also the sister of Charmides and niece of Critias who were both leading figures in the Thirty Tyrants, the brief oligarchic regime that ruled following the Peloponnesian War in 403 BCE.

Plato was not his given name. When he was born, he was named Aristocles but was given the name Plato, it is said, by his wrestling coach, Ariston of Argos, who nicknamed him 'Platon' which means 'broad', believed to be a reference to his large figure.

Ariston died while Plato was very young and Perictione married for a second time, to her uncle Pyrilampes who had been prominent in the political party run by the great Greek statesman, Pericles, who had died the year before Plato's birth. Pyrilampes had also been ambassador to the Persian court. Plato spent the majority of his childhood being brought up in Pyrilampes's house. He would also have known the philosopher, Socrates, from a very early age, as Critias and Charmides, both close friends of Socrates were also friends of Pyrilampes.

It is highly probable that, given his social class and connections, Plato's ambitions lay, as a young man, in politics. He was, in fact, canvassed by a conservative faction in Athens to join them, but he resisted their offers and encouragement and was soon glad that he had done so, given the violence to which the conservatives resorted soon after. When democracy was once again restored following the demise of oligarchy, he became optimistic but before long realised that there was no point in a man of conscience such as himself being involved in Athenian politics.

In 399, Socrates, a constant critic of Athenian society, morals and politics, was tried and condemned to death for corrupting the minds of the youth of Athens. Plato and other supporters were forced to take refuge temporarily at Megara with Eucleides, founder of the Megarian school of philosophy, following which he travelled extensively, visiting other parts of Greece as well as Egypt and Italy. He was forty years of age by this time and was disgusted by the sensuality of life he found in Italy.

Around the year 387, Plato felt it was safe to return to Athens and there he founded an institution – one of the earliest known schools in Western Civilisation – where men would be able to pursue philosophical and scientific research as well as teach others. It became known as the Academy because it was located on a plot of land in the Grove of Hecademus or Academeus. The Academy was in existence until 529 BC but was finally shut down by the Byzantine Emperor Justinian I who feared that it was inhibiting the spread of Christianity. During its time, however, it educated a great many well-known intellectuals, the most prominent probably being Aristotle.

Plato considered the Academy to be his greatest work, more so than his writings. When he compares written works with the living mind as a vehicle for philosophy in the *Seventh Letter*, he falls on the side of the living mind.

Every important piece of mathematical work done in the 4th century came from someone who had been taught at Plato's Academy. Theaetetus, the creator of a solid geometry, was a member, as was Euxodus of Cnidus, author of the doctrine of proportion to be found in Euclid's *Elements*, and inventor of a method of finding the area and volume of curvilinear figures by exhaustion.

He also devised an astronomical scheme of concentric spheres that Aristotle would later develop further. Speusippus, Plato's nephew and the man who succeeded Plato at the Academy, wrote on natural history and Aristotle worked in the field of biology at this early point in his career.

The Academy also featured jurisprudence and practical legislation. Former students such as Aristonymus, Xenocrates, Delios of Ephesus and Phormion went on to advise and counsel great kings such as Alexander the Great.

The Academy would continue to be a centre for learning for 250 years and can confidently be claimed to have been the first university.

While also being influenced by philosophers such as Heracleitus and the Pythagoreans, the greatest influence on the young Plato was undoubtedly the great philosopher, Socrates. Although he was in all likelihood not a 'disciple' of Socrates, he was a close friend and held him in great esteem. From him he took his commitment to philosophy, his rational method and his concern for ethical matters.

Plato wrote thirty-six works, none of which has been lost through the centuries. He wrote a series of *Dialogues* in which he himself did not appear, the greatest of which are without doubt, *Symposium*, *Phaedo* and *Republic*. The words in the books are uttered by real, historical characters, often with Socrates as the protagonist. It is difficult to know, therefore, if the words being spoken actually represent the opinions of the people saying them. In this way, of course, Plato was able to avoid committing himself to whatever was being said. However, some suggest that they were merely mouthpieces for his own opinions.

His best known and most influential work, studied by students of philosophy ever since it was written, is *Republic*. Written in approximately 380 BCE, it consists of a narration by Socrates, describing a discussion that had taken place the previous day at the house of Polemarchus at Piraeus near Athens. In it, Plato provides a description of the ideal community or state, ruled by philosopher-kings and with a rigid and well-defined social hierarchy. It also defines what a philosopher is and argues about different forms of government. He famously uses the Allegory of the Cave in which he imagines a group of people who have lived all their lives, chained up in a cave facing nothing but a blank wall. Onto the wall are projected the shadows of things passing the cave entrance and the inhabitants of the cave begin to ascribe forms to the shadows which are the only reality they have. Plato describes the philosopher as resembling a prisoner who is freed from the cave and realises that the shadows on the cave wall do not constitute reality because he can perceive the true form of reality rather than just the shadows the prisoners are seeing. In Plato's *Theory of the Forms*, to which this allegory is related, he asserts that the highest and most fundamental type of reality is not the ever-changing material world presented to us by our senses, but, rather, Forms or 'Ideas'. *Knowledge of Forms* is the only real knowledge.

The work of Plato has had a resonance from his time until today. He gave us the thoughts of Socrates and he helped to father generations of philosophers, scientists and mathematicians through the founding of the Academy. His influence on political and social thinkers cannot be underestimated and the changes he brought to the way people thought were both pervasive and profound.

BUDDHA

PRINCE GAUTAMA SIDDHARTA was probably born around 563 BCE and may have died around 483 BCE, although recent debate about the date of his death places it within twenty years either side of the year 400 BCE. Born into a life of luxury and indulgence, he would abandon it all and, as Buddha, he would lead a life of contemplation and deprivation and go on to found one of the world's great religions.

Much that is written about Buddha is couched in myth and it is extremely difficult to separate the truth from the legends and miracles that surround him. A great deal has been taken from Buddhist texts and his followers certainly put a great deal of effort into recording the events of his life as well as his teachings.

He was said to have been a handsome man and was strong enough as a young man to be asked by one king to join his army as a general. What seems to be known for sure is that Buddha's father was Suddhodana, Rajah, or king of a Nepalese warrior tribe, the Sakyas. En route to her father's kingdom, his mother Maya – a Koliyan princess – gave birth to Siddharta in a grove known as Lumbini, in the foothills of the Himalayas, at the foot of Mount Palpa, twenty-five kilometers from the city of Kapilavastu. She is said to have dreamed on the night of his conception that a white elephant with six white tusks entered her right side. She died seven days after his birth and Siddharta was brought up by her sister, Maha Pajapati.

As ever on such occasions there seemed to be numerous predictions about the future of the boy. The hermit prophet, Asita, claimed that he would be either a great king or a great holy man; eight Brahmin scholars are said to have agreed.

Desperate to prevent his precious son from undertaking religious vows, Suddhodana lavished all kinds of luxury on him. He gave him three palaces that he had specially built for him and shielded him from all religious teaching. Siddharta was allowed to experience all of the pleasures of the senses, married at the age of sixteen to his cousin, Yasodhara and had a son named Rahula. For the majority of the time, he lived in a sumptuous walled palace with gardens, fountains and evenings filled with music and dancing.

At the age of twenty-nine, however, he did just what his father feared – he abandoned his family and his luxurious lifestyle and began to devote himself to spiritual pursuits and yogic practices. His existence changed from one of contented indulgence to one of extreme austerity. It is said to have occurred because one day he succeeded in escaping from his luxurious walled compound with his servant, Channa, to observe the lives of the ordinary people of the nearby town. Seeing an old man, a corpse and a monk, made him realise that he would, like the old man and the dead man, succumb to old age and disease one day but could also mitigate the miseries of *samsara* (daily life) by achieving serenity like the monk.

He shaved his head, donned the saffron robes of the monk and left his palace on his horse Kanthaka, riding to a cave complex in the hills close to Rajgriha, capital of the kingdom of Magadha – an episode in his life known as 'The Great Departure'. In the caves lived many hermits who had renounced the everyday cares of the world and now sought enlightenment in ascetic isolation. Siddharta failed to find a satisfactory teacher amongst the hermits and neither did the yogic practices with which he experimented, such as breath control, help him. He then tried the path of self-mortification, denying himself worldly goods, including food. Eating a leaf or a nut a day, he almost starved himself to death and also almost died when he collapsed in a river and came close to drowning while bathing. This was obviously not the way to enlightenment, he reasoned.

He then recalled an incident from his childhood when he had fallen into a blissful, focused state as he watched his father start the season's ploughing. He decided to study meditation and the art of breathing properly. It was called the Middle Way, a moderate path to enlightenment.

Eventually, he arrived at the blissful state to which he had been aspiring, while seated under a banyan tree in Bihar, now known as the Bodhi tree. He had resolved not to rise until he had found the Truth and meditated there from sunrise to sundown, remaining there the next day and then the next. He remained there for forty-nine days in total and, aged thirty-five, he arrived at the state known as Nirvana, freedom from both suffering and from the cycle of re-birth; an awareness of life's real questions and a religious way of dealing with them. From that day on, he was known as Buddha – the Enlightened One – and became determined to share his new-found understanding of the nature and cause of human suffering with the world. His realisations would be categorised into the Four Noble Truths and after achieving Nirvana, he possessed the Nine Characteristics with which every Buddha is endowed.

The Four Noble Truths can be characterised as saying that suffering is an inherent part of existence; that the origin of suffering is ignorance and the results of that ignorance are attachment and craving; that attachment and craving can be stopped; and that following the Noble Eightfold Path will lead to a cessation of attachment and craving and, therefore, suffering.

The Eightfold Path is right understanding; right thought; right speech; right action; right livelihood; right effort; right mindfulness, and right concentration.

It has been said that the Buddha doubted whether he should teach the Dharma (Truth) to human beings, that it might actually be too difficult for them to understand. But, eventually, he decided to become a teacher and set about converting people to the Truth.

His first conversions were two merchants, Tapussa and Bhallika, who became lay disciples. He travelled to Varanasi (modern-day Benares) and delivered his first sermon to a group of five men with whom he had previously sought enlightenment. They became his first monks. In total, he created sixty disciples and sent them out to spread the word. His followers increased in number, drawn from every caste in India, from high-caste Brahmins to people of the lowest castes, and soon there were over a thousand in the sangha or community. They were obliged to become monks, if they wished to be full-time members of his order and there were strict rules of conduct.

For the remainder of his life, the Buddha travelled incessantly on the Gangetic Plain teaching and preaching his message to anyone who would listen. He converted nobility, murderers, street sweepers and many people who believed in other religions and faith systems. Race and class were irrelevant to him. What mattered was the Truth.

The only period of the year during which the *sangha*, in common with ascetics of other religions, did not travel, was during the four months of the rainy season. The constant rain and subsequent flooding was one reason, of course, but it was really so that they would not stamp on and kill any submerged animal life. This period was known as the *vassana*.

After the first *vassana*, at Varanasi, Buddha travelled to visit Bimbisara, King of Magadha. Here, his two most important disciples, Sariputta and Mahamoggallana, were converted.

By now, his father Suddhodana was beginning to hear stories about his son and he dispatched men to request that he return to Kapilavastu to visit. Buddha agreed and made the two-year journey by foot back to his home, preaching, needless to say, the length of the route. His father was horrified when his son arrived and started begging for food around the houses of the town, but Buddha explained that this may not be the way of his father's warrior lineage, but it was the way of his Buddha lineage. Nonetheless, he accompanied him to the palace for a meal. Many members of his family, including his father and his former wife, were converted during this visit. One cousin, Devadatta, became a monk, but made three attempts to assassinate his cousin. On the first, he hired a group of archers to kill him, but when they met Buddha, they were

21

immediately converted; the second time, he rolled a huge boulder down a hill, but it only injured the holy man on the foot; the third occasion involved an elephant being set loose that had been plied with alcohol – again Devadatta failed. He gave up and formed a breakaway *sangha*.

At the age of eighty, Buddha announced that he would soon reach the state known as Parinirvana – the final deathless state of abandoning the earthly body. One night he ate a meal and was taken violently ill and, after asking his disciples if they had any questions or doubts, he died. His last words were said to be: 'All composite things pass away. Strive for your own liberation with diligence.' His body was cremated and placed in monuments, some of which are believed to have survived to this day.

Nowadays, Buddhism is practically extinct in its country of origin, India, but it spread like wildfire throughout the sub-continent until in the 3rd century BCE, it was the dominant religion, a dominance encouraged by the conversion of the great King Asoka. It later went into decline as Buddhists were persecuted by Brahminism in the 7th and 8th centuries CE and as Islam arrived.

Nonetheless, it is followed in different forms in many parts of the world. Theravada Buddhism, using Pali as its scriptural language, is the dominant form in Cambodia, Laos, Thailand, Sri Lanka and Burma. In China, Korea, Taiwan, Singapore and Vietnam, Mahayana Buddhism, using Chinese scriptures, is practiced. Tibetan Buddhism can be found in Tibet, Bhutan, Mongolia, parts of China, Nepal and the Russian Federation.

It is estimated that Buddhism is practiced by at least 350 million followers and it is the fourth-largest religion in the world after Christianity, Islam and Hinduism.

PERICLES

IT IS INDEED rare for a period in history to be named after a person, but there are, of course, the 'Elizabethan Age' and the 'Victorian period'. One of the few other examples is the 'Age of Pericles', a period in ancient Greece from 461 until 429 BCE, when the influential Athenian statesman, orator and general led Athens, creating an empire. At the same time he made his city the cultural and artistic capital of the known world, helping it to become the birthplace of democracy of which he was a fervent advocate.

He was born in 495 BCE in the Cholargos suburb in the northeast of Athens. His father, Xanthippus, was a wealthy Athenian politician and general who had been ostracised in 484 BCE. Ostracism was an Athenian practice where someone could be expelled from the city for a period of ten years, usually to prevent dangerous confrontations between politicians, or to prevent a politician from becoming a tyrant. In Xanthippus's case, however, the ostracism lasted just five years and he returned to Athens to lead the Athenian troops taking part in the Greek victory over the Persians at Mycale.

Pericles is said to have been a quiet, self-controlled child, devoting his time to study with some of the most notable teachers of the day, amongst whom were the philosophers, Protagoras, Zeno of Elea and Anaxagoras who became an influential, close friend. He was the first philosopher to attribute the order of the world to intelligence rather than chance or necessity.

He was an extremely skilful orator and he became famous in Athens while still young. He entered politics around 472 BCE, joining the democratic party. Taking it very seriously, he lived frugally and gave up going out with friends or attending social events. He rarely appeared in public, only being seen on important occasions. When he did, however, his oratory astonished and impressed his audience.

The democratic party, to which Pericles belonged, became the dominant faction in Athenian politics and Pericles pursued a populist strategy in order to please the public. Pericles won the hearts of the people of Athens and they began to overrule the decisions of their elected representatives. Soon, Pericles, champion of the people, was the most powerful man in the city

Pericles continued to introduce crowd-pleasing policies such as one which permitted the poor to watch theatrical dramas free of charge with the state picking up the bill. He also increased the wage paid to people serving on the jury of the Athens Supreme Court. He did, however, introduce a controversial new rule of Athenian citizenship – namely, that to be a citizen of Athens, you had to have Athenian parentage on both your mother's and your father's side.

He is said to have tried to bring stability to Athens by giving the lower classes access to the political system and Athenian public offices. Previously, the very lowliness of their birth, or quite simply their lack of financial means, had barred them from these. Pericles believed that Athenian military might would come from the poor having these rights. Cimon, his rival, believed the opposite. He considered democracy to have peaked and that Pericles' reforms would only damage the state.

The murder in 461 BCE by a member of the opposition of Pericles' ally, the leader of the democratic party, Ephialtes, had left him as leader and the reforms begun by Ephialtes would be built upon and completed by Pericles in the course of the next few decades.

The first military action into which he led Athens was the First Peloponnesian War. Athens and Sparta had long been rivals, but an uneasy peace had prevailed for a while in the region, leading the Delian League.

A revolt of *helots* – slaves – in Sparta, precipitated the war. Sparta, unable to deal with it alone, summoned help from its allies in the

Delian League, an alliance of Greek states of which Athens, preeminent in the region, was leader. Athens sent the general, Cimon, a rival to Pericles, at the head of a force of 4,000 men, but when an attack on the helots was unsuccessful, the Spartans became suspicious of the Athenians' intentions and dismissed them. This failure led to Cimon's fall from grace and his ostracism. Athens responded angrily to the slight and the situation quickly escalated into war. When Cimon returned from exile in 451 BCE, he negotiated a five-year truce with Sparta, a truce proposed by Pericles.

This represents something of a policy shift by Pericles and it has been suggested that he and Cimon came to an arrangement where he would manage domestic affairs, leaving Cimon to handle foreign affairs, effecting a compromise and a political marriage between Periclean liberals and Cimonian conservatives.

The role of leading the conservatives fell to Thucydides who was an orator every bit as good as Pericles. The two engaged in a bitter personal rivalry and to ensure that he retained the support of the people of Athens, Pericles spent even more Athenian money on lavish plays, pagents and banquets. He created a very ambitious building plan, using public funds to construct the Periclean Acropolis, consisting of the Propylaea – the gateway to the Acropolis, the Parthenon and the golden statue of Athena, sculpted by Phidias, a friend of Pericles and one of the greatest of all Greek sculptors. He also financed from the public purse the refurbishment of all Athenian temples.

Much of the cost of the building work was paid for by money from Athens' allies who were happy to pay the Athenians for protection. Such expenditure, however, was severely criticised by Thucydides and his party. When Pericles offered to pay for it himself, however, the Athenians ordered him to use public funds. Eventually, Thucydides was ostracised, leaving Pericles in a position of unparalleled power, virtually a dictator.

The Athenians trusted him, however. He did not accept bribes and was dedicated to making Athens powerful and prosperous. In military matters, he took no chances and only entered a fight when the odds were stacked heavily in the Athenians' favour. However, the Athenian navy conquered many cities and islands and from them received the taxes vital to Pericles' work in Athens.

The defining relationship of Pericles' time in power was the one between Athens and Sparta, the other Greek states lining up behind one or other of the two great powers. They had already been at war during his rule, in the 450s and another confrontation seemed likely in 433 BCE. It came at a good time for Pericles. His friend Phidias and his companion Aspasia were both the targets of attacks by opposition politicians and commentators and Pericles' reputation was suffering. Phidias, in charge of all building projects, was first accused of embezzling and then of impiety in some of his carvings. Aspasia, a courtesan who probably ran a brothel, was accused of corrupting the women of Athens. There was even talk of impeachment. It has been suggested that Pericles hastened the war with Sparta in order to protect his position. It would not be the last time a politician used a war to deflect criticism at home.

The Pelponnesian War occurred, in part, due to Sparta's fear of the increasing power of Athens. Athens had become embroiled in the struggle between Corcyra and Corinth, sending a fleet to support the Corcyraeans. They fought in battles in 433 and 432 BCE. Critically, at this time, Pericles proposed the Megarian Decree, excluding Megarian merchants from selling their goods in the market at Athens and from using the ports of the Athenian Empire. This, of course, spelled disaster for the Megarian economy and angered Sparta, allies of Megara. The reason given for this action was that the Megarians had cultivated sacred land and had provided refuge for runaway slaves.

The Spartans sent a diplomatic mission to Athens demanding the retraction of the Megarian Decree and the expulsion from Athens of Pericles and his family. If these demands were not met, the Spartans added, war would follow. Pericles and the Athenians refused and in 431 BCE, the Spartans invaded Attica, the region around Athens. They found no Athenians, however, as Pericles had evacuated everyone to within the city walls. Then, in autumn of that year, Pericles led an army into Megara.

The Spartans returned to Attica in 430 BCE, but Pericles remained unwilling to engage them in battle, instead leading naval expeditions to plunder the Peloponnesian coastline. There was panic and uproar in the city when it was ravaged by a disease, but Pericles used a rousing oration to win the people round. However, his enemies gained ground and he was removed temporarily from his position as general, returning within a year and being re-elected as *strategos* or commander. In 429 BCE, he led all Athenian military operations.

The end came that year. Pericles' four sons – two legitimate and two illegitimate – all died of the plague that was devastating Athens. Pericles was shattered by this quadruple blow. Then he, himself, caught the disease and died in the autumn.

His name is forever linked with the principle of democracy, but, as Thucydides wrote, Athens was 'in name a democracy, but, [was] in fact, governed by its first citizen'. He acknowledges the manipulative power of Pericles' astonishing oratory, so essential to his position in Athens. Others have claimed him to be amongst the greatest statesmen and military leaders in history. He left a magnificent legacy of literary and artistic works created during his rule and, of course, the Acropolis, although in ruins, remains one of the wonders of the world.

With his death, Athens' golden age was over and it would never again achieve the greatness that it did during the glorious age of Pericles.

ALEXANDER THE GREAT

ALEXANDER THE GREAT was an extraordinarily gifted military commander and an inspirational leader of men. He had such a great military mind that it is believed he remained undefeated throughout the countless battles and campaigns he fought and during his life he ruled vast swathes of the known world in one of the greatest empires in history.

He was born on 20 July 356 BCE, in Pella, the son of King Philip II of Macedonia and his fourth wife, Olympias. His family already contained military genius -- he was a second cousin of the famous general, Pyrrhus of Epirus. Before his birth, according to the Roman historian, Plutarch, both his parents had disturbing dreams about their son. Olympias had dreamt of thunderbolts being sent by the god, Zeus and Philip had a dream in which he locked his wife's womb with the seal of the lion. These were interpreted to suggest that Alexander would be a great fighter. He enjoyed all the privileges of being a royal prince and as a child, was taught by such great men as Aristotle, the greatest thinker of his age. He is said to have already been assertive and confident at a very early age.

An early example of Alexander's courage concerns his horse Bucephalus. The horse, a beautiful thoroughbred, is said to have been brought to court to be sold to Philip, but was so wild that no one could ride him. Alexander, ten years old at the time, realised very quickly that the horse was frightened by his own shadow. He approached Bucephalus, turned him so that he was facing the sun, his shadow falling behind him and calmly climbed onto his back. He rode Bucephalus throughout his campaigns and when he died, he named a city – Bucephala – after him.

His father was so sure of Alexander's maturity while still youthful that when he had to leave Macedonia to wage a campaign in Byzantium, he appointed him regent at just sixteen years of age. That same year, Alexander commanded the left wing of the Macedonian army, acquitting himself excellently against an alliance of Athens and Thebes at the Battle of Chaeronea. His branch of the army faced the Sacred Band of Thebes, an elite group of soldiers that was thought to be invincible. It was believed that that the corps was made up of homosexual couples on the principle that they would fight more passionately for each other. Alexander annihilated them, and left their corpses 'heaped one upon another', as Plutarch reported.

As a result of this victory, Philip now ruled the entire Greek mainland, but two years later, at the wedding of his daughter, Cleopatra, he was assassinated by one of his bodyguards – the young nobleman, Pausanias of Orestis. It has been suggested that the assassin was a former lover of Philip but there are also suspicions that Alexander and his mother Olympias were implicated in the plot or might even have been its instigators.

So, at the age of nineteen, Alexander assumed the throne of Macedonia and leadership of the League of Corinth, a federation of most of the city-states of mainland Greece. The Greek city-states saw Philip's death and the promotion of a young and inexperienced king as an opportunity and rose up against Macedonian rule. Alexander went into action at once, putting down the rebellion of the southern Greek city-states and leading a campaign in 335 BCE against the Thracians and the Illyrians to the north, establishing the River Danube as the northern frontier of his Macedonian kingdom. He sent out a message to any Greeks wishing to question his rule by ordering the destruction of the rebellious city of Thebes. He spared only priests, Theban supporters of Macedonia and the descendants of the poet, Pindar, whose house was the only building left untouched. The remainder of the surviving inhabitants of the city were sold into slavery.

Before his death, Philip had planned an expedition against the Achaemenid Empire of Persia. Alexander was nominated as general by the other Greek states and put a plan devised by his father into action, leading around 42,000 troops across the Hellespont separating Greece from Asia Minor, and, in 334, winning a major victory over the Persians at Granicus in modern-day northwestern Turkey. Now the Greek cities of Asia Minor lay open to him.

At Halicarnassus, he staged a siege, forcing Memnon of Rhodes and the Persian satrap of Caria, Orontobates, to flee by sea. He then marched his army into the mountainous region of Lycia and the Pamphylian Plain in Southern Anatolia where he established control of the coastal cities. Moving inland, he is said to have undone the ancient 'Gordian Knot' in the ancient Phrygian capital, Gordium. Legend had it that whoever untied the knot would become king of Asia. Alexander, ever the pragmatist, like all before him, could not untie the knot. He simply took his sword to it and sliced it in half – a problem-solving technique that has become known as the Alexandrian Solution.

In 333, at Cilicia, he met the main Persian army led by Shah, or Emperor, Darius III, and comprehensively defeated it at the Battle of Issus. Darius fled, leaving a huge amount of valuable treasure behind, as well as his family. Alexander then proceeded to Damascus which he occupied and, in 332, he also captured the city of Tyre, after a seven-month long siege. As he had done in other conquered cities and countries, he treated the ruler and his family with great leniency.

In 332–331 BCE, Alexander arrived in Egypt which, long occupied by Persia, welcomed him as a liberator and pronounced him son of Zeus. There, he founded the city of Alexandria which would become the country's capital after his death. It was the first, and probably the best known of the many cities he would go on to found.

Marching eastwards, at Gaugamela, near Arbela in modern-day

northern Iraq, Alexander faced Darius once more, the Persian leading an even bigger army than the one at Issus. Once more Alexander defeated him, forcing him to flee the battlefield.

He next marched his troops into Babylon, capturing the legendary Achaemenid treasury of Susa. Then, towards the end of 331 BCE, he faced one of his most difficult opponents when the Persian military commander, Ariobarzan, held his army at bay for thirty days at the Battle of the Persian Gate. Victory here left the Persian capital and its vast treasury at Alexander's mercy. During his stay in the city, the royal palace was burned to the ground and it is said by some to have been the work of a drunken Alexander. Persepolis secured, he set out in pursuit of Darius, but by this time the Persian emperor had been taken prisoner by one of his own men, Bessus, who, hearing of Alexander's approach had Darius murdered. He then proclaimed himself Shah as Artaxerxes V and retreated into Central Asia where he launched a guerrilla campaign against the Greeks. Bessus was eventually killed by his own men in 329 BCE.

Alexander fought his way east, through Media, Parthia, and the lands that make up modern-day Afghanistan. He founded a number of new cities, all of which he named Alexandria. In the meantime, Alexander had married Princess Roxana of Sogdiana, a Persian province that he subdued in 328–327 BCE.

Around 330, Alexander had begun to sense hostility from a number of his associates and friends. One of his officers, Philotas, was executed for failing to bring to Alexander's attention an assassination plot; Philotas' father, Parmenion was also killed on Alexander's orders to prevent any attempts at revenge. In an infamous incident, during a drunken argument, Alexander killed his great friend, Cleitus the Black, who had saved his life at the Battle of Granicus.

In 326 BCE, Alexander moved against the Indian sub-continent, calling all of the chieftains of the former Persian-controlled territory of Gandhara, in modern-day northern Pakistan, to submit to his authority. Many of the hill clans refused and Alexander personally led an army against them. These were hard people to beat and Alexander was wounded in the shoulder by a dart at one point, but before long he had subdued them. He enslaved 40,000 Aspasoi after defeating them and in a fierce campaign in which he was again wounded, in the ankle this time, he defeated the Assakenoi whose army consisted of 30,000 cavalry, 38,000 infantry and thirty elephants. Alexander reduced the cities of Massaga and Ora to rubble, slaughtering the inhabitants and following the survivors to their mountain stronghold where, after four days of fierce fighting, he took the hill-fort and massacred those still alive. He is reported to have even killed many who had surrendered after he had promised them safety.

He was ready to push on, but faced with the powerful army of Maghada and exhausted by years of fighting, his army mutinied at the Hyphasis River and refused to go any further. They had feared crossing the wide Ganges where, it was said at the time, the kings of the Ganderites and Praesii awaited them on the other side with 80,000 horsemen, 200,000 infantry, 8,000 chariots and 6,000 fighting elephants. Alexander was forced to begin a return march, turning south to defeat the Malli clans, said to be amongst the best fighters in the whole of South Asia. At one point it is reported that Alexander jumped into a fortified city accompanied only by two of his bodyguards and was seriously wounded by an arrow. His troops thought he had been killed and took terrible revenge on the Malli, slaughtering all within the city; men, women and children. But Alexander had survived and the army proceeded on its journey home, conquering Indian tribes en route.

He sent his admiral, Nearchus, to explore the coast of the Persian Gulf, sent much of his army to Carmania in modern-day southern Iran and in 325, led the rest of his force back in the direction of Persia through the Gedrosian Desert in modern-day Baluchistan, suffering heavy losses on the way.

On his march back through territories he had conquered and in which he had installed satraps and military governors, he discovered that many of these had misbehaved in his absence and, furious with their behaviour, executed them. But, as he prepared to send a number of his older and injured troops back to Macedonia, there was another mutiny against the Persian customs that Alexander had adopted and the introduction into his army of Persian soldiers and officers. He executed the ringleaders and, in 324 BCE, in an effort to create harmony between his Macedonian and Persian subjects, staged a mass marriage of himself and many of his officers to Persian noblewomen at Susa. He also schooled a regiment of Persian boys in Macedonian customs.

Alexander returned to Ecbatana, capital of the Median Empire to collect the treasure that he had left there, but while quartered there, his lifelong friend – and lover, it has been claimed – the Macedonian general, Hephaestion, became ill and died. Alexander was heartbroken and mourned for six months.

On the afternoon of 29 May 323 BCE, Alexander was taken ill at the palace of Nebuchadrezzar II of Babylon. He had been drinking with colleagues and friends and it is likely that he was poisoned, although some say he suffered from a congenital illness or that he suffered from malaria which he had contracted in 336.

On 9 June his soldiers visited him, one at a time, as he lay dying in his tent. He would never carry out his plan to expand into the Arabian Peninsula and then lead his army to the west to conquer Carthage, Rome and the Iberian Peninsula. The following day, after twelve years of constant campaigning, during which he created an empire stretching from the Danube to India, Alexander the Great, possibly the greatest military leader the world has ever known, died.

HANNIBAL

IT MUST HAVE been an astonishing sight. An army including huge war elephants, marching over the Pyrenees and then the Alps and into northern Italy. It took a very special type of military commander to cajole his men and animals into performing such a feat. Hannibal was such a man, one of the greatest military leaders and tacticians the world has ever seen.

He was born, the son of the Carthaginian general, Hamilcar, in 247 BCE in Libyssa, Bithynia in the western part of modern-day Turkey. Carthage, in present-day Tunisia, and Rome were the two major Mediterranean powers in the 3rd century BCE. When Carthage had fallen to the Romans in the First Punic war, Hamilcar had gone to the Iberian Peninsula to subjugate the tribes there and safeguard Carthaginian possessions against the Romans. Hannibal, still a child, had begged to accompany him but was only allowed to go if he swore an oath to destroy Rome. He did and the remainder of his entire life would be devoted to that aim.

On the death of his father, killed in battle in 229 or 228 BCE, Hanibal's brother-in-law, Hasdrubal, assumed his command and began the consolidation of his father-in-law's conquests. In 221, however, Hasdrubal was assassinated and Hannibal, aged twenty-six, was proclaimed commander by the army. He married a Spanish princess, Imilce, and completed the conquest of Hispania south of the Ebro.

In the treaty between Rome and Carthage signed after the First Punic War, the River Ebro had been defined as the northern limit of Carthaginian influence in the Iberian Peninsula. In 219, Hannibal attacked the city of Saguntum, just south of the river, besieging it for eight months. But Rome had allied with Saguntum, declaring the city a Roman protectorate and they regarded Hannibal's attack as an act of war against them. They demanded the surrender of Hannibal who had been seriously wounded in the siege. When the Carthaginians refused, the Second Punic War began.

Hannibal prepared for the conflict that he had wanted all along in the seaport of Cartagena, the capital of Carthaginian Spain. His amazing and bold plan was to take the war to the Romans with a rapid march through the northern Iberian Peninsula across southern Gaul and over the Alps into northern Italy. He set off for the Pyrenees, leaving his brother, Hasdrubal, in command of a large army to defend the Iberian Peninsula and North Africa.

There are various reports as to the size of his army, but, although some say that it was more than 100,000 strong, it is more likely to have totalled around 50,000 men – 40,000 infantry and 12,000 cavalry. There were also a number of elephants, of course. He left Cartagena in late spring, 218 BCE, and battled through the tribes who lived in the north of Hispania. 11,000 troops were left to garrison the newly conquered region and he released another 11,000, who were reluctant to leave Hispania.

As he crossed southern Gaul, there was little resistance. He arrived at the Rhône before the Romans had time to react and crossed the river, having outmanoeuvred local tribesmen who had attempted to stop him crossing. He then succeeded in escaping from a Roman force, commanded by Consul and general, Publius Cornelius Scipio, by marching inland up the Rhône. When Scipio realised that Hannibal was going to make a crossing of the Alps, he returned to North Italy by sea to wait for him.

Hannibal's route across the mountain range has long been the subject of debate. He may have crossed by the Col de Grimone or the Col de Cabre, through the Durance basin or he may have travelled over one of two passes – the Mont Cenis or Montgenèvre into the upper Po valley, descending into the lands of the warlike

Taurini where he attacked their town, modern-day Turin. There is little debate, however, about this astonishing journey's status as one of the greatest achievements in military history. The climate was harsh and the terrain virtually impassable. Snow and ice made it perilous for both men and animals. Landslides were regular occurrences, holding the army up in the freezing cold. Furthermore, local Celtic tribes conducted a relentless guerrilla war against his army and this was all exacerbated by the fact that his army was a mixture of races and languages and difficult, therefore, to communicate with. After fifteen days in the mountains and a journey lasting five months from southern Hispania, he arrived in Italy with 20,000 infantry, 6,000 cavalry and only one survivor of the original thirty-seven elephants.

His army was exhausted and in no condition to face Scipio who had hurried to the Po to defend the new Roman colonies of Placentia and Cremona. Nonetheless when they met west of the Ticino River, Hannibal won, his cavalry playing a major role in the victory. Scipio was seriously wounded in the battle and was saved only by the courage of his son who rode back onto the field of battle to rescue his father. In December 218, after another Roman army, under the other Consul, Sempronius Longus, had arrived to bolster Scipio's men, the two armies met again south of Placentia. Hannibal displayed his innate tactical ability, wearing down the Roman infantry and then destroying it with an ambush from the flank.

Word spread of Hannibal's successes and apparent invincibility and others flocked to his side, such as the Gauls, the Ligurians and the Celts. His force back at its original strength of 40,000, he wintered with the Gauls before moving south. By spring 217, he had advanced as far as the River Arno in present-day Tuscany. Crossing the Appenines, Hannibal lost his right eye because of conjunctivitis and in the marshy lands around the Arno, he lost many soldiers and the last of his elephants.

By now, the Romans believed him to be advancing on Rome and Cnaeus Servilius and Gaius Flaminius, the new Roman Consuls, moved their armies into position to block his eastern and western routes. Hannibal outmanouevred Gaius Flaminius at Arretium and marched four days and three nights to Faesulae and Perugia. Flaminius had no choice but to attack him but it was a disastrous move and Hannibal's army, ready for him, annihilated his troops near Lake Trasimene. Thousands were killed in the fighting and thousands more were driven back into the lake where they drowned. Once again showing his tactical expertise, Hannibal had drawn Flaminius into battle by marching his army around the Roman army's left flank and cutting him off from Rome. It was the first recorded example of a turning movement in military history.

By now, however, Hannibal's troops were spent from their long, arduous march and numerous battles. He realised they were too exhausted to march on to Rome and could only hope for a rebellion by Rome's allies and a civil war. Sadly for him, it was a vain hope.

The winter of 217 was spent at Picenum, interrupted by raids on Apulia and Campania. There were brief skirmishes with the army of Quintus Fabius Maximus Cunctator. Unexpectedly, however, Hannibal advanced south in early summer to seize a large supply depot at Cannae where, in August he fought a numerically superior Roman force, estimated by some to number around 100,000 men. The Consul Varro was in command and was determined to defeat the Carthaginians but Hannibal's cavalry again won the battle for him, encircling the Romans at the rear while Carthaginian troops pushed in from the Roman right and across the rear, effectively hemming the Romans in and giving them no chance of flight. Hannibal's men surrounded the Romans and destroyed them. Around 50,000 to 70,000 Romans were killed or captured at Cannae and the list of dead carried the names of many prominent Romans – the Consul Lucius Aemilius Paulius, the two Consuls of the previous year, two quaestors (treasury officials), twenty-nine of the forty-eight military tribunes and eighty senators. It was one of ancient Rome's greatest military defeats and one of the bloodiest battles in history.

Many regions now feared that Roman power was on the wane and began to defect. Furthermore, Rome was facing difficulties elsewhere. Greek cities in Sicily revolted against Roman rule and the Macedonian king, Philip V, had pledged support for Hannibal, initiating the First Macedonian War against the Romans. Instead of taking advantage and advancing on the capital, however, Hannibal wintered in 216 at Capua.

Meanwhile, the Romans adopted a clever new strategy. It was obvious that they were incapable of defeating him in open battle. Therefore, they decided to embark on a war of attrition, defending the cities loyal to Rome and trying to recapture the ones that had fallen to the Carthaginians. In this way, they would stretch the Carthaginian army and its allies, making them fight in every theatre of war. Hannibal, for his part, was weakened by a decline in the number of troops who remained by his side and as a result was forced to adopt a more cautious and more defensive approach. Any hope of support from Carthage had faded, too, as the Romans controlled the Mediterranean and Hannibal's men had to forage locally for provisions. Hannibal had launched his campaign without the full backing of the Carthaginian oligarchy which was drawn from wealthy ruling families known as the 'Hundred and Four'. They were more concerned about the situation in Iberia where they had commercial interests than in Hannibal's campaign in distant Italy. Therefore, instead of being sent Carthaginian reinforcements, he was forced to reinforce his army with inadequately trained and less motivated mercenaries from Italy or Gaul.

Between 215 and 213 BCE, apart from the capture of Tarantum, Hannibal made little progress, winning only minor victories. The tide was turning and the Romans were now beginning to win back cities that he had taken. In 211, he marched to try to relieve a siege of his headquarters at Capua, but failed and Capua fell. That year, he also lost Sicily and Syracuse and in 209, Tarentum returned to Roman hands.

Back in Spain the Romans were also making progress. In 208, Hannibal's brother followed Hannibal's route across the Alps to reinforce him, but he was disastrously defeated and killed at Metaurus in northern Italy the following year. Hannibal's plan to join with his brother's army and march, finally, on Rome was gone. He was devastated and retired to Bruttium with his army.

Meanwhile, his old enemy, Scipio, struck at North Africa, defeating Carthage's main ally, the Massaesylian Numidians and threatening Carthage itself. Hannibal was ordered to abandon Italy after almost sixteen years campaigning there and return to North Africa to defend Carthage. Behind him he left a record of his expedition carved on bronze tablets at the Temple of Juno at Crotona.

In 202 BCE, the two great rivals Hannibal and Scipio met at a peace conference. But terms had already been agreed and Carthage would be permitted to retain its African conquests but would lose its European territories. It would also have to reduce the size of its fleet and pay reparations to Rome. Hannibal was furious and as the Roman envoys returned to Rome with the treaty they had concluded with the Carthaginians, he breached it. But his luck had finally run out. At the battle of Zama, his long-held invincibility was brought to an end with a crushing and humiliating defeat.

Hannibal had always enjoyed superiority in numbers of cavalry, but at Zama the tables were turned – the Romans had more cavalry and the Carthaginians more infantry. Scipio's numbers were also augmented by the troops of Masinissa, a former ally of the Carthaginians who had switched sides in 206 BCE with a promise from the Romans of land. As for Hannibal, he was now getting old and was exhausted by the constant warfare of the last twenty years.

The Roman cavalry began the battle well, limiting the effectiveness of the 80 African war elephants that Hannibal brought to the battlefield. It was a close-run battle and at one point it seemed that Hannibal's men were on the verge of victory, but Scipio rallied his men and after routing Hannibal's cavalry, made an attack from the rear. The Carthaginian formation collapsed and they were forced to surrender. In the carnage, 20,000 Carthaginian troops had lost their lives. Hannibal, his reputation in tatters, fled the battlefield and the Punic Wars were over.

Although tired and in bad health, Hannibal was still only forty-three. He swapped his role as a general for that of a politician and was elected chief magistrate in the now empire-less Carthage. He fought against a new enemy – the corruption that blighted the state, making reforms to the 'Hundred and Four'. He stipulated that its membership should be elected rather than co-opted, with a limit on the length of time a member could serve. Gradually, Carthage became prosperous again.

Its renewed prosperity alarmed the Romans and they demanded that Hannibal be handed over to them. To escape such a fate, he went into voluntary exile, travelling to Tyre and then to Ephesus in Syria where the king, Antiochus III, was preparing an army to fight the Romans. In 190 BCE, he was given command of a Seleucid fleet by Antiochus, but lost to the Roman fleet in a battle at the River Eurymedon in modern-day Turkey.

When it looked like Antiochus was about to betray him to the Romans, Hannibal fled to Crete before returning to Asia Minor where he served King Prusias I in a war against an ally of Rome. At one point, commanding a fleet, he is reported to have had large pots filled with poisonous snakes thrown into the enemy ships.

The Romans were still after him, however, and around the year 183 BCE he was once again about to be betrayed and handed over to the Romans. Rather than let himself fall into the hands of the people he had spent his life fighting, however, he poisoned himself and died, aged about sixty-four.

JULIUS CAESAR

To be in charge of Rome in 49 BCE was to be in charge of the world. Julius Caesar fulfilled that role brilliantly. He dominated Roman politics for many years and as well as being a great politician, was also a brilliant and inspirational general, leading his armies in the conquest of Gaul, extending the Empire to the North Sea, and, in 55 BCE, leading the first Roman invasion of Britain. So great a leader was Julius Caesar that his surname name itself came to mean 'emperor'. Thus, the titles, Kaiser, Czar and Tsar, derive from it and are all used to designate an emperor.

He is considered by military experts to have been one of the greatest military strategists and tacticians the world has ever known, with an ability to fight on any terrain, in any weather. His troops were intensely loyal to him, marching as much as forty miles a day and respecting his great abilities. He made use of the Roman army's formidable artillery as well its superb engineering skills. Once, during the Gallic Wars, when he was mounting a siege on a city on a plateau, his men tunnelled through solid rock, found the source of the spring that supplied the city with water and diverted it for their own use.

His ancestors were, indeed, noble. His patrician family were said to be descended from Iulus, the son of the legendary Trojan prince Aeneas who in turn was the son of the goddess Venus. He gained his name Caesar from the manner of his birth – by caesarean section which derives its name fro the Latin word to cut, *caedere*.

Caesar's father had been a *praetor*, or magistrate, governor of the province of Asia and Julius was born between 102 and 100 BCE. At the time of his birth, however, his family was neither wealthy nor

41

influential, although his aunt was married to Gaius Marius, a prominent politician.

Not much is known about Caesar's childhood, although it is known that his father died in 85 BCE and he became head of the household. The following year he was offered the position of *Flamen Dialis*, high priest of Jupiter. The holder of that position had to be not only a patrician, but also to be married to one and Caesar was consequently forced to break off his engagement to a woman named Cossutia to whom he had been betrothed since he was a child, and marry Cornelia, daughter of a politician of the Popular Party.

At that time, Rome was in turmoil, having fought the Social War with a number of her Italian allies between 91 and 88 BCE over the issue of Roman citizenship while the kingdom of Pontus, in modern-day Turkey, led by King Mithridates, was a formidable enemy, constantly threatening Rome's eastern border. In Rome itself politicians were split into two factions – the Optimates and the Populares. Neither was what could be called a political party in today's terms, with a common agenda. But the Optimates were pro-aristocratic and used traditional methods in the Senate to achieve their political goals; the Populares tried to achieve theirs through direct appeal to the people of Rome.

When Optimate dictator, Sulla, was in power, having been a great rival of Caesar's uncle Gaius Marius, he stripped Caesar of his inheritance, his wife's dowry and his position as high priest. He was also ordered to divorce Cornelia, but he refused and, instead, went into hiding. Eventually, Sulla relented, under pressure from Caesar's family and influential friends.

Instead of returning to his old life in Rome, however, he joined the army, serving with distinction under Marcus Minucius Thermus in Asia and Sevilius Isauricus in Cilicia in present-day Turkey. During this time, he was awarded Rome's second-highest military honour, the *Corona Civica* (Civic Crown).

Around 79 BCE, he was sent as an envoy to Nicomedes, King of

Blythnia, to obtain a fleet of ships. Having succeeded in his mission, rumours very quickly spread that he had only succeeded after sleeping with Nicomedes IV who was known to be a homosexual. These rumours would follow him for the remainder of his life, although he is said to have denied them under oath. It is probable, however, that they were spread by his political enemies.

When Sulla died, in 78 BCE, having restored the Consulship as the method of government in Rome, Caesar felt it was safe to return to the capital where he became a lawyer. His new career proved successful and he gained a reputation for the skill of his oratory and for prosecuting former governors who had been corrupt in office.

To improve his skills further still, he decided, in 75 BCE, to travel to Rhodes to study under Greek rhetorician, Apollonius Molon. On his journey, however, Caesar was kidnapped by Cilician pirates and taken to the Greek island of Pharmacusa where he was held in captivity while a ransom was sought. His attitude throughout was one of absolute superiority to his captors and it was reported that when he was told that they were asking for a ransom of twenty talents, he told them that he was worth much more than that, perhaps fifty. He promised them terrible retribution when he was freed, and he kept his promise, tracking them down and having them crucified as a warning to others. He was not all bad, however – as they had treated him fairly well during his captivity, he had their throats cut before the crucifixion so that they would not suffer too much.

Returning to Rome, he was called into military service again and served in Asia, repulsing another invasion from Pontus. In 72 BCE, he was elected military tribune and in 69 BCE was elected quaestor – a role dealing with the financial affairs of the empire – serving in Hispania (modern Spain) .

His wife died that year and he re-married in 67 BCE, his new wife being Pompeia, granddaughter of Sulla. He was elected *curule aedile*, a role in which he was responsible for the maintenance of public buildings and organising lavish festivals and games. He is also believed to have become interested in higher office with suspected involvement in two coup attempts.

In 63 BCE, he ran for office as Pontifex Maximus, the important role of chief priest. It was a messy election contest as he ran against two Optimates, the rival party to his, and there were accusations of bribery on all sides. Caesar, faced with the prospect of being forced into exile if he did not win, on account of the huge debts he had incurred, won by a comfortable margin. In 62, he became Praetor, and in the same year, divorced his wife Pompeia who had been suspected of being involved in a scandal with another man. When it emerged that the man had been acquitted of any crime, Caesar is said to have uttered the famous words, 'The wife of Caesar must be above suspicion.'

Caesar's debts were haunting him, however, and before he became a private citizen again, and opened himself to prosecution, he had to leave Rome for Hispania at the head of an army. There, he conquered the Celtic tribes, the Calaici and the Lusitani and was hailed as Imperator by his troops. He was now entitled to a triumph – a civic ceremony accorded to a successful military commander. However, if he had accepted the honour, he would have had to remain a soldier and he had his sights firmly set on being a Consul, the republic's most senior public position. He chose the Consulship and was elected with Bibulis for the one-year post in 59 BCE. Meanwhile, he allied himself with two very powerful Romans – Pompey and Crassus – an alliance that has become known as the First Triumvirate that controlled all public business in Rome. They effectively took over the government of Rome and Bibulis retired to his villa for a year. Caesar also married for a third time, to Calpurnia Pisonis.

He succeeded in obtaining a five-year term as Pro-consul of Gaul, a good way to raise cash to pay off his debts as well as a means of avoiding prosecution for his nefarious deeds as Consul when that term of office came to an end. He would be gone for nine years.

He had four legions under his command and with those and a couple more that he raised, he conquered most of central Europe, introducing these lands to Roman and Mediterranean civilisation. His conquests were a defining moment in European and world history, unifying the continent in a way that had not yet been achieved. His summers would consist of fighting and in the winter, he would return to quarters in Cisalpine Gaul (modern-day northern Italy) from where he would do his best to influence Roman politics through his supporters in Rome.

In 56 BCE, he held a meeting with Crassus and Pompey to renew the Triumvirate. In this meeting, Caesar's Pro-consulship was also extended by a further five years. Meanwhile, he continued to win victories against the tribes of central Europe, in 55 BCE defeating the Germanic tribes, the Usipetes and the Tencteri and building a bridge across the Rhine in order to cause panic in Germany with a show of strength.

In late summer, 55 BCE, he crossed into Britain from Gaul, on the pretext that the Britons had helped the Celtic tribe, the Veneti against the Romans the previous year in Brittany. He made a beachhead on the coast of Kent but could advance no further, returning to Gaul to winter there. In 54, he returned with more and better-prepared troops. As he was beginning to make progress, agreeing terms with some British tribes, news of rebellion in Gaul forced him to return there to re-establish stability.

Back in Rome, however, Caesar's relationship with Pompey was becoming strained, a situation was made worse when Crassus was killed in Parthia in 53. Rome was dangerously unstable and in an attempt to stabilise the situation, Pompey was appointed sole Consul, having now moved his political allegiance to the Optimate faction. Worse still, for Caesar, Pompey's wife Julia, Caesar's daughter, had died in childbirth and he re-married the daughter of Caesar's political rival, Quintus Metellus Scipio. Pompey invited Scipio to become his partner in the Consulship and the Triumvirate was no more.

By the following year, Caesar's conquest of Gaul was complete. The statistics of the conquest were staggering. His army had fought against three million men, of whom one million had died; 300 tribes had been subjugated, 800 cities destroyed, and in one case the entire population of 40,000 had been massacred.

He established a stable administration in the vast province and published his history, *The Gallic Wars*. But, he was told in no uncertain terms that if he returned to Rome as a private citizen he would be prosecuted. Pompey and he were now sworn enemies and neither would back down.

Finally, in 49 BCE, Caesar led his armies across the Rubicon River that marked the frontier of his province, an act that was tantamount to declaring war on Pompey whose troops were in Spain at the time. Pompey and the Senate retreated to southern Italy while Caesar marched on Rome, set up his own Senate and proclaimed himself dictator. He then unexpectedly marched to Spain to prevent a link-up between Pompey and his army. His campaign there was brief and, returning quickly to Rome, he was elected Consul.

He now set off in pursuit of Pompey who was, by this time in Greece. The two great generals met in the Battle of Pharsalus, undoubtedly one of Caesar's greatest victories. With only around 21,000 men, he defeated Pompey's 46,000 men in a remarkably short engagement. He was careful, however in victory. All Roman citizens taken prisoner were pardoned. Pompey, meanwhile, fled to Egypt with Caesar in hot pursuit. He landed in Alexandria with only 4,000 legionnaires, but was horrified to be presented with the head of his arch-rival who had been murdered by a former Roman officer serving at the court of King Ptolemy XIII.

Egypt was, itself, in the midst of civil war at the time, the twelve-year-old Ptolemy's co-ruler, Cleopatra VII having been driven out of Alexandria by supporters of the young king. Caesar took Cleopatra's side, defeating Ptolomy's forces in the Battle of the Nile in 47 BCE. He ordered the Egyptian fleet to be burnt, but his men accidentally burned down the famous 300-year-old library of Alexandria, the largest collection of books in the ancient world. Cleopatra was installed as sole Pharaoh.

Caesar and Cleopatra never married as Roman citizens were legally only allowed to marry other Roman citizens, but it is believed that he fathered a son by her, named Caesarion. She would visit Rome many times in the next fourteen years, staying in Caesar's villa on the outskirts of Rome.

In the middle of 47, Caesar decimated the army of King Pharnaces of Pontus in the Battle of Zela and then defeated various supporters of Pompey in Africa. He was also elected for third and fourth terms as Consul.

A canny political animal, Caesar had always taken care not to proscribe his enemies when he had defeated them, whether in battle or in the Senate and, for this reason, back in Rome there was really no serious opposition to him. Returning in September 45 BCE, he named his grandnephew, Gaius Octavius as his heir with Marcus Junius Brutus a reserve, in the event of Gaius Octavius dying before Caesar. He lived, however, and would rule as Octavian.

In 46 BCE Ceasar made important changes to the way that time was measured, introducing the Julian Calendar, featuring a 365-day year with a leap year every fourth year. It would remain in force until 1582 when Pope Gregory would reform it.

However, as dictator, he governed autocratically and his methods began to displease many Roman nobles. He would simply announce his decisions to the Senate without allowing the Senators the opportunity to debate them or vote on them. He caused further discontent when he celebrated a triumph over rebel Roman forces under the leadership of Pompey's son in Spain. Many believed that triumph ceremonies should be reserved for victories over foreign enemies and not Roman ones. Furthermore, he allowed statues of himself to be decorated like statues of the gods and appointed officials without reference to anyone else. Inscriptions such as 'to the unconquerable god' referring to him, were not uncommon and at official functions he always sat in a gilded chair.

The tensions between him and the Senate mounted as his pretensions to being king became more pronounced. He was nominated for nine consecutive terms as dictator and then made dictator perpetuo (dictator for life).

In 44 BCE, a contingent of Senators met him in the Temple of Venus Genetrix to inform him of new honours to be bestowed upon him, but he failed to stand up when greeting them. He later ascribed the incident to a bout of diarrhea, but was not believed. At the same time, he refused to accept various kingly symbols, such as a diadem that Marc Antony tried to place on his head.

On 15 March 44 BCE, although he had been advised not to, by his wife and friends, he attended the last meeting of the Senate before leaving to wage a campaign against the Parthians. The meeting was being held in the temporary venue of the Theatre of Pompey as the Curia had been burned down and was in the middle of reconstruction. Sixty conspirators, led by Marcus Junius Brutus, Gaius Cassius Longinus, Decimus Brutus Albinus, and Gaius Trebonius, tired of Caesar's royal airs and autocratic methods, attended the meeting with daggers concealed in their togas. They surrounded him and stabbed him around twenty-three times at the base of Pompey's statue, continuing to strike at him even as he lay on the ground, dying. Before he collapsed, legend, and William Shakespeare have it that he said, '*Et tu, Brute?*' (You, too, Brutus?) although some claim that he said nothing, merely pulling his toga over his head when he saw his protegé, Brutus amongst the conspirators.

Fear stalked Rome as the conspirators fled. Marc Antony, Octavian and others fought five civil wars in the aftermath of Caesar's death. They would culminate in the creation of the Roman Empire.

JESUS CHRIST

ALMOST A THIRD of the earth's population is Christian and since the 4th century, at least, Christianity has played a defining role in Western civilisation. The central figure in Christianity is Jesus Christ, revered as the Son of God and he appears as an important figure in other religions, too, Muslims, for instance, view him as a prophet.

To Christians, however, he is a divine being, the Messiah prophesied in the Old Testament, the Son of God who was crucified by the Romans and who was resurrected after death. He came to earth, they believe, to provide salvation to mankind by dying for their sins. They also believe that he was born to a virgin, Mary, that he performed miracles, that he ascended to heaven following his resurrection and that he will return to earth in the Second Coming.

Of course, as with the other major religious figures, Buddha and Muhammad, it is difficult to separate the facts of Jesus' life from the legends but academic scholars do concur that he existed, that he was a Galilean Jew who became a teacher and a healer. The main sources for the events and chronology of Jesus' life are the Gospels of Matthew, Mark, Luke and John in the Bible although each treats Jesus very differently to the others.

By the time of Jesus' birth, the Jewish people had been ruled by foreign powers for thousands of years – Egyptian, Syrian, Babylonian, Persian, Greek, Romans and others – and during that time had enjoyed only brief periods of independence. In the 1st century, the Romans ruled the area where Jesus was born. King Herod was king, but he was no more than a puppet of the Romans, following the orders of Rome and the Emperor at the time, Caesar

Augustus. The Jews hated the Romans who were often ruthless in the application of their laws.

The Jews were awaiting the birth of a Messiah or saviour, a leader they claimed had been promised by God and who would lead them not only to spiritual renewal, but also to freedom from the tyranny of foreign rule. Jesus' exact date of birth is unknown but is presumed to have been while Herod the Great was on the throne of Judaea and he is known to have ruled from 33 BCE until his death in 4 CE. The date of Jesus' birth is usually placed sometime between 6 BCE and 4 CE.

He was born in the town of Bethlehem to Mary who, according to the Gospels, had been visited by the Holy Spirit. She had been told by the angel Gabriel that she was carrying the Son of God. Shortly before the birth, Mary and her husband, Joseph, had to leave their home in Nazareth and travel to Bethlehem to take part in a census called by Caesar Augustus.

In Bethlehem, unable to find accommodation, they sought shelter in a stable which is where Jesus was born, a manger being used for his crib. The Gospel of Luke relates that the angel Gabriel told some shepherds that Jesus, the Son of God, had been born and they left their flocks to visit him in the stable, following which they spread the news of the birth of the Messiah. Other visitors to the stable were the Three Wise Men, or Magi, who had followed a bright star in the sky, believing it would lead them to the place where the King of the Jews was being born. They brought gifts of gold, Frankincense and Myrrh for the newborn child.

When news reached Herod that the King of the Jews had been born, he reacted angrily and ruthlessly, ordering that all boys in Bethlehem under the age of two be killed. To avoid this 'massacre of the innocents', as it is known, Mary and Joseph fled with their newborn son to Egypt and remained there until Herod's death in 4 CE. They settled in Nazareth in Galilee and until he reached the age of thirty, Jesus lived a quiet life, working as an artisan of some kind; he is usually believed to have been employed as a carpenter.

At thirty, Jesus' life changed irrevocably following his baptism by John the Baptist, a charismatic preacher who performed his baptisms in the River Jordan in anticipation of the arrival of the Messiah. John immediately recognised Jesus as the Saviour for whom he had been waiting and about whom he had been preaching for years. He at first refused to baptise him, saying that Jesus should actually be baptising him. Jesus told him to proceed with the baptism, however. 'It is proper for us to do this to fulfill all righteousness,' Matthew reports him as saying. Following his baptism, Jesus heard a voice from heaven announce to him; 'You are my beloved Son, in whom I am well pleased.' It was the moment that launched Jesus' ministry and he would spend the remainder of his short life wandering, teaching, healing and preaching.

Following his baptism, Jesus was led into the desert by God and fasted there for forty days and forty nights, being visited by the devil and tempted three times by him. On each occasion Jesus rejected the devil's offer. He now set out on travels during which he preached his message to increasingly large crowds as his fame spread. On his travels, he was accompanied by twelve main disciples, but there were many people who followed him, especially as news of the miracles he performed as he wandered the countryside spread.

He 'cast out demons', sometimes thought to be the curing of nervous and mental illness and John reports in his Gospel that he walked on water. One day, he sent his disciples on ahead of him in a boat to Bethsaida, a city east of the Jordan. When they were halfway across the lake, however, Jesus walked across the water to meet them and climbed into the boat.

The largest collection of miracles attributed to Jesus concern illness and disabilities. The Gospels describe him curing by merely saying a few words or by laying his hands on the sick or disabled person. Sometimes spit or mud are used. Variously in the Gospels, he is reported to have cured fever, leprosy, bleeding, withered hands, dropsy, deafness, blindness and paralysis amongst other things.

The Gospels also report many miracles in which he controls nature – the feeding of the 5,000 with only a few loaves and several fish, turning water into wine when it ran out at a wedding and making it possible for his disciples to make a large catch of fish.

He is also reported to have on several occasions displayed power over death. He woke up the daughter of Jairus who had died, saying she was only sleeping; he revived the son of the widow at Nain who was about to be buried, the supposedly dead man getting up out of his coffin when Jesus told him to and he raised Lazarus, of the town of Bethany, from the dead. And, of course, he, himself, rose from the dead.

Jesus' itinerant teaching led him to Capernaum on the northwest shore of the Sea of Galilee, where he lived in a house which some consider to have been treated as a base for his ministry and to which he would return from time to time. It is possible that he went there because it was a prosperous town that offered lots of opportunities to reach a bigger audience but it may just have been because his disciples lived there and he wanted to be close to them.

His message in his preaching was very similar to the one preached by John the Baptist – 'Repent, for the Kingdom of Heaven is near.' He taught in synagogues and in the open and, as his fame spread, people began to travel distances to hear him. Matthew lists members of his audiences having traveled from Deacapolis, Jerusalem, Judaea and Peraea – somewhere beyond the River Jordan.

Of all the sermons he delivered, one of the most famous is the Sermon on the Mount which he is estimated to have delivered in 30 CE to his disciples and a large crowd on the side of a mountain. Many famous and much-used phrases such as 'Turn the other cheek' and Judge not that ye be not judged' originate in this sermon. The Gospel of Matthew describes the opening of the sermon, a section known as the Beatitudes in which Jesus describes the qualities of the inhabitants of heaven. They begin with the lines 'Blessed are the poor in spirit: for theirs is the kingdom of heaven.'

In what is often said to have been April 30 CE, Jesus travelled to

Jerusalem, having already told his disciples that he would die soon. He arrived during the festival of the Passover and was welcomed into the city by large crowds as the 'King of Israel'. At Herod's Temple, he overturned the tables used by moneychangers there and argued with the priests for allowing them to do business there.

Later that week, he celebrated Passover by having a meal with his disciples, the meal known as the Last Supper, so famously recreated by Leonardo da Vinci in one of the history's most famous images. The meal is supposed to have been eaten either in the Room of the Last Supper on Mount Zion, located just outside the walls of Jerusalem or in what is now St. Mark's Syrian Orthodox Church in Jerusalem.

During the meal, Jesus took some bread and prayed before passing it to his disciples with the words 'This is my body which is given for you'. At the end of the meal he picked up a cup of wine, prayed again and passed it to his disciples saying 'this cup which is poured out for you is the New Covenant in my blood'. Thus, the ritual of the Eucharist was introduced. During the meal, he revealed, to the disbelief of the gathering, that one of them would betray him. In the Gospels of Matthew and John, the traitor is revealed as Judas Iscariot.

Following the Last Supper, Jesus and the disciples went to the Garden of Gethsemane to pray but temple guards arrived to arrest him, having been ordered to carry out the operation by night to prevent a riot, such was Jesus' popularity. When the guards asked which one of the gathered men was Jesus, Judas fulfilled Jesus' prophecy by kissing him to identify him. Another disciple, Simon Peter, grabbed a sword and attacked one of the arresting guards, cutting off his ear. According to Matthew, Jesus healed the man immediately and remonstrated with Simon Peter. 'All they that take the sword,' he said 'shall perish by the sword.' Jesus was led away and his disciples went into hiding.

He was tried before the Sanhedrin, a Jewish judicial body, the elders asking him whether he was, as claimed, the Son of God. When he replied that they were right in saying that he was, they immediately condemned him for blasphemy. He was handed over to the Roman authorities, headed by the Roman Prefect or Procurator of the Province of Judaea, Pontius Pilate. He was charged with sedition for telling people they should not pay their taxes and for claiming to be the King of the Jews. Pilate famously did not believe Jesus to be guilty of any particular crime against Rome, although when he asked him if he was indeed King of the Jews, Jesus replied, 'It is as you say.'

There was a tradition at Passover whereby the Roman governor could free one prisoner. When he offered the crowd a choice between Jesus of Nazareth and Barabbas who was either a bandit or a member of a Jewish movement seeking to overthrow the Roman occupying forces, the crowd chose Barabbas and Jesus was sentenced to be crucified, the usual punishment at the time for Jews believed to have betrayed Rome.

Jesus was painfully crowned with a crown of thorns and forced to carry his large wooden cross to the place of the Crucifixion, known as Calvary. His route was lined with baying crowds.

He was nailed to the cross and died late in the afternoon, his body being taken by the wealthy Judaean, Joseph of Arimathea, and placed in a tomb. On the third day following the Crucifixion, however, according to the Gospels, he came back to life and left the tomb, an angel having appeared to Mary Magdalene to announce the fact. During the next forty days, he is reported to have appeared to a number of people, amongst them two travellers on the road to Emmaus and his disciples. He told Peter he was the shepherd of new souls and Peter would, according to the Roman Catholic Church, become the first Bishop of Rome, or Pope.

Finally, Jesus ascended into heaven and was received by a cloud, as described in the Acts of the Apostles, leaving his followers to spread his word and await his Second Coming.

Following his death, Christianity was no more than a small Jewish sect. Several decades later, it had become distinct from Judaism. As

Nicene Christianity, it began to spread through the Roman Empire and, over the centuries, it became the main religion of Europe. During the years of exploration in the 15th and 16th centuries, Christian missionaries spread Christianity to the Americas and then the rest of the world.

It is estimated that, although church attendance is declining, Christianity now has anywhere between 1.5 and 2.1 billion adherents, split into 34,000 denominations. It is the world's largest religion.

BOUDICCA

'A TERRIBLE DISASTER occurred in Britain. Two cities were sacked, eighty thousand of the Romans and of their allies perished, and the island was lost to Rome. Moreover, all this ruin was brought upon the Romans by a woman, a fact which in itself caused them the greatest shame . . . the person who was chiefly instrumental in rousing the natives and persuading them to fight the Romans, the person who was thought worthy to be their leader and who directed the conduct of the entire war, was Boudicca, a Briton woman of the royal family and possessed of greater intelligence than often belongs to women.'

So wrote one Roman historian of the greatest leader ancient Britain ever had – the warrior queen, Boudicca.

She would undoubtedly have been an imposing sight. The only physical description of her – written by Cassius Dio, a Roman historian and public servant who, admittedly, died 175 years after her last battle, describes her as 'very tall, in her demeanour most terrifying, in the glint of her eye most fierce, and her voice was harsh; a great mound of the tawniest hair fell to her hips; around her neck was a large golden necklace; and she wore a tunic of divers colours over which a thick mantle was fastened with a brooch.'

Most sources agree that Boudicca was of royal descent, born around 25 CE to a Celtic family and in 48 CE married Prasutagus who would go on to become king, or chief of the Iceni tribe, a Brythonic or British tribe whose territory corresponded roughly to the modern-day county of Norfolk in the east of England. There are few solid facts about Boudicca's life. Our main sources are Cassius Dio and another Roman historian, Tacitus whose father-in-law was

Gnaeus Julius Agricola, a military tribune under Suetonius Paulinus, Military Governor of Britain during Boudicca's lifetime.

The Iceni enjoyed independence of sorts from the Roman conquerors of Britain, having concluded an alliance with them. They had welcomed the Romans a hundred years earlier when Gaius Julius Caesar had made the first forays into Britain in 55 BCE and 54 BCE. Six tribes had offered him allegiance and the Iceni had been one of them. The Romans had failed to establish themselves, however, and for the next ninety-seven years they had stayed away from this country with its pugnacious tribes and terrible weather. Finally, Emperor Claudius decided in 41 CE that it was time to return. Britain provided a ready supply of grain and other supplies needed by the Roman army and its conquest would also look good for the limping, stuttering Emperor who many thought to be weak.

Boudicca would have been around eighteen when the Romans returned at a time when Antedios was king of the Iceni. He adopted a neutral position towards the invaders while other tribes openly supported them; there was a lot to be gained from Rome, after all. Some, however, such as Caradoc, king of the Catuvellani whose land was to the south of the Iceni fought back and an alliance of tribes was formed to repel the Romans. It was only when the Emperor himself came to Britain and defeated the British tribes at Camulodunum – modern-day Colchester – that he gained the submission of the tribes and amongst the eleven tribal chiefs who submitted to the Emperor was Antedios.

The normal practice of the Romans in an occupied land was to allow a kingdom its independence during the lifetime of the incumbent ruler. At the end of that time, the kingdom would pass to the Emperor – Nero in this case – and in accordance with this practice, Prasutagus made the Emperor a co-heir, along with his wife and two daughters. However, in Roman law, inheritance could only pass through the male line of a family. Consequently, when Prasutagus died, the Romans, who considered them to have passed to the

Emperor, took his lands and property. They moved in and began to treat the Iceni land like an occupied territory. The nobles were treated like slaves and Boudicca was stripped and beaten in public and her young daughters raped. They demanded the repayment of loans that had been made to Prasutagus and Boudicca and her compatriots found themselves heavily in debt to the Romans.

It was 60 or 61 CE when the tribes decided they had had enough of marauding groups of legionnaires and the abuse of their land, property and persons.

The governor of the time, Gaius Suetonius Paulinus was in Wales, trying to subdue the rebellious tribes there. Boudicca joined with the neighbouring tribe, the Trinovantes and others who had suffered the same treatment as the Iceni and such was her passion and determination that she was elected leader of the combined force. They marched on Camulodunum where the Romans had appropriated land and buildings from the locals and had built a temple to Claudius that was particularly insulting and provided a focus for local resentment, especially as the people of the region had been forced to pay for it. When the Roman garrison in the city called for reinforcements in the face of Boudicca's advancing force, they were sent only two hundred soldiers. The British showed no mercy, annihilating out the garrison and razing the city to the ground. The IX Hispana Legion marched hurriedly towards Camulodunum from its camp at Longthorpe, some eighty miles away, led by Petillus Cerialis but, fresh from her victory at Camulodunum, Boudicca ambushed them and massacred them, Petillus Cerialis only just escaping with his life. It was a stunning victory.

Governor Suetonius rushed back from North Wales with his army to defend the relatively new and thriving town of Londinium which bustled with merchants, travelers and Roman officials and was even then the most populous town in the country. However, he did not yet have sufficient troops to defend the city and decided that discretion was the better part of valour, abandoning the town in order to save the province. Boudicca's force fell on Londinium and burned it to the ground, massacring any inhabitants who had been foolish enough not to flee. They then marched northwards to Verulamium – St. Albans – and meted out the same treatment as they had in Colchester and London. In the three cities, the Britons showed no mercy. Cassius Dio wrote that the noblest women were impaled on spikes and had their breasts cut off and sewn to their mouths, 'to the accompaniment of sacrifices, banquets, and wanton behaviour' in sacred places, particularly the groves of Andraste.

As Tacitus wrote: 'The natives enjoyed plundering and thought of nothing else. By-passing forts and garrisons, they made for where loot was richest and protection weakest. Roman and provincial deaths at the places mentioned are estimated at seventy thousand. For the British did not take or sell prisoners, or practice wartime exchanges. They could not wait to cut throats, hang, burn, and crucify – as though avenging, in advance, the retribution that was on its way.'

In all, around 70,000 people are believed to have been slaughtered by Boudicca's men in the three cities.

Suetonius rallied his men. He gathered the XIV Gemina legion, detatchments of the XX Valeria Victrix and any other auxiliaries he could find. His army numbered some 10,000 legionnaires and took its stand in an unknown location somewhere in the West Midlands along the Roman road, Watling Street. It may have been at Mancetter, where there was already a Roman camp, midway between Wales and Londinium.

The Romans were heavily outnumbered but had the advantage of being better organised, disciplined and trained and they also possessed superior weapons. They carefully chose a location where the British could not make full use of their superior numbers – a gorge with a wood behind them.

The British warriors approached, an unprecedented host of 230,000 men, according to some accounts, and although this is likely to be something of an exaggeration, it was still a massive army. Boudicca was standing up in her war chariot, her daughters beside her, driving in and out of her troops, exhorting tham, reminding them that their cause was just, that they were avenging their lost freedom, the rape of their women and the atrocities wrought on them by the Romans. She reminded them that they should not fear the Romans – they had after all already defeated one legion.

The location was decisive, however. The narrowness of the area available to fight in limited the number of troops she could send forward at any one time. The Romans were drawn up tightly in the centre with the auxiliaries on the flanks and the cavalry on the wings. The Britons rushed forward, screaming abuse at their enemy and singing battle songs. The Romans were silent and disciplined as they released a deadly flurry of two metre-long iron javelins – the pilum. They held their ground and tens of thousands of Britons died rushing forward. The next wave faced an unrelenting wall of Roman shields from behind which their owners stabbed with their lethal short swords. The Romans then began to advance in wedge-shaped formation, hacking at the Britons as they ploughed through them, killing them or driving them back. The British chariots made for the Roman archers but were repulsed by a volley of arrows. Lacking breastplates or armour, many of Boudicca's men were killed and wounded. Now the Roman infantry charged at full speed, breaking through the British ranks as those British still alive tried to retreat, but found themselves trapped between the Romans and a ring of wagons holding their own families which blocked the perimeter of the battlefield. It turned into a rout and the Romans butchered everyone, even the women at the rear.

The casualty numbers vary, but Tacitus claims that eighty thousand British troops died that day while only four hundred Romans lost their lives. It was a crushing and decisive defeat.

As for Boudicca, her bold attempt to restore the dignity of the British tribes was at an end. Reports vary as to what became of her after the battle. Some say that she died of her wounds, but others claim that defeat was more than she could stand and that she poisoned herself.

MARCUS AURELIUS

ROME HAD ITS share of feckless or downright wicked emperors over the centuries that the Roman Empire wielded power across Europe. Between 96 and 180 CE, however, it enjoyed one of its most prosperous periods. The great historian, Edward Gibbon wrote of it in *The History of the Decline and Fall of the Roman Empire*: 'If a man were called to fix the period in the history of the world during which the condition of the human race was most happy and prosperous, he would, without hesitation, name that which elapsed from the death of Domitian to the accession of Commodus.' During this period, the Empire fell under the stewardship of the 'Five Good Emperors' – five consecutive emperors who provided just and virtuous rule. These were Nerva, Trajan, Hadrian, Antoninus Pius and the last of them, from 161 to 180 CE, Marcus Aurelius Antoninus Augustus, known to us as Marcus Aurelius and often with the epithet 'the Wise' appended to his name.

Not only was he a great leader, however, he was also a great thinker and one of the most important of the philosophic school of Stoicism, created in Athens in the 3rd century BCE by Zeno of Citium.

Born Marcus Annius Catilius Severus on 26 April 121 CE, he was the only son of Marcus Annius Verus, a man of Spanish origin, who served as a praetor, but died when Marcus was just three years old. His mother, Domitia Lucilla, was a woman of noble birth whose grandfather served three times in Rome's highest-ranking elected role of Consul, a rare distinction. Following his father's death, Marcus was brought up by his mother and his paternal grandfather

Marcus was taught philosophy and rhetoric and was intelligent and conscientious. His family was very well connected, his aunt, Vibia Sabina being married to the Emperor Hadrian. He was also related to the previous Emperors, Trajan and Antoninus Pius. The Emperor Hadrian took an interest in him while he was still young and is said to have nicknamed him 'Verissimus' – most truthful. It is thought that Hadrian had already picked him out at this early age as a possible successor to him.

In 137 CE, the aged and ailing Hadrian announced his successor to be Lucius Ceionius Commodus, who would rule as Lucius Aelius Caesar. Commodus had no military experience but had been a Senator and had powerful political allies. His health, however, was weak, and he did not outlive the Emperor, dying in 138. Next in line was Antoninus Pius whom, as was customary, Hadrian adopted as his son. He only did it, however, on condition that Antoninus, in turn, adopted Marcus Aurelius and Lucius Commodius's son, also called Lucius Ceionius Commodius as his sons and ensure that they were next in the imperial line. Antoninus named them as his successors in February 138 when Marcus Aurelius was just eighteen years old.

Hadrian died in the summer of 139 CE and Antoninus Pius became Emperor, his reign of twenty-two years becoming one of the most peaceful and prosperous in Roman history. He never once left Italy throughout that time partly because of his lack of enthusiasm for military adventures. However, this meant that neither of his two young heirs benefited from any military experience, something of a disadvantage for a prospective Roman Emperor. They made their way through the public life of Rome and Marcus was Consul in 140, 145 and 161 CE and began to play an increasing role in decision-making with Antoninus. He had also married Antoninus's daughter, Annia Galeria Faustina in 145, bonding himself even closer to the Emperor and his family.

He had been educated by the greatest scholars of his day – Geminus taught him drama, Andron taught geometry, Caninius

63

Celer and Herodes Atticus taught him Greek oratory, Alexander of Cotiaeum, Greek language and Marcus Cornelius Fronto tutored him in Latin. In correspondence that has survived, Marcus's burgeoning interest in philosophy comes across.

On the death of Antoninus in March 161 CE, Marcus was offered the imperial crown, but refused to accept it unless Hadrian's and Antoninus's wish was carried out and that Commodus, now re-named Lucius Aurelius Verus be offered it, too.

There were sound political reasons for this joint emperorship. There were wars to be fought on several fronts, and it would be difficult for the Emperor to fight on different fronts. Previous experiments with the appointment of strong generals – Julius Caeasr and Vespasian being prime examples – had only led to them seizing control of the Empire on the back of their military successes. So, Verus marched off to command the legions on the Parthian front to the east while Marcus Aurelius took command of the German front to the north. Marcus reasoned that Verus enjoyed sufficient power not to want to overthrow him and he was right.

The challenges Rome faced at the time were, indeed, great and with Marcus's elevation to the imperial throne, the famous Pax Romana – a long period of peace and minimal expansion – came to an end and, to some extent, so, too did the glory of ancient Rome. Newer races were striving for recognition and for freedom from suppression and tyranny whether by occupying armies or by invaders from the east. There had been problems in Britain where the warlike Picts had begun to threaten the Antonine Wall that had been constructed to keep them out of Roman Britain. This was crushed, as were similar rebellions and raids along the Danube. But, the threat from the east was much more dangerous and the destruction of an entire legion – the XXII Deiotariana – at Eleigia emphasised the serious of the situation .

The Parthians had originated in the northeastern part of modern-day Iran and relations with the Romans had deteriorated in recent years until in 161, Parthian king, Vologases IV, taking advantage of Antoninus's death, declared war on Rome and re-conquered Armenia which had served as an effective buffer state between the two empires. Marcus Aurelius sent Verus to lead an expedition against the Parthians, ensuring that he was accompanied by some of the best Roman generals. The campaign, known as the Bellum Armeniacum et Parthicum was waged over a wide area including Syria, Cappadocia, Armenia, Mesopotamia and Media and it was successful and decisive; most of Parthia's important cities and strongholds were destroyed. By 166 CE Parthia had surrendered and a candidate of the Romans now occupied the Armenian throne. Verus's return was triumphant, both emperors parading through Rome and their sons and daughters joining the procession.

The Parthian war, however, was punishing for a people who had been at peace for a long time. Not only did it tax all their resources, the withdrawal of troops from the northern frontier of the Empire, along the Danube river, provided an opportunity for trouble there. Warlike Germanic tribes and other nomadic peoples had been marauding along the northern frontier, attacking Gaul and the towns and villages along the Danube. They were, in reality, part of a great migration known as the 'Wandering of the nations' and many of them were simply moving in response to invasions of their own territory from the east.

In 162 CE, the Chatti, an ancient Germanic tribe that had settled in Hesse and Lower Saxony, were repulsed by the Romans. In 166 CE, however, a mixture of tribes crossed the Danube, the first time Italy had been invaded since the late 2nd century BCE. They included the Bohemian Marcomanni, a tribe who had been conquered by the Romans in 19 CE, and a smaller tribe, the Quadi. At the same time as this was happening, the Sarmatians, people of Iranian origin, were launching an attack to the east, between the Danube and the Tisza rivers.

Rome was also facing disaster on its own doorstep. The army that had returned from the Parthian War had brought back with it a plague, known as the Antonine Plague, or sometimes the Plague of Galen. Believed to be either smallpox or measles, the pandemic ravaged Rome between 165 and 180 CE, killing thousands, including Verus who died as he rode north with Marcus Aurelius in 169 CE to deal with the threat on the northern frontier. Grief-stricken at the loss of his adoptive brother, Marcus returned with his body to Rome and buried him with all honours. He then hurried northwards again to fight on and rule alone.

Following Verus's death, Marcus personally led his men into battle and was now engaged in campaigns to protect the Empire for the remainder of his life. The plague, famine and earthquakes that had ravaged the Empire in recent years, coupled with casualties of war, had decimated the army and even slaves were mobilised to increase its strength. At first the tribes were successful against the Romans and they crossed the Alps and inflicted defeats on them before laying siege to the principal Roman city in the Italian north-east. The Dacian tribe, the Costoboci, invaded in the east, attacking Moesia, Macedonia and Greece, but Marcus forced them to retreat, although many settled in the area.

It was an expensive campaign and it took a long time. He had to create two entirely new Roman legions and construct numerous new camps. In 174 CE an extraordinary victory was won against the Quadi, an incident known as the Thundering Legion. The Roman army was hopelessly surrounded, with no chance of escape, when suddenly there was a cloudburst. Refreshing rain is said to have poured down on the Romans while the enemy were scattered in disarray by lightning and terrible hailstorms and consequently defeated.

But his steady campaigning was interrupted in 175 when a rival to the imperial crown appeared. Roman general, Avidius Cassius, governor of Syria claimed the empire for himself. It has been suggested that he was involved in a conspiracy with Marcus's wife, but this has never been proved and it may be that he simply heard a rumour that Marcus had been killed and seized the opportunity that presented itself. Marcus's reaction was to immediately leave for the East, but Avidius was killed before he arrived. He took advantage of his journey, however, inspecting his provinces and, in Athens, being initiated into the Eleusinian Mysteries, the secret rites, ceremonies and beliefs that included promises of divine power and rewards in the afterlife to which both Hadrian and Verus had been introduced before him.

Returning to Italy, he headed for the northern frontier once again, taking with him his 16 year-old son, Commodus, whom he had decided would succeed him as Emperor. In 180 CE, however, while making plans for the annexation of Bohemia he fell ill. On 17 March, he died of the same illness that had killed Verus.

Marcus Aurelius was one of the most remarkable men of antiquity, but not just for his campaigns against Rome's various enemies. He was a philosopher-Emperor, and left behind a series of 'Writings to Myself' called *Meditations*, twelve volumes that can be said to be like a modern self-help book. These are personal reflections and aphorisms, written for his own personal enjoyment throughout his life of public service. They were written in his tent at night after a long march or after a battle and demonstrate the tenets of his philosophy, Stoicism. He believed that inner freedom is to be gained from submission to providence and rigorous detatchment from everything over which we have no control. Stoicism believed that the denial of emotion frees a man from the pains and pleasures of the material world. He writes: 'He who fears death either fears the loss of sensation or a different kind of sensation. But if thou shalt have no sensation, neither wilt thou feel any harm; and if thou shalt acquire another kind of sensation, thou wilt be a different kind of living being and thou wilt not cease to live.'

EMPEROR HADRIAN

ROMAN EMPEROR HADRIAN, who reigned from 117 until 138 CE, has often been described as the most versatile of all Roman emperors, a man equally at home in the fields of the arts as he was in military matters. He also, of course, made a major impact on Britain, known to the Romans as Britannia, having initiated the construction of Hadrian's Wall, a stone and turf fortification, stretching across northern England to both mark the furthest western limit of the Roman Empire and to keep out the marauding hordes from the north.

Although some say that he was born in Rome, it is more likely that he was born Publius Aelius Hadrianus in Italica in the province of Hispania, modern-day Spain. His father, Publius Aelius Hadrianus Afer, was a senator who spent much of his time in Rome and was a cousin of future Emperor Trajan. His mother, Domitia Paulina, also came from a family of noble Romans.

When his parents died in 86 CE, when Hadrian was ten, he became a ward of Trajan and Publius Acilius Attianus who would later be appointed to the senior position of Praetorian Prefect by Trajan when he became Emperor.

He fought and did well in the wars between the Romans and the Dacians with the rank of Legate of the V Macedonia legion. Later, he accompanied Trajan on his expedition against Parthia, being given his own command at this time. Trajan was very ill, however, and left Hadrian in charge of guarding the Roman rear in Syria while he went home to recover. He did not make it, dying at Selinus, a Greek colony in Sicily.

Although Hadrian was an obvious successor to Trajan, he may have owed his actual elevation to the imperial throne to Trajan's wife, Plotina. Trajan had not named his successor, but Plotina, who nursed her husband in his final illness, probably forged an adoption document, signed by her and not by the Emperor, that made Hadrian his son, and next Emperor.

The new Emperor quelled a Jewish uprising in the Middle East before returning to Europe to stabilise Rome's Danube frontier and eliminate some political rivals, principally four prominent Senators that he discovered to be plotting against him. They were all put to death and it is probably no coincidence that they were all Trajan's men. But, Hadrian was loved by the army and with that kind of support, forged adoption papers and political rivals meant little.

His reign was not characterised by much in the way of major military conflict. Rather, he was a brilliant military administrator and strengthened the Roman border against attacks with fortifications such as Hadrian's Wall and a series of forts and outposts. He maintained a very hands-on approach to the army, personally inspecting them and establishing intensive drill routines to prevent his troops from becoming bored as well to instill discipline in them.

Hadrian spent more than half of his reign away from Rome, becoming one of the most-travelled of Roman Emperors, riding far and wide across the Empire to inspect his legions. Travelling and remaining in contact with the furthest reaches of his Empire became the way he governed, in the same way that the Holy Roman Emperor Charlemagne would do some 800 years later. He did this with the support of the Roman Senate and, it is suggested, a secret police force, the Frumentarii.

He left his mark wherever he went, handing out instructions and funds for the construction of new public buildings, significantly improving the Empire's infrastructure and by doing so, strengthening it against hostile forces, a more efficient way, he believed than by waging war and conquering enemy peoples.

His entourage was huge and of administrators, officials, architects and builders who would help him develop his plans. Countries were almost bankrupt as they passed through, given the huge amount of supplies it took to keep them on the road.

In 121, he travelled north towards Germania, providing funds to strengthen the defences in that part of the world but then, hearing of a revolt in Britannia, he headed to this remote corner of the Empire the following year. The rebellion had been going on since 119 and it may be the reason he built his famous wall, although the true reason for its construction is uncertain. It may merely have been a monument to Hadrian or, cynically, might have been a project dreamed up to occupy the time and the energy of an army bored with its stay in a cold and inhospitable country. Whatever the reason, it stands as a monument to his method of governing, using fortification and infrastructure rather than force and violence.

At the end of the year, he sailed from Britannica to Mauretania on the coast of northwest Africa where he led his troops against local insurgents. Receiving messages, however, that there was an uprising in Parthia – a region in what would be modern northeastern Iran – he hurried around the Mediterranean, paying a visit to Cyrene in present-day Libya, where he provided the necessary monies to establish a military training school for the sons of the noble Roman families who had settled there.

Arriving eventually at the Euphrates river, Hadrian characteristically negotiated a settlement with the Parthians before sailing along the Black Sea coast. Wintering in Nicomedia, the capital of Bythynia, he funded the reconstruction of buildings following a devastating earthquake. His popularity in the region soared.

It was around this time that he is reported to have fallen in love with a good-looking boy named Antinous who became an imperial favourite. He then voyaged through Anatolia, founding, en route, a new city, Mysia. He also built an impressive temple to his predecessor, Trajan, using dazzling white marble.

By autumn of 124, he was in Greece. Hadrian was a famous lover of all things Greek, well-versed in Greek culture and history to the extent that, when younger, he had been named Graeculus, or Little Greek. He participated in the famous Eleusinian Mysteries, initiation ceremonies held every year for the cult of Demeter and Persephone at Eleusis, that were the most important of the many such ceremonies held in Greece. After travelling around Greece, he arrived in Athens in March 125, initiating a construction programme, including the completion of a temple to Zeus that had been ongoing for some years under a number of Emperors.

Back in Rome for the first time since the early months of his reign, he was pleased by the completed Pantheon, a temple to honour all the gods whose re-building he had instigated after its destruction by fire in 80 CE. He did not rest long in his newly completed villa in the Sabine Hills, however, setting off on a tour of Italy in March 127. He decided to divide the country into four regions governed by legates with the rank of Consul, an unpopular innovation that disappeared shortly after his death.

Although ill, he set off for a visit to Africa in spring 128, inspecting his troops and funding building projects as usual. A few months later, he was back in Rome, but soon set off on his travels again and this time he would be gone for three years.

He firstly went to Greece to once again participate in the Eleusinian Mysteries and also to establish his grand new vision for Greece, the Panhellenion, a council of all the rival cities of Greece, meeting in his grand new Temple of Zeus in Athens. The Panhellenion was an idea far ahead of its time, a parliament by any other name, although it failed despite his efforts.

Tragedy struck in 130 when, Antinous, by now his lover, drowned while they were sailing on the Nile in Egypt. The cause of his drowning is unknown and it has been speculated that it might have been murder, suicide or part of a religious sacrifice. The Emperor was broken-hearted, immediately declaring his dead lover a god. He ordered cities to be named after him and medals depicting him to be fashioned. Statues of Antinous were erected everywhere and temples re-named in his honour. The city of Antinopopolis was founded where he died.

In 130, Hadrian visited the ruined city of Jerusalem which had been devastated by the First Roman-Jewish war, fought between 66 and 73 CE. He made a promise that the city would be rebuilt and re-named it Aeli Capitolina, after himself and the main Roman god, Jupiter Capiolinus. It is probable that Hadrian remained in Athens during the winter of 131 to 132, but he definitely led his troops personally against yet another Jewish revolt in Judaea in 133. The rebellion had been induced partly by his banning of the Jewish tradition of circumcision and it took additional troops from Britannia and from the Danube to quell the revolt, but not before the Roman army had suffered substantial losses. The rebellion was ended in 135 but according to Roman sources of the time, the three years of fighting had resulted in 580,000 Jewish soldiers dying and fifty fortified towns and 985 villages being destroyed. The Jewish cause was irreparably damaged and Hadrian persisted in persecuting them, attempting to wipe out Judaism by executing Judaic scholars and prohibiting the law of the Torah as well as the Jewish calendar. He even re-named Judaea, calling it Syria Palestina and Jews were forbidden from entering its capital for five years.

Hadrian's patronage of the arts was exemplary. He was responsible for the construction of many great and influential buildings, the Pantheon being just one of these, its domed structure wielding influence over the architects of the Italian Renaissance and the Baroque periods. He had always shown an interest in architecture but also wrote poetry in both his native Latin tongue and in Greek. An autobiography, that he wrote has now been lost.

Curiously, he was the first Roman Emperor, apart from Nero, to sport a beard and Emperors after him are mostly depicted wearing beards. He had begun wearing one as a sign of his love for Greek culture and history, but he started a new fashion that lasted for many years.

In his philosophy, he is most often described as an Epicurean. Epicure did not believe in superstition or divine intervention. He believed that the greatest good was to be gained from seeking modest pleasures, from knowing how the world worked and understanding the limits of our desires. Through this, a state of tranquility and freedom from fear could be achieved.

Hadrian did not actually abolish slavery from Roman life but the lot of the slave was improved under his rule. He humanised the legal code and torture was outlawed by him.

The final years of this great and much-loved Emperor were passed in Rome. His health began to fail and, like all of his predecessors, he had to deal with the eternally vexed matter of his succession. He firstly adopted Lucius Aelius Caesar, who died in January 138 and then took another adoptive son and heir, Titus Aurelius Fulvus Boionius Arrius Antoninus, who would become Emperor Antoninus Pius.

Hadrian died, most probably of heart failure, on 10 July 138 in his villa at Baiae, aged sixty-two. He was initially buried at Puteoli, near Baiae but his remains were transferred to Rome and re-buried in the Gardens of Domitia, near to the site of a mausoleum that was being built for him. The building was finished in 139 and his ashes and those of his wife, Sabina, and his first adopted son, Lucius Aelius, were interred there.

His reign had enjoyed moments of real glory after a faltering start and his tomb, now known as the Castel Sant'Angelo, stands as a magnificent monument to a glorious reign.

ATTILA THE HUN

THE SCOURGE OF God they called him. One of the most fearsome of the enemies of the eastern and Western Roman Empires, he rampaged across Europe from east to west and created an empire that stretched from Germany to the Ural River in Kazakhstan and from the Danube to the Baltic. He is reported by many to have been the embodiment of evil; cruel and rapacious. According to others, however, he was a great and noble king, a proud and powerful leader of men.

Attila the Hun became leader of the Hunnic Empire in 434. The Huns were probably a confederation of nomadic tribes from Central Asia and Europe that some experts trace back to Turkic origins, believing them to have been descended from the legendary Xiongnu tribes that as early as the 5th century BCE threatened China to such an extent that the Emperor Qin Shi Huangdi built a section of the Great Wall specifically to keep them at bay.

They first appeared in Europe in the 5th century CE, moving from southern Russia westwards, great fighters always ready for battle, fine horsemen and with superior weapons to their European opponents such as the composite bow, made from different materials – each ideally suited to its purpose – laminated together.

In 434, the Hunnic leader, Rugila, died and was succeeded by his nephews, Attila and Bleda, who assumed control over all of the united Hun tribes. Discontent amongst the Huns at the brothers' assumption of the leadership led to several Hunnic nobles being forced to take refuge in the Byzantine Empire. Attila and his brother met the Emperor Theodosius II's envoys and negotiated not only on the return of the renegade nobles, but also a doubling of the tribute they were paid by the Byzantines, the opening of their markets to Hun traders and an agreed ransom for each Roman captured by the Huns. It was a good deal and marked an auspicious beginning to the brothers' joint rule.

For the next few years, Attila turned his attention to the riches to be won in the east, leading a force against the Persian Empire. Defeat at the hands of the Sassenid Persians in Armenia brought this adventure to an end, however, and Attila returned to Europe.

In 440, a major Hun force menaced the frontier of the Roman Empire on the River Danube, attacking merchants at the market on the river's northern bank, the same market that had been established by Attila's earlier treaty with the Romans. He led his army across the river and attacked Illyrian cities and forts. The Romans were at their mercy as they were facing attacks in both Armenia and the important province of Africa which had Carthage as its capital. The Sassenid Persian Shah Yazdegerd II invaded Armenia in 441 and threatened the Eastern Empire.

The Western Empire was experiencing trouble in its province of Africa, the richest province of the empire and, critically, its main source of food. Its main city, Carthage, had been taken by the Vandals led by Geiseric and Rome had been forced to strip its Danube frontier and fortresses in Illyria, to send an army to try to re-take the province. Consequently, Attila faced little opposition, enjoying a clear path with little resistance right through to the Balkans which he invaded in 441. He sacked the important cities of Margus and Viminacium and then captured Singdunum, modern-day Belgrade and the important town of Sirmium where he halted.

In 442, Emperor Theodosius brought in reinforcements from Sicily and ordered a huge new issue of coins that he used to finance his campaign against the Huns. Attila, meanwhile, launched a campaign along the Danube, attacking and capturing military bases at Ratiaria. He also began to introduce sophisticated new weaponry and fighting techniques entirely new to the Huns. During his siege of the city of Naissus, for example, he used battering rams and mobile siege towers.

His advance continued along the Nisava river, capturing Serdica – modern-day Sofia – Philippopolis (Plovdiv) and Arcadiopolis. Meeting a Roman army not far from Constantinople, Attila's army annihilated it, but Theodosius had spent 442 reinforcing the walls of Constantinople, adding a sea wall to its defences and the Huns were unable to breach it. However, Attila defeated another Roman army in the vicinity of Callipolis – modern-day Gallipoli – and Theodosius was forced to negotiate. Attila demanded harsh terms, the Emperor agreeing to give the Huns almost two kilos of gold and trebling the annual tribute payment, as was the ransom to be paid for the freedom of each Roman captive the Huns took.

Attila was an ambitious man and around this time, 445, decided he was not entirely happy sharing the throne with his brother, a situation he remedied by arranging a hunting accident for Bleda. He now reigned alone.

In 449, he again rode south into the Roman Empire. At the Battle of the Utus he defeated Arnegisculus and his Roman army, but not without severe losses. Once again, though, the Huns were unopposed and marched through the Balkans to Thermopylae, capturing dozens of cities and killing a large proportion of their populations. As they passed they attacked monasteries and convents, murdering anyone they found, regardless of whether they were men or women. Only the intervention of the prefect Flavius Constantinus saved Constantinople. He reconstructed the city's defences, damaged by an earthquake, and built entirely new fortifications where necessary.

In 450, Attila turned his attention to the west, to the powerful Visigoth kingdom of Toulouse. By this time, he had befriended the Western Roman Emperor, Valentinian III, forming an alliance with him and providing troops to fight the Goths and the Bagaudae. He had earned the honorary title of magister militum, the most senior Roman military rank.

However, good relations with Rome did not last long. Valentinian's sister, Honoria, was about to become the victim of an arranged marriage to a Roman senator and in desperation had sent her engagement ring to Attila in a plea for help. He understood her message to be a proposal of marriage and accepted, asking for half of the Western Empire as a dowry. Valentinian, discovering the marriage plans, exiled his sister and wrote a letter to Attila in which he denied the legitimacy of the marriage proposal. Attila, offended, sent an ambassador to the Emperor, claiming the opposite and stating that unless Velentinian agreed, he would come and claim what was rightfully his – half of the Western Empire.

Attila gathered his tribes, amongst whom were the Gepids, Ostrogoths, Rugians, Scirians, Heruls, Thuringians, Alans and Burgundians and marched west. He arrived in Belgica with a massive army in 451, seeking to extend his empire across Gaul – present-day France – to the Atlantic Ocean.

In early April, he took Metz and came close to occupying Aurelianum – modern-day Orléans. The Roman general, Aetius, gathered an army drawn from the Franks, the Burgundians and the Celts and was joined by Theodoric I, King of the Visigoths. They had reached Orléans in advance of Attila and when he turned back, Aetius pursued him, catching his army near to modern-day Châlons-en-Champagne. The ensuing battle resulted in a Pyrrhic victory for the Romans. Theodoric was killed and Aetius failed to press his advantage, fearing the consequences if the Visigoths won, as much as he feared a defeat. Attila retreated in complete disarray. Remarkably, it would be the only defeat he ever suffered.

The following year, 452, he invaded Italy, again seeking to claim his marriage to Honoria. He sacked a number of cities – Padua, Bergamo, Milan and Verona amongst them. The city of Venice was founded when the residents of the area fled in the face of his advance to the many islands in the lagoon and began to live there. The city of Aquileia was destroyed completely and it is said that he built a castle on a hill nearby so that he could watch the city burn. This castle became the modern-day city of Udine. Finally, disease and famine brought his army to a halt at the River Po.

A meeting was arranged between Attila and Pope Leo I, the Consul Avienus and the Prefect Trigetius at Mincio near to Mantua. The Pope got Attila to promise to withdraw from Italy and make peace with Valentinian, prophesying, it has been said, that one of his descendents would receive a holy crown. Attila also superstitiously feared the fate of Alaric, who died shortly after sacking Rome in 410.

He re-traced his steps across the Danube, planning now to attack Constantinople to reclaim the tribute that Marcian was refusing to pay following the death of Thodosius. However, Attila died suddenly in his sleep the night of his marriage to the young and beautiful Ildico. He is said to have suffered a severe nosebleed and choked to death although other versions have him dying of internal bleeding after a bout of heavy drinking or being stabbed by another of his wives.

His cavalry rode around his tent singing dirges before he was buried in a triple coffin made of gold, silver and iron under the river bed of the Tisza which had been temporarily diverted for that purpose. Buried with him were treasures from his conquests and the men who buried him were killed to prevent them from divulging the location.

His three sons fought over his empire but in their disarray were defeated the following year by the Ostrogoths, and the Gepids at the Battle of Nedao. The great empire of Attila the Hun was gone.

HATSHEPSUT

HATSHEPSUT, BORN DURING Egypt's 18th Dynasty which lasted from 1550–1292 BCE, was one of the greatest leaders, male or female, of her time. She rose through the ranks from princess to queen and finally became the fifth pharaoh of her dynasty and one of the greatest pharaohs of them all, despite the constraints that arose from being a woman. She would bring great wealth to her country through an expansion of trade and this wealth would enable her to instigate the construction of great buildings that would only be matched a thousand years later in the architecture of Classical Greece. Remarkably, however, she was only able to achieve this by claiming the rights of a male and by strapping a golden beard to her chin and wearing male clothing. Not for nothing was she known as the Crown prince of Egypt during her rise to power.

She had begun to undertake the role of a male gradually, wearing the appropriate clothing – the *shendyt* kilt, the *nemes* headdress with its *uraeus* – the stylised, upright form of an Egyptian spitting cobra worn on the headdress – the *khat* head cloth and false beard. She gave up those titles that only a woman could hold and even dropped the female ending to her name – the letter 't' – shortening her name to Hatshepsu.

She was the daughter of Thutmose I who reigned from 1493 to 1479 BCE and was educated more or less as a prince would have been. The position of women in Egypt was a complex one. Economically and legally, they had the same status and rights as men, but were still viewed as being responsible mainly for reproduction and the maintenance of the home. Her ambition and eventual achievement, therefore, were remarkable for her time.

On the death of her father, as was the custom, she married her half-brother, Thutmose II, assuming the customary title of Great Royal Wife. This title was given to the chief wife of a male pharaoh on the day of his coronation and her status in the royal line of succession was essential to his gaining the position of pharaoh. Thutmose was pharoah for between three and thirteen years – it is not known for certain how long – and, Hatshepsut being a strong individual, is surmised to have wielded a great deal of influence during her husband's reign.

Not only would she have been Great Royal Wife of the pharaoh, however. She would also have occupied the position of the God's Wife. In this sacred role, which was passed from mother to daughter, she would have officiated at the rites in Egyptian temples and would have acted as a priestess.

Thutmose left only one son, Thutmose III, to inherit his title, the son of Isis, another of his wives. With Hashepsut he had only a daughter, Neferura, who was made ready to accept the roles of her mother and is thought to have become the royal wife of her half-brother. The couple had one son, Amenemhat who died before his father.

Thutmose was young when he inherited the throne and, as his mother, Hatshepsut undertook the role of regent, governing in his place, while Neferura took over her religious duties. Hatshepsut, taking all the responsibilities of state, crowned herself co-pharaoh, relinquishing her title as God's Wife which was inappropriate for a pharaoh and which was passed on to Neferura. There had been many female rulers before, but none had taken for themselves the title of pharaoh and she was recognised as such until she died, following a reign estimated to have lasted around twenty-two years.

She firstly re-established trade networks. These had collapsed about three hundred years earlier during a period of disruption in Egypt. An expedition was planned to the Land of Punt, a fabled place, once believed to be somewhere in the Horn of Africa, where gold was produced and from where aromatic resins, African blackwood, ebony, ivory, slaves and exotic wild animals could be found.

Hatshepsut sent five sailing ships, each of which measured seventy feet long and carried 210 men, thirty of whom were rowers. Punt provided the riches that she had anticipated, amongst which were frankincense trees – in the first recorded attempt to transplant trees, they would be planted in the courtyards of her mortuary temple complex at Deir el Bahri.

As was customary, she had monuments constructed at the Temple of Karnak, and importantly, carried out restoration work on the Precinct of Mut that had been destroyed by foreign rulers several hundred years previously. She ordered the construction of twin obelisks, at that time the tallest in the world, at the entrance to the temple where one of them stands to this day.

Deir el Bahri, on the West Bank of the Nile, near the entrance to the Valley of the Kings, was one of the great achievements and undoubtedly the masterpiece of her reign. Constructed on the site of an even older temple – Mentuhotep I's mortuary temple from the 11th Dynasty – she built it to symbolise her divinity, given to her, she claimed by the god, Amun-Ra, and used the very latest building techniques in its construction. Its architect blended it in with the cliffs that surrounded it, creating a three terrace edifice with porticoes, and chapels to the gods Hathor, Anubis, Ra-Horakhte and, of course, Amun-Ra. Its terraces would once have been covered by lush gardens and amongst the many inscriptions are the words: 'welcome my sweet daughter, my favorite, the king of upper and lower Egypt, Maatkere, Hatshepsut. Thou art king, taking possession of the two lands.' It is one of the great buildings of the ancient world.

Numerous scenes of her time as pharaoh were depicted, including some references to military activity which is believed to date from early in her reign. She is said to have led successful military campaigns, gaining credibility among her people as a warrior queen. However, on the whole, her reign brought peace to Egypt.

Hatshepsut, the female pharaoh, died of unknown causes as she approached middle age, probably in 1458 BCE.

II
MEDIEVAL AND RENAISSANCE

MUHAMMAD

MUHAMMAD IBN 'ABDULLAH was born in 570 CE in the historic region of Hejaz in the present-day Saudi Arabian province of Makkah. He would grow up to become the principal human figure at the centre of the religion of Islam, regarded by Muslims as both the messenger of God and his prophet. In the temporal world, he worked as many things – merchant, diplomat, philosopher, orator, legislator, reformer and brilliant military general.

His life story is well documented, although every detail is not known. Nonetheless, the holy book of Islam, the Qur'an, serves as a good source of biographical information and it is also believed by scholars to contain an actual record of words spoken by Muhammad.

He lived the first fifty-two years of his life in Mecca, the town of his birth, a member of a prominent family in the city, the Banu Hashim, although its prosperity seems to have arrived later in the Prophet's life. Soon after his birth, he was sent to live with a family of Bedouin in the desert, a practice customary amongst families of the region; the desert life was thought to provide a much healthier environment for children. He returned home aged two, but in the meantime his father, Abdullah had died. He became an orphan aged six when his mother, Amina, became ill and died. He was taken into the care of his grandfather on his mother's side, Abd al-Muttalib, but within two years, he, too, was dead. His next guardian was the leader of the Hashim clan, his uncle, Abu Talib, but times were hard and, although his guardian ensured that Muhammad was fed, he had to more or less fend for himself.

His uncle began training him in commerce, allowing him, when he was still young, to accompany him on trading trips to Syria. On one of these trips when Muhammad was about twelve years old, the caravanserai in which he and his uncle were travelling, is said to have passed by the cave of a Christian monk named Bahira. Bahira invited the merchants to share a meal with him, but when he saw the young Muhammad, he noticed certain stigmata on him. Other versions say that he noticed a strange cloud movement or that the boy was constantly in the shadow of a branch of a tree, regardless of the time of day. He informed Muhammad's uncle and warned him to protect him from people who might want to do him harm, prophesying that he would be a prophet of God.

Muhammad eventually became a merchant, plying his trade between the Indian Ocean and the Mediterranean. Unusually for the time, he was honest and fair in his dealings with others, earning the nickname 'Al-Amin' (faithful or trustworthy). Others employed him to mediate in disputes, knowing he would be fair and just. In 595 CE, he married a forty year-old widow, Khadijah.

Muhammad took himself off to meditate for several weeks every year in a cave on Mount Hira, not far from Mecca. It was there, according to Islamic tradition, that the Archangel Gabriel first communicated with him in 610 CE. He was startled by this miracle and is said to have considered jumping off the mountain, but Gabriel explained to him that he had been chosen as a messenger of God. Returning to his family, he was consoled by Khadijah. For three years he had no further revelations, but devoted a great deal of time to prayer and meditation. The revelations resumed.

It was his wife who first believed him to be a prophet. Then his ten year-old cousin, Ali ibn Abi Talib, friend Abu Bakir and his adopted son, Zaid also began to believe.

In 613, he began preaching the message he had received in his revelations. In Mecca, however, he was largely ignored by those who did not laugh at what he was preaching. Those who did follow him were the young, those who had fallen out of the first rank of their families and the weak, mostly foreigners.

There was also violent opposition to what he was preaching – denouncing idol worship and polytheism, the worship of multiple gods and goddesses. He threatened to overthrow the focal point of Meccan religious life, the Kaaba, a huge cuboid building of granite, believed by Muslims to date back to the time of Abraham or possibly even earlier than that. It is to the Kaaba that Muslims face when they pray. Needless to say, there was wealth to be gained by local people and their rulers through having such a vital religious symbol in the midst of their city. Local merchants tried to bribe him to stop preaching against the traditions, but he refused to do so.

The first follower of Muhammad to die as a martyr was a slave, Sumayyah bint Khabbab. She was stabbed with a spear by her master for refusing to renounce the Muslim faith. Another slave, Bilal, was tortured by having a heavy rock placed on his chest, in order to make him give up Islam.

Muhammad was himself protected by his membership of the Banu Hashim family but in 617 CE, two other clans began a boycott of Hashim goods which they said they would only withdraw on condition that they stop providing protection for the Prophet. They refused and it endured three years before eventually collapsing.

The year 619 CE became known as 'the Year of Sorrows' as both Muhammad's wife, Khadijah and his uncle Abu Talib died. Unfortunately for Muhammad, the leadership of his family passed to one of his enemies, Abu Lahab, who immediately withdrew the Hashim protection that he had enjoyed for so long. It was now effectively open season on him. He tried to find others who would protect him, but none was available until a man called Mut'im ibn 'Adi offered the protection of his family, the Banu Nawfal.

Muhammad relocated with his followers to Yathrib – later called Medina – still in the region of Hejaz. There he made many converts who would meet with him covertly by night. They made the *Second Pledge of al-'Aqaba*, also known as the *Pledge of War*. It included an oath of obedience to Muhammad, 'enjoying good and forbidding evil' and a promise to respond when called to arms.

Tradition says that in 620, Muhammad, accompanied by the angel Gabriel, travelled from Mecca to what was called 'the Furthest mosque', usually stated to be the Al-Aqsa Mosque in Jerusalem. He is then said to have visited heaven and hell and spoken to ancient prophets – Moses, Abraham and Jesus. Some commentators present this experience as a spiritual journey, while others insist it was an actual physical journey.

Muhammad was invited by the clans of Medina to serve as chief arbitrator for the community, a necessary role because for around a hundred years there had been fighting between Jewish and Arab inhabitants of the town and the Arab tribes had also been engaged in destructive blood feuds. One unsavoury incident, the 617 CE Battle of Bu'ath, between the Banu Anus and the Banu Khazraj had ended inconclusively and an uneasy truce had been in place. They believed only a man with the authority of Muhammad could mediate between these warring clans and they offered him their protection if he agreed to accept the role.

Muhammad agreed and sent his followers to Medina but the Meccans, alarmed at the disappearance of the Muslims from their city, tried to assassinate the Prophet. He escaped, however, in the company of Abu Kakr and by 622 was established in Medina.

He began his work by devising the Constitution of Medina, a document that created a federation of the eight Median tribes and the new Muslim immigrants. It specified the rights and duties of all citizens and, although it had a religious element to it, it was a practical document that helped to preserve the legal traditions and customs of the old Arab tribes.

Gradually, the clans began to convert to Islam, following the conversion of Sa'd ibn Mu'adh, a prominent tribal leader. Opposition to the conversions was dealt with when two men who had composed verses ridiculing the Muslims – Asma bint Marwan and Abu 'Afak – were murdered, some claiming on the orders of the Prophet, others denying such claims.

Meanwhile, the Meccans began seizing the homes of the Muslims who had gone to Medina. The Muslims responded by attacking Meccan caravans and war broke out between the two sides. Muhammad provided Qur'anic verses that permitted the Muslims to fight the people of Mecca and the Muslims began to become wealthy from their plundering and, as the Meccans became economically weaker, the Muslims hoped they might use this to convert them.

In 624 Muhammad led a raid by 300 warriors on a Meccan caravan but a force from Mecca arrived to protect it. The opposing sides met at the Battle of Badr in March of that year and although they were outnumbered by more than three to one, the Muslims crushed the Meccans, killing many of their leaders. Muhammad went on to form alliances with many of the Bedouin tribes in the area to provide further protection for his community from attacks from the northern part of the Hejaz region.

As the Muslims carried out more attacks on Mecca's caravans and on tribes who supported their enemy, the Meccans were anxious to avenge the humiliation they had suffered and, in 625, their leader, Abu Sufyan, mobilised a huge army of three thousand men to launch an attack on Medina.

When a scout alerted Muhammad of the huge force advancing on them, a council of war was held at which there were arguments about how best to deal with the threat. While Muhammad and many of the senior Medina figures argued for remaining in Medina and fighting there, the younger members argued that while they remained in the city, the Meccans were destroying their crops and disdained them as cowards. They won the day and Muhammad assembled his force and led them to the Mountain of Uhud on 23 March.

Once again, in this battle the Muslims were heavily outnumbered but they gained the early initiative and forced the Meccans back. The Meccan camp was now unprotected and the Muslims launched an attack. However, the Meccan cavalry were waiting for them and took them unawares, rampaging through their ranks and killing many, including Muhammad's uncle, Hamza. It represented a significant setback for Muhammad and his men. He produced Qur'anic verses blaming the defeat on disobedience and suggested it was a test of their steadfastness.

The Meccans had won the battle but had failed in one respect – they had not achieved their objective of wiping out the Muslim threat for good. In pursuit of this aim, Abu Sufyan negotiated the support of nomadic tribes from the north and east of Medina while Muhammad worked to destroy such alliances.

In late March 627 CE, Abu Sufyan led a mighty force of 10,000 men against Medina, Muhammad having only 3,000 men at his disposal. He had, however, devised a new and original form of defence that had never before been employed in Arabia. He ordered his men to dig a trench wherever there was a chance that Meccan cavalry would attack the city. The ensuing battle became known as the battle of the Trench. The Meccans lay siege to Medina for two weeks but were unable to penetrate Muhammad's defensive system. Eventually, they were forced to give up and return to Mecca, their prestige in tatters and many trading partners abandoning them.

Meanwhile, Muhammad exacted revenge on some of the Meccans' allies. The Muslims besieged the Banu Qurayza for twenty-five days and when they finally surrendered, all the men, apart from some who converted to Islam, were beheaded.

Muhammad had delivered Qur'anic verses ordering Muslims to perform the Hajj, the pilgrimage to Mecca. For obvious reasons, they had not carried out this obligation for some time. In 628 CE he ordered his followers to prepare for a pilgrimage to Mecca, saying that God had promised him the fulfillment of his goal in a vision where he was shaving his head after performing the Hajj. Approaching Mecca, he entered into negotiations with the pagan Meccans and concluded a treaty – the Truce of Hudaybiyya. Its main points included the cessation of hostilities, the postponement of Muhammad's pilgrimage until the following year and an agreement to send back any Meccan who had gone to Medina without his protector's permission.

Muhammad next led an expedition against the Jewish oasis of Khaybar to deal with the Banu Nadir who were inciting hostility against the Muslims and wrote to numerous foreign rulers – including Heraclius of the Byzantine Empire, Khosrau of Persia – asking them to convert to Islam.

After two years, the Truce of Hudaybiyya with Mecca was broken when two tribes, one allied to Mecca, the other to Medina, attacked each other. The Meccans declared the treaty null and void, but then, realising their mistake, sent Abu Safyan to renew it. Muhammad refused and began preparations for a new campaign against the Meccans. He marched on Mecca in 630 CE with 10,000 men and captured the city with ease. In the spirit of reconciliation, however, he declared an amnesty for all Meccans and the majority of the city's inhabitants converted to Islam.

Muhammad now turned his attention to a threat emerging from the confederate tribes of Hawazin, based around Taif in the Arabian Peninsula. Heavily outnumbered, the Muslims defeated them at the Battle of Hunain, capturing huge amounts of valuable spoils. Meanwhile, numerous Bedouin and other tribes submitted to Muhammad.

Finally, ten years after leaving Mecca for Medina, Muhammad performed his pilgrimage to Mecca, teaching his followers, in the process, the regulations and rites of the various ceremonies of the Hajj. He followed this with a speech known as the 'Farewell Speech' in which he dealt with many issues of the Muslim faith, including the treatment of women and blood feuds, all of which he abolished.

Several months after his pilgrimage, the Prophet became ill with head pains and weakness. On 8 June 632, he died in the city of Medina and was buried in a tomb now housed inside the Mosque of the Prophet in Medina. The tomb next to his is empty. Muslims believe it awaits the body of Jesus.

CHARLEMAGNE

IT WAS CHRISTMAS Day 800 and Charlemagne, King of the Franks, was kneeling in prayer in St. Peter's Basilica in Rome. As he knelt, Pope Leo III approached him and unexpectedly placed a crown on his blond locks, proclaiming him to be *Imperator Romanorum*, Emperor of the Romans. It was not only a defining moment in Charlemagne's life; it was also a defining moment in the history of Europe.

Charlemagne's powerful kingdom, Francia, had been Christianised by the 6th century CE and ruled since by the Merovingian dynasty. The Merovingians went into decline, however, and a court official, the Mayor of the Palace, began to take a leading role in affairs, virtually running the country. One such Mayor, Pippin of Herstal, rose to stage a coup in the Frankish Kingdom in the late 7th century. His son, Charles Martel (Charles 'the Hammer') succeeded him in 737 but did not call himself 'king'. His sons, Carloman and Pippin the Short, father of Charlemagne, succeeded him in 741. However, the brothers decided to put Childeric III, a Merovingian on the throne, to prevent trouble in the kingdom. Childeric, a weak ruler, would be the last of the Merovingians to rule.

Carloman, a devout man, retired to a monastery in 747, leaving Pippin in sole control of Francia and when Childeric died, in 753, Pippin was elected King of the Franks by an assembly of Frankish nobles, having first gained the recognition of Pope Zachary. On the death of Pippin in 768, as was customary, his realm was divided between his two sons, Charles – to be known as Charlemagne – and Carloman.

Charlemagne had been born around 742 but little is known about his childhood. The division of the kingdom on his father's death left him with Neustria – most of the north of modern-day France – western Aquitaine and northern Austrasia – Germany, Belgium, Luxemburg and the Netherlands. Carloman, on the other hand, was given southern Austrasia (roughly, southeastern France), eastern Aquitaine, Burgundy, Provence and Swabia – land on the present-day German-Italian border.

Charlemagne's first challenge was an uprising by the people of Aquitaine and Gascony, in 769, no doubt to gauge the strength of their new, young monarch. His brother, Carloman, refused to help and Charlemagne led his army to Bordeaux which was enough to make the leader of the rebels, Hunald, flee. His flight took him to the court of Lupus II of Gascony, but Lupus also feared the power of the Franks and handed Hunald over to Charlemagne. Charlemagne sent him to a monastery and Aquitaine was subdued.

In 770, Charlemagne married a Lombard princess, Desiderata, daughter of King Desiderius, but after less than a year, divorced her and re-married, this time to the thirteen-year-old Swabian, Princess Hildegard. Desiderata's father was, naturally, furious and for a moment it looked as if he might make an alliance with Carloman, and go to war with Charlemagne. Suddenly, however, Carloman died, reportedly of a severe nosebleed, and Charlemagne found himself in sole control of the huge Frankish empire.

Pope Hadrian I's pontificate began in 772, but he found himself immediately in a war with King Desiderius who had captured a number of papal cities. He even looked at one point as if he was going to march on Rome. Hadrian dispatched envoys to Charlemagne, pleading for help and the Frankish king set off at once across the Alps, chasing the Lombards back to the city of Pavia. While that city was besieged, Charlemagne led part of his army to Verona where Desiderius's son, Adelchis, was busy raising an army. The Frankish king pursued him to the Adriatic and the prince was forced to flee to Constantinople and the protection of Emperor Constantine V.

Victorious, Charlemagne headed for Rome where the Pope

granted him the title patrician, making him a member of Rome's elite class. Returning to Pavia, he accepted the surrender of the imprisoned Lombards, sending Desiderius to a monastery and learning that Adelchis, the heir to the Lombard throne, had died. Charlemagne was crowned King of Lombardy, with the famous Iron Crown of Lombardy. Within a couple of years he was back in Italy quashing rebellions by Dukes Hrodgaud of Friuli and Hildeprand of Spoleto. Northern Italy was now completely under his control.

In those days, it was always a good idea for a monarch to have his sons crowned in order to ensure there would be no succession dispute on his death and Charlemagne had his two younger sons crowned by the Pope – Carloman being re-named Pippin and being crowned King of Italy and Louis being crowned King of Aquitaine.

While Charlemagne retained power in his son's kingdoms, they supported him in battle many times. His daughters, however, remained at home and were never allowed to marry, probably so that they did not start new branches of the family that might result in difficulties and disputes later in the form of challenges to the main line of descent.

In the late 770s, the Moorish rulers of Zaragoza, Gerona, Barcelona and Huesca in the Iberian Peninsula made approaches to Charlemagne, seeking his help against Abd ar-Rahman I, Umayyad Emir of Córdoba. Charlemagne saw a great opportunity to expand the frontiers of Christendom and led the Neustrian army across the Western Pyrenees. Meanwhile an Austrasian, Lombard and Burgundian force traversed the mountains in the east. He arrived at Zaragoza but realised that there was a danger of losing the battle that was about to take place. Accepting that discretion as the better part of valour, he retreated north. En route, however, as he made his way through the Pass of Roncesvaux, a force of Basques attacked the rear of his army, wiping it out and the baggage train that accompanied it. Many famous men of the age died in this skirmish and amongst them was Roland, the Warden of the Breton March. From his death and this event, the most famous song of the Middle Ages and the oldest extant work of French literature, was created – the *Song of Roland*.

The Iberian Peninsula was not the only contact that Charlemagne had with the Saracens. His son, Pippin, had been fighting them in southern Italy, Charlemagne having conquered Corsica and Sardinia. In 799, he also conquered the Balearic Islands which were regularly under attack from the Saracens. In Hispania, his son Louis kept the Saracens at bay and even succeeded in extending the Frankish kingdom as far as Gerona which he captured in 785. Gradually, Frankish control in the region spread until a number of northern territories were united in 795 to form the Spanish March, as a bolster against Moorish incursions. 797 saw the capture of Barcelona, but the Umayyads recaptured the city two years later. Nonetheless, the Franks continued pressing southwards and took Tarragona in 809 and Tortosa in 811.

Throughout his life, Charlemagne was constantly fighting, always riding at the head of an elite group of knights, the Scara, who acted as bodyguards, and always with his sword 'Joyeuse' at hand. There were numerous legends about Joyeuse – that it contained the lance of Longinus, the weapon that was used to pierce Jesus's side during the Crucifixion or that it was forged from Roland's sword, Durendal or Curtana, the sword that had once belonged to the legendary Danish hero, Ogier.

One of the longest of his campaigns was the thirty-year long conflict that made up the Saxon Wars, lasting from 772 until 804. During that time there were no fewer than eighteen battles. The Saxons resolutely resisted annexation into the Frankish Empire and launched countless raids into Frankish territory as soon as Charlemagne focused on another problem elsewhere. In the end, they acceded to Charlemagne's terms, renounced their customs and religious practices and accepted Christianity, becoming part of Francia.

Other expeditions included one against the Avars, a pagan horde who had settled in modern-day Hungary and from there invaded

Friuli and Bavaria, both Frankish possessions. Charlemagne marched down the Danube and rampaged through their territory. He left his son, Pippin, to prosecute the campaign on his behalf, sending back huge amounts of Avar treasure which Charlemagne distributed both amongst his followers and amongst other rulers, including King Offa of Mercia in England. Before long, the Avars had submitted and become Christians. Meanwhile Charlemagne had launched an attack on another people from the east, the Slavs, who surrendered almost immediately.

The greatest moment in Charlemagne's reign occurred in 799. Pope Leo II was unpopular with the Roman nobles and had been set upon by them during a papal procession, coming close to having his eyes and tongue cut out. Following this narrow escape, he turned to Charlemagne for help. Charlemagne obliged, travelling to Rome and restoring Leo to the papal throne. It was for this reason that Charlemagne found himself being crowned Emperor on Christmas day, 800. He was now seen as the man who could restore the Roman Empire to its former glory; the Pope was transferring the position of Roman Emperor from Byzantium, with whom he had fallen out, to Charlemagne.

Although Charlemagne is known as a great warrior, he was also an effective and innovative administrator. He did, of course, hold the final say in all matters. His capital was at Aachen and it was there that, twenty years into his reign, he built a palace, the palace chapel becoming Aachen Cathedral. He ruled from there over the 350 counties into which he had divided his empire.

Each county was ruled by a count who served as judge and administrator. A system of *missi dominici* (envoys of the lord or ruler) was established whereby the count was supervised by local bishops and royal legates who toured the realm to ensure that the royal will was being applied. Charlemagne was careful, however, to make sure that local customs were respected and, often, local leaders retained much of their power.

Oaths of loyalty were sworn at annual assemblies in Aachen, attended by the elite of the empire – bishops, counts and the rich and a new international elite class emerged, basking in royal favour and often united by marriage.

Charlemagne also oversaw a cultural revival. He employed the greatest scholars of his day, men such as the English monk, scholar, poet and teacher, Alcuin of York, who became the most prominent teacher at Charlemagne's court, teaching many of the most notable men of the Carolingian era, even Charlemagne himself, at the Palace Academy. The grammarian, Peter of Pisa and the theologian, Agobard of Lyons, also contributed to the remarkable intellectual renaissance of Charlemagne's reign. The text of the Bible was revised during this period and countless books were published – grammars, histories and collections of ballads.

One of the most lasting and most visible signs of this cultural revival can be seen in the great buildings of the time. Carolingian architecture abandoned the Byzantine style, introducing the rounded arches and vaults of the Romanesque style.

In 813, aged about seventy-two, in another effort to prevent arguments about the succession when he died, Charlemagne crowned his only surviving legitimate son, Louis, as co-emperor before sending him back to Aquitaine. He spent the autumn of that year hunting, returning to his palace at Aachen on 1 November. In the following January, he became ill with pleurisy and on 21 January took to his bed. Seven days later, on 28 January, he took Holy Communion and at nine in the morning, he died. He had been on the throne for forty-seven years and had been engaged in warfare during almost every single one of those years.

He was buried that same day in Aachen Cathedral, interred seated on a throne, wearing a crown and holding a scepter. In 1165, however, Frederick I had his tomb opened and re-interred him in a sarcophagus under the floor of the cathedral. Then, in 1215, Frederick II put his remains in a casket made of gold and silver.

Charlemagne's empire only lasted another generation, with his son, Louis, at its head. On his death, it was divided between his three sons by the Treaty of Verdun, and the great nation states of Europe began to take shape.

ALFRED THE GREAT

THE EXACT BIRTH-DATE of the great Anglo-Saxon king and military commander, Alfred the Great, is not known for certain, but is believed to have been sometime between 847 and 849. He was born in Wantage in present-day Oxfordshire, the youngest of five sons of King Aethelwulf of Wessex, the kingdom of the West Saxons, and his wife, Osburga. Each of the couples five sons would go on to become King.

At the age of five, Alfred accompanied his father to Rome, following a visit to the court of Charles the bald, King of the Franks, to be confirmed by the Pope at the time, Leo IV. In 856, however, when they returned, Aethelwulf was deposed by his son Aethelbald. Aethelwulf would die two years later.

Aethelbald ruled only until 860 when he died, aged thirty-five, and was replaced by Aethelwulf's third son, Ethelbert. His reign felt the full force of the Viking invasions that were taking place at the time. The Vikings, fearless and ferocious fighters who had fast, mobile armies that travelled in shallow-draught longships, had begun raiding many parts of Europe in search of plunder. They attacked and looted Kent and raids were also carried out in Northumberland. They had penetrated as far as Winchester during the early years of his reign. Their raids often evolved into permanent settlements and in 867 they had captured York and established a settlement in the southern part of Northumbria.

Alfred's remarkable family continued to reign when Ethelred I, fourth son of Aethelwulf took the throne on Ethelbert's death in 865. Ethelred found it difficult to withstand the Danes whose raids were increasingly disrupting life in England and lost heavily to them in January 871 at the Battle of Reading. He did defeat them at the Battle of Ashdown several days later but was again defeated at Merton in April of that year, a battle in which he lost his life.

Although Alfred was fairly anonymous during the reigns of Aethelbald and Ethelbert, his name had began to come to the fore during the time that Ethelred was king, and he had been recognised as next in line to the throne. In times when hereditary succession was not guaranteed, it was often the custom in medieval times to recognise the next in line to the throne while his predecessor was still alive, in order to avoid damaging, and often violent succession disputes. Alfred, a strong-minded, but highly strung individual, fought alongside his brother against the Danes in West Mercia in 868 before the Vikings were paid a substantial sum to stop their attacks.

In late 870 and throughout 871, Alfred fought in nine battles, the date and location of two of which have never been recorded. He fought at Englefield, Reading, Ashdown and Merton with his brother. At Englefield, Alfred's men waited at the valley-fort, now known as Alfred's Castle at Ashbury with Ethelred's force not far away. Meanwhile, the Danes had made their camp at Uffington Castle. They met on 8 January 871, where a single, ancient throrn tree stood, which, according to legend, had been worshipped by Druids. The armies were each in two columns, the Danes commanded by their Kings, Bagsecg and Halfdan Ragnarsson. They stood facing each other, jeering and shouting abuse. At that point, Ethelred is said to have left the battlefield to pray in the little church at Aston and refused to return until he had finished. The Danes had already deployed their forces in an advantageous position and Alfred had to decide what his course of action would be. In the absence of his brother, with his troops becoming increasingly impatient, he gave the order to attack.

The Saxons won a brilliant victory, mainly due to the military genius of Alfred who drove his men in an unconventional, but unexpected and fiercely fought uphill assault. The Danes were pushed back to the east across Berkshire leaving thousands of bodies behind on the chalky slopes.

When Ethelred died in the Battle of Merton, there was little doubt that Alfred would succeed him as King of Wessex over Ethelred's young sons. The kingdom needed a strong man with military experience and ability to rule the country in troubled times when it was constantly under attack. In his absence, however, while he was burying his brother, the Danes defeated the English in battle at an unknown location and then, even when he had returned to the fray in May, the Danes won again at Wilton.

There was peace for five years following Wilton as the Danes raided and plundered in other parts of England, but in 876 they arrived in the south once again, with a formidable new leader, Guthrum. He had consolidated his position as king over the other Danish chieftains in the parts of England controlled by the Danes and had captured parts of Mercia and Northumbria.

Following an initial skirmish close to the Welsh border, Guthrum slipped past the English army and launched an attack on Wareham in Dorset. Marching westwards, they then captured Exeter in Devon. Alfred instigated a blockade and, a relief fleet having been caught in a storm, the Danes were forced to surrender and withdraw to Mercia. In January 878, however, they launched a surprise attack on Chippenham where Alfred had been spending Christmas. He only just managed to escape.

Alfred constructed a fortified base at Athelney in the Somerset marshes and reassessed his tactics. It was from this time that the legend of King Alfred and the Cakes derives. According to the legend, he was given shelter by a peasant woman who was unaware that she had the King beneath her roof. She left him to look after some cakes she was baking on a fire, but Alfred, preoccupied with the great problems he was facing, accidentally allowed the cakes to burn. She was very angry on her return, but on learning the identity of her guest, apologised profusely. On the contrary, Alfred insisted, it was he who should apologise.

From Athelney, Alfred waged a campaign against the Danes

whilst rallying men from the surrounding areas of Somerset, Wiltshire and Hampshire. In May 878, he led a force to Edington in Wiltshire and challenged the Vikings to a battle. Using a protective wall of shields, in imitation of the way soldiers of the Roman Empire used to fight, Alfred inflicted a heavy defeat on Guthrum. Alfred's contemporary biographer, Bishop Asser describes the battle: 'Alfred attacked the whole pagan army fighting ferociously in dense order, and by divine will eventually won the victory, made great slaughter among them.' The Danes fled to their own territory before surrendering at Chippenham after being besieged by Alfred for fourteen days. Guthrum submitted to Alfred and, along with twenty-nine of his men, was baptized, the Englishman accepting the role of godfather to him. It was the turning point in Alfred's long war with the invaders.

The two kings signed a treaty – the Treaty of Wedmore – creating the Danelaw, the formal division of England between the Danes and the Saxons. The Danes retained control of lands north of a line drawn roughly between London and Chester.

There was peace for several years as the Danes busied themselves in Europe, but in 884 or 885 there was a Viking raid near a hamlet called Plucks Gutter in Kent, defeated by Alfred's men and recognised as the Royal Navy's first victorious engagement of an enemy, Alfred having established England's first navy. When the East Anglian Vikings rose up, encouraged by the unsuccessful Kent raid, Alfred took steps to quash them, capturing London in 885 or 886, in the process. Peace returned for a while but in autumn 892 or 893, the Danes launched another, much bigger raid, consisting of 330 ships. They dug in at Appledore and Milton in Kent and, having brought with them wives and children appeared to be making a serious attempt at the colonisation of the southern part of England.

As Alfred entered into negotiations with the leader of the Group based at Milton, the reputedly ferocious and cruel Viking chieftain, Haeston, the other group, based at Appledore broke out and marched northwards. Alfred's son, Edward set off in hot pursuit and defeated them at Farnham in modern-day Surrey. The Vikings fled and sought refuge on an island on the River Colne in Hertfordshire but eventually surrendered.

Meanwhile, Alfred went to Exeter to lift a siege laid by East Anglian and Northumbrian Danes. Haeston's army, en route to assist their compatriots in the west were defeated by troops from Mercia, Wiltshire and Somerset. The remnants of this force were reinforced and made for Chester but the destruction of all the sources of food in the area persuaded the Vikings to return to Essex in 895. The Danes sailed their boats up the Thames and the Lea, building a camp and digging in some twenty miles north of London. Alfred, however, cunningly obstructed the river, blocking them in and completely outmanoeuvring them. Defeated and exhausted, they headed for Bridgenorth where, the following year, they gave up, returning to Northumbria and East Anglia or sailing back to the European mainland.

To prevent further attacks, Alfred focused on creating a bigger and more effective navy. He was even responsible for the design of a ship that was much faster than previous vessels. However, these new ships are reported to have run aground or foundered in storms. Nonetheless, the Royal Navy claims King Alfred as its founder.

He was a great military innovator. One of the secrets of his astonishing military success was the manner in which he organised his troops. His main force was called the Fyrd and it was split in two with one half always at home while the other was out engaged in campaigns. The half left at home was used to provide food for those at home and the army out fighting. He also upgraded the defences of his forts. There were no standing armies in those days and once a war was fought, the troops would return home to farm the land and the forts would be left largely undefended and prey to enemy attack. Alfred instituted the ingenious practice of creating a number of fortified boroughs throughout Wessex and nowhere in the kingdom would be more than twenty miles from one of these strongholds. Thus, in the case of attack, local people could seek refuge in a place of safety. They also became places of residence and trade.

Alfred's legal code was one of his greatest legacies. Called the *Deemings* or *Book of Dooms* (Book of Laws), it was an amalgam of the laws of King Offa and others, those of the kingdoms of Mercia and Kent and his own administrative regulations. It formed a definitive body of Anglo-Saxon law.

A deeply devout man, Alfred was also deeply conscious of the damage that had been done to learning in his kingdom with the Vikings' plundering of the monasteries. In order to improve literacy, therefore, he arranged the translation of a handful of books from Latin into Anglo-Saxon. He thought these to be 'most needful for men to know, and to bring it to pass . . . if we have the peace, that all the youth now in England . . . may be devoted to learning' The books concerned dealt with history, philosophy and included Pope Gregory the Great's handbook for bishops, *Pastoral Care*. He was also patron of the *Anglo-Saxon Chronicle*, the great history of the Anglo-Saxons designed to celebrate Wessex and Alfred.

By the 890s, Alfred was unassailable, being styled 'King of England'.

He died, aged fifty, on 26 October 901 and, although his cause of death is unknown, he did suffer throughout his life from a painful illness, possibly the debilitating condition known as Crohn's disease, an inflammatory disease of the digestive system.

He was buried initially in the Old Minster in Winchester, the traditional resting place of members of the West Saxon royal family, but was moved to the New Minster which may even have been specially built to house his remains. He was moved to Hyde in 1110 and in the reign of Henry VIII his crypt was looted during the dissolution of the monasteries and his bones were re-buried in the churchyard. In 1788, during the construction of a prison, his bones were scattered, but bones discovered in 1866 were declared to be his and re-interred in Hyde churchyard.

Alfred's actions not only stopped the advance of the Vikings into the whole of England, but also initiated the process by which his successors began to extend control over other Anglo-Saxon kings until England was unified. For these reasons, he is reckoned to be one of England's greatest kings and it is for these reasons that he bears the much-deserved epithet 'the Great'.

GENGHIS KHAN

HE WAS BORN Temüjin around the year 1162 in a nomad Mongol tribe in present-day Mongolia and would go on to create the greatest empire the world has ever seen.

His family was amongst the leading families of its time, related on his father's side to Qabul Khan, leader of the Mongol Federation. Qabul was killed in 1161 and Temüjin's father, Yesükhei, took his place but his position was not unchallenged, the rival Tayichi'ud clan also claiming the leadership. Temüjin was Yesükhei's third son and he had three brothers, a sister and two half-brothers.

As was customary, when he reached the age of nine a marriage was arranged for him and he was sent to live with the bride's family who were part of the Onggirat tribe. He basically worked as a servant to the head of the household, his future father-in-law until he was twelve, recognised as marriageable age. At twelve he returned home to learn that his father had been poisoned by the rival Tatars, but his tribe were unwilling to be led by such a young man and he, his mother and brothers and sister were forced to leave their protection to embark upon a life of poverty, subsisting on whatever they could find to eat. Hunting provided a great deal of their food and it was after one expedition that Temüjin is said to have killed one of his half-brothers in an argument over their catch. At thirteen, he found himself head of the household.

Life was difficult and dangerous on the plains and in 1182 Temüjin was kidnapped by the rival Tayichi'uds for whom he was put to work as a slave, before escaping. His reputation was greatly enhanced by the boldness of his escape.

At the time, tribal warfare was rife in Mongolia and raids by rival tribes were an everyday occurrence. Furthermore, there were foreign forces to be dealt with, especially the Chinese dynasties to the south. The only way that individual tribes could survive was if they formed alliances with their neighbours to put up a united front. It was a lesson that Genghis took to heart early in his life as he watched the chaos around him.

Marriage was one way of cementing an alliance and the marriage that Temüjin's father had arranged all those years ago was one such. At sixteen, he married Börte of the Konkirat tribe. They would have four sons – Jochi, Chagatai, Ögedei, and Tolui and she would be his only empress, although as was common, he would also have children by other women.

Central Asia at the time of Genghis Khan consisted of tribes or confederations amongst whom were the Naimans, Merkits, Uyghurs, Tatars, Mongols and Keraits. Genghis succeeded by allying himself with as many of these rival tribes as possible, unifying them into a powerful force. It took a long time to achieve, beginning when he allied with the Khan of the Kerait, Toghrul. When Temüjin's wife Börte was kidnapped by the Merkits, it was to Toghrul that he turned for help. Toghrul provided 20,000 warriors, Börte was freed and the Merkits were annihilated. Toghrul would, however, later betray Temüjin and the Keraits would be brought down because of his betrayal.

His approach to conquest, which was the way he brought some of these tribes under his control was different to his predecessors. Instead of massacring them, he would take the conquered tribe under his protection, welcoming its members into his own tribe. Moreover, once part of his tribe, they found that he organised things differently to others. Rewards and positions were given in exchange for loyalty and on the basis of merit, rather than because of family ties.

In 1201 he faced a challenge from the Naiman Mongols with whom a former ally and blood brother of Genghis – Jamuka – had taken refuge. Jamuka was elected Gur Khan, 'Universal Ruler', and formed a coalition of tribes to march against Temüjin. The two former friends met in several battles won by Temüjin and Jamuka was eventually handed over to the Mongols by his own men in 1206. When Temüjin offered Jamuka the chance to live and fight by his side again, his old friend rejected the offer, saying he would rather die. As the noblest death was believed by the Mongols to be one in which no blood was spilt, he was killed by having his back broken. It was different to the manner in which Temüjin normally executed his opponents – he would boil them alive.

With the defeat of Jamuka and the Naimans, Temüjin was by 1206 the ruler of the entirety of the Mongol plains. At a Kurultai, a council of Mongol chiefs, he was officially recognised as 'Khan' of the consolidated tribes and took the new title 'Genghis Khan'. There was now peace between the warring tribes and Genghis Khan was at the head of a massive political and military force.

As a general, he was unlike any that had gone before. He was insistent on the collection of good intelligence on his enemy and managed an extensive spy network that fed him information about his enemies' numerical strength and positions, but also gave him a thorough understanding of their motivations and morale. He was also quick to adapt the new military techniques, such as siege warfare, that he learned about from the Chinese. He is reported to have personally led his army from the front, but there is no absolute certainty that this was the case.

To the west of the Mongol plain was the Tanguts' Western Xia Dynasty. To the south was the Jin Dynasty, founded by Manchurian Jurchens, traditionally overlords of the Mongols. Genghis set his sights on enlarging his empire and attacked the Xia first. The Jin having refused to come to their aid, he had beaten them into submission by 1209.

In 1211 he slaughtered the Jin army at Badger Pass and in 1215, he sacked the Jin capital of Yanjing, modern-day Beijing, forcing the Jin Emperor to flee, moving his capital south to Kaifeng and leaving the northern half of his kingdom to Genghis.

Next in line was the Kara-Khitan Khanate to the west. It had been usurped by the deposed Khan of the Naimans, Kuchlug, who had fled when his tribe were defeated by Genghis. After a decade of continuous fighting, the Mongol army was exhausted. Therefore, Genghis sent only 20,000 men against the Kuchlug, under the command of one of his young generals, Jebe who defeated Kuchlug west of Kashgar. Kuchlug was captured and put to death. Genghis's vastly increased empire now extended to the border of another huge empire – the Muslim Khwarezmid Empire, ruled by Shah Ala ad-Din Muhammad that stretched from the Caspian Sea to the west and the Persian Gulf and the Arabian Sea to the south.

To begin with, it seemed to Genghis to make more sense to nurture the Khwarezmid Empire as a commercial partner rather than to invade and he initially sent 500 men in a huge caravan to establish a trading relationship with the Shah. But on its journey, a Khwarezmian governor attacked it, claiming that it was all part of a plot by Genghis. When Genghis then sent a delegation to discuss the matter with the Shah, he beheaded them. Insulted and furious, Genghis assembled one of his largest armies, around 200,000 men and led it personally into the Khwarezmid Empire. He carefully studied intelligence reports before splitting his force into three. One third, led by his son, Jochi, rode into the northeast of the empire; a second, commanded by his general, Jebe, marched into the southeast and formed a pincer attack with the first section on the capital, Samarkand. Genghis meanwhile, led a force from the northwest.

The Shah made the fundamental error of splitting his army into small groups to defend individual cities, allowing the Mongols to fight these small groups rather than one large army. Eventually, he fled, a Mongol force pursuing him. The Governor who had killed the members of the caravan was captured and molten silver was poured into his ears and eyes.

Genghis took terrible revenge – even by his brutal standards – on the Khwarezmid Empire. He ordered everything to be destroyed, from royal palaces to farmland. The Shah's birthplace was eradicated from the map when he diverted a river to make it flood the town. Genghis put his third son, Ögedei, in command of what was left of the Khwarezmid Empire.

It was 1220 and the Mongol surge continued. Genghis led an army into Afghanistan and Northern India while another force marched into Russia through the Caucasus. Another force of 20,000 men, commanded by Jebe and Subutai penetrated deep into Armenia and Azerbaijan. They sacked Georgia and then, after wintering near the Black Sea, were attacked by about 80,000 badly trained troops under the command of Mstislav the Bold of Halych in western Ukraine and Mstislav III of Kiev. At the Battle of the Kalka River in 1223, Subutai defeated this huge force, but then lost to the Volga Bulgars at Samara Bend. Genghis's grandson, Batu would lead the Mongol force known as the Golden Horde in the ultimate conquest of the Volga Bulgars and Kievan Rus' in 1240.

From prisoners taken in the latter battle, the Mongols learned of the rich pickings that lay beyond the land of the Bulgars and resolved to conquer Hungary and the rest of Europe. Meanwhile, news of this incredible expedition of Jebe and Subutai, one of the most illustrious in military history, spread to other, understandably fearful European nations. By 1225, all the divisions of the Mongol army had returned home, adding Transoxiana and Persia to Genghis's empire en route.

While the Mongols had been focusing on the west, the Western Xia and Jin Dynasties had united to form a coalition against them. In 1226, however, Genghis led a force against the Tanguts of Western Xia, defeating them in a number of battles and destroying the Tangut capital, Ning Hia. He advanced to take Lintiao-fu, Xining Province, Xindu-fu and Deshun Province in the spring of 1227. Following the death of the ruler, Ma Jianlong, the new emperor surrendered. Genghis had the entire royal family executed and the Tangut royal dynasty was brought to an end.

As Genghis got older, the question of who would succeed him became pressing. His son, Jochi, was the most senior of his offspring but his paternity was questionable. He had been born after his mother had been kidnapped and it was always whispered that he had been conceived in captivity. Therefore, his other brothers were reluctant to accept him as next in line for the throne. He died in 1226, having been poisoned, quite possibly on the orders of his father. Genghis's third son, Ögedei, was proclaimed as heir. However, Genghis was concerned about the rivalry between his sons, worrying that after his death this rivalry might erupt in a struggle for control of the empire. He decided, therefore, to divide the empire between them, making them all Khans in their own right, with Ögedei in charge.

The great Genghis Khan died in 1227 but it is not known conclusively how his life ended. Some histories report that he was killed when he fell off his horse while being pursued by enemy troops in Egypt, while others say he died of a long illness, possibly pneumonia. One chronicle claims that he died fighting the Tanguts.

He ordered that his body should be buried in an unmarked grave, according to the custom of his tribe. It was returned to Mongolia, probably to the place of his birth in Khentii province and is assumed to lie near the Onon River, close to the Burkhan Khaldun Mountain. As was the practice, all involved in the burial were killed to ensure secrecy and it is said that a river was diverted to flow over the burial site so that it could never be located.

If measured in terms of square miles conquered, Genghis Khan was the greatest conqueror of all time. His empire was four times the size of that conquered by Alexander the Great. In 1241, his son, Ögedei's army stood at the gates of Vienna when Ögedei died and they retreated to Mongolia, leaving Europe to breathe a huge sigh of relief.

ROBERT THE BRUCE

BORN AT TURNBERRY Castle in Ayrshire on Scotland's west coast in 1274, Robert Bruce, Earl of Carrick, is, without doubt, the greatest of all Scottish heroes. The very nature of his victories, achieved against the odds and, more often than not, against an enemy vastly greater than whatever force Bruce had assembled, serves as a metaphor for the Scottish nation. With great cunning and tremendous courage and patience, he achieved his ambition to be undisputed King of Scotland, righting what he saw as an injustice committed against his grandfather when the English King Edward I had handed another Scot the crown during turbulent times in 1292.

The struggle for the Scottish throne had begun in 1286 with the death of Alexander III that left his grandchild Margaret, the infant daughter of the King of Norway as his heir. Edward I, keen to seize control of the kingdom on his northern border suggested a marriage between Margaret and his son, Edward. A treaty was signed that guaranteed that Scotland would remain a separate kingdom but the young Margaret died on her way to Scotland, throwing the succession to the Scottish throne open to a number of claimants. In spite of a sound claim from Robert Bruce, grandfather of Robert the Bruce, Edward selected an English baron who also had a claim – John Balliol who, to the great anger of the Bruce family, became King of Scotland in 1292. In exchange, of course, Scotland would be in subjugation to the English. Balliol, however, concluded a treaty with France and made plans to invade England. Edward marched north and received homage from many Scottish lords, among them the twenty-one-year-old Robert the Bruce. Balliol punished Bruce's

111

treachery by seizing his lands and giving them to the rival Comyn family who had supported his claim against the old Robert Bruce.

Nationalist feeling became rampant in Scotland, led by a young Scottish knight, William Wallace, and Robert the Bruce was amongst Scottish nobles who rose up against the English that year. Unfortunately, their revolt was ended by the Capitulation of Irvine in 1297 when, waiting to do battle with the English, bickering broke out amongst the Scots. No battle ensued and they were forced to swear allegiance to Edward.

Bruce was not completely loyal to the Scottish cause – he did whatever was necessary to retain his lands and there has always been suspicion surrounding the fact that, following William Wallace's defeat at the Battle of Falkirk in 1297, unlike those of many other Scottish nobles, Bruce lands were not confiscated. Some – principally the film *Braveheart* – have even suggested that Bruce actually fought on the English side at Falkirk. It is more likely, however, that Edward realised he would need some support in Scotland and left Bruce's lands alone for that reason.

Scotland was now being governed by Guardians and following the disaster of Falkirk the Scottish lords elected Bruce and John Comyn of Badenoch, known as Red Comyn, to jointly hold that position. It is hard to see how it could ever work. The Bruces and the Comyns had been at each other's throats for generations, since the Comyns had supported Balliol's claim to the throne in preference to the Bruce claim. Bruce, tired of the bickering, resigned from the position in 1300.

Yet another English invasion in 1301 resulted in a truce a year later and an oath of allegiance to Edward by most of the Scottish nobility, including Bruce. Further invasions in 1303 and 1304 led to Guardian John Comyn agreeing peace terms with Edward.

Meanwhile, Bruce was little trusted either in Scotland or in England where Edward believed that he was plotting against him. However, the Scottish crown remaining vacant, Bruce inevitably had his sights set on it.

John Comyn remained a problem, however, and the two men agreed to meet to see if they could come to some sort of understanding as to how the country should be governed. They met in the neutral territory offered by the Church of the Grey Friars in Dumfries on 10 February 1306. But it ended badly. Bruce fled the church, having argued with Comyn and stabbed him, probably because he refused his support in an uprising against the English. One of his supporters went into the church and finished off the seriously wounded Guardian.

There was revulsion at Bruce's act. It had been committed in front of the altar of a church, after all. Nonetheless, Bruce launched his long campaign to become undisputed King of Scotland, firstly grabbing Comyn strongholds. He also obtained absolution for the stabbing of his rival from the Bishop of Glasgow but it seems certain that the Scottish Church was already on his side.

Although there was no coronation regalia or Stone of Destiny – they had all been taken south by Edward I – Robert the Bruce was made King of Scots on 25 March 1306.

All-out war with the Comyns ensued and Edward I weighed in on the side of Bruce's enemies, immediately sending an army north and declaring Bruce and his supporters to be outlaws. He also managed to persuade Pope Clement V to excommunicate Bruce for Red Comyn's murder.

In June 1306, Bruce was surprised and defeated by a Comyn force, many of his troops being killed in the fighting, although he managed to escape. Then, in July, he faced further disappointment when he and his followers were trapped in a valley near Tyndrum on the southern edge of Rannoch Moor by John MacDougall of Lorn, Red Comyn's son-in-law. His remaining followers were wiped out and Bruce was left virtually alone, his dream in tatters.

Worse still, the English took revenge on his family. Two of his brothers were hung, drawn and quartered, a sister, Mary, was suspended in a cage from the battlements of Roxburgh Castle for four years, as was Bruce's mistress, Isabella Countess of Buchan from the ramparts of Berwick Castle. Meanwhile, his sister, Lady Christian Bruce and daughter, Marjorie, were both sent to nunneries and his wife was imprisoned in a royal residence in Yorkshire, treated rather more leniently because she was the daughter of a supporter of Edward I.

Bruce went into hiding, living for a while in a cave on the island of Rathlin, off the Northern Irish coast. From this time comes the famous story of the spider. Bruce is said to have observed a spider weaving and re-weaving its web, never giving up until it was completed. The story is more than likely apocryphal, but it is said that Bruce drew strength from the spider's determination and resolved to continue the struggle for Scottish independence.

When the fugitive king returned to action, the renewed campaign did not start well. In February 1307, Bruce's brothers, Thomas and Alexander, landed with a force of warriors from Ireland and Kintyre at Loch Ryan but they were ambushed and slaughtered by the men of Galloway under Dougal MacDowall. Robert landed at Turnberry and in March 1307 and succeeded in defeating a larger English force that had been searching for him. On 10 May, he engaged a force of 3,000 English troops at Loudon Hill with only 600 men and also defeated them. Scots rallied to his cause.

On 7 July, Edward I died at the border as he led an army north to engage Bruce. His weak son, Edward II, assumed the throne and virtually ignored Scotland for the first three years of his reign. Bruce, on the other hand, was busy, waging a brilliant guerrilla war across Scotland, against English supporters and, of course, against the Comyns. In rapid succession, he took Inverlochy, Urquhart, Inverness, Nairn and Elgin Castles, mostly through subterfuge, without lifting a sword.

On 22 May 1308, Comyn's men fled the battlefield near Inverurie, rather than face Bruce's troops and Bruce took terrible revenge on his old enemy, burning villages and massacring countless members of the clan. He captured Aberdeen and then took MacDougall of Lorn's Dunstaffnage Castle. He now controlled northern Scotland, apart from Stirling Castle, Perth and Dundee. However, in the next few years, he would take Edinburgh, Perth, Dumbarton and Linlithgow and would begin making raids into the north of England.

Stirling was still in English hands, however, but Edward was on his way north with the largest army ever to cross the border, around 20,000 men. They arrived at the Bannock Burn on 23 June, a few miles south of Stirling Castle where Bruce's 7,000-strong army awaited them. The English attacked immediately, but were surprised by the anti-cavalry spikes the Scots had dug into the ground. Bruce was himself specifically targeted, but he fought off his assailants with a battle-axe. The English threw themselves forward once more, but once more were repelled by the determined Scots.

The following day, the main battle took place with English knights charging the assembled ranks of Scottish spearmen. It was ground unsuited to the heavy cavalry of the English, however, and, at the same time, the English longbowmen were unsuited to the close, hand-to-hand fighting that developed and fled. Bruce sent his Highlanders forward, followed by his reserves and suddenly the Scottish army seemed to be larger than it actually was. The English army broke ranks and fled the field, Edward II only just making it to safety.

Stirling was captured, the English had been routed and Robert I was unchallenged King of Scotland. Moreover, he was able to exchange the Earl of Hereford, who he had taken prisoner, for his wife, sister and daughter.

He sent his brother Edward to Ireland where he defeated the English and became High King in 1316, before being killed in 1318. He also re-conquered Berwick-upon-Tweed and undertook frequent raids into the north of England.

On 6 April 1320, the Scots made the first declaration of independence by any nation when they sent the Declaration of Arbroath to Pope John XXII. This historic document was intended to persuade the pope to recognise Robert the Bruce as King of Scotland and to endorse Scottish independence. It was also hoped that such recognition would put pressure on the English to do the same. It was a document that would resonate through the centuries, influencing both the American and the French Revolutions and it worked. The pope brokered a truce and peace negotiations between the two warring neighbours.

Inevitably, the negotiations collapsed and the Scots resumed their pillaging of the northern counties of England. In 1324, however, news came that the pope had recognized Robert the Bruce as King of the Scots.

With Edward III now on the English throne, peace talks resumed in 1327 and were concluded with the signing of the Treaty of Edinburgh and Northampton, signed by Robert at the Palace of Holyroodhouse in Edinburgh on 17 March and by Edward on 3 May 1328. By this treaty, Edward renounced all claims on the throne of Scotland, also promising the return of the Stone of Destiny, something that would not actually happen until almost 700 years later. The Scots paid compensation for their raids with provision being made for a marriage between Bruce's son, David and Edward's sister, Joan.

By this time Bruce was too ill to attend his son's wedding in July 1328. Just over a year later, on 7 June 1329, he died at Dumbarton and was succeeded by David I, his son. His excommunication had been lifted in October 1328 and he died leaving behind Scotland as a sovereign state.

The only disappointment in Robert the Bruce's life was said to have been the fact that he was always too busy fighting for independence to go on a Crusade to the Holy Land. But following his burial at Dunfermline Abbey, Sir James Douglas carried the great king's heart in a silver casket when he went to Spain to fight against the Moors. Robert the Bruce's last wish had been fulfilled and on his return, Douglas buried his heart in Melrose Abbey.

TAMERLANE

IN ISFAHAN HE built a pyramid of skulls from the people he beheaded; outside Aleppo, it was 20,000 skulls high. In Damascus, he herded thousands of the city's inhabitants into the Cathedral Mosque and set it on fire. He ordered the beheading of 70,000 in Tikrit and 90,000 in Baghdad. They say that in his many campaigns and wars, as many as seventeen million people lost their lives. He was Tamerlane, also known as Timur the Lame, the 14th century conqueror of much of Western and Central Asia, founder of the Timurid Empire that stretched from the Mediterranean in the west to India in the east and Russia in the north. The Timurid Dynasty he founded ruled until 1857 as the Mughal dynasty in India.

He was born in 1336, in Transoxiana, on the plain of Kesh, some fifty miles south of Samarkand in modern-day Uzbekistan, to Taraghay, the head of the nomadic Barlas tribe who wandered the steppes of Central Asia. Amongst his forebears was the great Genghis Khan, founder of the Mongol Empire in the 12th and 13th centuries and his tribe was descended from those of Genghis's invaders who had remained in the area, embracing Turkic or Iranian languages and customs.

Tamerlane rose through the political and military ranks of the Chagatai Mongols in Central Asia, despite his lowly birth and a physical disability resulting from wounds to his right arm and leg. Genghis Khan's huge empire had been divided on his death in 1227, amongst his sons, each receiving a territory to rule, known as an *ulus*. Gengis's second son, Chagatai was given Transoxiana and Moguistan. By Tamerlane's birth, however, Mongol power in the Chagatai lands was very weak and minor chieftains wielded local power. Tamerlane used this lack of leadership in the area to build his own power base and by 1369, having assassinated his long-time supporter, his brother-in-law, Husayn, he had become the ruler of Transoxiana with Samarkand as his capital city.

Samarkand, which Tamerlane had moved south of its previous location, became a thriving commercial centre, half of the trade of Central Asia passing through its markets. Leather, linen, spices, silk, precious stones, exotic fruits and many other goods were sold. Tamerlane also brought in great scholars of the time as well as the best craftsmen and artists and built great architectural monuments. In fact, whenever he conquered a city, he would send the artisans he found there back to Samarkand to work there. There were stone-masons and stucco-workers from Azerbaijan, Isfahan and Delhi; Mosaic-workers from Shiraz; weavers, glass-blowers and potters from Damascus. And Tamerlane liked nothing better, on those rare occasions when he was not on a campaign, than to supervise the construction work in his capital.

In his conquered cities, too, Tamerlane left his mark with fabulous buildings. In Shahr-i-Sabz, for example, he constructed a magnificent Aq Saray – White Palace – and in Turkestan he erected a mosque and mausoleum in honour of the famous 12th century poet and Sufi Sheikh, Hoja Ahmed Yasavi. But, it was in Samarkand that he built his most impressive structures. He filled his capital with both secular and religious monuments, as well as abundant gardens, featuring stone walls and floors with elaborate patterns and palaces adorned with gold, silk and exotic carpets.

He was interested in the other arts, too. His calligrapher, Omar Aqta, is said to have transcribed the Koran using letters so small that it could be fitted onto a signet ring. He also created a huge version with gold lettering that required a wheelbarrow to transport it.

He was an avid chess player – not surprising in a man with such a tactically astute mind. He even invented his own version, known as Tamerlane Chess, using more pieces and a larger board.

On his coronation, Tamerlane declared himself a Mongol and a direct descendant of Genghis Khan whose empire he swore to restore to its former glory. For the next thirty-five years he would wage constant war across Asia, subjugating his rivals at home and extending his empire with foreign conquests.

The first additions to his empire were modern-day Turkmenistan, Khorosan – northern Afghanistan – and Persia, all in the 1380s and all formerly parts of the Mongol empire. He carried his campaigns into the Russian Steppe where he faced his great rival, Tokhtamysh, who, with Tamerlane's support had invaded Russia and in 1382, captured Moscow. Tokhtamysh became Khan of the Golden Horde but turned against Tamerlane, invading Azebaijan in 1385. The two great leaders now began a titanic struggle that only ended in 1395 when Tamerlane finally defeated his erstwhile friend and ally at the Battle of the Kur River. Tamerlane had led an army of 100,000 men for 700 miles into the uninhabited steppe and had then advanced west for 1,000 miles in a front in excess of ten miles wide. The army was exhausted and starving by the time they cornered Tokhtamysh's men and destroyed them. In a second campaign against Tokhtamysh, Tamerlane destroyed Sarai and Astrakhan, wrecking the Golden Horde's economy, dependant upon the trade that passed along the Silk Road.

There were financial considerations in Tamerlane's programme of conquest, of course. He sent back treasure from all the countries and cities that fell to his armies and he was also trying to gain control of the valuable trade routes that linked east and west. To this end, he made the long march to invade the area of the Delhi Sultanate, ruled by Nasir-u Din Mehmud of the Tughlaq Dynasty. Tamerlane claimed that he was invading because he thought the sultan treated his Hindu subjects too leniently – Tamerlane had a special disdain for what he called 'idolatrous Hindus'. However, that was no more than a mask to hide his real reason – the great wealth of the sultanate.

He crossed the Indus at Attock and the campaign proceeded as normal – villages were attacked and then looted, the inhabitants massacred and the women raped. Survivors were converted en masse from Hinduism to Islam. He met resistance here and there, but nothing to really worry about and easily defeated the armies of Sultan Mehmud on 17 December 1398. Delhi was looted and reduced to ruins by his troops. More than 100,000 Hindus were executed.

In his memoirs, Tamerlane himself describes the horror of that day: 'In a short space of time all the people in the Delhi fort were put to the sword, and in the course of one hour the heads of 10,000 infidels were cut off. The sword of Islam was washed in the blood of the infidels, and all the goods and effects, the treasure and the grain which for many a long year had been stored in the fort, became the spoil of my soldiers. They set fire to the houses and reduced them to ashes, and they razed the buildings and the fort to the ground . . . All these infidel Hindus were slain, their women and children, and their property and goods became the spoil of the victors. I proclaimed throughout the camp that every man who had infidel prisoners should put them to death, and whoever neglected to do so should himself be executed and his property given to the informer. When this order became known to the ghazis of Islam, they drew their swords and put their prisoners to death.'

It would take Delhi more than a century to recover from the violent excesses of Tamerlane's invasion.

He brought back a huge amount of valuables from Delhi to Samarkand. It is reported that it required ninety elephants to carry the looted precious stones, alone.

In 1400, it was the turn of Armenia and Georgia to experience the power and cruelty of Tamerlane's army. In these campaigns he collected some 60,000 slaves and many areas were completely depopulated.

In 1401, he captured Baghdad, directing that every soldier should return with at least two severed heads. He then launched a campaign against the Ottoman Sultan, Bayezid I, saying that he wanted to restore the Seljuk Turks as the rightful rulers of the empire; they had ruled during Genghis Khan's time and once more Tamerlane expressed his desire to restore that Mongol Empire of his ancestor. He invaded Anatolia in 1402 and the Ottomans were defeated in the Battle of Ankara at which Bayezid was captured. He died in captivity.

Tamerlane's skill as a military commander was phenomenal. His army generally consisted of cavalry armed with bows and swords leading spare horses loaded with supplies for long campaigns. He was one of the first leaders to employ propaganda as an instrument of war, sending spies in advance of his army into territories that he was about to attack or invade. These men would not only collect vital information about the fortifications and the area's preparedness for war, they would also spread terrifying rumours about the size of Tamerlane's army and the cruelty with which they treated the enemy. The morale of the targeted area would by devastated and often panic spread amongst defending troops.

He was also meticulous in his planning with campaigns being planned years in advance. He did not pay his troops, but inspired tremendous loyalty in them by caring for them and by displaying personal bravery. Anyway, they needed no payment when they were incentivised by the prospect of highly lucrative looting. They would bring back fabulous bounty, including horses, wives, precious stones and rare metals.

He was no politician, however, and, failing to establish a stable government apparatus in his conquered territories, often found himself having to return to put down rebellions. He saw his captured territories merely as sources of loot and opportunities for his men to rape and pillage.

Although the European monarchs were delighted to see the Ottoman Empire receive a bloody nose – he was celebrated in Europe for centuries on account of this – they also feared that Tamerlane would become an even bigger threat and made diplomatic contact with him. Letters exist from him to King Charles

VI of France, written in Persian and discussing trading matters. He even received tribute from countries beyond his grasp. The Sultan of Egypt and even the Byzantine Emperor, John I, showed him respect in this way. One of the envoys, Ruy Gonzalez de Clavijo, sent by the King of Castile, was present as Tamerlane made preparations for his most ambitious venture yet, the reconquest of China.

In 1368, the Mongol Yuan dynasty that had ruled China was deposed by the Ming dynasty, led by its first Emperor, Hongwu. Hongwu received tribute and homage from many Central Asian rulers, but Tamerlane was insulted by the Chinese Emperor's treatment of him as a vassal. He decided to teach the Chinese a lesson and in 1404 began a campaign against them, making alliances with the Mongols of the Northern Yuan Dynasty.

It was not to be, however. While camped near the Syr Darya River, he developed a fever. He died at Otrar in modern-day Kazakhstan in February 1405.

His empire was divided, as was the custom, between his sons and grandsons, but it fell apart with various tribes and warlords competing for dominance. The Western Empire was destroyed in 1410 by the Black Sheep Turkmen, but Tamerlane's youngest son, Sharukh, was able to secure control in Persia and Transoxiana from around 1409. He controlled the main trade routes between east and west, including the Silk Road and became fabulously wealthy as a result.

JOAN OF ARC

SHE HEARD VOICES and sometimes she called them her 'counsel'. At first it was simply a voice, as if someone had spoken standing next to her, but there was something else – a flash of light. She had heard them for the first time in 1424 when she was about twelve years old. Later, she could just make out the people who spoke to her. They were St. Michael, usually surround by other angels, St Margaret, St Catherine and others. She did not like to speak about them and she certainly said nothing to the priest who heard her confession. At her trial in Rouen in 1431, she refused under persistent questioning to describe the voices that had told her to drive the English out of France and bring the Dauphin, heir to the throne, to Reims to be crowned King of France.

England and France had been at war since 1337, engaged in the series of conflicts that came to be known as the Hundred Years' war. It had all started over a dispute about the succession to the vacant French throne between the French House of Valois and the English House of Plantagenet, also known as the House of Anjou. The Plantagenets, from England, claimed the thrones of both France and England and the Valois claimed the throne of France. Confusingly, French soldiers fought on both sides throughout the war, Burgundy and Aquitaine providing support for the Plantagenets. It actually went on for 116 years, but it was interspersed by periods of relative peace.

Almost all of the fighting took place on French soil and the French people, already devastated by the Black Death that had ravaged Europe in the previous century, suffered further as the English burned and pillaged their way across their lands. Furthermore, by the time of Joan's birth, the French had not won a victory for a generation and the incumbent French monarch, Charles VI, suffered from mental instability and was often incapable of governing his country. Internal feuding over the regency during Charles's incapacity led to the assassination of one of the candidates, the Duke of Orléans, by his rival, the Duke of Burgundy in 1407.

Such chaos encouraged the English king, Henry V, to invade France in 1415 when he won one of the most famous of English victories at Agincourt. When the Duke of Burgundy sided with the English after the murder of his predecessor, John the Fearless, large sections of France were conquered.

The Treaty of Troyes in 1420 granted succession to Henry V and his heirs, but both Charles VI and Henry died within two months of each other in 1422. The infant Henry VI of England was now the nominal King of both France and England.

By 1429, all of northern France and parts of the southwest were under foreign rule, the English holding Paris and the Burgundians holding Reims, the traditional site of French coronations. The English were besieging Orléans, the last loyal French city to the north of the River Loire. The fate of France depended on what happened to Orléans.

Joan's parents owned land in Domremy in Champagne, a village that had always been loyal to Charles in the struggle, despite the fact that it came under the control of the Duke of Burgundy who supported the opposing side. She was the youngest of five and her father was a poor, peasant farmer. She was a pious and very serious child, and could often be found deep in prayer at the local church.

The voices that had been commanding her to get rid of the English for four years became more insistent around 1428 when she decided to present herself to Robert Baudricourt, commander of Charles's troops in the neighbouring town. However, when she made the journey to see him, he showed no respect for her mission or for her and told her to go home. But as defeat came ever nearer for Charles's men at Orléans, the voices grew more urgent. She returned to Baudricourt, and, remaining in the town for a while, began to make an impression on him. On 17 February 1429, she proclaimed that the French had been defeated outside Orléans. Their defeat in the Battle of the Herrings was announced a few days later and all were impressed by her advance knowledge.

Eventually, she was given permission to travel to Chinon to have an audience with the King. For the journey she dressed in male clothing, probably to safeguard her in the male environs of the camp. Arriving at Chinon on 6 March, she was admitted into Charles's presence but to test her he had disguised himself and hidden amongst his attendants. She had no hesitation in pointing him out immediately, even though she had never seen him before.

Gradually, in spite of opposition to her amongst his entourage, he began to half-believe in her. Before he would allow her to engage in any military activity, however, he put her through another test. She was sent to Poitiers to be examined by a panel of bishops and doctors. Once again, she gave a good account of herself and returned to Chinon with their support.

At this time, King Charles's mother was funding an expedition to relieve Orléans and Joan volunteered to go with it as long as she could do so in the armour of a knight. She borrowed or had donated her armour, sword, horse, banner and entourage and before leaving she boldly ordered the King of England to withdraw his troops from French soil, the audacity of her demand infuriating the English knights. She arrived at the besieged city of Orléans on 29 April 1429.

Although Jean d'Orléans, the acting head of the Orléans ducal family, tried to exclude Joan from every war council and engagement with the enemy, she made sure she was ever-present. Of course, there is dispute about to what extent she took part in actual fighting. Some historians say that she was no more than a standard-bearer who served as a morale boost to the demoralised French troops. Others, however, endow her with great tactical and strategic skills. What is certainly clear, however, is that from the moment this poor, illiterate farm girl, entirely untrained in military matters, arrived on the scene, the French army put together an astonishing series of victories.

At the head of the troops, remarkably aged just eighteen, she over-turned the cautious approach that the army had taken in the conflict so far, attacking and capturing the fortress of Saint Loup on 4 May and taking a second fortress the following day. The next day she argued with Jean d'Orléans in a war council. She wanted to make another assault, but he did not, ordering the gates of the town to be locked to keep her from making her attack. She persuaded someone to unlock the gates and rode out to capture another fortress. Then, ignoring a decision by the council to await reinforcements before engaging in further action, she attacked the English on 7 May. She was wounded in the neck by an arrow, but continued to lead the charge.

French spirits were now soaring and it was suggested that Paris should be re-taken or that the army should advance on Normandy. Joan persuaded Charles to make her joint commander of the army with Duke John II of Alençon and gained approval for a bold plan to recapture the bridges on the Loire before advancing on Reims, deep in enemy territory, where the coronation could be held.

She had now won over her fellow commanders, following her extraordinary performance at Orléans. She further enhanced her reputation when she saved Alençon's life at Jargeau which was re-captured on 12 June. She herself was struck on the helmet by a stone cannonball as she scaled a wall. They took Meung-sur-Loire on 15 June and Beaugency two days later. On the 18 June at Patay, she faced a relief English force, headed by Sir John Fastolf. It was a humiliating rout in favour of the French who lost few men.

En route for Reims, the French army accepted the surrender of Auxerre on 29 June and many more did likewise along the route. Troyes, the location of the signing of the shameful treaty that had disinherited Charles VII, was taken after a four-day siege.

On 16 July, they marched through the open gates of Reims and

Charles was crowned King of France the following day. Joan was now eager to march on Paris, but the King preferred to pursue a peace treaty with the Duke of Burgundy. While they negotiated the treaty, however, Philip the Good, Duke of Burgundy, used the time to reinforce his defences around Paris.

They attacked the capital on 8 September and fighting ensued all day, Joan receiving a leg-wound from a crossbow bolt. Next morning, however, she was unaccountably ordered to withdraw. There were skirmishes in November and December and while she waited through the winter, she and her family were ennobled by the King, and known from then on by the name Du Lis, taken from the lilies on her coat of arms. It was not until April 1430 that she was involved in a serious action again, helping to defend the city of Compiègne against a besieging force of English and Burgundian troops.

She was captured on 23 May. Having ordered the retreat, she was amongst a rearguard who were stranded outside Compiègne when the commander of the city, Guillaume de Flavy, panicked and ordered the raising of the drawbridge. Joan was pulled from her horse and became a prisoner of a follower of John of Luxemburg.

In such a situation, it was the habit for the family of a captured prisoner of war to pay a ransom for his or her release. Of course, Joan's family did not have the means to pay and, inexplicably and shamefully, after all she had achieved for him, the King did not intervene and make the payment on their behalf. He even had English prisoners such as the Earl of Suffolk for whom the enemy would undoubtedly have exchanged Joan, but he failed to do so.

She was imprisoned in a seventy feet-high tower in Vermandois and tried several times to escape. She once jumped, landing in the soft earth of the tower's dry moat, but was re-captured. They then moved her to Arras but the English purchased her from the Duke of Burgundy with the intention of trying her for heresy.

The English were eager for a conviction in order to cast doubt on the legitimacy of Charles's coronation for which she, of course, had been responsible. It began on 9 January 1431 at Rouen, headquarters of the English occupation and was dubious from the outset. The judge was Pierre Cauchon, Bishop of Beauvais, who was merely a tool of the Burgundians and who breached ecclesiastical law by denying her the right to a legal advisor. It soon became clear that no evidence had been found to support a charge of heresy.

As ever, however, Joan performed brilliantly, displaying great intellect and evading the traps set for her in cross-examination. She wore women's clothing, but when she was sexually assaulted in prison during the trial, she returned to wearing male attire to avoid further molestation.

Needless to say, she was sentenced to death and on 30 May 1431, after making her confession and receiving Communion, she was led out to a tall stake in the ground. She asked two clergymen to hold a crucifix in front of her and a peasant also gave her a small cross that she placed inside her dress. They lit the fire and she burned to death.

After her death, they raked the coals to expose her charred and burned body so that everyone present could see that she was dead and had not escaped. The body was then burned twice more until it was reduced to ashes to prevent anyone from collecting relics that could be used as a rallying point for the French cause. The ashes were thrown into the Seine.

The Maid of Orléans' extraordinary military adventure was over and, remarkably, she was still only nineteen years old when she died.

ISABELLA I

SHE WAS RESPONSIBLE, along with her husband, Ferdinand II of Aragon, for the *Reconquista* of Spain – the re-capture of Spanish territory occupied by the Moors; she sponsored Christopher Columbus's voyages, thereby taking the first steps in the exploration of the New World that would make Spain immensely wealthy and powerful; and she began the moves that would lead to the unification of Spain by her grandson, the Holy Roman Emperor, Charles V. Isabella is, for good reason, considered to be one of the most important sovereigns who ever lived.

The daughter of King John II of Castille by his second wife, Isabella of Portugal, she was only three years of age when her father died in 1454. Her much older half-brother, the dissolute and frivolous Henry IV, came to the throne and immediately exiled her and her other half-brother Alfonso in Segovia with her stepmother. When she was thirteen, however, Henry summoned them back to the royal court, ostensibly for them to complete their education, but, in reality to prevent them from becoming a rallying point for the country's dissatisfied nobles who held Henry in contempt. The nobles had increasingly gained power in recent years, taking advantage of young or weak monarchs. Now they demanded that Alfonso, Isabella's half-brother be named as heir to the throne, instead of Henry's daughter, Joan. There was some doubt, anyway, about whether Joan was even the daughter of Henry, a suspicion made worse by the common knowledge that Henry's second wife, also called Joan, had been having an affair with his favourite, Beltran de la Cueva. Joan was even given the nickname of 'La Beltraneja' in recognition of the fact that her parentage was dubious. Henry initially agreed to their demands on condition that Alfonso married Joan. A few days later, however, he changed his mind and rejected their demands.

The two sides went to war at the inconclusive Battle of Olmeda in 1467. All was rendered futile, however, when Alfonso died, possibly poisoned, aged just fourteen. The nobles now focused their aspirations on the young Isabella, offering her the throne. Showing astonishing maturity for one so young, however, she rejected it, saying that she would never accept the title of queen while her brother was alive. Henry, however, went part of the way to satisfying the nobles' demands, excluding his daughter from the succession naming his young half-sister as his heir – or Infanta – on 19 September 1468 in the Treaty of the Bulls at Guisando. Isabella was unhappy, however, with Henry's plans to marry her to Don Carlos, Prince of Viana, oldest son of King John II of Aragon, heir to the throne of Navarre. At the same time, John wanted to marry her, instead, to his younger son, Ferdinand. Negotiations stalled, but were brought to a hasty conclusion by Don Carlos's untimely death. Isabella refused to marry any of the candidates suggested by Henry, including Don Pedro Girón, Master of Calatrava, a member of the powerful Pacheco family, Richard, Duke of Gloucester, brother of Edward IV of England, and the Duke of Guienne, brother of Louis XI of France. When, finally, she refused the hand of Afonso V of Portugal, Henry threatened to imprison her in the royal palace of the Alcazar of Madrid. Fearful of the strength of her support, however, he realized this would be a foolish thing to do. He was about to make a journey to Andalusia and he made her promise not to discuss marriage with anyone while he was away.

Isabella was resourceful and determined, however. As soon as he was gone, she travelled to Valladolid and sent emissaries in search of Ferdinand who, on the death of his brother, had been crowned King of Sicily and had been proclaimed heir to the throne of Aragon. Ferdinand returned quickly and they were married on 19 October

1469 in the Palace of Juan de Vivero. It would be one of the most important unions in the history of the Iberian Peninsula.

When Henry IV died in December 1474, Isabella was at last proclaimed Queen of Castile. In 1475, however, La Beltraneja had married Afonso V of Portugal, her uncle. He considered his wife the rightful heir to the throne of Castile and proclaimed himself King. He was further encouraged by the fact that when he learned that Isabella had married Ferdinand without his permission, King Henry had revoked the Treaty of Guisando that had made Isabella his heir, thus legitimising La Beltraneja's claim to the throne. A number of nobles who had previously opposed La Beltraneja now supported her claim and as a consequence, Spain and Portugal went to war for the next five years.

Isabella's husband Ferdinand defeated Afonso at the Battle of Toro in 1476, following which he attempted unsuccessfully to obtain the support of the French king, Louis XI. Afonso would never recover from the defeat and deeply depressed by his lack of success against the Spanish, abdicated in favour of his son in 1477. During the war Isabella was constantly in the saddle, encouraging her men, exposing herself to constant danger.

The war ended in 1479 with an alliance and La Beltraneja at last abandoned her claim to the Castilian throne, retiring to a monastery in 1480. Isabella is said to have walked barefoot through the town of Torddesillas to give thanks at the church in the town. She now ruled unchallenged about her right to do so.

Meanwhile, Ferdinand had acceded to the throne of Navarre and the two kingdoms were united, the two monarchs agreeing to hold equal authority, as expressed in their motto – '*Tanto monta, monta tanto; Isabel como Fernando*' (As much as the one is worth so much is the other; Isabella as Fernando).

They immediately took steps to rein in the overwhelming power of the nobles. They founded the Santa Hermanda (Holy Brotherhood) – a permanent, organised military force supported by municipal councils, to protect people and property against the violent excesses of the nobles. They also reformed the administration of justice, everyone being permitted the right of appeal to the royal council and they centralised the coining of currency, which until that point could be done by a number of people, and re-drew currency laws to facilitate commerce. They revoked grants allowed to nobles by previous monarchs, distributing half of the money saved to the widows and orphans whose husbands and fathers had died for her cause in the recent war, demolished the nobles' castles as a menace to public peace and order and gave the crown the leadership of military orders. Finally, and more sinisterly, they obtained the permission of Pope Sixtus IV to establish the Inquisition, to suppress heresy and opposition to the teachings of the Catholic Church. The nobles, of course, were angered by these actions and threatened an insurrection, but she stood up to them and they eventually submitted to her authority.

The threat of the nobles dealt with at home, they moved their focus to the *Reconquista* whose progress had stalled since the reign of Alfonso IX in the 14th century. It would take them ten years but they prepared well for it. It took three years to reorganise the army, sent for skillful armourers from France to make weapons and imported gunpowder from Sicily and Portugal.

Granada was held by the Muslim Nasrid dynasty but there was dissent amongst the Muslims. Isabella played a large part in the war, not only ruling at home while Ferdinand was leading his army in the south, but also repeatedly visiting his camps, and encouraging the troops with her presence. Undaunted by the danger, she would kneel and pray with them in the middle of a battlefield or close to it. The army consisted of men from many countries who had flocked to Isabella's cause and she had ensured that they were equipped with the best and most up-to-date cannons and weaponry.

Isabella made sure that the wounded of her army were well cared for. Large mobile tents were provided, called the 'Queen's Hospital'.

Everything needed to care for the wounded was there – surgeons to dress wounds and even priests to administer the last rites to any soldier who was not going to survive. It was the first example of the field hospital, later such an essential part of warfare.

She threw herself into the war effort, re-constructing roads, bridging rivers where necessary, cutting passes through hills and mountain gorges and raising money in every way that she could. She begged funds from the Pope and, appealing to their patriotism, her nobles. She even sold some of her own royal domains and some of the crown jewels.

In 1485, her troops besieged and captured the town of Ronda and the following year they took Loja, capturing the Sultan of Granada, Boabdil. By the next year, they had captured the western half of the Nasrid kingdom. Baza fell in 1489 and the siege of Granada began in the spring of 1491. It surrendered at the end of the year and on 2 January Isabella and Ferdinand entered Granada. The principal mosque was re-consecrated as a church and the gate by which Boabdil left the city for the last time, was walled up at his request. The territorial unity of the Spanish monarchy was established.

Meanwhile, in Rome, there was great celebration of the expulsion of the Muslims from Spain and the Pope endowed Isabella and Ferdinand with the title 'The Catholic Kings'. From that point on, Isabella signed all documents and letters 'Isabella the Catholic'.

The Treaty of Granada later that year was designed to confirm freedom of worship for the Muslims. It would not last, however, and in 1502 a policy of expulsion was instituted, if Muslims refused to convert to Christianity.

They were even-handed in their religious persecution, however, although Isabella is understood to have resisted the bad treatment of the Jews. They pursued a policy of religious unity, trying to bring the country together under one faith, Catholicism, and the leader of the Inquisition – which had been established for just this purpose – Tomas de Torquemada, persuaded them to take harsh measures against the Jews. Three months after the fall of Granada, on 31 March 1492, the Alhambra Decree was issued, expelling all Jews from Spain – around 180,000 people – claiming that their cities had admitted the Muslims in the 8th century and designating them a danger to the independence and security of the nation. No native Jewish child would be born in Spain until 1966.

Europe had for many years enjoyed overland trade with the east, India and China, transporting silk, spices and other exotic items along roads. Christopher Columbus, a sailor of Genoese origin, believed, however, that he could find a way to the east by sea but had seen his plans rejected in Genoa, Venice and Portugal. Eventually, he petitioned Isabella, but she too rejected his plan three times before finally acceding to it. He was made Admiral, was permitted the governorship for him and his descendants of any lands that he discovered, as well as ten percent of any profits. Isabella provided him with the means to equip three caravels and on 3 August 1492, he set sail from the port of Palos, arriving not in India, but on the Bahamas in the Americas on 12 October. When he returned to Spain the following year, he received a hero's welcome and to Isabella's delight brought back with him gold and natives of the lands he had visited. Spain's Golden Age began and its discoveries abroad were matched by the development of manufacturing – cloths, silks, glass, steel weapons, leather and silverware. Meanwhile Spanish agriculture prospered and commerce went through the roof.

Isabella and Ferdinand had created an empire as well as unity and vast wealth for their country. Their later years were consumed by the management of this empire as well as securing their legacy through their family. They worked hard to link the Spanish crown with other European monarchies. The Crown Prince, Don Juan, married Margaret of Austria, establishing an important relationship with the Habsburgs that would influence Spanish history for centuries. Their eldest daughter, the Infanta Isabella, married the Portuguese king,

Manuel I and her sister, the Infanta Juana married yet another Habsburg prince, Philip of Burgundy. Unfortunately, however, these unions were ill-fated. Don Juan died not long after his wedding, the Infanta Isabella died in childbirth and her son Miguel survived her by only two years. Queen Isabella's titles would eventually be passed on to Juana who became known as 'Juana la Loco' (Juana the Mad). She is thought to have possibly been schizophrenic and her relationship with her husband Philip was understandably troubled. Nonetheless she gave birth to six children, two of whom would become emperors and four of whom would be queens.

Catherine of Aragon, another of Isabella's daughters, famously married King Henry VIII of England and gave birth to Queen Mary I of England. He would, however, divorce her to marry Anne Boleyn.

In the autumn of 1504, Isabella was attacked by a fever which killed her on 26 November. She was fifty-three years old.

QUEEN ELIZABETH I

GLORIANA, THE VIRGIN Queen, Good Queen Bess – in her day she was a cult figure, celebrated in literature and much painted. She is recognised as one of England's greatest queens, having reigned during a golden age for the country in which England ruled the waves through the offices of such great seamen as Francis Drake and John Hawkins and in which William Shakespeare and Christopher Marlowe were writing. Not for nothing is the time in which she lived and ruled named in her honour – the Elizabethan era.

Appropriately, Elizabeth was born in the Chamber of the Virgins, in Greenwich Palace on 7 September 1533. She was the second legitimate child of Henry VIII and her mother was his second wife, Anne Boleyn. Elizabeth became heiress-presumptive to the English throne, her half-sister Mary having lost her position as heiress to the throne when Henry had annulled his marriage to her mother, Catherine of Aragon in order to marry Anne Boleyn. After two miscarriages and failure to produce the son that Henry wanted to maintain the Tudor line, Anne Boleyn was arrested and imprisoned on trumped-up charges of adultery, incest and treason. She was beheaded on 19 May 1536 when Elizabeth was just under three years old.

Princess Elizabeth was declared illegitimate, just as Mary had been and Henry even took away her title of princess. He married Jane Seymour eleven days after Anne Boleyn's execution and she at last delivered him a son, Prince Edward. Unfortunately, however, Jane died giving birth.

Elizabeth was given into the care of Catherine 'Kat' Ashley who taught her English, Latin and Italian. Her tutors were among the best available. Her first, William Grindal, taught her Greek and French and when he died, she was passed to English scholar and educational theorist, Roger Ascham. She has been described as probably the best-educated woman of her generation.

Meanwhile, Henry VIII continued with his series of marriages. Following Jane Seymour, Henry married Anne of Cleves whom he divorced. He then married Catherine Howard whom he beheaded and finally he took Catherine Parr as his sixth wife.

When Henry died in January 1547, his son became Edward VI and Elizabeth became vulnerable to inscrutable elements who saw her as something of a political pawn. She was taken into the household of Thomas Seymour who Catherine Parr, Henry's last wife, had married. Seymour was the uncle of Edward VI and brother of the Lord Protector, Edward Seymour, Duke of Somerset. After some unseemly goings-on with Seymour, in one of which Catherine Parr caught him in an embrace with the fourteen-year-old Elizabeth, she was sent away. When Catherine died in childbirth in 1548, Seymour turned his attentions to Elizabeth again, seeking to marry her and gain the throne of England. In January 1549, he was arrested on suspicion of trying to marry Elizabeth and overthrow Edward. Under suspicion, Elizabeth successfully defended herself at the age of fifteen against alleged involvement in Seymour's plot. He was beheaded in March 1549.

King Edward died at the age of fifteen in July 1553, leaving a will declaring Lady Jane Grey, granddaughter of Henry VIII's sister, Mary, to be his heir. After just nine days on the throne, however, she was deposed and executed. Mary and Elizabeth rode triumphantly at each other's side into London.

Princess Mary became Mary I, but she very quickly fell out with her sister. Mary was a staunch Catholic and resolved to stamp out the Protestantism that had flourished in England after the reformation and after Henry VIII had broken with the Catholic Church. Elizabeth, a Protestant, had to pretend to be Catholic and attended Mass. However, Mary's attitude towards religion was unpopular, and there was an uprising in England, known as Wyatt's rebellion, led by Thomas Wyatt, with the objective of removing Mary from the throne and replacing her with Elizabeth. The proposed marriage of Mary to Prince Philip of Spain did nothing to soothe the people's anger.

At this time, suspected of being involved in the Wyatt plot, Elizabeth was arrested and imprisoned in the Tower. She passionately pleaded her innocence of any wrongdoing but some argued that while she was alive, the throne of England would not be safe and that she should be tried and executed as quickly as possible. Mary was persuaded to spare her sister's life, however. Elizabeth was taken from the Tower to Woodstock Manor in Oxfordshire where she remained under house arrest for a year. Finally, Mary's husband, now Philip II of Spain, persuaded Mary to let her go to her childhood home at Hatfield. He may have done this, however, because the precarious state of his wife's health made him fear that Elizabeth would soon be queen and he wanted to ensure good relations between his country and England. He also preferred her to the other likely candidate, Mary Queen of Scots who was betrothed to the Dauphin of France, heir to the French throne.

It was evident that Mary was never going to have a child and by 1558, Elizabeth was preparing for government. On 6 November of that year, eleven days before she died, Mary formally recognised her as her heir. Elizabeth, the unwanted daughter of Henry VIII who had been cast aside by the court many years previously, and who had even had her royal title taken away from her, was Queen of England, aged twenty-five.

Her accession to the throne was warmly greeted by the people of England and on 15 January 1559, amidst great pomp and the wild acclaim of her subjects, she was crowned queen at Westminster Abbey.

There was little doubt that Elizabeth would embrace Protestantism on behalf of England but she sought a solution to the country's religious issues that would not upset her Catholic subjects so much that they would resort to rebellion. Thus, Parliament brought in legislation that allowed for a Church based on the Protestant settlement of Edward VI, with the Queen as its head. There was some resistance from the House of Lords, but eventually she got her way, even if she had to accept the title of Supreme Governor of the Church of England instead of Supreme Head, the title enjoyed by her father, Henry VIII.

Of course, one of the big issues of the day was whom she would marry. There were, of course, many who were attracted to the idea of being king-consort to the Queen of England, but she refused to commit herself, possibly because of what had happened to the women in her father's life, or possibly because of her treatment at the hands of Thomas Seymour. Some have suggested that she was infertile, while others say that she was afraid of childbirth, a frequent cause of death amongst women in those days. It is not as if there were not fairly serious suitors and one of them, Robert Dudley, came as close as anyone did to marrying her. Dudley was a childhood friend, had been imprisoned in the Tower at the same time as her and for many years was her favourite of all the nobles at her court. In 1559, the rumour spread through court that their relationship had turned serious and that she was sharing a bed with him. Then, when Dudley's wife, Amy Robsart, was found dead in suspicious circumstances, at the foot of a flight of stairs with her neck broken, a scandal erupted. Many suspected he had ordered her murder to marry the queen and, already unpopular due to the fact that his father, the Duke of Northumberland, had been executed for putting Lady Jane Grey on the throne, he became even more unpopular.

The marriage question never went away and Parliament repeatedly petitioned her to marry. She kept it open, but used it only to suit herself, or for diplomatic purposes. The problem, of course was the succession. If she had no heir or had not named a successor, there was a great risk of civil war following her death. However, she stubbornly refused to either marry or name her heir. Of course, her stubbornness in refusing to name a successor may just have been political expedience. If she had named one, she would have been vulnerable to a coup. Keeping people in the dark gave her political strength.

Catholics believed that the daughter of Elizabeth's cousin, James V of Scotland, the Catholic Mary Queen of Scots, was the true queen of England. They considered Elizabeth to be illegitimate and there were many plots to replace her with Mary who, after a disastrous reign in Scotland, had been forced to flee Scotland and seek refuge in England. Elizabeth had, instead, imprisoned her for nineteen years in Fotheringay Castle. Many around Elizabeth agitated for Mary to be executed, but only when a plot, led by Thomas Babington was uncovered, implicating Mary, did Elizabeth sign a death warrant for her cousin who was finally executed in February 1587.

Mary's execution persuaded Philip II of Spain to cast envious eyes on the English throne. He disagreed with Elizabeth's political and religious agendas and by 1588 they were sworn enemies. On 12 July of that year, he launched a huge fleet, the Armada, against England. It would bring a Spanish invasion force under the Duke of Parma to the coast of south-east England. However, it encountered an English fleet off Gravelines which dispersed it to the northeast. Many ships foundered on the Irish coast and the remnants of the fleet limped home.

Before this great English naval victory, Elizabeth, inspecting her troops at Tilbury, clad in a silver breastplate over a white velvet dress, famously said: '...I know I have the body but of a weak and feeble woman, but I have the heart and stomach of a king, and of a King of England too, and think foul scorn that Parma or Spain, or any Prince of Europe should dare to invade the borders of my realm.'

The nation went into paroxysms of delight when it heard of the failure of the invasion. Elizabeth was driven through celebrating crowds lining the streets on her way to a service of thanksgiving at St Paul's Cathedral. The nation felt itself to be invincible under its virgin queen and believed that their victory was a sign from God.

War continued with Spain, however, and the results were not always as favourable to England. It was fought largely at sea and featured raids by English ships on Spanish ports, especially by Captain Francis Drake, knighted by Elizabeth for his circumnavigation of the globe from 1577 to 1580.

Her foreign policy was on the whole a defensive one. She did preside over the establishment of the first English colony in North America – named after her 'Virginia' – but in Europe, she did not enjoy great success. In 1562-63 she disastrously occupied Le Havre in France but it would be 1585 before she ventured into Europe again. Following the deaths of her allies, William the Silent, Prince of Orange and Francois, Duke of Anjou in 1584, she sent an army to help the Dutch Protestant rebels against the Spanish. The English, fearing Spanish domination of the Channel coast, signed the Nonsuch Treaty with the Netherlands, promising to provide military support for the Dutch against Spain. The Anglo-Spanish War would carry on until 1604.

Sir Walter Raleigh was of the opinion that Elizabeth's caution had prevented England from an outright victory over the Spanish; '…her Majesty did all by halves, and by petty invasions taught the Spaniard how to defend himself, and to see his own weakness.'

She faced inevitable difficulties in Catholic Ireland which, though part of her kingdom, was consistently rebellious and there was always the threat that the Irish would provide a base for enemies such as Spain. The English reacted to a series of uprisings by pursuing a destructive scorched-earth policy in Ireland, burning and killing wherever they went. In Munster in 1582, following a rebellion by the Earl of Desmond, it is estimated that 30,000 Irish people starved to death. Elizabeth described Ireland as 'that rude and barbarous nation.'

Tyrone's Rebellion between 1594 and 1603, led by Hugh O'Neill, Earl of Tyrone, enjoyed Spanish support and was difficult to quash. It was finally defeated by Charles Blount, Lord Mountjoy a few days after Elizabeth's death.

As Elizabeth grew older, her public image began to change. She looked unreal in her portraits, made to appear younger than she actually was. She had suffered an attack of smallpox and it had left her half bald and her skin badly scarred. But, her courtiers continued to praise her beauty as if she was still a young girl and she played the part. She became fond of the young Earl of Essex but he became increasingly irresponsible, deserting his command in Ireland in 1599 and returning to England against her express orders. He was put under house arrest and in 1601 attempted to start a rebellion against Elizabeth. There was little support, however, and he was arrested and beheaded. She very much blamed herself for the way things had turned out and it was said that 'Her delight is to sit in the dark, and sometimes with shedding tears to bewail Essex'. Nonetheless, that year she delivered her famous 'Golden Speech' to Parliament.

As she grew older, concern increased about the succession. Robert Cecil became her most trusted advisor but, in the absence of a declaration from her, he proceeded in secret, negotiating with James VI of Scotland who had a strong claim to the English throne through his mother, Mary Queen of Scots. Cecil taught James how to impress and flatter the old queen in his correspondence with her and it worked, although she never, at any time voiced her feeling that he should follow her on the throne.

In autumn and winter of 1602, Elizabeth was knocked by a series of deaths of friends. Following the death in February 1603, of her cousin and close friend, Catherine Carey, Countess of Nottingham, she became ill. She died quietly on 24 March at Richmond Palace between two and three o'clock in the morning. A few hours later James VI of Scotland was proclaimed King James I of England.

SIR FRANCIS DRAKE

HIS FELLOW NAVAL commanders considered him to be an upstart. He was a rich man, certainly, but a common one as shown, they sneered by his West Country accent and lack of the etiquette one would expect of a gentleman. Some things about him were never in doubt, however – his leadership, his seamanship, his courage and his hatred for the Spanish. Even Lord Burghley, Queen Elizabeth I's chief adviser, who disliked Drake intensely, was forced to admit that 'Sir Francis Drake is a fearful man to the King of Spain.' Indeed, he was; the king placed a reward of 20,000 ducats (more than £5 million in today's terms) on his head.

Drake has become something of a symbol of all that is good about the English. His sangfroid, tenacity and ability to improvise in any situation, coupled with a sense of fair play, demonstrated in his celebrated courtesy towards prisoners, have all come to be recognisable facets of the English character. Of course, the legend of Francis Drake has been massaged through the centuries to make us believe all these things but, even if some of it is wishful thinking on the part of a nation that loves its heroes, he remains an extraordinary figure whose achievements will always make his countrymen's hearts beat a little faster.

He was born in 1540 in the parish of Crowndale, close to Tavistock in Devon, the oldest of the twelve sons of Edmund Drake, a Protestant farmer and his wife Mary. He was named after his godfather, Francis Russell, 2nd Earl of Bedford, of whom his father was a tenant.

In 1549, Drake's family are said to have fled to Kent during the Prayer Book Rebellion that broke out in Devon and Cornwall as a result of the introduction of the unpopular Book of Common Prayer which presented the theology of the English Reformation. Others say, however, that Francis's father got involved in a spot of petty crime and had to flee on account of that.

Drake seems to have gone to sea around the age of thirteen, apprenticed to a small boat that traded in the Bay of Biscay and to the Channel ports.

At the age of eighteen, he went to sea with the Hawkins fleet, seizing shipping off the French coast and by the 1560s, he was sailing on ships trading with Africa. He was in command of his own vessel on behalf of the Hawkins fleet in 1568, illegally trading slaves in the Spanish colonies of the Caribbean. It was at this time that his dislike of the Spanish first came to light. He believed that they had wronged him in some way, possibly because they so tightly regulated their trade and restricted his activities.

His second voyage to the West Indies did not go well, however. At San Juan de Ulua off the coast of Mexico, the Spanish attacked the Hawkins vessels while they were being re-supplied and repaired in port. Two were sunk and a number of men were killed. Drake managed to escape and travelled back to England commanding the Judith, a small ship. He now had even more reason to be angry at the Spanish.

The one good thing to come out of this particular financial disaster, however, was that Drake's name came to the attention of Queen Elizabeth who had invested in the slave trading venture.

Drake made a couple of further voyages to the West Indies, as he put it, 'to gain such intelligence as might further him to get some amend for his loss.' Then, in 1572, he obtained a privateering commission. This meant that he was free to plunder Spanish shipping whenever he encountered it. He set sail for the Americas in command of the seventy-ton *Pasha* and the twenty-five-ton *Swan* with crews made up mainly of Frenchmen and Maroons, African slaves who had escaped from the Spanish and had a score to settle.

His first objective was to capture the town of Nombre de Dios in Panama. The attack was, however, a failure and Drake was wounded in the attack but although they failed to take the town, they still managed to get away with a significant amount of plunder, especially after they attacked a mule train carrying silver from the mines. Drake captured a fortune in gold although he was forced to leave behind still more because it was too heavy.

At some point in the midst of all this, Drake stood on a piece of high ground on the Isthmus of Panama, gazing at the Pacific Ocean, the first Englishman to set eyes on it. As he stood there, he dreamed of sailing an English ship across that ocean.

He returned to England both a rich man and a hero but only to discover that although Elizabeth was, of course, delighted with his success, she had signed a temporary truce with Philip II of Spain and was, therefore, unable to officially acknowledge his success. Drake exercised extraordinary discretion and sailed to Ireland to take orders from the Earl of Essex who had gone there to colonise Ulster. There he was involved in a shameful episode when around 600 men, women and children were massacred on Rathlin Island after they had surrendered. They were the families of the followers of the Scottish chieftain, Sorley Boy MacDonell who was fighting the English in Ulster. Drake was commanding the Falcon, with the task of preventing Scottish ships from landing reinforcements on the island.

In 1577, Drake began the greatest adventure of his career. Elizabeth chose him to lead an expedition, backed by her, to voyage around South America, through the Strait of Magellan, the narrow and difficult passage that ran between the Chilean mainland and Tierra del Fuego. He was then to explore the coast beyond that point. For the first time, as he prepared for the trip, he met Elizabeth who told him what he wanted to hear, that she 'would gladly be revenged on the king of Spain for divers injuries that I have received.' It was a voyage in which he had been given permission to indulge his two favourite pastimes – piracy and fighting the Spanish.

He set out in December of that year with five small ships with total crews of only 164 men and by spring 1578, he was off the Brazilian coast. His flagship on this voyage was the 100-ton *Pelican*, but later, as he prepared to enter the Strait of Magellan, he would give it the name under which it became one of the most famous ships in English naval history, the *Golden Hind*. However, the crossing of the Atlantic had been arduous and he scuttled two of his ships, the *Christopher* and the *Swan* due to the loss of a large number of their crews.

As he arrived in South America with his three remaining ships, Drake displayed his qualities as a strict disciplinarian when he accused his co-commander and close friend, Sir Thomas Doughty, of treason and witchcraft. Doughty demanded that he be taken back to England and tried, but Drake refused and he was tried with members of the ship's crew as the jury. They found him guilty and sentenced him to death, some of them reluctantly. Remarkably, before his execution, Doughty requested that he and Drake receive Communion together and the two men also dined together. On 2 July 1578, Doughty was beheaded.

He lost another vessel to violent storms in the Strait and another had turned back for England. The *Golden Hind* continued alone north, up the Pacific coast of South America, attacking Spanish ports it passed and raiding coastal towns, including the port of Valparaiso. He was seriously wounded on a visit to Mocha Island, off the coast of Chile when he was attacked by hostile Mapuche natives.

Off Lima in Peru, he captured a treasure-laden Spanish galleon, taking gold that would be worth, in today's terms, about £7 million. He pursued and captured another Spanish treasure ship, the *Nuestra Señora de la Concepción*, this time looting eighty pounds of gold, a golden crucifix, jewels, thirteen chests full of royal plate and an astonishing twenty-six tons of silver. This was an important capture, however, as it revealed to the world that the Spanish were active in territory in the Far East that the Pope had awarded to the Portuguese in his document *Inter Caetera*, in which he had divided the world up between the two great Iberian seafaring nations. As a result, Philip II of Spain invaded Portugal and seized the crown later that year.

In June 1580, Drake progressed beyond the Spanish Empire's most northerly point and landed in order to re-supply and make repairs to the *Golden Hind*. He claimed the land in the name of the queen and named it Nova Albion. He is also believed to have left some of his men behind in a small settlement.

It is not known for certain where exactly Nova Albion was. Some say California and others suggest that it was further north – Oregon or even Vancouver Island. However, all the records of the voyage were lost when Whitehall Palace was destroyed by fire in 1698 and the exact location remains a matter of speculation.

From Nova Albion, Drake set out to find the fabled Northwest Passage – a sea route north of America connecting the Atlantic and the Pacific Oceans – which would have represented a fantastic and highly lucrative coup for the English crown. However, Drake was driven back by the extreme cold he encountered as he sailed north through the icy seas.

He headed off across the Pacific, reaching the Moluccas in the southwest Pacific, a few months later. It was a difficult time – the *Golden Hind* came close to being lost when she hit a reef but Drake waited patiently, dumped inessential cargo and after three days the ship floated off the reef on the tide.

He sailed on towards the Cape of Good Hope at the bottom of Africa, stopping many times en route and he sailed into Plymouth a hero with fifty-nine surviving crew members and a ship laden with booty on 26 September 1580. The wealth he handed over to the Queen following this voyage – a half-share – was greater than the crown's income for the entire year. He was hailed as the first Englishman to circumnavigate the earth and was knighted by Queen Elizabeth on board the *Golden Hind* while it was at Deptford in the Thames estuary.

In 1581, Drake became Mayor of Plymouth, an office that he treated with great seriousness. His first wife Mary died in 1583, after fourteen years of marriage and he re-married Elizabeth Sydenham, heiress to the fortune of a local Devonshire businessman, Sir George Sydenham. He purchased a large house, Buckland Abbey, close to Plymouth.

Drake was never popular with his fellow naval commanders. Men such as Sir Richard Grenville and Sir Martin Frobisher detested him, but the only thing that mattered was that Queen Elizabeth liked him. In 1585 she proved it by putting him in command of a fleet consisting of 25 ships. England was once again at war with Spain and Drake's mission was to do as much damage as he could to the Spanish fleet and Spanish ports in the Americas. This he did happily, plundering a slew of them.

In 1586, Philip of Spain was assembling a fleet to attack England with the Pope's blessing. The Pope wanted the English crown to be returned to the Catholic fold and blessed the Spanish king in his enterprise. The Queen similarly gave Drake her blessing to 'impeach the provisions of Spain.' In 1587, he attacked the Spanish ships at anchor at Cadiz in southern Spain, destroying a large number of them. He famously laughed the venture off as 'singeing the king of Spain's beard.' It was an important action because it delayed the Armada for a year but in July 1588 that force of ships was sailing up the English Channel.

It was at this time that the most famous – and probably apocryphal – story of the many that surround Francis Drake, emerges. He was reported to have been playing a game of bowls on Plymouth Hoe when he was informed of the approach of the Spanish Armada and is reputed to have said nonchalantly that there was plenty of time to finish the game before defeating the Spaniards. In reality, Lord Howard was in command when the Armada was defeated and Drake was vice admiral. He did not play a major role in the battle, but did succeed in pursuing and capturing one Spanish galleon, the *Rosario* that was carrying a large amount of cash to pay Spanish soldiers fighting in the Netherlands.

In 1589, Drake and Sir John Norreys sailed on an ill-fated mission to seek out the surviving Spanish ships and provide support for the Portuguese who were rebelling against Spanish rule. They succeeded in destroying a few Spanish vessels at Coruña, but lost a great number of ships and a huge number of lives.

Sir Francis Drake continued fighting the Spanish until the age of fifty-six when he died of dysentry while his ship was at anchor off the coast of Puerto Bello, Panama. This greatest of all English seamen was buried at sea in a lead coffin.

MARY QUEEN OF SCOTS

THE EXECUTIONER'S BLOCK stood on a black-draped platform three feet off the ground, in front of a silent crowd of people in the hall at Fotheringhay Castle. She climbed the steps accompanied by two servants. The executioners knelt before her and, as was customary, begged her forgiveness. She forgave them and went on, 'You are about to end my troubles.' The servants and executioners helped her to disrobe, removing her black outer gown, two petticoats and a corset, to reveal a red chemise, the colour symbolic as it represented martyrdom in her beloved Catholic Church. Remarkably, she smiled at her executioner at one point, saying quietly, 'Never have I had such assistants to disrobe me, and never have I put off my clothes before such a company.' They slipped a blindfold over her eyes and she knelt down in front of the block with a cushion beneath her knees. She bent down, positioning her neck in the slot on the block and stretched her hands out of the way behind her.

It apparently took the executioner two swings of the axe. The first drove into the back of her head, at which point she is said to have been heard whispering, 'Sweet Jesus', but the second struck true, although her head remained connected to her body by a thin sinew. The executioner sawed it off completely with the razor-sharp blade of the axe. He picked up the head, holding it aloft to the crowd and shouting 'God save the Queen!' As he held it by its long, auburn hair, the head came away from the hair and fell to the ground. She had been wearing a wig and underneath it her real hair was short and grey.

At forty-four years of age the extraordinary life of Mary Queen of Scots was over. It had been a life of royal privilege – she had become Queen of Scotland a mere six days after her birth and Queen consort of France, aged just sixteen. However, it had also been a life of intrigue, murder, kidnap, love, long incarceration, betrayal and, ultimately, disappointment.

Although in the 14th century, it had been stipulated that only male children of a king could inherit the throne of Scotland, Mary took the throne in 1542 because she was the only surviving legitimate child of James V. She had been born at Linlithgow Palace on 7 December 1542 to James and the French Mary of Guise. James is famously supposed to have said on hearing that he had a daughter, 'It came with a lass and it will pass with a lass!' predicting the fall of the House of Stuart that had arrived on the throne when the high steward of Scotland, Walter Stewart, married the daughter of Robert the Bruce, Marjorie, in 1314. His prediction did come true but not until 1714 when George Louis of Hanover, son of Sophia of Hanover, daughter of Elizabeth Stuart, became King of Britain, replacing the House of Stuart with the German House of Hanover.

As Mary was so young, a regent was required to govern Scotland and James Hamilton, 2nd Earl of Arran, who was next in line for the crown after her, performed this task until 1554. Then, the Queen's mother, Mary of Guise, took over and continued to hold the reins of government until 1560 when she died.

The English had been agitating for Mary to be betrothed to Prince Edward, the son of the English king, Henry VIII. The Treaties of Greenwich signed between the two countries in 1552 agreed on this point, meaning that their children would inherit the kingdoms of both Scotland and England.

Mary of Guise, along with many Scots, however, was opposed to such a move and she hid with Mary in Stirling Castle where, on 9 September 1543, the coronation of the ten-month-old baby took place.

Henry VIII now proceeded to undertake what has become known as the 'Rough Wooing' of the young queen. He demanded that she live in England until the marriage with his son and also insisted that the Scots end their alliance with the French, the Auld Alliance. He backed up his demands with raids over the border, a costly exercise in terms of both finance and human life. In May 1544, the Earl of Hereford attacked Edinburgh Castle with the intention of capturing Mary and taking her to England. Mary of Guise had, however, spirited Mary out of the castle and taken her to Stirling where they hid again in the deep and secret passages of Stirling Castle.

Eventually, when matters began to go very badly for the Scots following a catastrophic defeat by the English at the Battle of Pinkie Cleugh, Mary of Guise had no option but to turn to her countrymen for help. The recently crowned French king, Henry II came up with a solution that was eminently acceptable to her. He would send help if she would agree to Mary marrying his son, the Dauphin François, uniting the Scottish and French crowns instead of the Scottish and English. She agreed and with the English on their way back to continue the Rough Wooing, she took Mary to Dumbarton Castle where a marriage treaty with the French was signed in June.

Mary Queen of Scots was dispatched to France in 1548 and she would live there at the French court for the next thirteen years in the company of four little girls who were sent with her to keep her company. The daughters of Scottish nobles, the girls were all called 'Mary' and have become known as 'the Four Marys' – Mary Beaton, Mary Seton, Mary Fleming and Mary Livingston.

Mary became popular at the French court. She proved herself to be intelligent, bright and vivacious and she received a good education from the best teachers available at the time, learning French, Latin, Greek, Spanish and Italian. She was taught to play musical instruments as well as becoming proficient in horsemanship, falconry and needlework.

Although not a great beauty while young, she would develop into a tall, attractive woman who would later beguile a number of men. The first of these was the Dauphin François, who was far shorter than her five feet eleven inches, but with whom she got on very well.

The teenage couple were married at the cathedral of Notre Dame in Paris on 24 April 1558; he became King Consort of the Scots.

On 10 July 1559, François' father, Henry II died and he became King of France while Mary took on the role of Queen Consort of France.

Mary was seen by many Catholics as the true heir to the throne of England. They considered Henry VIII's daughter, Elizabeth, whose mother had been the executed Anne Boleyn, to be illegitimate and, indeed, she had been declared illegitimate when her mother was executed three years after her birth. However, the Third Succession Act was passed, confirming Elizabeth as the next Queen of England, following the death of Mary I and, anyway, Henry VIII had stipulated in his will that he wanted Stuarts to be excluded from assuming the throne of England.

Mary's life was turned upside-down, when, in December 1560, her young husband, François, died when an ear infection developed into an abscess in his brain. He was just sixteen years old.

She returned to a dangerously divided Scotland, regarded suspiciously by many of her subjects, but also perceived as an on-going danger by Elizabeth I. The Treaty of Edinburgh had been signed by Mary's representatives with English forces in July 1560 and in it Mary and all her descendents were excluded from the English throne. She would never ratify the treaty.

There had been a religious revolution in favour of Protestantism in Scotland and it made Catholic Mary's attempts to govern very difficult. She accepted the status quo, tolerating the Protestant ascendancy, and gradually life improved for Scottish Catholics. Nonetheless, firebrand preachers such as the influential John Knox and her illegitimate half-brother, James Stewart, Earl of Moray, leader of the Protestant faction, railed against her and her religion.

She made entreaties to the Queen of England, inviting Elizabeth to Scotland, an invitation that was, of course, refused, and sending an envoy to plead her case. There was an arranged meeting that was cancelled. Elizabeth then suggested that if Mary married someone of her choosing – such as the Protestant Robert Dudley, Earl of Leicester – she would pronounce her as next in line to the throne after her. Needless to say, Mary rejected her offer.

Instead, on 29 July 1565, Mary married her first half-cousin, Henry Stuart, Lord Darnley, making Elizabeth furious as she believed that her permission for the union should have been sought first. Given that Darnley also felt he had a claim to the English throne, she felt even more threatened.

It was a step too far for the Protestant lords of Scotland who openly rebelled but she routed their forces in the action known as the Chaseabout Raid, forcing Moray and other lords into exile in England.

Darnley became arrogant and violent towards Mary and extremely suspicious of her private secretary, David Rizzio. With a group of the very nobles who had fought Mary in the Chaseabout Raid, he murdered Rizzio in March 1566 in front of the Queen. Darnley would later betray his accomplices but the marriage was effectively over.

Mary had a son, James, in June 1566 and began to hatch a plot to dispose of her increasingly difficult and unpleasant husband. In February 1567, he was found dead in the garden of a house in Edinburgh following an explosion at the house. The explosion had not killed him, however. By the time the bomb had gone off, Darnley had already been murdered.

The 4th Earl of Bothwell, who had become a favourite of Mary's, was charged with the murder but his trial was a charade and he was acquitted of all charges. Bothwell now persuaded some Scottish nobles to sign the Ainslie Tavern Bond that stated that Mary should marry a Scotsman and in April 1567, while Mary was travelling fom Stirling to Edinburgh, she was kidnapped by Bothwell and taken to Dunbar Castle where she was allegedly raped by him. As a result, she became pregnant with twins which, sadly, later miscarried. Bothwell took her to Edinburgh and on 15 May, a few days after he had scandalously divorced his wife, he married her in a Protestant ceremony at the Palace of Holyroodehouse.

The country was seriously divided by news of the marriage, but an army was raised at once by the Scottish nobles who confronted Mary and her new husband at Carberry Hill a month after the wedding. There was no battle, however, as Mary said she would go with them if they let Bothwell go. Bothwell fled and she never saw him again. Imprisoned in Denmark, he would die, insane, in 1578. Meanwhile, instead of being treated properly by the lords, as promised, Mary was imprisoned in Lochleven Castle. Escaping from her incarceration almost a year later, on 2 May 1568, she raised an army but was defeated at the Battle of Langside on 13 May. She fled to England and threw herself on the mercy of her cousin, the English queen. Elizabeth did not know what to do with her, however, incarcerating her initially at Carlisle, before moving her to Bolton Castle in July and then transferring her to Tutbury Castle in January 1569.

After eighteen years' imprisonment, Mary had become a danger that Elizabeth could no longer tolerate. The Scottish queen's name came up in a number of plots to assassinate her but the principal one was the Babington Plot for which she was put on trial. Of course, there was some doubt as to the authenticity of this plot, many surmising that it was actually created by the Elizabethan 'spymaster', Sir Francis Walsingham, and the English Secret Service to entrap Mary. The verdict, however, was never in doubt and inevitably she was sentenced to death by beheading at Fotheringhay Castle on 8 February 1587.

Mary Queen of Scots died as she lived – courageously and holding true to her beliefs.

III
THE ENLIGHTENED WORLD

NZINGA MBANDE

THE CONFERENCE WAS ready to start. The Portuguese had seated themselves but they neglected to offer the envoy of the Ndongo ruler, the Ngola (King) Mbande, a chair to sit on. Instead they had insultingly thrown a mat on the floor for her. But Nzinga Mbande was not prepared to sit on a mat. That was what servants did and she was no servant of the Portuguese. She turned to one of her entourage and ordered her to crouch on the ground on her hands and knees. Nzinga sat on her back and waited for the talking to start.

She was born around 1582 in modern-day Angola, southwestern Africa, to Ngola Kiluanji and Kangela and had three siblings – two sisters, Kifunji and Mukambu, and one brother. She was much loved by her father who allowed her to observe as he governed his kingdom and even carried her with him when he went to war.

She grew up at a time when the Portuguese were strengthening their grip on Africa. Their empire had been the earliest of all the European colonial empires, Portuguese explorers first mapping the coast of Africa as early as 1419 as they tried to find a sea route to Asia, the source of many exotic items much desired in the west, such as spices. By 1488, Bartolomeu Dias had rounded the Cape of Good Hope and in 1498, Vasco da Gama reached India. With the beginning of the exploration of Africa, by 1434, slaves were being brought back and slave trading became one of the most lucrative parts of Portuguese commerce. Trade outposts and fortified bases were established on the coast and increasingly in the interior.

The conference that Nzinga was attending was to persuade the Portuguese to withdraw one such base, the fortress of Ambaca which had been constructed on Ngola Mbande's land on the orders of a former Governor, Luis Mendes de Vasconcelos. The Ngola also wanted a number of his subjects who had been taken as slaves to be returned. Furthermore, he wanted Nzinga to discuss with the colonial power the marauding of mercenaries of the warrior Imbangala tribe who were in Portuguese service.

She must have been persuasive because the governor, João Correia de Sousa agreed to what she requested. The sticking-point arose, however, over the question of whether Ndongo submitted to Portugal. Nzinga stood her ground refusing to agree to such a humiliation for her brother's kingdom. Nonetheless, she had achieved much and relations with the Portuguese were improved and in order to show goodwill to them regarding their agreements, she agreed to become a Christian, adopting the name Dona Anna de Sousa on her baptism in honour of the Governor's wife who became her godmother.

As often happened, however, the Portuguese failed to honour the agreements they had made with Nzinga. The fortress at Ambaca remained in place and the Ndongo slaves remained in captivity. They also failed to do anything about the Imbagala who continued to cause a great deal of trouble to the Ndongans.

Ngola Mbande, Nzinga's brother, was devastated by the failure of the agreements and believing there was nothing he could do to recover what had been lost in the war with the Portuguese, killed himself. There were malicious rumours that Nzinga had actually poisoned him, but these are likely to have been spread by the Portuguese to persuade the Ndongans to block her path to the throne.

Her son was heir to the throne but was far too young to accede. Therefore, she ruled as regent. At the time of her brother's suicide, the boy was living with an Imbangala band commanded by a man named Kaza and Nzinga contacted them, requesting that the boy be returned to her care. She then assumed the full powers of the Ngola, styling herself in correspondence as 'Senhora de Andongo' (Lady of Andongo). By 1626, however, she was calling herself 'Rainha de Andongo' (Queen of Andongo).

It is said that after becoming queen, she kept a large, all-male harem. Men are said to have fought to the death in order to be able to spend a night with her but after a single night, they were put to death.

When a new Portuguese Governor, Fernão de Sousa, arrived in 1624, Nzinga pressed him on the issues that had been agreed at the conference, but he, too, refused to honour them. Nzinga felt she had no option but to declare war.

It started badly, however, and she was driven from her island capital, Kidonga, that year. In 1627, she re-captured it but the Portuguese drove her and her people out again two years later, capturing one of her sisters in the process. Pursued to the district of Baixa de Cassange, Nzinga escaped only by climbing down steep cliffs.

She came to the conclusion that the only way she could win was with the help of other tribes and tried to form an alliance with an Imbangala tribe led by a chief called Kasanje. When he refused to accord her equal status to himself, she abandoned this idea. Instead, she raised another army and by 1631 had taken over another kingdom, Matamba. She had, during this time, allied herself with an Imbangala band led by her son, Njinga Mona.

To bolster Matamba's power, she offered sanctuary to runaway slaves and Portuguese-trained African soldiers and recruited them into her army. She introduced the kilombo, a military structure in which young men renounced their families and were brought up communally in the militia. At the same time, she encouraged rebellion in Ndongo to destabilise the Portuguese-installed puppet regime there.

In those times great exaggerations were made about the customs and rituals employed by native peoples. It provided a justification for the enslavement and harsh treatment meted out to them by colonial powers. Thus, Portuguese Capuchin priests working in the area accused Nzinga and her people of indulging in such barbarities as cannibalism and infanticide. Nonetheless, Imbangalas were also accused of these atrocities by African witnesses, giving slightly more credence to them. It remains unclear, however, whether Nzinga was ever involved in such things and, although she presented herself as an enemy of Christianity because of the things done in its name to her people, she is said to have treated priests respectfully when they were captured. She even permitted Portuguese prisoners of war and Christian Africans to have the sacraments.

She became respected for personally leading her men into battle and banned her subjects from calling her 'Queen', insisting, instead, that they addressed her as 'King'.

In 1639, the Portuguese Governor sent envoys to her to discuss the internal borders of the territory, but no formal agreement was reached, Nzinga perhaps wary of any settlement with the people who had reneged on the last one.

The Dutch were in direct competition with the Portuguese in several parts of the world and Africa was one of these. Working in alliance with the west-central African Kingdom of Kongo, they had captured the city of Luanda and it was to Luanda that Nzinga sent an envoy to conclude an alliance against their mutual enemy, Portugal. She moved her capital to Kavanga in the north of her old Ndongo land and in 1644, defeated the Portuguese at Ngoleme. Two years later, however, she in turn lost to them at Kavanga, losing her remaining sister to captivity. The Portuguese discovered when they captured her private archive that her captive sister had been conducting a secret correspondence with Nzinga, and had revealed Portuguese plans to her. They were furious and drowned the unfortunate woman in the Kwanza River.

With Dutch reinforcements, Nzinga crushed a Portuguese army in 1647 and then besieged the city of Masangano. Meanwhile, the Portuguese took Luanda back from the Dutch and in 1648 Nzinga beat a retreat to Matamba and continued to fight a rearguard action against the pursuing Portuguese. She continued to do so, leading her troops into battle personally, until she was well into her sixties.

At last, in 1657, time caught up with her. Exhausted by her

decades-long struggle, she concluded a peace treaty with Portugal and then tried to re-construct her kingdom, seriously damaged by the years of war. She tried to assure that the succession to the throne of her combined kingdom of Ndonga and Matamba did not fall to the Imbangala after her death, attempting to marry her surviving sister to a man called João Guterres Ngola Kanini, the scion of a powerful family. The marriage was not permitted by Catholic priests, however, who claimed he already had a wife.

Finally, she returned to the Catholic Church and allowed Catholic missionaries to preach to her people. She also devoted her energy to helping resettle former slaves and resisted numerous attempts to oust her from the throne, especially by the Imbangala, Kasanje. She developed Matamba as a trading power, capitalising on its position as the gateway to the Central African interior and by the time of her death, it was a formidable commercial power, dealing with the Portuguese colony on an equal footing.

Incredibly, after her decades of warfare, Nzinga Mbabde died peacefully at the age of eighty on 17 December 1663 in Matamba.

Immediately following her death her kingdom erupted in civil war but eventually Francisco Guterres Ngola Kanini carried on her royal line. Portugal would continue to struggle to subdue the region and did not establish full control of the interior for another 400 years.

In time, even the Portuguese began to respect the achievements of this warrior queen who was a brilliant military commander, a resourceful politician and a skilful diplomat.

CARDINAL RICHELIEU

THE EXOTICALLY NAMED Armand Jean de Plessis de Richelieu, Cardinal Duc de Richelieu, can be said to have been the world's first prime minister. He was appointed Chief Minister by King Louis XIII when in 1624, aged thirty-nine, and would retain control of affairs in France until his death in 1642. During his rule, he tried to consolidate the power of the king by reducing the power of the nobles, making France into a strong, centralised state that wielded a huge amount of power in the face of the threat from the Austro-Spanish Habsburg dynasty. To do so, he governed ruthlessly, eliminating all opponents, censoring the press and creating a huge network of spies and informers both in France and abroad.

Richelieu was also a great patron of the arts, writing a good many works himself and funding the careers of a number of writers. Although it was not considered a respectable art form at that time, he was a great lover of the theatre and he was a patron of several playwrights, including Pierre Corneille, widely recognised as the founder of French tragedy. Richelieu was also the founder of the highly respected Académie Francaise, the pre-eminent body for regulating the French language. Already existing informally, Richelieu formalised it with letters patent in 1635. He was the principal of the Sorbonne, presiding over its renovation and overseeing the construction of its chapel where his body would eventually be laid to rest.

He was born into a good family in Paris, his father a soldier who held the psition of Grand Provost of France and his mother the daughter of a prominent lawyer. However, when he was five, his father was killed in the French Wars of Religion, a period of civil war between the French Catholics and Protestant Huguenots. The family was left in debt but received payment from the royal coffers which eased their situation and at the age of nine, the future Cardinal was sent to study philosophy at the College of Navarre in Paris, before training to be a soldier.

Richelieu's father had been awarded the Bishopric of Luçon for his participation in the war and Richelieu assumed the position in 1607. He was actually too young, at twenty-two, to become a bishop, but he had travelled to Rome to obtain special dispensation although some say that he actually lied about his age to the Pope. As Bishop, he was soon being hailed as a reformer, the first bishop in France to introduce reforms devised at the Council of Trent almost seventy years previously.

In 1614, he was elected by the clergy of Poitou to represent them at the States-General, France's legislative assembly where he argued vigorously in a famous speech that bishops and prelates should be appointed to the royal council, the ruling committee of France, that the distribution of ecclesiastical benefices to lay people should be prohibited, that the clergy should be exempt from taxation and that the reforms of the Council of Trent should be introduced across the country. In the speech, he reassured King Louis XIII that it was the wish of the clergy to consolidate royal power so that it would be 'comme un ferm rocher qui brise tout ce qui gheurte' (like a firm rock that crushes all that opposes it). In a way, he was predicting the manner in which he would later govern when he became Louis Chief Minister.

The young Cardinal began to make political progress, working as almoner for Queen Anne and then serving Concino Concini, the Italian politician who was the most powerful minister in France at the time. This led to his 1616 appointment as Secretary of State and he was given responsibility for foreign policy. He also acted as one of the advisers to Marie de Medici who had been acting as Regent to her son, Louis XIII since he had been nine and had remained in that position even after he had attained his majority. However, when in 1617, Concini was assassinated and Marie was overthrown, Richelieu was left powerless, dismissed from his position and banned from the roayal court. He was forced to accompany Marie to Blois and then, in 1618, the king, still harbouring suspicions about his intentions, sent him into exile in Avignon where he wrote a catechism entitled *L'Instruction du Chrétien*. It was a much valued book in a country in which there was still a great deal of ignorance about religion, intended to be read at every church in every parish in France every Sunday after the priest had delivered his sermon.

When Marie de Medici escaped from imprisonment in 1619 to head a rebellion of French nobles, the king recalled Richelieu and asked him to try to dissuade her from her action. He mediated successfully between mother and son and the Treaty of Angoulême freed the Queen who was restored once more to the royal council of ministers.

Richelieu now began to rise through the political ranks, especially following the death of the royal favourite, the Duc de Luynes in 1621. In 1622, he was made Cardinal and he became increasingly indispensible to the king as an adviser. In 1624 he was appointed to the royal council and won the principal position in the government following the arrest of Charles, Duc de La Vieuville for corruption. Of course, the scheming Richelieu was behind the accusations made against de La Vieuville.

As Chief Minister, he took on the problems of checking Habsburg power and suppressing the power of the nobles in France. He immediately opposed the Spanish Habsburgs in the Valtellina, a valley in northern Italy, supporting the Protestant Swiss canton of Grisons and driving out the Catholic garrisons. The Spanish sarcastically nicknamed him 'Cardinal of the Huguenots'.

Back home, he made himself hated by the nobility for ordering the demolition of all fortified castles, removing the nobles' means of defending themselves against the army of the King.

Meanwhile, the religious divide in France threw up further problems, the Huguenots remaining at war with the crown with a huge military force at their disposal and Charles I of Great Britain declared war on France in support of their struggle. Richelieu personally commanded the French troops who besieged the port of La Rochelle, a Huguenot stronghold, and defeated an expedition by the Duke of Buckingham to relieve the city. The war continued, however, and did not come to an end until a year after La Rochelle capitulated. The Peace of Alais finally permitted the continuance of religious toleration for Protestants granted by the 1598 Edict of Nantes.

The Spanish Habsburgs, like the British, had tried to exploit the Huguenot situation, funding them and hoping by doing so to keep the French preoccupied. Characteristically, after the fall of La Rochelle, Richelieu led his army south into northern Spain to serve as a warning to them.

Meanwhile, at court, Marie de Medici, fearing that Richelieu's influence over her son was becoming greater than hers, and with the support of the King's brother, Gaston, Duc d'Orléans, tried to persuade the king to dismiss his Chief Minister. On the day in November 1630, known as the Day of the Dupes, they believed they had succeeded, enemies of the Cardinal gathered to celebrate in the apartments of the Luxembourg Palace. Richelieu, however, had followed the King to Versailles where he persuaded him to retain his services. The King assured him of his unswerving support and the Queen was sent into exile at Compiègne, never to return.

The last effort to unseat Richelieu was an uprising in 1632 led by Henri, Duc de Montmorency which was swiftly suppressed. Montmorency was executed on Richelieu's orders, sending the Cardinal's enemies a strong message; he would brook no opposition. Meanwhile, his huge network of spies kept him fully informed of everything that was going on.

The Thirty Years' war began before Richelieu came to power. One of the most destructive wars in history, in terms of both property destroyed and lives lost, it took place mainly on German soil but involved almost every country in Europe at some stage. Largely a war between Catholics and Protestants, it developed into a conflict between the Bourbons of France and the Habsburgs of Spain and the Holy Roman Empire. Entire regions were destroyed, millions lost their lives and mercenary armies roamed across what would later become modern Germany.

There is no doubt that at this time, if France had allowed the Habsburgs to advance their ambitions in Europe, her very existence would have been in danger, encircled as she would have been by Habsburg enemies. Holy Roman Emperor, Ferdinand II, had beaten his Protestant rivals in his empire and he also had ambitions in northern Italy. Richelieu was never afraid to align France with Protestant countries and he incited the Swedes to attack Ferdinand, providing him with the necessary funds to do so. Of course, many accused him of betraying the Catholic Church and in the beginning it looked as if his efforts would come to nothing, the Spaniards and the Empire winning a number of battles. However, before long the war had entered a stalemate and it would still be going on when Richelieu died.

Back home, he made few friends with the people of the Third Estate – the bourgeoisie and peasants – on whom the tax burden was already excessive. The war was a drain on royal finances and Richelieu responded by raising taxes on salt and land, the classes that did have the money – the clergy and the military – being exempt from paying the higher taxes. There was a great deal of unrest amongst the peasants. Needless to say, Richelieu dealt with them in the ruthless manner in which he customarily dealt with anyone opposed to his policies.

Cardinal Richelieu was never the greatest supporter of the Vatican and towards the end of his life he was angered by Pope Urban VIII's refusal to appoint him papal legate to France. The rift was partly healed by the appointment as Cardinal of his political ally, Jules

Mazarin, in 1641. However, in spite of his problems with the Church in Rome, at no point did Richelieu argue for the abolition of papal authority in France.

He did have to face several more attempts to remove him from power before his death. A young man, Henri Coiffier de Ruzé, Marquis de Cinq-Mars, had been introduced to Louis' court and Richelieu, a friend of the young man's father, hoped to use him to exercise even greater influence over the King. Cinq-Mars had become a member of Louis' inner circle by 1639, but Richelieu found him to be not as easy to control as he had hoped. Furthermore, Cinq-Mars, an ambitious man, realised that the wily Cardinal was never going to allow him to make any progress in royal politics. In 1641, he took part in a failed plot by the Comte de Soissons to remove Richelieu from power. The plot which involved the King's brother, the Duc d'Orléans, was to murder Richelieu and then, with him out of the way, to depose the King. His role in that plot undiscovered, he took part in another the following year, a plan to raise a rebellion against the King. He had signed an agreement with the King of Spain to help the rebels but Richelieu's extraordinary network of spies discovered the plot and Cinq-Mars was arrested and executed.

By now, however, aged fifty-seven, Richelieu's health was fading. Realising death was near, he named Jules Cardinal Mazarin as his successor. Cardinal Richelieu, one of the greatest European statesmen who ever lived, died on 4 December 1642 and was buried in the church at the Sorbonne.

Richelieu's foreign policy prevented the hegemony of the Habsburgs over all of Europe and in this way, he helped to create the Europe we have today. He also transformed France from a largely feudal kingdom to a centralised modern state where local and even religious interests were less important than those of the state as a whole. Whether he is seen as a power-hungry maniac, or just a patriot, a war-mongerer or a statesman fighting in his country's best interests, he is rightly called the 'father of the modern nation-state'.

OLIVER CROMWELL

ON 30 JANUARY 1661, three years after he had died, the body of the former Lord Protector, Oliver Cromwell, embalmed and wrapped in cloth, was exhumed at Westminster Abbey. Along with two others who had also run the country during its only period as a republic, it was transported to the gallows at Tyburn in London and hanged in chains for a day. The heads of the three bodies were then cut off and stuck unceremoniously on poles and displayed at Westminster Hall. They were treated thus as a warning to others. It was quite a warning – Cromwell's head remained on display for twenty years until it was blown off in a gale and appropriated by a sentry.

Oliver Cromwell was born on 25 April 1599 in Huntingdon, to Robert and Elizabeth Cromwell, lower gentry who owned a house in Huntingdon as well as some land. From school, Cromwell went to Sidney Sussex College, Cambridge where, although not very academic, he showed an aptitude for sport and games. It was rendered irrelevant, however, in June 1617 when Robert Cromwell died and Oliver had to return home to manage the family's affairs and look after his mother and seven sisters. In the meantime, he studied law at Lincoln's Inn in London. In 1620, he married Elizabeth Bourchier, daughter of a London merchant. Their marriage would prove long and fruitful, nine children being born to them.

Elizabeth's father, owner of a great deal of land in Essex and with strong connections to puritan families living there, provided Oliver with an entrée to the London merchant community and to the world of politics. Cromwell, however, remained uninfluenced by Puritanism.

He became Member of Parliament for Huntingdon in 1628 but does not seem to have made much of an impression during his first term. It would be his only term for some time, as Charles I proceeded to dissolve Parliament, deciding to rule without it.

In 1631, Cromwell sold his properties in Huntingdon and moved to a farm in St. Ives, probably as a result of a dispute over a new charter for Huntingdon which led to him being summoned to appear before the Privy Council in 1630. St Ives was a long way from anywhere and Cromwell remained in the wilderness for a number of years. His time there, however, appears to have brought on something of a spiritual crisis and by 1638 he was writing to friends that the Reformation that had sought to reform the Catholic Church across Europe had not done enough and that the Church needed to change still more. He had become a Puritan.

By 1640, King Charles was in trouble. He had tried to impose the Anglican prayer book on the Scots and they had angrily refused it. The Scots had invaded England as a result and the rebellion known as the Bishops' Wars had broken out. The wars had bankrupted him and if he wanted to continue fighting, he needed to raise money. Consequently, he was forced to summon Parliament in order to raise enough funding to finance an army to march against the Scottish rebels. Cromwell was elected to this Parliament – it would become known as the Long Parliament – as member for Cambridge. He consorted with a powerful group of MPs – the Earls of Essex, Warwick and Bedford, Oliver St John – whom the King made Solicitor-General – and Viscount Saye and Sele. They were intent on reformation and envisioned a monarch kept in check by parliament. Cromwell played a major role, proposing, for instance, the second reading of the Annual Parliaments Bill in May 1641. He was also heavily involved in the drafting of the Root and Branch Bill advocating the abolition of episcopacy which was defeated in August 1641.

The Long Parliament passed legislation intended to prevent Charles from ruling absolutely again and impeached several of Charles's advisors. On 22 November 1641, Parliament presented the

King with the Grand Remonstrance, listing more than 150 things that Charles had done wrong during his reign. The King rejected it and proceeded to order the arrest of five MPs whom he suspected of encouraging the Scots to invade and of working against him. The five had fled, however, and Charles left with his supporters to convene in Oxford as the Oxford Parliament. The Long Parliament continued to sit without its Royalist members. In the autumn of 1642, civil war broke out.

Oliver Cromwell had had very limited military experience up to this point, mainly as a member of his local militia. Nonetheless, he recruited a cavalry troop in Cambridgeshire and fought at the inconclusive Battle of Edgehill in October of that year. During the following winter, he built his troop into a regiment and it took its place as part of the Eastern Association Army, led by the Earl of Manchester.

His tactics were not particularly innovative, but it is worth remembering that this was a war fought largely by amateurs, not by professional soldiers. But what Cromwell did possess was an intuitive ability for leading men and for training and instilling discipline. He was also deeply respected by his men and carried with him an air of moral authority.

Cromwell's military experience and standing among the Roundhead forces grew rapidly as he took part in a number of successful actions, such as the Battle of Gainsborough in July 1643. He was promoted to Colonel and made Governor of Ely.

By July 1644 he was Lieutenant General of Horse and he and his men contributed hugely to Parliament's victory at Marston Moor, breaking through the ranks of Royalist cavalry and attacking their infantry from the rear. Cromwell was wounded in the head in the battle but the victory secured the north of England for Parliament and severely damaged Royalist ambitions.

When the Battle of Newbury ended inconclusively, Cromwell entered into a serious dispute with the Earl of Manchester, accusing him of having thrown away an excellent chance of victory.

His dispute with Manchester was short-lived as Parliament passed the Self-Denial Act early in 1645, forcing Members of Parliament and the House of Lords to choose whether they wanted to be administrators or military commanders. The only man to reject a return to Parliament was Cromwell whose commission was given regular extensions. The army was also 'remodelled' by this statute, becoming a national army, rather than one made up of lots of local county militia. The New Model Army emerged in April 1645, Sir Thomas Fairfax in command and Oliver Cromwell as lieutenant general in charge of cavalry, effectively second-in-command of the army.

The sheer size of the New Model Army – it was twice the size of the Royalists' – began to tell almost immediately when they inflicted a crushing defeat at the Battle of Naseby. When they also crushed the King's army at Langport, all hope looked lost for the Royalists and it was a matter of simply capturing their remaining strongholds in England. Cromwell besieged Basing House in Hampshire in October 1645 and was accused of killing 100 of the 300 Royalists who surrendered there. He took part in a number of subsequent sieges across southern England, ending up in Devon and Cornwall in the first few months of 1645.

Charles I surrendered to the Scots in May 1646 and Cromwell and Fairfax accepted the Royalists' formal surrender at Oxford in June that year.

Illness kept Cromwell away from the political world during February 1647 and he returned to the fray to find much debate about how the country should proceed and, in particular, what should become of the King. In Parliament, both houses favoured paying off the Scottish army, disbanding the New Model Army and restoring the King in return for a Presbyterian settlement of the Church. However, Scottish Presbyterianism was not to Cromwell's liking and the Army, angry because its wages had not been paid, was also against it. Parliament sent Cromwell to negotiate with them, but to no avail.

He persisted in his efforts to curb the powers of the executive, attempting to introduce regularly elected parliaments and secure a religious settlement. Eventually, no solution in sight, a Second English Civil War broke out in 1648. Cromwell defeated Royalist rebels in South Wales, capturing Chepstow Castle and Tenby. He took Pembroke Castle after a siege lasting eight weeks. Marching north, he faced a pro-Royalist Scottish army at Preston, in sole command of an army for the first time. His 9,000 men defeated an army twice its size.

By this point in his life, aged forty-nine, Cromwell was becoming increasingly spiritual. His correspondence is littered with biblical quotes and he truly believed that God was against the King and his supporters and that he was controlling events through 'chosen people', of whom, of course, he was one. Cromwell's victories were, therefore, signs of God's approval for his actions.

Back in Parliament, in December 1648, Colonel Thomas Pride prevented those who wished to negotiate with the King from entering the chamber and those who did constituted what was termed the Rump Parliament. They decided that Charles should be charged with treason and tried. Acknowledging that only the King's death would bring the civil war to a conclusion, Cromwell wholeheartedly approved of this decision.

Thus, King Charles I was beheaded at the Palace of Whitehall on Tuesday 30 January 1649 and Oliver Cromwell's name was the third of fifty-nine on the death warrant.

A republic was declared, to be called the Commonwealth of England, the Rump Parliament retaining legislative and executive powers and supported by a smaller Council of State. The Royalists had not completely gone away, however, and a number of them had gathered in Ireland, allying themselves with the Irish Catholic Confederation, which governed two-thirds of Ireland. Cromwell was ordered by the Rump Parliament to invade Ireland which he did at the end of July after several months' preparation.

The fact that his opponents were the Catholics he despised so much, plus the memory of massacres of Protestant settlers by Irish Catholics in a rebellion of 1641, served to harden Cromwell's resolve in this campaign, going some way to explaining the cruelty he and his men displayed.

The campaign lasted nine months and was well-supplied and reinforced as necessary. Prior to his arrival, the Parliamentarian presence in Ireland was desultory – merely outposts in Dublin and Derry. When he left, they occupied most of the east and north of the country. However, in achieving this, he massacred 3,500 people after the siege of Drogheda, including Catholic priests and many civilians. At Wexford, 2,000 Irish soldiers and around 1,500 civilians were put to the sword.

On 26 May 1650, having learned of the arrival of Charles II in Scotland where he had been proclaimed King by the Covenanting Presbyterian regime, he returned to England. The Irish campaign carried on without him and within a couple of years, the country had capitulated.

A few months after returning to England, Cromwell invaded Scotland. It started badly, but victory for his army of veterans at Dunbar led to him taking Edinburgh. The following year, 1651, when Charles and his Scottish army invaded England, Cromwell destroyed them at the Battle of Worcester. Cromwell's men went on the rampage towards the end of the campaign in Dundee, massacring 2,000 of its population of 12,000. Scotland was now an occupied country, ruled by England.

But, back in London, there was furious in-fighting and Cromwell's efforts to obtain decisions on elections and other matters came to nothing. On 20 April, accompanied by about forty armed men he cleared Parliament and dissolved it.

After a brief parliament known as the Barebones Parliament, General John Lambert proposed that a new constitution be proposed and that Oliver Cromwell become Lord Protector for Life, effectively dictator of Britain. He took the oath on 16 December 1653, dressed entirely in black. Despite his rejection of all monarchical accessories, he signed his name 'Oliver P' just as Charles would have signed his 'Charles R' and was styled 'Your Highness'. He had the power to convene and dissolve parliaments with the majority vote of a Council of State. He was paid a massive £100,000 a year.

During his Protectorship, he tried to bring order back to the country, made peace with England's bitter rivals, the Dutch, and reduced taxes. He also launched a crusade to promote spiritual and moral reform in the country.

In 1657, Parliament offered him the crown. He thought about it for six weeks but, in spite of the stability he saw that it could offer, he declared that God was against the office of King and rejected it. Instead, he was re-installed as Protector with increased powers in a ceremony at Westminster Hall that was a coronation in all but name.

He had contracted malaria during the Irish campaign and also had also suffered from problems with his kidneys and urinary tract. In 1658, he became very ill and died at Whitehall on 3 September. His recently acquired royal ways followed him in death; his elaborate funeral was based on that of a previous king, James I.

Richard Cromwell, Oliver's son succeeded him as Lord Protector, but he enjoyed the support of neither the army nor Parliament and was forced to resign in May 1659. Following a short period when general George Monck, head of the army governed, Charles II was restored as king on 23 April 1661.

PETER THE GREAT

HE HAD THE mind of a genius and the body of a giant. At six feet eight inches, he was abnormally tall for his time, a giant amongst his contemporaries. He was also so strong that he is said to have once crumpled a silver plate as if it was aluminium foil and when annoyed by someone, was perfectly capable of knocking him out. However, he did not have the stature that would be expected in a man of that size. His hands and feet were small, as was his head. He was also the victim of serious facial tics and it is thought that he suffered from the condition *petit mal* – a form of epilepsy.

Nonetheless, this odd-looking, disabled man became one of the Russian Empire's greatest leaders.

He was the product of the second marriage of Tsar Alexis who had lost his first wife in childbirth. Born on 1 February 1671, there was great rejoicing when he was born in the Kremlin, the fortified central area of the capital, Moscow, an apparently healthy baby boy.

When he was four, in 1676, his father caught a chill during the annual service to bless the waters of the Moscow River and died and Peter's half-brother, Feodor, became Tsar as Feodor II. Feodor was a semi-invalid, however, and reigned for only six years. Ten year-old Peter now assumed the throne, under the regency of his mother, Natalya.

A few weeks after he became Tsar, Peter faced his first challenge. His half-sister, Sophia, instigated a rebellion by the *streltsy* – the Russian elite military corps in favour of her feeble-minded brother, Ivan, who had been passed over in the succession to the throne. Peter would never forget standing on the staircase of one of the palaces of the Kremlin watching his supporters being thrown from the top down onto the halberds of the *streltsy* waiting below. Ivan was proclaimed senior co-ruler with Peter, with Sophia acting as regent. She literally became the power behind the double-seated throne when she had a large hole cut in it through which she was able to listen and pass messages as Peter talked with his nobles. She ruled autocratically for seven years.

Natalya moved Peter out of the Kremlin to a modest estate near Moscow and he lived there for the remainder of his childhood, returning to Moscow only for state occasions. He did not waste his time, however. In the nearby German quarter, he found men who taught him trades and the Dutchman Franz Timmerman was hired as his tutor. He learned to sail and began a lifelong fascination with ships and the sea.

Around the age of seventeen, he learned that Sophia wanted him killed and fled to a monastery. With the help of friends he began to plot a coup against his half-sister. There was considerable support for him, as she had been weakened by two campaigns in the Crimea that had ended in failure. When she found out what he was planning, she began to devise a counter-plot. He fled in the middle of the night to the impregnable monastery of Troitsky from where he gradually began to gather support. He overthrew Sophia, sent her to a convent and continued to rule jointly with his half-brother.

But, he was still not fully in charge of Russia. With Sophia out of the way, his mother, Nataliya, took her place and acted as regent until her death in 1694. Two years later, Ivan died and Peter was at last sole ruler.

He inherited a country that was uncivilised, that based many of its practices on superstition and that seemed a million miles away from the sophistication of normal European society, economy, and politics.

His first objective as ruler was to introduce reforms to modernise his huge country. Opposition to his policies was ruthlessly crushed and all of the rebellions that he faced, including a serious one led by the Don Cossack Kondraty Bulavin, were suppressed immediately and ruthlessly.

Peter also had ambitions to make Russia a maritime power for the first time. To achieve his maritime ambitions, however, he had to first find access to the sea, his only access at the time being to the White Sea at Archangel. The Baltic was controlled by Sweden and the Ottoman Turks controlled the Black Sea to the south. He first targeted the Black Sea, realising that he would have to expel the Tatars from the areas around it – no mean task. He went to war with the Khan of the Crimea and the Ottoman Sultan.

He planned a campaign to take the Ottoman fortress of Azov, near the River Don in 1695, but failing in his attempt, he returned disappointed to Moscow and began the construction of a large navy. Launching thirty ships against the Ottomans in 1696, he finally took Azov and later in the year founded the first Russian naval base at Taganrog.

Peter knew that he could not defeat the Ottoman Empire without help and, consequently, in 1697 he embarked upon a remarkable 18-month journey to Europe, incognito – an adventure known as the 'Grand Embassy' – to solicit the support of European monarchs. His bold plan was in vain, however. France was already allied with the Ottomans and the Austrians were too busy with wars in the west and the Spanish succession to be concerned about launching a campaign in the east.

Nonetheless, in spite of his diplomatic failures on his journey, Peter persisted, learning a great deal about the culture and life of the west. In Holland, he studied shipbuilding techniques, spending four months in the shipyard belonging to the Dutch East India Company, at the time the largest and most advanced shipyard in the world. He employed many experts to take with him back to Russia – builders of locks, fortresses, shipwrights and seamen. He employed the Dutch-Norwegian, Cornelius Cruys, a vice-admiral who would become Peter's advisor on maritime affairs. Bizarrely, he also learned how to draw teeth and catch butterflies, amongst other things.

He travelled to England and had a meeting with King William III.

He visited Greenwich and Oxford and watched a naval review at Deptford. In Manchester, he learned about city planning, lessons he would apply to his re-building of the city of St Petersburg.

He travelled on, to Leipzig, Dresden and Vienna, meeting with August the Strong, the Elector of Saxony, and the Holy Roman Emperor, Leopold I. In 1698, however, he had to rush back to Russia. The *streltsy* had rebelled once again and were trying to put Sophia on the throne.

On his return, he dealt with the rebels in a characteristically harsh manner. They were killed and their bodies put on public display as a warning to others. The *streltsy* were disbanded and Sophia was banished yet again.

Peter now favoured western customs and fashions and, to the disappointment of his courtiers, he forced them to adopt western fashions, shaving off their long beards and wearing western-style clothes. Anyone refusing to shave his beard had to pay a beard tax of 100 roubles for the privilege. Arranged marriages, customary among the Russian nobles, were banned and the New Year celebration was moved from 1 September to 1 January.

Meanwhile, his maritime ambition for Russia was beginning to become a reality. The peace Peter made with the Ottoman Empire had allowed him to retain the fortress at Azov and he now focused on creating a powerful Russian navy.

The Swedes had seized control of the Baltic fifty years earlier and he was keen to divest them of it. He declared war and was supported against the Swedish king, Charles XII, by Denmark-Norway, Saxony and the Polish-Lithuanian Commonwealth. The Great Northern War began badly for the ill-prepared Russians and they lost heavily during a snowstorm at the Battle of Narva in 1700. Charles, however, focused on fighting the Polish-Lithuanian Commonwealth after the battle, giving Peter time to re-group and reorganise his forces.

In 1703, he founded the city of St Petersburg, having captured the land on which it was located from the Swedes. All building of stone edifices was banned in Russia while he was constructing the city – he wanted all of the country's stone masons to be concentrated on his ambitious venture. At the same time, he took a mistress, Martha Skvronskaya who, on secretly marrying Peter in 1707, converted to the Russian Orthodox Church and changed her name to Catherine. He would marry her officially in the full view of the people of the Empire in St Isaac Cathedral in St Petersburg in 1712.

The Poles were losing their war with Sweden and in 1706, King August II abdicated. The Swedish king now directed his forces at Russia, launching an invasion in 1708. He defeated Peter's army at Golovchin in July of that year but Peter avenged himself at Lesnaya and Charles was forced to abandon his march on Moscow. Instead, he invaded Ukraine. Peter, meanwhile, adopted a scorched-earth policy as he retreated southwards. As a result, in the winter of 1708–09, the Swedish army, exhausted and starving, was forced to halt its advance. In June 1709, as they moved forward once again, Peter's forces won a decisive victory at the Battle of Poltava and Charles was forced into exile in the Ottoman Empire. Meanwhile, back in Poland, King August II took the throne again.

In 1711, Peter made a mistake when he attacked the Ottomans again, anticipating support from his Balkan allies which never materialised. Disastrously, he lost the Black Sea ports he had gained in 1697 and Charles XII was able to return to Sweden, Peter being forced to grant him safe passage as he travelled through Russia. In 1714, however, Peter won the Battle of Gangut against the Swedes and captured most of Finland.

In 1716 and 1717 he returned to the Netherlands and visited France once again. He made successful diplomatic overtures to the Electorate of Hanover and the Kingdom of Prussia, but peace with Sweden was still a long way off. Following the Battle of Aland, Sweden made peace with everyone except Russia, until the Treaty of Nystad finally ended the Great Northern War in 1721. By that treaty, Russia acquired Ingria, Estonia, Livonia and a large part of Karelia.

In return, Peter gave up Finland and paid a substantial sum of money to Sweden. Most importantly, he was permitted to hold on to some Finnish territory close to St Petersburg – now his capital – giving him access to a warm-water port which made trading with the west much easier.

On 22 October 1721, he was proclaimed Emperor of All Russia, a title that, although accepted by a few such as August of Poland, irritated a number of the European monarchs who believed that the name 'Emperor' connoted superiority over mere 'kings'. There was a fear that he would claim sovereignty over them in the same way that the Holy Roman Emperor had once claimed it over all the nations of Christendom.

As Peter grew older, his reforming ways did not stop. He reformed the Orthodox Church, abandoning the office of Patriarch of Moscow, leader of the church, and replacing it with the Holy Synod, a council of ten clergymen. He also made a law that no man could become a monk under the age of fifty – too many able men were opting for the monastic life in preference to the army, he thought. As few people lived beyond the age of fifty, there were very few new monks in the Russian church.

In 1722, he introduced the Table of Ranks, a new order of precedence. Instead of birth, merit and service to the Emperor became the determining factor in nobility. Of course, behind this lay a determination to reduce the power of the boyars – the nobles. Remarkably, for the time, he also introduced a decree that made education in basic mathematics and geometry compulsory for all children of nobles, government clerks and lesser officials.

In 1724, Peter's second wife, Catherine was crowned Empress of Russia. By now all his male children had died. Shamefully he had had his eldest son, Alexei, tortured and murdered in 1718 because he had disobeyed him and opposed his policies. He had also treated his first wife Eudoxia harshly, trying her on charges of adultery and his mistress, Anna Mons, was similarly mistreated in 1704.

Peter had never been the healthiest of individuals and by the winter of 1723, he was experiencing problems with his urinary tract and bladder. He had surgery in summer 1724 that released a reported four pounds of blocked urine but he remained incapacitated until late autumn.

Ironically, his eventual death came from his love of the sea and sailing. He wanted all of the people of St Petersburg to share his passion and issued an order that everyone should own a boat and that if people could not afford one, they would be helped by public finance. Furthermore, all visitors to the Winter or Summer Palace had to arrive by boat. In 1723, he brought his own boat to St Petersburg and it became known as 'the Grandfather of the Russian Navy'. On Sundays people enjoyed the river as vodka flowed and bands played.

One day in November 1724, however, Peter saw a boat run aground that looked like it was going to capsize. He leapt into the freezing river and tried to help the crew, later coming down with a bad cold, as a result. He was well enough to enjoy Christmas but afterwards suffered a relapse. He died in his wife's arms on 28 January 1725.

CATHERINE THE GREAT

SHE WAS BORN Sophia Augusta Frederica von Anhalt-Zerbst in 1729 in the city of Stettin where her father, Christian August, Prince of Anhalt-Zerbst, a general in the Prussian army, was Governor for the King of Prussia.

When a wife was being sought for the prospective Tsar of Russia, Grand Duke Peter of Holstein-Gottorp, a great del of diplomacy went on, involving such aristocratic personages as Frederick II of Prussia, Peter's aunt, the incumbent Empress, Elizabeth, and Count Lestocq, a French adventurer who wielded a great deal of influence on Russian foreign policy on Elizabeth's behalf. There was a great deal of intrigue as Lestocq and Frederick wanted to strengthen Russia's link with Prussia at the expense of her relationship with Austria which was supported by Russian Chancellor, Count Alexei Bestuzhev-Ryumin. Empress Elizabeth relied greatly on Bestuzhev and Lestocq was keen to weaken his position in the government.

Fortunately for Sophie, Elizabeth took a shine to her and agreed to the marriage. The young woman threw herself into it, learning Russian, joining the Russian Orthodox Church and adopting a new, Russian name – Catherine (Yekaterina or Wkaterina in Russian). On 21 August 1745, aged sixteen, she married Grand Duke Peter in St Petersberg. They moved into their new home in the beautiful palace of Oranienbaum, on the Gulf of Finland, west of St Petersberg.

Unfortunately, the marriage was not a happy one. Peter had a mistress from a celebrated Russian family, Elizabeth Vorontsova and not to be outdone, Catherine, as she now was, formed liaisons with a number of men – Count Sergei Vasilievich Saltykov, a Russian officer who she suggested was the father of her son Paul who would be Paul I of Russia; Grigory Grigoryevich Orlov, another Russian officer with whom she had a child, Aleksey Bobrinsky; Stanisław August Poniatowski, the future and last King and Grand Duke of the Polish-Lithuanian Commonwealth and others.

After the death of Empress Elizabeth in January 1762, Catherine's husband, Peter, succeeded to the Russian throne as Peter III. The royal couple moved into the new Winter Palace in St Petersberg. Catherine was now Empress Consort of Russia. Peter immediately courted the disapproval of his nobles by withdrawing his troops from the Seven Years' War and making peace with Prussia. The war was being fought by all of the European powers at the time, Prussia, the Electorate of Brunswick-Lüneburg, Portugal and Great Britain, fighting against France, Spain, Austria, Sweden, Saxony and the Russian Empire. The nobles were especially irritated by the fact that Russia which had at one point occupied Berlin and was winning the war, gained nothing from the peace settlement.

In July 1762, Peter went with his Holstein-born courtiers and relatives to Oranianbaum, leaving Catherine in St Petersberg. On the 13 and 14 July, the Leib Guard, the personal bodyguards of the Emperor and Empress, revolted, fearing that he was about to impose harsher discipline on them. They deposed Peter and, with the support of a number of the nobility, proclaimed Catherine Empress. She was relieved as she had become convinced that he was about to divorce her in order to marry his mistress and make her Empress.

Peter is said to have acquiesced to the change in his fortunes, calmly requesting only an estate and the company of his mistress. However, while being held in custody at Ropsha, he was murdered, it is said by Alexei Orlov, the younger brother of her lover, Gregory Orlov. Many have suggested that Catherine, herself, gave the order to kill her husband, but there was no real reason for her to have done so. Nonetheless, she made no effort to punish those responsible.

Although not Russian-born, Catherine justified her succession to the throne by claiming it had been done by 'unanimous election' of the Russian nation. She was crowned in a lavish ceremony at the Kremlin in Moscow on 13 September 1762. The streets of the old city were decorated with statues, plants and mile upon mile of ribbon and several triumphal arches were specially built for her arrival. Her carriage, decorated with gold, was followed by an entourage clad in gleaming liveries with gold thread sewn into them. Tens of thousands crowded the streets, cheering as she passed.

The ceremony took place at the Assumption Cathedral in the Kremlin where she sat on a throne under a canopy, clad in magnificent scarlet robes, the Order of St Andrew pinned to breast. More than sixty bishops and archimandrites – senior abbots – of the Russian Orthodox Church looked on as the archbishop offered her the cross to kiss. Meanwhile, the Metropolitan of Moscow sprinkled her with holy water. As the crown was placed on her head, a canon outside the cathedral fired a salute and continued to do so as she processed to the Annunciation Cathedral to pay tribute to the Russian holy personages buried there. She then moved to the Palace of Facets in the Kremlin where a banquet was held with singers and musicians providing entertainment. At midnight, she reappeared to see the fireworks that lit up the Moscow sky for the entire night. Six days after the ceremony, Catherine threw a huge party for the people of Moscow, providing food, drink and entertainment. The celebrations carried on for a week.

Nonetheless, a large number of nobles were still opposed to her, believing her rule to be legitimate only during the minority of her son, Grand Duke Paul; they regarded her as a regent and hoped that they could establish him as a constitutional monarch – a ruler legally bound and limited in power by a constitution. They even thought of deposing her, but nothing ever came of this.

Catherine extended the frontiers of Russia during her reign, extending the Empire to the south and west to incorporate an extra

200 square miles of territory – New Russia, an area in modern-day southern Ukraine, southern Russia, Bessarabia and Transnistria; Crimea; Ukraine on the right bank of the Dnieper River Belarus; Lithuania and Courland, a region in modern-day Latvia.

Russia became the dominant power in southeastern Europe, enjoying greater success in that area than it had even during the reign of Peter the Great. Catherine's armies inflicted some of the greatest defeats in Ottoman history on Turkish troops during the Russo-Turkish Wars which took place between 1768 and 1774, and 1787 and 1792. In the First War, the Russians won stunning victories at the Battles of Chesma and Kagul in 1770. With these victories, Russia gained access to the Black Sea and in southern Ukraine she founded the new cities of Odessa, Nikolayev and Yekaterinoslav. She annexed the Crimea in 1783 and gained other new territories including a strip of the Black Sea coast between the Dnieper and the Bug rivers.

The Ottomans launched the Second Russo-Turkish War in 1787, hoping to re-capture their lost territories. It proved disastrous. The Treaty of Jassy brought hostilities to an end with Russia formalising its hold on the Crimea.

While this war was fought, Russia engaged in another, with Sweden. Catherine's cousin, King Gustav III sought to take advantage of the fact that the Russian army was busy in the Crimea and attempted to attack St Petersberg. The Russian Baltic fleet proved too strong for the Swedes and matters took a turn for the worse when Denmark declared war on Sweden later that same year. By the 1790 Treaty of Värälä, all conquered territories were returned to their pre-war owners.

The partitioning of Poland was the brainchild of Prussian King Frederick the Great. Poland had descended into anarchy in the 18th century, making it vulnerable to foreign intervention. When Augustus III of Poland had died in 1763, Catherine invaded in order to stop any destructive succession disputes developing. She installed her former lover, Count Stanisław Antoni Poniatowski, on the throne and Europe waited to see if she would then marry him and bring Poland under her complete control. She had no intention of marrying him, however. All she wanted was to establish a government that was controlled by Russia. However, by the 1790s, following the French Revolution, she feared that the increasing democratic factions inside the Polish-Lithuanian Commonwealth might become a threat to her and the other European monarchies and decided to intervene. She provided support for the Targowica Confederation, an anti-reform group and defeated the Polish loyalists in the Polish War in Defence of the Constitution in 1792, quashed the Kościuszko Uprising of 1794 and finally partitioned Poland, sharing it with Prussia and Austria.

As a monarch of the Enlightenment, Catherine considered herself a 'philosopher on the throne'. She corresponded with some of the great thinkers of her time, such as Voltaire, Diderot and d'Alembert. She corresponded with Voltaire for fifteen years, mourned his death bitterly in 1788 and placed a collection of his work in the Imperial Public Library. When she heard, a few months after her accession to the throne, that the French government was threatening to stop the publication of the *Encyclopédie*, the great French encyclopedia, she told its compiler, Diderot, that he could complete his work under her patronage and protection in Moscow. She wrote comedies, fictional stories and memoirs. She established the Free Economic Society in St Petersberg and invited foreign economists such as the Englishman Arthur Young and French statesman Jacques Necker to be members. Great scientists, too, became visitors to her court in Moscow – men such as the pioneering Swiss mathematician and physicist, Leonhard Euler, and German physician, Simon Pallas. She expanded Russia's universities in order to increase the number of scientists in the country.

In 1766, in an effort to incorporate the tenets of the Enlightenment into the Russian legislative system, she convened a Grand Commission made up of 652 people representing every class and nationality in the Empire. She asked it to consider what the Empire needed and how it could be delivered and provided guidelines upon which it should work taken from the work of the great European thinkers of the time, men such as the French social commentator and political thinker, Montesquieu. His work, *L'Esprit des Lois* (The Spirit of the Laws) provided inspiration. The Commission held more than two hundred sittings, but nothing concrete really emerged, although she did later reorganise the legal system along rational lines. Like a number of other 'enlightened despots' as monarchs influenced by the principles of the Enlightenment came to be known, she applied Montesquieu's view that prisons should rehabilitate inmates, reducing, for example, the number of executions and abolishing torture. Nonetheless, her enlightened views did not extend to the treatment of the millions of peasant serfs in Russia whose harsh existence carried on unchanged.

During her life, Catherine the Great took a great many lovers. They would be elevated to high office and would remain there just as long as she remained interested in them. They would then be retired to large estates with numerous serfs to work for them. It is said that they were selected by her advisor, Grigori Alexandrovich Potemkin who had also once been in a relationship with her. They were chosen for their physical beauty but also had to have sufficient intelligence to retain her interest. Her last lover, Prince Zubov, who became the most powerful man in Russia during the last years of her reign, was forty years younger than her.

Catherine's behaviour towards her son, Paul, was undeniably harsh and there is little doubt that she intended to exclude him from the succession to the throne, passing her crown on her death to her favourite grandson, Alexander. She often claimed that her husband Peter was not Paul's father and that he had been sired by one of her lovers, Sergei Saltykov. However, Paul's physical resemblance to Peter belied her claim which was undoubtedly made for purely political reasons. She distrusted Paul and was not prepared to allow him to dispute or share her authority which is why he was kept like a captive at his estates, Gatchina and Pavlovsk.

Catherine had a stroke on 16 November 1796 and died at 9.20 the following evening without regaining consciousness. She was buried at the Peter and Paul Cathedral in St. Petersberg and would have been irritated to learn that her son, Paul, did, indeed, succeed her as Emperor.

VOLTAIRE

THERE IS A degree of irony in the fact that the thinking of the Enlightenment writer, essayist and philosopher, Voltaire, had a great influence on the people who created the French Revolution in the late 18th century. The Revolution, beginning eleven years after Voltaire's death, was driven by the masses whom he quite simply dismissed as ignorant and uneducated. He was unstintingly opposed to democracy in any form and espoused a system based on constitutional monarchy of the kind he saw during his enforced three-year exile in England.

After centuries of tyranny and repression, there was a growing desire for a world based on Reason rather than the mystery of religion or superstition and mysticism. The institutions of religion were denigrated and the freedom of the individual became paramount to thinkers such as the Swiss Jean Jacques Rousseau and the English John Locke. Locke had claimed that people are born equal and are no more than the sum total of their experience. Rousseau claimed rather more directly that 'Man is born free, but everywhere is in chains.'

To Voltaire, only an enlightened despot could achieve the best for all and his thinking persuaded several European monarchs to go some way down the road towards enlightened despotism. Where once they had been absolute monarchs, ruling by divine right, now the ideas of the Enlightenment interested them and they tried to apply them to the government of their countries. They abolished torture, improved their countries' legal systems, liberalised prisons, reduced the number of executions and founded schools. Voltaire's thinking was key to the changes taking place in European society.

His life was extraordinary. He was a great polemicist and relentlessly denounced the hypocrisy of the ruling elite, especially the Catholic Church. He did it all at great risk to himself and during his life was imprisoned and exiled because of what he was unafraid to say. Eventually, however, he realised the true danger of what he was writing and began to deny that the works were actually his.

He was born in 1694 in Paris as François Marie Arouet, a sickly child who surprised everyone by living beyond his first few days. His father, also François, worked in the Treasury and was fairly well off and his mother, Marie Marguerite d'Aumard, was well-connected in society. She was a close friend of the Abbé de Chateauneuf who became his tutor. He taught the young François to eschew the superstition with which society was suffused at the time and taught him deism, the belief in God based on Reason and observation of the natural world. The Abbé also introduced him to literature.

He was sent to the Lycée Louis-le-Grand in Paris a couple of years after the death of his mother, remaining there under the tutelage of the Jesuits for seven years. He was a studious boy, preferring the company of his teachers to his peers and began to write poetry. He also had his first experience of the theatre which made a huge impression on him.

He left college determined to be a writer, but his father had other ideas, finding him a job as an assistant to a lawyer. François, however, spent more time writing satirical poetry, essays and historical studies than he did studying law and his father stepped in again, obtaining a position for him as secretary to the French ambassador in the Netherlands. Once again, François disappointed his father by falling in love with Catherine Olympe Dunoyer who was nicknamed Pimpette. Pimpette had no money, was Protestant and her mother was a writer whose reputation was scurrilous. François' father obtained a *Lettre de Cachet* to prevent the two from marrying. This was a sealed warrant issued by the king which often sent people to prison without trial. Before the letter could be served, however,

Pimpette brought the relationship to an end. He returned to France, heart-broken, finding employment in the office of a lawyer again, but was soon in trouble once more for spending his time writing libelous poetry. He was sent to the country where instead of studying law, he wrote.

The death of Louis XV in 1715 coincided with François' return to Paris where people were dancing in the street at the news of the king's death. His reign had been characterised by food shortages, brutal repression and misery and there was hope that with a new king things would change for the better. By now François Arouet's bold and witty work was becoming widely known and he was welcomed into the literary salons of the capital. However, when he ridiculed the Prince Regent in a wickedly satirical poem, he was once again sent into exile in May 1716. He went firstly to Tulle and then Sully but within a year was back in Paris. His reputation went before him, however, and he was falsely accused of authoring two libels that had been published anonymously, the *Puero Regnante* and *J'ai Vu*. This time they threw him into the Bastille prison, where he languished for eleven months. He wasted no time there, however, composing his first play, *Oedipe*, a tragedy that became a commercial success, earning him a considerable amount of money.

Around this time, he adopted the name 'Voltaire'. There are several theories as to where the name came from, but it is probable that it is an anagram of 'Arovet l.i' which was the Latin version of 'Arouet le Jeune' (Arouet the Young). From this time, he was popularly known as Arouet de Voltaire or simply Voltaire.

Oedipe ran for a remarkable forty-five nights in Paris and at the age of only twenty-three, he was a successful and critically acclaimed playwright. He was even awarded a pension by the Prince Regent, but it made no difference to Voltaire as he persevered with his criticism of church and state. He found himself in the Bastille for a second time in 1725 when he ran foul of a well-connected young noble, the Chevalier de Rohan. De Rohan had insulted him and

Voltaire had retaliated with a scathing verbal attack. De Rohan had his men beat Voltaire up and Voltaire responded by challenging him to a duel. Before the duel could take place, however, through his connections de Rohan had him arrested and incarcerated once again in the Bastille.

Voltaire was not keen on an extended period in prison, opting rather for exile. He travelled to England where he would spend almost three years, learning English, and observing the greater tolerance that existed in England for freedom of speech and religion. The success of England's constitutional monarchy made a deep and lasting impression on him and he would remain a monarchist until his death.

He made more money in England, publishing a bestselling English edition of his work, the *Henriade* and met many of the important people of the time, including the poet Alexander Pope and the playwright, William Congreve. He also studied the work of the philosopher, John Locke and the great scientist, Isaac Newton. Meanwhile, needless to say, he wrote – an *Essay Upon the Civil Wars in France* and an *Essay Upon Epic Poetry*. He also produced a biography of the Swedish king, Charles XII, espousing the notion that man, not God, controls his own destiny – dangerous thinking for the time.

He published *Letters Concerning the English Nation* in 1733, praising the tolerance of English society and its constitutional monarchy. It caused a scandal and the publisher was thrown into the Bastille. Voltaire fled Paris yet again, resolving never again to accept responsibility for his work.

He moved to Chateau de Cirey in eastern France at the invitation of a young woman he had met, Emilie de Breteuil, Marquise de Chatelet and with whom he had become close. She was twelve years younger than him and married, but her husband did not seem to mind their relationship. They would remain together for fifteen years until her death in 1749.

With Madame de Chatelet, Voltaire began exploring the natural sciences, performing experiments in his laboratory and the pair considered themselves 'Newtonians', followers of Isaac Newton. They also devoted time to studying philosophy and history. They assembled a remarkable library of 21,000 books. She was herself an accomplished mathematician and scientist and together they produced important and ground-breaking work.

Meanwhile, Voltaire spent time at court, befriending, in the process, the king's mistress, Madame de Pompadour. He also worked as an ambassador-spy in 1740 at the Prussian court, following which he was in Brussels from 1742 until 1743.

He was now acknowledged by many to be France's greatest poet and playwright and had been invited to be a member by such organisations as the Royal Society in England. In his native France, however, the prestigious Académie found him to be too controversial and he was not given the recognition he so badly desired in his homeland. Eventually, however, some of his most powerful supporters, such as Madame de Pompadour and the king, ensured that at last he was welcomed into the organisation.

When Madame de Chatelet died in 1749 during childbirth, Voltaire was, naturally, devastated with grief. He was fifty-five years old by this time and had little idea what to do next. Finally, he accepted an invitation from Frederick of Prussia who had been trying for years to persuade him to come to his court and with whom Voltaire had enjoyed a lengthy correspondence.

However, the two men did not get on nearly so well in the flesh as they did on the page of a letter and Voltaire remained in Potsdam for only two years. Refused permission to return home to France, he instead purchased an estate near Geneva in Switzerland, Les Délices. He used his wealth to establish himself in great comfort there, having a theatre built in the grounds of his property and buying other properties in the area. He entertained generously and staged his own plays, performing in them himself.

In 1758, he bought an even bigger property on the French side of the border on the edge of Lake Geneva and it was at Ferney that he would spend the remainder of his life. A year later, he published what is without doubt his best known work, the entertaining satire, Candide. The young and innocent hero of the book, *Candide*, undertakes a series of adventures in which he falls victim to a sequence of disreputable characters, all the while trying to remember the philosophy he had been taught by his teacher, Dr. Pangloss, and reconcile it with the experiences he had. Needless to say, the book presents an opportunity for Voltaire to rail against hypocrisy, greed and stupidity.

1764 saw the publication of his greatest philosophical work, the *Dictionnaire Philosophique* in which he discussed his idea of what religion should be. As usual, he denied that he was the author of the work, realising that the views he was expressing could conceivably land him in trouble once again.

By 1778, it had been nearly twenty years since Voltaire had set foot in Paris. That year, his play, *Irene*, was to be performed at the National Theatre and Voltaire wanted to be there to see it. The eighty-three-year-old writer returned to an amazing hero's welcome, people lining the streets as his carriage passed. Unfortunately, however, the journey and the excitement of it all was too much for him and he became very ill. He pulled through, however, and made it to a performance of the play. He was acclaimed when he arrived at the theatre.

He decided to live in Paris but by May he had once again fallen seriously ill. He died on 30 May 1778, having refused to sign a retraction of all his works, as a result of which he was refused a Christian burial. Nonetheless, his body was buried secretly at the Abbey of Scellieres in Champagne. When asked on his deathbed by a priest to renounce the devil and accept God, Voltaire is said to have refused, saying, 'Now is no time to be making new enemies'

Voltaire was the perfect example of the Enlightenment man, a renowned playwright as well as a figure who achieved much in the scientific field. Not least of his achievements, however, are his ideas and writings about civil rights and freedom of thought and expression which made a huge contribution to some of the most momentous events of his time and of the years following his death.

GEORGE WASHINGTON

HE IS THE only American to have a state named after him – Maryland, the Virginias, the Carolinas and Georgia are all named after British monarchs. Thousands of buildings, bridges, streets and institutions bear his name and his head, which adorns the one-dollar bill and the quarter coin, has come to symbolise America almost as much as the Stars and Stripes and the White House. George Washington – America's first President – is often recognised as its greatest.

Born on 22 February 1732, in Westmoreland County, Virginia, his father died when he was eleven and the young George helped his mother to run their plantation, Ferry Farm, learning to grow tobacco and look after cattle. His irregular formal education ended when he was around fifteen years old, by which time he could read and write and had a proficiency in mathematics. He was sent to the Shenendoah Valley as an assistant to the official surveyor by Lord Fairfax who owned large amounts of land in the British colony of Virginia and he began to see something of the land in which he lived. In 1749, with Fairfax's help, he became official surveyor of Culpepper County, a position he retained for two busy years. On a number of occasions, he had to make journeys into the western wilderness and his experiences during these trips toughened him up and taught him to be resourceful. He also became passionate about the development of the west, remaining so for the remainder of his life.

Washington's older half-brother, Lawrence, suffered from tuberculosis and to try to improve his health, George accompanied him to the warmer weather of Barbados in 1751, the only time in his life that George Washington set foot outside the land that would become the United States. Whilst there, George suffered from an attack of smallpox, but when he recovered the pair returned home to Lawrence's estate, Mount Vernon. It was merely a brief respite in his illness, however, and he died the following year. When his daughter, Sarah died a few months later, George inherited Mount Vernon.

For the next twenty years, Mount Vernon and his other estates were the focus of George Washington's life. He introduced crop rotation, made sure the land was properly fertilised and kept abreast of the latest developments. He employed slaves on his estates – by 1760 he had forty-nine working for him – but he did not fully approve of the practice. When he died, he bequeathed all his slaves to his wife, with instructions that on her death they should all be freed. After his death she freed them anyway.

In 1752, he was appointed adjutant by Lieutenant Governor Robert Dinwiddie to the southern district of Virginia and a year later he was appointed to the same position for Northern Neck and Eastern Shore. When, in October 1753, Dinwiddie wanted to warn the French regarding encroachments they had made into Ohio land owned by the British Crown, he sent Washington on the dangerous journey to deliver the message. The French commander, however, made it clear that he was going to take Ohio, and Washington returned with this message to Dinwiddie, having been fired on by Indians and having almost died of hypothermia when he fell into an icy river.

Dinwiddie sent Washington's report to London and began preparations to send an expedition to hold Ohio. Washington was appointed lieutenant colonel and was sent with 160 men to reinforce the fort at what would later become Pittsburgh in Pennsylvania. Before they arrived, however, they learned that the French had already captured the fort, renaming it Fort Duquesne. Washington marched to within forty miles of the fort and established a base at Great Meadows and from there attacked a French detachment of thirty men on 28 May 1754, killing ten men, including the commander. It marked the start of the French and Indian War, the

North American chapter of the Seven Years' war between Great Britain and France.

Washington was immediately promoted to colonel, in command of a sizeable contingent of troops from Virginia and North Carolina, as well as Indian auxiliaries. He needed them because the French attacked Great Meadows, laying siege to the fort with 700 men against his 350 and forcing him to surrender. He was allowed to return to Virginia but not before he had signed a document promising that the colonials would not build a fort on the Ohio territory for a year. Nonetheless, he returned to a warm welcome and learned that his name had been appearing in the London newspapers as a result of his report that had been sent there.

He resigned his commission in October 1754 in protest at the low pay of colonial officers and their insulting treatment at the hands of the British, but he desperately wanted to play a part in the war. Consequently, when General Edward Braddock offered him the post of his personal assistant with the rank of colonel, he eagerly accepted it. He was at Braddock's side en route for Fort Duquesne when the colonial army was ambushed and heavily defeated. During the battle, Washington was everywhere, rallying the troops despite being ill with fever. He had two horses shot from under him and had four bullets rip his clothing without being injured. Braddock died of wounds received in the fighting and Washington was promoted to the command of all Virginia's troops. For the next few years he commanded an ill-disciplined force of only 700 men who had to patrol a 400-mile border and they had to do it without the support of the Virginia legislature. It was almost inevitable that he would become ill and when he did, he was ordered home to Mount Vernon. It was 1757.

In 1758, he returned to the army, now a brigadier general, and took part in the expedition led by the British general, John Forbes, that finally drove the French out of Fort Dusquesne. At the end of the year, however, Washington retired from active service and for the next sixteen years led the life of a Virginia planter and local politician.

Within a year, he was married, to a wealthy widow, Martha Dandridge Custis, to whom he was introduced by friends. She brought two children from her previous marriage but they never had children of their own, Washington having been rendered sterile by bouts of smallpox and tuberculosis. He was now the wealthiest man in Virginia and was elected to the Virginia provincial legislature, serving as a justice between 1760 and 1774. In August 1774, he was elected as a delegate to the First Continental Congress which was convened to discuss the colonies' relationship with Britain. He was, by this time, a radical and advocated a hard line against the British, attending the meetings of the Congress in his military uniform.

On 14 June 1775, the Congress created the Continental Army and there was little doubt who its commander would be. Accordingly Washington was appointed Major General and Commander-in-Chief. He reorganised and re-equipped the army and drove the British from Boston without firing a shot, simply by putting artillery on the hills overlooking the city.

Meanwhile, as he moved his troops to New York, the British praised his courage and military skills, declaring that he displayed qualities as a commander that were severely lacking in their own generals.

The British launched a massive attack on New York in August 1776 by both land and sea. For the first time an army of the independent United States – the declaration of independence had been made on 4 July – took the field. The Battle of Long Island was the largest of the war but it ended in defeat for Washington with his army retreating in disarray to New Jersey. A counter-attack on Trenton on 25 December, however, was successful as was another at Princeton in January. He lost at Brandywine in September 1777 and when Phildelphia fell to the British, Washington came close to being relieved of his command. The nature of the war changed, however, when British General Burgoyne was forced to surrender his entire army at Saratoga, persuading the French that it was time to enter the war on the side of the Americans.

After wintering at Valley Forge, where 2,500 of his force of 10,000 men died of exposure and disease, Washington emerged and defeated the British at the Battle of Monmouth. It was the second of two battles in which Washington's men faced British Regulars on straightforward terms, in a set-piece field battle and were not defeated.

Eventually, in October 1781, following a French naval victory, a joint American and French force, led by Washington, trapped a British army that surrendered at Yorktown. It was a decisive victory and the American Revolution was virtually over. The Treaty of Paris signed in September 1783 recognised the independence of the United States of America.

On 23 December 1783, Washington resigned his command and at the age of fifty-one, retired once more to his beloved Mount Vernon where he presumed he would live his remaining days as a gentleman farmer.

The newly independent nation was struggling to hold itself together, however, and Washington feared for its future, writing in May 1786 that 'something must be done, or the fabric must fall, for it is certainly tottering'. In 1787, he was elected as a delegate to the Constitutional Convention in Philadelphia that had sprung from meetings he had at Mount Vernon. He was unanimously chosen as president of the convention and for four months presided over it, speaking only once. A constitution was ratified by all thirteen states of the Union and Washington sincerely believed that, following this agreement, he would be permitted to retire quietly to Mount Vernon once again.

But, when the question arose as to who would be the first President of the United States, as detailed in the constitution, all eyes turned to him. He was the only man who commanded the respect of all parties and he enjoyed the additional benefit of being respected throughout Europe. His name brought prestige to the new republic.

He was unanimously elected president by the Electoral College, the only president ever to have been accorded such an overwhelming show of support and it occurred again in 1792.

He took the oath of office on 30 April 1789 after a journey to New York which became a celebratory procession as the inhabitants of every town and village through which he passed came out to greet him. A month later, Martha joined him.

Throughout his presidency he was criticised for his style. He and Martha would ride in a coach-and-four, a bit too much like monarchs for some people, he refused to shake visitors' hands and he received them on a raised platform, wearing a sword at his hip. He would attend receptions dressed in a black velvet suit with gold buckles, with yellow gloves, powdered hair, a cocked hat with an ostrich plume, and a sword in a white leather scabbard. However, it was a brand-new role and he was defining it, giving it some substance. One of the first things he decided was that he would be addressed as 'Mr President', as every president since has been addressed.

He turned out to be a good administrator, holding regular meetings of his cabinet and selecting the most able people for government positions. He was not a member of a political party and hoped that American politics could stay free of the factionlism and conflict that political parties engendered. Very soon, however, two factions had formed, establishing the way in which American politics would go.

He endeavoured to build a strong central government that would fund the national debt, implement an efficient tax system and create a national bank. He made the Proclamation of Neutrality in 1793 that was designed to keep the United States out of any foreign war and signed the important Jay Treaty, making peace with Britain for ten years.

Washington had been re-elected in 1792, but when offered a third term in office, declined. He was tired, and disheartened by the abuses of the opposition. His Farewell Address is one of the most influential statements of American political values. In it he spoke of the importance of national union, the value of the Constitution, the law, the iniquities of the political parties he loathed and the virtues of a republican people. He warned against foreign interference in American affairs and American interference in Europe.

He retired, for a third time to Mount Vernon in March 1797 and the last two and a half years of his life were devoted to his family and his farm. There was one final flourish when, with war with France looming, he was appointed commander-in-chief of the provisional army, but the threat of conflict passed.

On 12 December 1799, he had been out riding in bitterly cold, snowy weather. He returned home and neglected to change his wet clothes. The next day, he suffered an attack of acute laryngitis. He was bled several times and given various other remedies, but his strength was fading fast. After giving instructions to his secretary about his funeral, he died at ten in the evening of 14 December, aged sixty-seven. His last words were 'Tis well'.

The entire country mourned his passing. The US army wore black armbands for six months, the British navy lowered its flags to half-mast and Napoleon Bonaparte ordered ten days of national mourning in France.

In the United States Bicentennial year, 1976, George Washington was posthumously appointed to the rank of General of the Armies of the United States, giving him the position of the highest-ranking officer in United States military history.

MAXIMILIEN DE ROBESPIERRE

THEY CALLED HIM 'L'Incorruptible' (the Incorruptible). He was the exquisitely attired and impeccably well-mannered Maximilien François Marie Isidore de Robespierre, one of the most important and influential figures of the French Revolution and a leading player during the violent and destructive period known as the Reign of Terror that occurred fifty months after the outbreak of revolution, the result of conflict between the political factions, the Girodins and the Jacobins.

He was born the oldest of four children in Arras in May 1758, the son of a lawyer, François, and his wife, Jacqueline, whose family had been brewers. When Jacqueline who suffered from tuberculosis, died during childbirth in 1764, Robespierre's father abandoned his young family and began travelling, dying eventually in Germany thirteen years later. The children, meanwhile, were sent to live with relatives, the two girls to their father's family and the two boys to their mother's.

As head of the family in his father's absence, Maximilien became a serious child, something of a loner who preferred his own company to that of others. He threw himself into his studies and at the age of eleven with the help of the Bishop of Arras, gained a scholarship to study at the demanding Lycée Louis-le-Grand run by the Jesuits in Paris. There he would meet future fellow revolutionary, Camille Desmoulins.

After eleven years, he left the school with a law degree and began to work as a lawyer in Arras. His view of his job was very different, however, to that of other members of the legal profession. He accepted jobs not for the benefit – either professionally or financially – of himself. He saw his job as being to help people and he was good at it. Meanwhile, he soaked up the ideas of the great thinkers of the Enlightenment, philosophers and social thinkers such as Jean Jacques Rousseau and Voltaire.

He harboured aspirations to become a writer and was a member of a literary society whose members called themselves the 'Rosati'. He wrote poetry and entered literary competitions.

Towards the end of the 1780s, France was experiencing a major financial crisis with food shortages and prices for what food there was going through the roof. The greatest tax burden was imposed on the Third Estate, the commoners, while the clergy – the First Estate – and the nobility – the Second Estate – enjoyed a light tax burden. Naturally, the First and Second Estates rejected any ideas of reform to the system to make it more equitable. Louis XVI, desperate to bring some much-needed money into the royal coffers, called a meeting of the Estates General, a convention of all the different levels of society, on 5 May 1789.

By the time the assembly was called, Robespierre was at the summit of his legal achievement, having won some notable cases. He put himself forward as a candidate to be the Arras representative, writing some remarkable pamphlets in support of his candidature in which he called for the king to initiate revolutionary changes to the governance of France, reconciling the political and moral nature of his rule.

His reputation as 'L'Incorruptible' had made him popular with the people of Arras and they trusted him enough to elect him as their representative on 26 April 1789. He was excited at the prospect of helping to change France for the better and to introduce some of the ideas of the Enlightenment.

Inevitably, Louis' treatment of the Third Estate was poor – he kept them waiting for hours when he was supposed to be introduced to them and then they were marched past him quickly, as if he was bored. They soon felt neglected and, realising that their presence represented no more than a token gesture, began staging their own meetings where they aired their numerous grievances. They called their meetings the National Assembly but the king and the other estates began to fear them and banned them, closing the building in which they were held. The National Assembly began to meet in the king's tennis court where they swore the Tennis Court Oath – an undertaking to remain in session until they had created a new constitution for France.

Meanwhile, on the streets of Paris, people were becoming restless due to the lack of progress. It was Camille Desmoulins, Robespierre's old school friend who was the catalyst. He jumped on to a table in the garden of a cafe in the garden of the Palais Royal and announced the king's dismissal of Finance Minister Jacques Necker, a politician sympathetic to the plight of the Third Estate. He became leader of a mob that gathered in the street and gained arms by force at Les Invalides before marching on the Bastille to find powder for their weapons. It was the beginning of the French Revolution.

Robespierre began to gain influence through his oratory where he spoke in support of concepts such as universal suffrage, the abolition of slavery and free education provided by the state. He aligned with the Jacobins who were on the political left of the numerous factions that were forming. But, to begin with, he favoured a constitutional monarchy. In 1790, he was voted President of the Jacobin Club.

Louis, meanwhile, although seemingly happy with the way things were going, was looking for outside help to bring to an end the revolutionary changes that were occurring. Finally, in June 1791, he tried to flee the country with his family. They were sensationally stopped at Varennes and the country was scandalised by his flight. By this time, Robespierre, disillusioned with the idea of a constitutional monarchy, became a republican.

A constitution was drafted that Louis swore to uphold, resulting in his restoration to the throne. The Legislative Assembly now ruled

France and for several years, Robespierre no longer had a role to play. He continued to speak in opposition, however. He had called for Louis to be deposed and was disappointed at the way things had turned out. When soldiers opened fire on demonstrators in the Champs de Mar, he was forced to flee the Jacobin Club and go into hiding with the family of a carpenter, and Jacobin supporter, called Duplay. He would remain with this family for the remainder of his life, even after his need to conceal his whereabouts had faded.

The threat of foreign invasion of France or war with its enemies – Austria and its allies – loomed large in 1792. The king and the Girodins were eager for it, the king because he anticipated a surge in his popularity as a result. The Girodins were eager to spread revolution throughout Europe; this would also strengthen the Revolution in France. Robespierre, however, was against any wars with foreign powers while the domestic situation was still unstable. Nonetheless, war was declared on Austria in April 1792.

On 10 August, insurgents representing the new, revolutionary Paris Commune, attacked the Tuilleries, taking the king and queen prisoner. The monarchy was suspended by the Legislative Assembly. Meanwhile, the Commune sent gangs into the prisons to butcher the inmates, other French cities being invited to do likewise. A new governing assembly, the Convention, met in September, charged with devising a new constitution. On 21 September, the monarchy was abolished and France was declared a republic.

Robespierre was horrified, but not surprised by the violence. His popularity was undiminished, however, and he was the first deputy to be elected for Paris. As ever, in keeping with his status as 'L'Incorruptible', he refused to accept remuneration for his work, and continued to live on his low salary of 600 livres per annum. He became famous; his portrait hung in salons and he received hundreds of letters. Some were about political matters, but in others women proposed marriage to him or told him they were naming their sons after him.

As the Jacobins began to gain increasing influence in the Convention, Robespierre began to gain more power, becoming one of the assembly's most prominent members. He voted, like many others, for the death penalty for Louis XVI and the king was executed on 21 January 1793.

The Committee of Public Safety was established by the Convention in July 1793 and became the de facto executive branch of the French government during the period known as the Reign of Terror that lasted until 1794. Denunciations, trials and executions were centralised under this body and Robespierre became the leader of its twelve members, elected in July 1793 to replace Danton. He expanded the list of the enemies of the Revolution to include moderates and what he termed 'false revolutionaries'. Anyone who was not in total sympathy with the actions of the Committee was purged from the Convention. This policy, resulting in the execution of many of the Revolution's original and strongest advocates, including his predecessor, Georges Danton and his old friend Camille Desmoulins, has sometimes been suggested to have been intended more to further Robespierre's political ambition than to improve the government of France.

The people of Paris – the *Sans-culottes*, as they were known – were hungry for blood, desperate to wreak revenge on the nobles at whose hands they had suffered for centuries. Robespierre indulged them, showing no mercy to his enemies. 'Uncertainty of punishment encourages all the guilty', he said. He published the *Report on the Principles of Political Morality*, a tract that urged the furtherance of the Revolution at all costs. It also called for political equality, universal suffrage and abolition of privilege.

He worked hard in 1794 to extend his power base, using his followers to dominate the Paris Commune and the French army. Meanwhile, the Terror upped its pace. On 10 June the radical Law of 22 Prairial was passed. This gave the Revolutionary Tribunal the power to condemn without witnesses, carte blanche for getting rid of any opposition. Until his death, 1,285 victims were guillotined in Paris as a result of this law.

He wished to establish a spiritual regeneration in France and introduced a law in May 1794 that established the notion of a Supreme Being. This was based on the ideas of Rousseau and was a long way from the Catholic view of religion.

Of course, holding such power, he was accused of being a dictator or a tyrant and defended himself against such accusations in the Convention in July 1794. He also spoke of a conspiracy against the Republic although he steadfastly refused to name the members of the plot. On 26 June, he had saved a woman called Catherine Theot from the guillotine. Bizarrely, she had claimed to have had visions of Robespierre and declared him to be a Messiah, a saviour. This had done nothing to allay fears of a dictatorship with Robespierre at its head. Suspicions about his intentions gained ground and the Sans-culottes began to feel that he was ignoring their wishes.

It came to a head on 27 July 1794 when he was accused and not permitted to defend himself – as he had done with so many of his enemies – at the Convention. He and his supporters, Saint Just, Couthon and his brother, Augustin, were arrested. However, troops from the Paris Commune who were loyal to Robespierre, freed them and marched against the Convention which ordered its own troops out to face them. Robespierre and his supporters gathered at the Hotel de Ville and were declared outlaws by the Convention. This implied that on arrest they could be killed within 24 hours without a trial. The Commune troops began to desert as the Convention force approached, eventually leaving Robespierre and his men undefended.

Augustin killed himself by leaping from a window, Couthon was crippled by a fall and another supporter, Philippe-François-Joseph Le Bas shot himself.

Robespierre also tried to shoot himself but managed only to shatter his jaw and was discovered semi-conscious at his desk. He was held at the Hotel de Ville for the remainder of the night before being moved to the same prison cell in the Conciergerie prison where Marie Antoinette, wife of Louis XVI was held prior to her execution.

The following day, 28 July 1794, Maximilien de Robespierre was guillotined without trial in the Place de la Revolution. When the executioner removed the bandage keeping together his shattered jaw, he let out a piercing scream and continued screaming until the blade fell. It is said that he was the only person to ever be guillotined face up – so that he could see his death coming.

Robespierre's reputation has remained controversial. Some say that he was no more than a bloodthirsty tyrant who manipulated the Revolution for his own ends and to further his own political ambitions. Others claim that he was basically a good man who remained true to his revolutionary beliefs, 'L'Incorruptible' to the bloody end.

SHAKA ZULU

THE LEGENDARY ZULU chief, Shaka Zulu, took the death of his mother, Nandi, very badly. He ordered that people should not plant any crops during the year after her death, and they were forbidden from using milk. Women who became pregnant were killed, as were their husbands. Anyone not deemed to be mourning sufficiently was put to death and cows were slaughtered so the calves they left behind would know what it was like to lose a mother.

He was, by this time, no longer the same man who had ruled over 250,000 people and could raise an army of 50,000 warriors with the snap of his fingers. His ten-year reign over the Zulus had cost around ten million lives and no one can be certain exactly how many died during the punishing mass migrations that occurred to escape his marauding armies.

He was born illegitimately in 1787, to a Zulu chief and a woman from a lower class clan and, as a child, was treated as an outcast. His name is testament to his status at that time, meaning 'intestinal parasite' or, often just 'bastard'. In spite of his treatment, however, he was ambitious. He was also intelligent and absolutely ruthless, a necessary quality for the advancement of a career amongst the Zulus.

Shaka and his mother wandered for many years before settling eventually with the Mtetwa, a confederation of tribes and clans. Aged sixteen, Shaka joined the ibutho lempi (warrior force) of Dingiswayo, Chief of the Metetwa to whom Shaka's people the Zulus were, at the time, paying tribute. The Chief became his mentor, teaching him military organisation and tactics. Meanwhile, Shaka distinguished himself on numerous occasions, serving for around ten years.

He learned much from Dingiswayo who had introduced new ideas of military and social organisation. He invented the *ibutho* -- a regiment or troop – which radically changed the way his men fought.

Shaka's father died in 1816 and Dingiswayo sent Shaka back to his homeland to claim his inheritance, the leadership of the Zulus. He also helped him to defeat his brother, and assume the leadership. He started out with just 350 men and by the end of his first year as Chief, there were 2,000 Zulu warriors in his ranks. Shaka immediately began to consolidate his position, making alliances with neighbouring tribes in an effort to form a united front against the Ndwndwe tribe who were marauding from the north. Initially, it was this diplomatic approach that he employed, that and assassinations where necessary.

Regarding his warrior force, Shaka began to apply the lessons he had learned from Dingiswayo, introducing the ibutho regimental system, and introducing heavy-bladed thrusting spears – *i-klwas* – to be used in close combat to replace the light javelin-like assegais. The name of the *i-klwa* derived from the sound it made as it went into and was then withdrawn from an enemy's body. He introduced a much heavier shield made of cowhide and every warrior was trained in the most effective use of this shield, how to use it to push an opponent's shield to the right, exposing his left side. Then the *i-klwa* would come into its own.

Close combat was fundamental to the way Shaka wanted his warriors to fight, as was discipline. He made his men discard their sandals to toughen them and forced marches – or runs – for distances of fifty miles over rugged terrain in the heat of a southern African day.

His army was supplied by teams of young boys who joined aged six or over to carry supplies, cooking implements and sleeping mats. Eventually, when they were old enough or strong enough, they would become warriors. Shaka divided his army into age groupings. And activities were distributed according to age. Each age grouping was organised into a regiment with its own encampment, or kraal, and its own insignia and name.

His tactics in battle included the famous 'buffalo horns' formation, designed to encircle and trap an enemy force. The horns on the right and left wings of his force were made up of younger members of his army and they would carry out the encirclement in which they would have been very well trained. The main force, made up of the best fighters, was called the 'chest', and was responsible for charging into the centre of the opposing force. The 'loins', consisting of the older warriors, were reserves or reinforcements who would be brought up to the battle as and when they were required. Controlling the entire strategy were regimental izinduna – chiefs -- who communicated to their warriors with hand signals and messengers. The simplicity of the strategy ensured that in battle each warrior knew exactly what his role consisted of.

In 1818, Shaka, now thirty-one, fought the first defensive engagement of his military career at the Battle of Gqokli Hill, when he was advancing to support Dingiswayo in battle against the Nwandwe. Dingiswayo was killed in the battle and Shaka was furious, resolving to exact revenge on the Ndwandwe Chief, Zwinde. The revenge was, indeed, terrible. He kidnapped the Chief's mother and had her mauled and then eaten by jackals.

He had himself only just avoided defeat in the battle in which Dingiswayo had died and was forced to fight numerous small engagements in the following year in order to add the defeated men to his depleted army. Eventually, he was ready and less than a year after Gqokli, his warriors massacred the Ndwandwe in a brutal two-day battle at the Mhlatuzi Fords. Following this victory, he introduced a new tactic to African warfare – the scorched-earth policy. He left nothing alive or capable of living in his wake, burning crops and homes and killing every living thing.

With Dingiswayo's death, Shaka was now on his own. He had relied greatly on the experience, power and influence of his friend but now he had to establish himself. He moved his people southwards, away from the Zulu heartland and settled in Bulawayo in Qwabe territory.

By now the Zulus were developing the warrior outlook on life for which they became renowned. Only by conquering and controlling other tribes, Shaka taught them, could you ensure that you became powerful and successful. And Shaka was most certainly both of these. The Zulu nation grew to 250,000 and he led an army of 40,000 warriors. The Zulu Kingdom covered an area of two million square miles, stretching from Cape Colony in the south to modern-day Tanzania in the north.

In 1824, a visiting Englishman, H. F. Flynn, gave Shaka medical treatment after he had been wounded in a battle, and Shaka reciprocated by allowing English traders to work in his kingdom, under his protection. At one point, he even tried to exchange ambassadors with the British king, George III.

His erratic behaviour after the death of his mother was merely an extension of the customarily harsh way he treated his people anyway. His subjects were terrified of him – understandable, given that you could be executed for 'smelling like a witch'. On occasion, entire villages were massacred on a royal whim. His army, too, became tired of the constant warfare and campaigning to which he subjected them. These took them further away from home every time as he sought new peoples and lands to incorporate into his kingdom. Added to this was the fact that Shaka insisted on the celibacy on his warriors, a condition not guaranteed to improve their morale.

His mother's death also led to him no longer going out at the head of his army as he had always done and which had always instilled confidence in his warriors and in his people.

His half-brothers, Dingane and Mhlangana, had already made several attempts on his life. But his enemies did not, of course, lie merely within his own people. They may have enjoyed the support in their efforts of the disaffected Mpondo and iziZende peoples.

He was killed by three assassins – his half-brothers and an inDuna called Mbopa – on 23 September 1828, when his warriors were away fighting to the north, leaving his kraal critically unguarded. His body was unceremoniously buried in an empty grain pit, the location of which is unknown.

The Zulu Kingdom did not wane with the death of its greatest figure. His brother Dingane, having killed Mhlangana, picked up the reins and breathed fresh life into it. Over the next few years, he purged Shaka's supporters and as a result ruled for twelve years. Shaka's organisation and tactical innovations helped him to maintain Zulu power and ensured they remained the dominant force in the region.

The buffalo formation was still being used successfully fifty years after the death of its inventor, the greatest military leader Africa has ever produced.

IV

THE
NINETEENTH
CENTURY

THOMAS JEFFERSON

ON HIS EXPLICIT instructions, his tombstone reads simply: 'author of the Declaration of American Independence, of the Statute of Virginia for religious freedom, and Father of the University of Virginia'. This in spite of the other astonishing achievements in one of the greatest of American lives. There is no mention, for instance, of the fact that he had been Governor of Virginia, US Minister to France, Secretary of State under George Washington, Vice President to John Adams or President of the United States from 1801 to 1809.

This extreme modesty also meant no mention for the other prodigious talents of this extraordinary polymath – architect, naturalist, linguist and wine connoisseur.

Born in Shadwell, Virginia on 13 April 1743, Thomas Jefferson was a scion of one of Virginia's first families through his mother, Jane Randolph Jefferson, who had come to the New World as a child with her family. His father, Peter, was a wealthy landowner. Coming from such a privileged background, Jefferson naturally enjoyed a good education, attending the College of William and Mary from 1760 to 1762 before going on to study law with George Wythe, the first professor of law in the United States, who was known as the 'Father of American Jurisprudence.' Wythe also taught another future American President, James Monroe. In 1769, Jefferson began six years as a representative in the Virginia House of Burgesses which was the very first elected lower house in a legislative assembly in America.

In 1768, he had begun the building of a home at Monticello, designed personally in every detail by Jefferson himself in the Palladian style fashionable at the time. It was on a plot of land given to him by his father and he moved into it in 1770. He married Martha

Wayles Skelton two years later and they would have six children, only two of whom survived into adulthood.

Jefferson first began to make a name for himself when he published a pamphlet, *A Summary View of the Rights of British America*, in 1774. In it, he claimed the allegiance to the king was, in fact, voluntary. Espousing the views of the Enlightenment that would inform the American Revolution and the country's eventual independence, he wrote that 'The God who gave us life, gave us liberty at the same time: the hand of force may destroy, but cannot disjoin them.'

On 10 May 1775, a convention of delegates from the thirteen American colonies met in Philadelphia. The first shots of the American War of Independence had just been fired and the Second Continental Congress was designed to manage the war effort. Elected to the Congress on behalf of Virginia, Thomas Jefferson was appointed head of a committee of five given the task of drafting a *Declaration of Independence*. Its members, apart from Jefferson, were John Adams of Massachusetts, Robert R. Livingstone of New York, Benjamin Franklin of Pennsylvania and Roger Sherman of Connecticut. Adopted on 4 July 1776, a year after hostilities had broken out, and written principally by Jefferson in just seventeen days, the Declaration is a formal explanation of why Congress had decided on 2 July the previous year to declare independence from Great Britain. It is also one of the most important documents ever written.

The writing of the *Declaration* immediately made Jefferson internationally famous and although John Adams described the ideas it contained as hackneyed, Jefferson wrote of it as 'Neither aiming at originality of principle or sentiment, nor yet copied from any particular and previous writing, it was intended to be an expression of the American mind.'

In late 1776, he returned home to Virginia and, until 1779, continued to serve on the Virginia House of Delegates which had been established by the state's new constitution in 1776. His colleagues in the House numbered among them his old teacher, George Wythe, future US President James Madison and George Mason, the man who would become known as 'the father of the Bill of Rights'. Together, they attempted with a series of bills to liberalise Virginia's laws, efforts fiercely resisted by more conservative elements who represented the interests of Virginia planters. Importantly, however, Jefferson achieved changes in the laws of inheritance. He wrote that 'These laws, drawn by myself, laid the ax to the foot of pseudaristocracy.'

Although he succeeded in revising the Virginia criminal code, enacted in 1796 an attempt to create a system of tax-supported elementary education for all except slaves and his effort to create a public library were amongst those that failed.

One initiative struck a raw nerve in Virginia – his bill on religious liberty stirred up a debate that lasted for eight years. It would have been a first not only in America but also in the world as no country at the time had ever legislated to allow complete religious freedom. His bill stated 'that all men shall be free to profess, and by argument to maintain, their opinions on matters of religion, and that the same shall in no wise diminish, enlarge, or affect their civil capacities,' but it was regarded by many Virginians as nothing more than an attack on Christianity, not being passed until 1786, largely because of the efforts of James Madison. Jefferson, by then in France, congratulated him with the words 'it is honorable for us to have produced the first legislature who had the courage to declare that the reason of man may be trusted with the formation of his own opinions.'

He was elected Governor of Virginia in 1779 but his term in office was criticised by his opponents who claimed that he was unprepared for war, especially in the defence of Richmond in 1780 to 1781. The city was burned to the ground by the British and Jefferson was forced to flee, even though he had known that an attack was imminent. They accused him of cowardice and in June 1781 he retired from the governorship. However, a subsequent inquiry exonerated him and he was actually afforded a resolution of appreciation of his conduct. He remained bitter, nonetheless and jaded by the vicissitudes of public office.

He was further troubled when his wife, Martha, died in September 1782, but he returned to Congress the following year, making a further vital contribution to the new nation. He advocated the use of a decimal system of money in his Notes on the Establishment of a Money Unit and of a Coinage for the United States which led to the adoption of the dollar as the unit of currency.

His advice regarding the government of the United States' lands to the west represented the most progressive and liberal colonial policy of any nation in history. In effect, he suggested that they be self-governing and should be admitted to the Union only when they attained a certain size. He further proposed the abolition of slavery in all of those territories after 1800. He was, however, a slave owner himself but believed it should not be allowed to spread. This last proposal was only narrowly defeated.

In 1785, initially sent to Paris the previous year to help negotiate commercial treaties, he succeeded Benjamin Franklin in the important role of Minister to France. In France he witnessed the beginnings of the French Revolution but was doubtful as to whether the French could replicate the American model of Republican government. Instead, he advised, the French should adopt the British model and establish a constitutional monarchy.

In Paris he lived on the Champs Elysées and spent a great deal of time exploring the wonders the city had to offer. He moved in high social circles, attending salons and dinners and also threw parties. He and his daughters were accompanied to France by two black slaves, James Hemings, who trained to be a chef while in Paris and his sister Sally who was there to look after the girls. It is thought that during this time, Jefferson began his long-term relationship with Sally Hemings.

Returning to the USA in September 1789, he was appointed by Congress as Secretary of State in the new nation's first administration, led by the country's first President, George Washington. Jefferson, however, was reluctant to accept the position and only did so on the insistence of the President. He was hesitant mainly because of the ceremony that was attached to the executive office but he trusted Washington and relented.

In that first government, however, he was suspicious of the proposals of Alexander Hamilton, Secretary of the Treasury. He found them to be contrary to the principles of liberty with which the United States had been established. Hamilton was a member of the emerging Federalist Party and Jefferson suspected that it had monarchist ambitions. The two men even opposed each other on foreign affairs, Hamilton pro-British, Jefferson inclined to be pro-French. Twice Jefferson threatened to resign, frustrated with his minor position in the Cabinet. On the third occasion, on 31 December 1793, his resignation was accepted.

He spent the next three years at home occupying himself with his farm and his family, experimenting with new farming machinery and building a nail factory. He also resumed work on Monticello and welcomed foreign guests who were queuing up to see the man who had written the Declaration of Independence.

He followed events on the political stage, both at home and abroad with a mounting sense of foreboding, however. He was concerned about the grip that the Federalists seemed to have on Washington and was annoyed by what he perceived to be an unnecessary use of force when the Whiskey Rebellion of 1794 in Washington, Pennsylvania, was ruthlessly put down.

When Washington announced that he would not run for a third term in 1796, Jefferson was pleased. He became a reluctant candidate of the Democratic-Republican Party but was probably relieved when the Federal, John Adams narrowly defeated him by seventy-one electoral college votes to sixty-eight. The system at the time, however, ensured that he became Vice President.

At least, he must have thought, Adams hated Alexander Hamilton as much as he did. Even with that, however, it was not a marriage made in heaven and Jefferson was disappointed by a deterioration in relations with France. New taxes were imposed and the authoritarian Alien and Sedition Acts threatened the freedoms of American citizens. Jefferson, with the help of James Madison, secretly wrote the Kentucky Resolutions, in favour of states' rights, in opposition to these two acts, their participation not being discovered until many years later.

In 1800, Jefferson was again put forward as a candidate for the presidency, facing the incumbent, John Adams. However, each elector in those early days could vote for two people and Jefferson and his running mate, Aaron Burr, received the same number of votes. The outcome was decided in the House of Representatives, Hamilton's influence helping to make Thomas Jefferson the 3rd President of the United States.

During his presidency, he reduced taxes, cut military spending, allowed the Alien and Sedition Acts to lapse and made plans to do away with the national debt. The watchwords of his administration were simplicity and frugality and his greatest achievement in office was the Louisiana Purchase when he acquired for the United States more than 800,000 square miles of territory from the French for a total cost of just over $15 million. It was a stroke of genius that, even though it was felt to be unconstitutional, would effectively prohibit France or Spain from ever blocking American access to the port of New Orleans. On completion of the deal, Napoleon Bonaparte, Emperor of France said, 'This accession of territory affirms forever the power of the United States, and I have given England a maritime rival who sooner or later will humble her pride.' The country was swept with a wave of enthusiasm for the purchase and Jefferson won a second term with a landslide, winning all states bar two.

During his second administration, the explorers Lewis and Clark, sent by him to explore the continent, returned in triumph and the newly-founded US Navy fought its first engagements in the

Tripolitan War against the Barbary States in North Africa, a conflict that was favourably settled by Jefferson. His old rival Aaron Burr engaged in a bizarre conspiracy for which he was tried and acquitted. The main business of the second term, however, was the Napoleonic Wars. Britain and France consistently violated US territory and sovereignty and Jefferson responded with appeasement and economic sanctions.

He ended his presidency in 1809 and returned to Virginia where he founded the University of Virginia at Charlottesville, conceiving, planning and designing it as well as supervising its construction.

Ironically, Thomas Jefferson died on the 50th anniversary of the adoption of the Declaration of Independence, on Independence Day, 4 July 1826. To add even further irony, one of the other architects of the historic document, John Adams, died just a few hours later.

HORATIO NELSON

TO PRESERVE IT, Nelson's body was placed in a cask of brandy that was mixed with camphor and myrrh. This was then tied to the mast of his ship HMS *Victory* and an armed guard was placed upon it. The body was transferred to lead-lined coffin after the battle and news of his death was taken to England aboard HMS *Pickle*. On arrival, news was taken to Lady Hamilton and the King is said to have shed tears when he was informed. 'We have lost more than we gained,' he is reported to have said.

Nelson's coffin returned to England on board the *Victory*. It was taken to Greenwich where it was put in another lead coffin and then that was put inside a wooden one that had been crafted from the mast of the French flagship *L'Orient* that had been salvaged after the ship was blown up at the Battle of the Nile. The body lay in state for three days and was then transported upriver on a barge on board which were the Prince of Wales, and the Admirals, Lord Hood and Sir Peter Parker. It rested in the Admiralty the night before the funeral, attended by Nelson's chaplain, and the following day one of the most impressive funerals ever seen in Britain took place. His funeral procession consisted of thirty-two admirals, more than 100 captains and 10,000 troops. The funeral service at St Paul's lasted four hours, after which he was laid to rest inside a sarcophagus carved originally for Thomas, Cardinal Wolsey.

Nelson was a man who provided Great Britain with some of its proudest moments in warfare. During the Napoleonic Wars, he won for Britain at sea while Wellington swept all before him on land. He was an inspirational leader, an inveterate maverick and an unconventional tactician who has been held in great esteem by the British people in the two hundred years since his death at the Battle of Trafalgar.

Horatio Nelson was born in 1758, son of the Reverend Edmund Nelson and Catherine Nelson, at Burnham Thorpe, Norfolk. He was the sixth of eleven children but his mother died when he was nine.

His naval career began in January 1771 when he enlisted in the Royal Navy at just twelve years of age, joining the *Raisonable* as an Ordinary Seaman and coxwain. The commander of the vessel was his uncle, Captain Maurice Suckling and before long, Nelson was training to be an officer, all the while fighting back the seasickness from which he suffered for the rest of his life at sea.

Captain Suckling was promoted and helped Nelson's advancement in the navy, having him dispatched to serve aboard the ships belonging to a company called Hibbert, Purrier and Horton that traded with the West Indies. He gained invaluable experience of life at sea, twice crossing the Atlantic before returning to work for Suckling again, as commander of his longboat. He next served as a midshipman aboard HMS *Carcass*, which set out on an expedition to survey a passage in the Arctic by which India could be reached. The expedition was unsuccessful, thick ice forcing the Carcass to turn back.

Nelson next sailed on HMS *Seahorse* to the East Indies to escort merchant shipping. It was on this tour of duty, in early 1775, that he experienced his first taste of action when the *Seahorse* was attacked by two enemy Indian ketches while carrying a shipment of money. In 1776, he contracted malaria and, seriously ill, was discharged from the *Seahorse* to return to England.

Fully recovered by the time he arrived home, his influential uncle now obtained for him a posting on board HMS *Worcester* which was preparing to set sail for Gibraltar on convoy escort duties. He returned to London in April 1777 and passed his lieutenant's exam, receiving an appointment to HMS *Lowestoft* sailing to Jamaica.

They arrived on 19 July but while the ship cruised in Caribbean waters, there was ample opportunity, provided by the outbreak of the American War of Independence, for Nelson to cover himself in glory. His ship captured several enemy boats. One of them, the tender, *Little Lucy*, was taken into service and Nelson was given command of her.

He had made a good impression during these voyages and was soon given a commission on board HMS *Bristol*, the flagship of the commander-in-chief in Jamaica, Sir Peter Parker. Parker campaigned successfully in the Caribbean, especially following the entry into the war of the French, and Nelson made a lot of money from the ships they captured. His reward came on 8 December 1778, when he was given command of his first ship, HMS *Badger*. On 11 June, the following year, he became post-captain of the twenty-eight-gun, *Hinchinbrook*, which had recently been captured from the French. Once again, Nelson distinguished himself, taking a number of American ships and leading a successful attack on a Spanish look-out post.

His next command was the forty-four-gun frigate, HMS *Janus*, but he had by this time become seriously ill after spending time in the jungles of Costa Rica and was discharged and sent home to recuperate.

In August 1781, he returned to sea in command of HMS *Albemarle*. After hunting American privateers, he sailed in the fleet of Admiral Samuel Hood and spent the remainder of the war cruising in the seas around the West Indies, capturing a number of French and Spanish ships. Finally, at the end of the war, Nelson was ordered home. It was June 1783.

He considered standing for Parliament, as a supporter of William Pitt the Younger, but, unable to find a seat, he returned to sea as commander of the frigate *Boreas* which had been given the task of enforcing the Navigation Act around Antigua. During this time, Nelson came close to imprisonment following his capture of several American vessels off the island of Nevis. He was sued by the captains for illegal seizure and was unable to leave the *Boreas* for eight months until the suits were rejected by the court. In the meantime, however, Nelson found distraction in Frances 'Fanny' Nisbet, a widow born on

Nevis. The pair were married in March 1787 and he returned to England soon after with his new wife.

They settled at his childhood home of Burnham Thorpe in 1788 and Nelson endeavoured to obtain a command, no easy task in peacetime. When the French Revolutionary government annexed the Austrian Netherlands in 1792, he was recalled and given command of the sixty-four-gun *Agamemnon*. On 1 February 1793, France declared war on Great Britain.

Nelson sailed with Lord Hood with the objective of securing the Mediterranean. At Toulon, in southern France they found a city controlled by moderate republicans and royalists and undertook to protect it against the forces of the National Convention. Nelson was dispatched to Sardinia and Naples, seeking reinforcements but while in Naples, he met for the first time the beautiful new wife of the British ambassador to Naples, William Hamilton. Emma was a woman with a fascinating past. She had worked as a maid, strip-tease artist and artist's model before marrying Hamilton. She would re-enter Nelson's life, changing it completely, a few years later.

When Toulon fell in December, with the loss of eighteen British ships, Nelson was blockading the French garrison at Corsica. Despite disagreements with army commanders, he took Bastia after a forty-five-day siege and then, in August 1794, Calvi followed. During the fighting, Nelson was at one of his forward batteries when a shot struck one of the sandbags protecting the position, spraying sand and stones onto the troops, including Nelson. He was hit in the right eye which was so seriously damaged that he would eventually go blind in that eye.

Having occupied Corsica, Nelson was ordered to Genoa to establish good relations with what was hoped to be a good ally. He then sailed with the new admiral, William Hotham. Off Corsica, they ran into some French vessels that were planning to invade the island. The French ship, the *Ça Ira* was a much larger vessel than Nelson's *Agamemnon*, with 1,060 men to his 344 and it carried much heavier guns, but Nelson moved in close and the two ships exchanged broadsides for two and a half hours. Two other French ships arrived and he was forced to flee, but not before he had inflicted serious damage on the larger ship. Later, they met again in the Battle of Genoa, the French being forced to surrender and return to port.

The year 1780 saw the first example of Nelson's disregard of orders from his superiors. Engaging a Spanish fleet off Cape St Vincent in southern Portugal while commanding HMS *Captain*, he found himself a long way from the action at the rear. Frustrated, he broke ranks and attacked three Spanish ships. He led a boarding party onto the *San Nicolas* and then onto the *San Josef* which had come to her aid, capturing both. He was not reprimanded, but neither was he mentioned in the report of the battle, even though of the four Spanish ships taken, he had captured two of them. However, the victory was well received and he was made a Knight of the Bath.

In July 1797, he was personally involved in hand-to-hand fighting off Cadiz in which he twice almost lost his life and then he attempted to capture a large treasure ship, *Principe de Asturias* at Santa Cruz de Tenerife. His attempt failed and, worse still, while he was leading an amphibious assault, he was hit in the right arm by a musketball, leaving him with multiple fractures. On arriving back on his ship, he declared to the surgeon: '...the sooner it is off the better!' The surgeon amputated most of the arm and within thirty minutes, Nelson was back on deck, issuing orders to his men.

He feared the end of his naval career – what use was a one-armed admiral, after all? – but was greeted with a hero's welcome on his return to Spithead on 1 September, and instead of blaming him for the defeat, the public blamed it on the politicians. He was awarded the Freedom of the City of London and an annual pension of £1,000 a year.

Appointed to the command of the seventy-four-gun HMS *Vanguard* in 1798, he went hunting the French once more in the Mediterranean, finding them in August 1798 in Abu Qir Bay off Egypt. He knew that they held a good position and that they were better armed than his fleet. Realising the disadvantageous position in which his fleet found itself, he had earlier said: 'Before this time tomorrow, I shall have gained a peerage or Westminster Abbey.'

He made a surprise attack late in the day and instead of the conventional attack on the centre from the starboard side, the French found themselves being attacked on both sides. At one point, Nelson was hit on the forehead by a piece of French shot and thought he was blinded and dying, but it was only a flap of skin that had fallen over his good eye. He was patched up and immediately returned to the deck. The flagship *L'Orient* was bombarded and exploded. The British had won the Battle of the Nile, a major blow to Napoleon's ambitions in the Middle East as the forces he had brought to Egypt now found themselves stranded. Although the Battle of Trafalgar is better known, many historians regard the Battle of the Nile as Nelson's greatest achievement.

Nelson sailed to Naples where he was enthusiastically welcomed. But during his stay, others noticed the attention he was paying to the ambassador's wife, Emma Hamilton, who was constantly at his side and with whom he had fallen deeply in love. Meanwhile, back in Britain, the news of his victory was greeted with wild scenes of celebration across the country. Church bells rang and victory feasts and balls were held. Nelson was created Baron Nelson of the Nile. He was disappointed, however, having expected to be made a viscount.

The French were making progress in Italy and eventually, Nelson had to evacuate the royal family and the Hamiltons. He also arrested a group of Neapolitan officers who had accepted an amnesty offered by the French and, despite pleas for clemency by the royal family and the Hamiltons, he had the officers executed. For helping his family to escape, King Ferdinand of Naples made him Duke of Bronte.

Nelson was now the senior officer in the Mediterranean but his health was not good and rumours were circulating in London of his relationship with Emma Hamilton. He was ordered to return to port, the Hamiltons accompanying him. On this voyage, he and Emma conceived an illegitimate daughter, Horatia and when he returned home, his wife, Fanny, issued an ultimatum. He had to choose between her and Emma. He never lived with his wife again.

Nelson was promoted to Vice Admiral on 1 January 1801 and

sailed for Denmark with his fleet. On his arrival he urged Admiral Sir Hyde Parker to allow him to make a pre-emptive attack on the Danish fleet that was at harbour in Copenhagen. Permission granted, on 2 April, he advanced on the Danish fleet but things did not initially go well, some of his vessels running aground and all coming under heavy fire from shore batteries. Parker sent a signal, ordering Nelson to withdraw. However, on board HMS *Elephant*, when he was informed of the signal, Nelson turned to his flag captain, Thomas Foley and said: 'You know, Foley, I have only one eye. I have a right to be blind sometimes.' Raising the telescope to his blind eye, he said 'I really do not see the signal.' The battle continued for three hours before Nelson sent a letter to the Danish commander, suggesting a truce. The next day he was given the honour of entering Copenhagen to open negotiations, the result of which was a fourteen-week armistice. Nelson, now commander-in-chief of the Baltic Sea, sailed for England.

He was next detailed to guard the English Channel against invasion by Napoleon before spending time in the company of the Hamiltons following the Peace of Amiens signed between Napoleon and Britain in October 1801. William Hamilton died in 1803 and shortly after, war broke out again between the two countries once again. Nelson returned to sea as commander-in-chief of the Mediterranean on board his flagship, the expensively re-fitted 104-gun HMS *Victory*.

For eighteen months he blockaded the port of Toulon and was promoted to Vice Admiral of the White while still at sea, making him the 6th highest-ranked sailor in the Royal Navy. However, having pursued the French fleet across the Atlantic, he was unable to bring it to battle and returned to England in July 1805, disappointed and fully expecting to face criticism. Again, though, he was warmly welcomed. He spent time with Emma, and prepared plans for an all-out attack on the enemy. He was given command of the fleet blockading the French at Cadiz and left on board *Victory* on 27 September, with enthusiastic crowds lining the quayside.

French commander Pierre-Charles Villeneuve had thirty-three warships and Napoleon had planned for them to sail into the Channel to help in the invasion of Britain. When that had to be abandoned, Napoleon had been disappointed at Villeneuve's reluctance to engage Nelson's fleet. He sent Vice-Admiral François Rosily to relieve him of his command, but Villeneuve slipped out of Cadiz harbour before he arrived, heading west.

At four in the morning of 21 October, Nelson ordered his fleet of twenty-seven ships to battle stations and they turned to face the approaching French fleet. After going below deck to make out his will he returned to give his signals lieutenant one of the most famous messages in British history: 'England confides that every man will do his duty.' The signalman suggested that 'expects' would be a better word than 'confides' and it was quicker to signal. Nelson agreed and the wording was changed.

He then refused the suggestion of the *Victory*'s captain, Thomas Hardy, that he remove the medals from his coat as they made him an obvious target and turned down the offer by Captain Henry Blackwood for his ship, the *Temeraire*, to lead the line rather than the *Victory*. Battle was joined off Cape Trafalgar in southwest Spain.

The *Victory* immediately came under fire and in the first minutes of the battle, Nelson's secretary was killed by a cannonball. Another killed eight marines. When the buckle of Hardy's shoe was dented by a splinter, Nelson observed: 'This is too warm work to last long.'

The *Victory* attacked the French eighty-gunner, the *Bucentaure*, but came under fire from the seventy-four-gun *Redoutable* and the 140-gun *Santisma*. While Nelson and Hardy walked around the deck issuing orders, snipers were constantly firing on them from the rigging of the enemy vessels.

Just after one o'clock, Hardy looked round to find Nelson not at his side but kneeling on the deck, resting on one hand and then falling onto his side. He rushed over to him to find Nelson smiling: 'Hardy, I do believe they have done it at last ... my backbone is shot through.' A sniper's bullet had entered his left shoulder, pierced a lung and come to rest at the base of his spine. He was carried below, still issuing orders, but then placed a handkerchief over his face so as not to cause panic amongst the crew. He was made comfortable and asked to see Hardy, still on deck. He asked him to take care of 'poor Lady Hamilton' and then uttered the famous words: 'Kiss me, Hardy.' Hardy leaned forward and kissed him on the cheek.

At last, he closed his eyes. He died at 4.30 and his last words were recorded as: 'God and my country,' although they were more likely instructions to those trying to ease his pain – 'fan, fan ... rub, rub ... drink, drink.'

DUKE OF WELLINGTON

THE NAPOLEONIC ERA produced many great men, men who are amongst some of the most potent leaders of men the world has ever seen. They fought great and important battles that determined not just the future of their own countries, but the very future of the world. Amongst the greatest of these was Field Marshal Arthur Wellesley, 1st Duke of Wellington whose victories in the Peninsular Wars against the French helped to liberate the Iberian Peninsula from occupation and whose ultimate victory at the Battle of Waterloo brought to an end once and for all the rule of Napoleon Bonaparte.

Wellington was born Arthur Wesley – the family name would later be changed to the ancient spelling Wellesley – probably in Dublin in 1769, the fourth son of Garret Wesley, 1st Earl of Mornington. He studied at a religious seminary in Ireland before being sent to Eton in 1781. His three years there, however, were not adorned with academic glory and that fact, plus the burden of the cost of such an education, led to him being sent to study in Brussels. It was only when he was enrolled at the French Academy of Equitation in Angers that he began to show some distinction. He became an excellent horseman and learned to speak French, a useful skill later when he spent years fighting French armies.

Returning to Ireland, in March 1787, he joined the army as an ensign in the 73rd Regiment of Foot and was given the position of aide-de-camp to the Lord Lieutenant of Ireland, Lord Buckingham. At the end of that year he was promoted to lieutenant and by 1789 he was transferred to the 12th Light Dragoons. He was also elected to the Irish House of Commons as member for the rotten borough of Trim. In 1791 he was promoted to the rank of captain and was transferred to the 18th Light Dragoons.

It was a decisive time in his life. He was interested in a woman, Kitty Pakenham who was the daughter of the Earl of Longford. When he asked for permission to marry her in 1793, her brother, the Earl, turned him down, saying that his prospects were not good enough. Wellesley was devastated and determined to pursue a military career. Borrowing money from his brother, he purchased the rank of lieutenant colonel, a practice that was common in those days.

He saw his first action in 1793 when he was sent Flanders in an allied army led by the Duke of York to invade France. He fought near Breda, not long before the Battle of Boxtel and spent the winter defending the Waal River. It was not a successful campaign, but by the time he returned to England in 1795, he had learned a great deal, especially the importance of having the support of a strong navy. He was horrified by the poor leadership and lack of organisation and resolved never to put himself in such a position.

Declining the position of Surveyor-General of the Ordinance – he had been hoping for Secretary of War – in the new Irish government, he returned to his regiment which was being sent to the West Indies. However, a storm sent their ships back to port and they were sent, instead, to India, Wellesley by this time having been promoted to colonel.

From Calcutta, where he arrived in February 1797, he was sent on a brief expedition to the Philippines before returning to take part in a campaign to expand the territory ruled by the British East India Company. In 1798 fighting broke out in the Fourth Anglo-Mysore War against Tippoo Sultan, Sultan of Mysore. Under orders from his brother, Richard, Lord Mornington, by this time Governor-General of India, he set out with a force to capture Seringapatam, bolstered by 24,000 troops under the command of General George Harris. At the Battle of Malavelly, Wellesley led his men to victory, forcing Tippoo to retreat. The Battle of Srirangapatna was less successful after he was ordered to mount a night attack on the village of Sultanpettah. The attack failed and he lost twenty-five men. He attributed the failure to inadequate daylight reconnoitering of the enemy's fortifications and the darkness that caused considerable confusion amongst his troops.

Several weeks later, however, Seringapatam fell and Tippoo Sultan was killed in the fighting. On entering the city, Wellesley was disappointed to notice discipline amongst his men crumbling as they went on a drunken rampage through the captured city. He put a stop to this ill-discipline by having a number flogged and four hanged.

He was made Governor of Seringapatam and Mysore but, remarkably, was still only thirty years old. He reformed the area's tax and justice systems and dealt with opposition ruthlessly. However, when he defeated one rebel, Doondiah Waugh, who lost his life in the battle, Wellesley promised to pay for the future care of the dead man's son.

His health was not great during this time, due to the hardships of the Indian climate but was cheered by news that he had been promoted to major-general.

He was next sent to lead a force of 24,000 men in the Second Anglo-Maratha war, fighting an army that was vastly superior to his in numbers. He concluded that the only way to defeat the enemy in this case would be to be bold. He captured a Maratha fort on 8 August 1803 and proceeded in pursuit of the main Maratha army. On 23 September, he defeated them brilliantly at the Battle of Assave, having two horses shot out from under him and losing 1,584 of his men to 6,000 losses on the enemy side. He always said it was the best battle he ever fought although the loss of so many men saddened him.

He inflicted another heavy defeat on the Maratha army at Argaum – 5,000 were lost, while the British casualties only amounted to only 361. The war was won.

Wellesley returned to England, much-changed. He had learned a huge amount about the organisation of a fighting army, about tactics and strategy and about the value of intelligence, using scouts and spies.

His dress style, too had changed and he now wore the clothes he would become famous for – white trousers, a dark tunic, Hessian boots and, in particular, a black cocked hat. He was awarded a knighthood.

His circumstances had also changed. In India he had amassed a fortune – around £42,000 – and he was now permitted to marry Kitty Pakenham. They married in April 1806.

Following a junior command of an expedition to Denmark in 1807, he was promoted to lieutenant general. He also entered the British Parliament as MP for Rye in Sussex and then Newport on the Isle of Wight. He was appointed Chief Secretary for Ireland and served for two years, becoming a Privy Counsellor. But military duty soon called again. He had been penciled in to take a force to Venezuela to support the Latin American freedom fighter, Francisco di Miranda, in the fight for the liberation of Venezuela. But Napoleon was reaching the height of his power and had now invaded the Iberian Peninsula. In 1808 Wellesley embarked on the mission that would secure his place in history as one of Britain's greatest generals.

He won a couple of battles almost at once – at Rolica and Vimeiro – but his commanding officer, General Sir Hew Dalrymple, linked his name with a shameful incident, the Convention of Sintra. In this it was stipulated that the Royal Navy would carry the French army out of Lisbon, together with their loot. Wellesley was summoned back to Britain to explain himself, but it emerged that although he had signed the preliminary armistice with the French, he had not signed the Convention. He was cleared of any blame and allowed to return, post-haste, to Portugal.

Meanwhile, the Spanish and the Portuguese were revolting against French rule and Napoleon himself led an army across the border to try to crush the rebellion. At Corunna in January 1809, Britain lost the commander of its forces in Spain, Sir John Moore. However, Wellesley devised a plan for the defense of Portugal and Foreign Minister Lord Castlereagh approved it. He also put Wellesley in command of British forces in Portugal, an army of 26,000 men.

He immediately went on the attack, routing the French at Porto. With a Spanish army added to his force, he then won the Battle of Talavera, as a result of which he was informed that he was being made Viscount Wellington of Talavera and of Wellington.

In 1810, a larger French army invaded Portugal, making many fear that the country would have to be given up and the British force would have to evacuate. However, after halting the French advance at Buçaco, Welleseley had his soldiers secretly construct defensive earthworks known as the Lines of Torres Vedras. With the Royal Navy guarding the flanks, the starving French troops had no option but to retreat after six months. Welleseley's men chased them ingloriously out of Portugal.

He defeated the French again at the Battle of Fuentes de Oñoro and he was promoted to general. He now attacked the Spanish fortresses of Ciudad Rodrigo and Badajoz that controlled the mountain passes leading to Portugal. Following his victory at Badajoz, he broke down as he surveyed the carnage.

In Spain, he defeated a French army of 50,000 at Salamanica – one of the biggest French defeats in recent years – and liberated Madrid. In quick succession, he was made Earl and then Marquess of Wellington and made commander-in-chief of all the allied armies fighting in Spain.

When the French abandoned Andalusia and combined their various armies into a powerful force, Wellington, as he now was, sensing danger, retreated to Portugal. Marshal Soult, commander of the French forces could have attacked with superior numbers, but held back, seemingly in awe of Wellington.

In 1813, using the element of surprise, Wellington moved his army through the hills north of Burgos, suddenly switching his supply line from Portugal to Santander on the northern coast of Spain. He bamboozled the French army under Napoleon's brother, the King of Spain, Joseph Bonaparte, at the Battle of Vitoria, outflanking them and personally leading a feint charge. He was promoted to field marshal and Beethoven wrote a piece of music called *Wellington's Victory*.

A further series of wins – the Pyrenees, Bidassoa and Nivelle – over the French left him free to invade southern France. He had just won at Toulouse when news of Napoleon's abdication arrived. On being told, he is said to have executed a jig, spinning round and snapping his fingers with delight.

He was elevated yet again to Duke of Wellington, and appointed ambassador to France. He took Castelreagh's place at the Congress of Vienna which ended the Napoleonic Wars and sought to re-draw the map of Europe in such a way that peace would ensue. Interestingly, while other wished to punish France, he was keen to allow it to retain its place as one of Europe's major powers.

But, Napoleon was not yet done with Europe, or with Wellington. As the Vienna Conference proceeded, he escaped from the island of Elba to which he had been exiled. Returning to Paris, he re-established control of France and built an army. An alliance, headed by Wellington, was hastily put together, featuring troops from Britain and Prussian troops led by Field Marshal Gebhard Leberecht von Blücher. They met the French army at the little Belgian town of Waterloo.

Napoleon tried and failed to prevent the British and Prussian forces coming together on the battlefield but the well-disciplined and exhaustively trained British and Prussian troops won the day, sending the French army from the field in disarray and then pursuing it all the way back to France.

Later when it was said that the Battle of Waterloo was a messy affair, Wellington replied that his strategy was always very clear. His troops had to maintain their position against everything that Napoleon threw at them and they were then to counter-attack, ending the battle and, at last, the Napoleonic Wars.

Wellington now entered public life, appointed master-General of the Ordinance in 1819 and in 1827 being made Commander-in-Chief of the British Army.

In 1828, he became Prime Minister.

His main concern as leader of the government was that the events of the French Revolution should not be allowed to happen in Britain but he fought against electoral reform throughout his term of office. He became known as the 'Iron Duke' but not because of his determination on the battlefield. Rather, it was because he had to put iron shutters on his residence, Apsley House, to prevent reform demonstrators from smashing his windows.

He was responsible for the controversial Catholic Emancipation Bill that granted almost full civil rights to Catholics. His government fell, however, as a result of his intransigence on reform in 1830, as a wave of riots swept the country – the Swing Riots.

He would briefly be in control of the country again in 1834 when the Tories were brought back to power. Wellington declined to be Prime Minister, but the next in line, Robert Peel, was abroad, in Italy, and Wellington acted as caretaker, performing the roles of most ministers until Peel returned. He then served as Foreign Secretary and Minister Without Portfolio as well as Leader of the House of Lords.

He retired in 1846, aged 77, although still Commander-in Chief of the British armed forces. He enjoyed another brief moment in the spotlight when he helped in the organisation of a force to protect London during Europe's year of revolution, 1848.

He died in 1852 at Walmer Castle, his residence as Lord Warden of the Cinque Ports. His body was transported by train to London where he was given a state funeral, the last heraldic state funeral to be held in Britain. The poet Lord Tennyson wrote an Ode on the Death of the Duke of Wellington and he was buried in St Paul's Cathedral, next to Britain's other hero of the Napoleonic Wars, Horatio Nelson.

NAPOLEON
BONAPARTE

NO BONAPARTE HAD ever been a professional soldier. How incredible, therefore, that Napoleon Bonaparte, born on the island of Corsica on 15 August 1769, should grow up to become one of the greatest military commanders in history and one of the most powerful men of all time.

Born in 1769, he was the second of eight children born to Carlo Buonaparte and his wife Letizia Ramolino, both members of the Corsican-Italian gentry. Carlo had taken part in the struggle for Corsican independence but was a lawyer by trade who had served as a prosecutor and then a judge following the French occupation of the island, eventually being made a count. The young Napoleon benefited from his father's influence as Corsican representative to the court of Louis XVI from 1777, in Paris and received an education at Brienne and at the Ecole Militaire in Paris from which he graduated in 1785, aged 16. He joined the artillery as a second lieutenant.

After the outbreak of the French Revolution, Napoleon returned to Corsica, being appointed lieutenant-colonel in the Corsican national Guard. However, when the Corsicans, taking advantage of the turmoil in Paris, declared independence, he fled with his family to Marseille. There, with the rank of captain, he fought in the siege of the city of Toulon which, with British help, was rebelling against the new French republic. The British were put to flight, Toulon fell and Napoleon was rewarded with promotion to brigadier-general.

In October 1795, Napoleon distinguished himself again when he saved the revolutionary government by dispersing a pro-royalist uprising. He was promoted again, to the command of the Army of the Interior. The following March, he married for the first time, to Josephine de Beauharnais.

In March 1796, Napoleon was sent at the head of a small army to fight a campaign in northern Italy against the Austrians and Sardinians. He defeated the Sardinians and they ceded Savoy and Nice to France and he followed that by besieging Mantua in 1797 and bringing the Austrians there to submission. He created the Cisalpine Republic in north Italy and delighted the French government with the valuable treasures he looted.

In 1798, in order to strike a body-blow at British trade with the east, he invaded and conquered Egypt, controlled at the time by the Ottoman Turks. He and his army were stranded, however, when British Admiral, Horatio Nelson, defeated his fleet, destroying all but two of Napoleon's ships in the Battle of the Nile. He spent his unexpected time there reforming Egyptian law and the government, abolished serfdom and feudalism and guaranteed basic human rights to all Egyptians. He failed to conquer Syria, but won a crushing victory over the Turks at Abkir.

Meanwhile, the European powers formed a new alliance in an effort to stop the French Republic. Great Britain, Austria, Russia, Portugal, Naples, Sicily and the Ottoman Empire lined up against the French. Bonaparte received reports of French defeats by this new grouping and despite having received no orders to do so, decided to return to France.

Back in Paris, in 1799 he joined a *coup d'état* against the government of the Directorate and he and two associates, Jean Jacques Régis de Cambacérès, and Charles-François Lebrun, seized power, establishing a new regime to be known as the Consulate. He was given, as First Consul, almost dictatorial powers and became without question the most powerful person in France. In 1801, he concluded the Concordat with the Catholic Church, designed to make peace with the Vatican after the quarrel that had arisen during the Revolution and to pacify the mostly Catholic population of France. He introduced his Napoleonic Code, considered to be the first successful codification of the law. It guaranteed the rights and liberties won in the Revolution, gave everyone equality before the law and guaranteed freedom of worship. The Napoleonic Code has strongly influenced the legal systems of many countries and historians have described it as one of the few documents to have influenced the whole world. In 1802 the constitution was altered to make him Consul for Life.

In 1800, Napoleon returned to Italy which had been re-conquered by the Austrians while he was in Egypt. He defeated them at the Battle of Marengo and following that victory, his brother, Joseph, led the peace negotiations. However, they did not go well and Napoleon ordered his general, Moreau, to strike again at the Austrians. Moreau defeated them at Hohenlinden and a peace treaty was signed in 1801. French gains were confirmed and increased.

In 1803, Great Britain went to war with the French again on the seas and in 1805, a Third Coalition was formed, comprised of the powers involved in the Second Coalition with the addition of Sweden but without the Ottoman Turks.

Napoleon had been planning an invasion of England at this point, but abandoned that idea and marched his newly formed Grande Armée east to face the Austro-Russian forces who had been lining up to invade France, defeating them at the Battle of Austerlitz on 2 December 1805 and bringing the Third Coalition to an end. However, Nelson defeated the French fleet again, at the Battle of Trafalgar, confirming British control at sea.

By now, he was Emperor. He had uncovered a plot by the Bourbons, the family of the previous monarchs of France and used it to re-establish a hereditary monarchy in France, with him as Emperor. This, he believed, would put an end to any hopes of a Bourbon restoration. He crowned himself Emperor and Josephine Empress on 2 December 1804 at the cathedral of Notre Dame de

Paris. The following May, he was crowned King of Italy with the ancient Iron Crown of Lombardy at Milan Cathedral.

In 1806, he seized the Kingdom of Naples, installing his brother, Joseph, as king. He re-named the Dutch Republic the Kingdom of Holland and made another brother, Louis king. He also amalgamated the German states into the Confederation of the Rhine. When Prussia allied with the Russians to attack the Confederation, Napoleon defeated them at Jena and Auerstadt and, for good measure, he also defeated the Russians at Friedland. New states were added to his huge empire – Westphalia which he gave to his brother, Jerome, the Dutchy of Warsaw and others.

Napoleon loathed the British, famously describing them as 'a nation of shopkeepers' and set out to break the country economically with a blockade of British goods, known as the Continental System. The conquests continued, however, at breathtaking speed. Portugal fell in 1807 and in 1808, he made his brother Joseph King of Spain. However, the Spanish would not take this lying down and a rebellion began that escalated into the Peninsular War. It was a five year-long war of attrition with the British joining in to support the Spanish who fought an arduous guerrilla war against Napoleon's men. It would cost 300,000 French lives and untold fortunes and would contribute a great deal to Napoleon's eventual demise.

Elsewhere in Europe, he was still winning, defeating the Austrians at Wagram in 1809 and annexing the Illyrian Provinces, lands on the north and east coasts of the Adriatic Sea.

By 1810, his empire was at its peak. Into each country he added to the empire, he introduced the Napoleonic Code, abolished feudalism and serfdom and permitted freedom of religion. Each was granted a constitution, universal male suffrage, a parliament and a bill of rights, many of the principles for which the revolutionaries had fought in France. Education was centralised and free public schools were created. Higher education was made available to all who qualified for it. Each state opened an academy or institute for the promotion of the arts and sciences and eminent scholars were given incomes. The people of Europe, long tyrannised by war, taxes and military conscription imposed on them by greedy governments had never had it so good.

He divorced his first wife, Josephine and married the Habsburg Archduchess Marie Louise, daughter of the Emperor of Austria, linking the Bonaparte dynasty with the oldest ruling house in Europe. By doing this, he hoped to gain acceptance for his son, born in 1811, and his descendants.

But the rot had already set in and his disastrous 1812 invasion of Russia spelled the beginning of the end. Russia had allied itself with France but by 1811 relations were decidedly tense. The Tsar, Alexander I was being pressured by the Russian nobles to break off the alliance and when the Continental System blockading British commerce was relaxed in Russia, Napoleon was furious. Russia began to consider invading and re-conquering Poland and advisors were even suggesting to Alexander that he invade France itself. By 1812, 300,000 Russian troops massed on the Polish border.

Napoleon responded by increasing the strength of the Grande Armée from 300,000 to more than 450,000 and he already had 300,000 troops in the Iberian Peninsula. Many told him it would be madness to invade a country as vast and as distant as Russia. He ignored all advice.

The invasion was launched on 23 June 1812 but the Russians cleverly avoided an all-out confrontation with the French, retreating deep into their territory, stretching Napoleon's supply lines and putting his troops in danger of being exposed to the extreme cold of the Russian winter. As the Russians retreated, they made it even more difficult for the French by employing a scorched-earth policy, burning crops and any source of food as they passed. Eventually, close to Moscow, the Russians offered battle. Over 44,000 Russians died in the bloody Battle of Borodino and 35,000 Frenchmen also lost their lives. It was a hard-fought French victory, described thus by Napoleon: 'Of the fifty battles I have fought, the most terrible was that before Moscow. The French showed themselves to be worthy victors, and the Russians can rightly call themselves invincible.'

Napoleon entered Moscow as the Russians retreated beyond it, but the Muscovites torched the city. After a month, Napoleon and his army left, worrying about what might be happening back in France. It was a harrowing retreat through the cold of the Russian winter. Of the 450,000 who had set out on the campaign, fewer than 40,000 returned.

A new coalition – the Sixth – was formed but Napoleon continued to chalk up victories, defeating the Allies at the Battle of Dresden in August 1813. However, the numbers began to tell, especially as Austria and Sweden were now part of the coalition. A force twice the size of the French army cornered it at the Battle of Leipzig in October of that same year, a battle in which 90,000 died. He withdrew to France, vastly outnumbered and surrounded by his enemies. Paris fell to the Allies in March 1814 and, as his generals began to mutiny, Napoleon decided to abdicate in favour of his son. This was unacceptable to the Allies, however, who would understandably accept nothing less than unconditional surrender. Five days later he abdicated unconditionally.

He was exiled to the island of Elba, an island in the Mediterranean, twenty kilometres off the Italian coast, being given sovereignty over the island and allowed to retain the title of Emperor. Humiliated, he had tried to poison himself but the pill he took had weakened and he survived.

Meanwhile, in France, the Bourbons were restored, in the shape of Louis XVIII. Napoleon, cut off from his wife and son who were under Austrian control, short of money as his allowance had been stopped and aware that he was going to be exiled in an even more remote location in the Atlantic, escaped from Elba on 26 February 1815, landing two days later on the French mainland.

A regiment of French soldiers had been sent to intercept him, but he approached them alone on horseback, dismounted and shouted 'Here I am. Kill your Emperor if you wish.' The reply from the soldiers was 'Vive l'Empereur!' and one of the most extraordinary adventures in history began. They marched with him to Paris where he picked up the reins of government once more. He would govern for another hundred days. The Allies, meeting at the Congress of Vienna, to redraw the map of Europe after the years of war, declared him an outlaw and determined to raise an army of 150,000 men to end his regime once and for all. He, too, was assembling an army and by the beginning of June, he had 200,000 men ready to do battle.

He went on the offensive, in the hope of driving a wedge between the British and Prussian armies of Wellington and Von Blücher. But when they met at Waterloo on 18 June 1815, he was comprehensively defeated, the British troops withstanding repeated attacks by the French and the Prussians breaking through Napoleon's right flank. The French troops were driven from the battlefield in total disarray and the Coalition forces entered France once more to restore Louis XVIII to the throne.

After considering an escape to the United States, Napoleon surrendered off the port of Rochefort to the British Captain Frederick Maitland on board HMS *Bellerophon* on 15 July.

This time there was no escape from his exile. St Helena was situated in the middle of the Atlantic Ocean, a remote rocky outcrop 2,000 kilometres from the nearest land. Napoleon lived there in Longwood House until his death in May 1821.

SIMÓN BOLÍVAR

IS THERE A historical figure more celebrated in statues, street names and squares than Simón José Antonio de la Santísima Trinidad Bolívar Palacios y Blanco? He is more commonly known as Simón Bolívar, one of the most important leaders of Spanish America's struggle for independence from Spain.

He was born in Caracas on 24 July 1783 to a well-to-do family of Basque origin who had arrived in Venezuela in the 16th century and whose wealth had derived from gold, silver and copper mining. The income from mining would prove useful to Bolívar later in life as he tried to finance his revolutionary wars. The young Símon was given an excellent education, soaking up the thoughts of the thinkers of the Enlightenment as well as learning about classical Greece and Rome.

However, by the age of nine, both his parents had died and he was looked after by an uncle, Don Carlos Palacios. Aged fourteen, he joined the White Militia in the Aragua Valley, a detachment that had been commanded by his late father. It was here that he first underwent some practical military training, rising to second lieutenant within a year. Meanwhile, at an academy established in Caracas by the Capuchin monk, Francisco de Andujar, he studied mathematics, topographic design and other subjects. In 1799, his uncle sent his young ward to Spain with a friend, Esteban Escobar to further his education. At fifteen, he was already a passionate advocate of Spanish American liberation, as the Viceroy of New Spain was alarmed to discover when he met the boy en route in Mexico City.

In Spain, he received the education of a young gentleman with a bright future ahead of him and he threw himself wholeheartedly into his studies. Furthering his knowledge of academic subjects, he was also taught fencing and how to dance. He also enjoyed a busy social life, attending parties and social gatherings.

Bolívar returned to Venezuela in 1803 with Maria Teresa Rodríguez del Toro y Alaysa whom he had married in Madrid the previous year. Tragically, however, his new young wife contracted yellow fever and died soon after arriving in Venezuela. He was devastated and vowed never to marry again. He never did.

He returned to Europe the following year with another friend, Simón Rodríguez. who was also his tutor, ending up in Paris. It was a momentous time in Europe as it underwent great political change. Napoleon Bonaparte was proclaimed Emperor of France that year and was then crowned King of Italy. Like many, however, Bolívar believed that the Corsican had betrayed the ideals of the French Revolution and lost all respect for him. His own ideals were intact, however, and he is said to have affirmed them by vowing on top of the Aventine Hill, one of Rome's famous seven hills never to rest until America was free from the Spanish. Meanwhile, he continued to mix a frenetic social life with attendance at conferences and courses.

In 1807, after a brief visit to the United States, he returned home. By this time Napoleon had installed his brother, Joseph on the Spanish throne and the great powers were lining up to fight the Peninsular War. In South America, resistance to the new power took the form of regional juntas, or committees, and people became restless. Bolívar was right in the centre of things. He was aware that the adventurer and revolutionary, Francisco de Miranda, was beginning the struggle to liberate his own country, Venezuela, and he wanted to be part of it.

The Caracas junta declared independence from Spain in 1810 and Bolívar was sent with two others on a diplomatic mission to England to obtain British recognition and, if possible, aid. Returning in 1811, he delivered a passionate speech in favour of independence to the Patriotic Society in Caracas. In July 1811 Venezuela was declared a republic with de Miranda as leader and its new flag was raised in

Caracas. Bolívar, meanwhile, had entered military service, rising to the rank of colonel and seeing action in Miranda's raid on the city of Valencia in Venezuela.

Things went badly wrong, however. In breaking from Spain, Venezuela had lost its main market for its principal export, cocoa, precipitating a serious economic crisis. Then, on 26 March 1812, a major earthquake struck the country that not only killed many people but was also interpreted as a sign that the revolution was doomed. It did not help that it happened on Maundy Thursday, the anniversary of the founding of the Caracas junta. The country swung back to the royalists. Bolívar was disappointed when Puerto Cabello, a town under his command, fell. When Miranda attempted to flee on a British warship, having concluded an armistice with the Spanish, Bolívar and others declared that his action was treasonable, arrested him and handed him over to the Spanish. Bolívar apparently had to be prevented from shooting Miranda. Nonetheless, his surrender of the former leader of the revolution allowed him to negotiate his escape.

He fled to Cartagena de Indias in New Granada – present-day Colombia – where he wrote the famous Cartagena Manifesto, in which he detailed why he thought the Venezuelan First Republic had failed. He also demanded that New Granada should help in the liberation of his country. The Congress of New Granada agreed and in May 1813 he led an invasion of Venezuela, launching the famous Admirable Campaign. Leading a small army, he took the city of Cúcuta and began the liberation which would take a mere three months to accomplish.

He entered Mérida on 23 May and occupied Trujillo on 9 June where he was welcomed as *El Libertador*. On 15 June, he issued his Decree of War to the Death which permitted murder and atrocities to be commited against the Spanish, other than those actively assisting South American independence. It exonerated Latin Americans who had already committed such murders and atrocities.

His home city of Caracas was captured on August 6 and the

Second Republic was proclaimed. The following year, however, the royalist, José Tomás Boves, led a counter-revolution in which he displayed particular brutality towards those who had supported Bolívar. *El Libertador* left the country, returning to New Granada.

His revolutionary work was far from over, however. He took command of a Colombian nationalist force and captured Bogota in 1814. He was unable to take his revolution further, however, when he fell out with the government of Caratgena and was forced to flee. He spent the months from May to December of 1918 in Jamaica where he wrote his Jamaica Letter that presciently analysed the past, present and future of the continent. There was much to consider. Napoleon had finally been defeated in Europe and with the menace at home dispensed with, a large Spanish army, led by General Pablo Morillo had landed in Venezuela, giving encouragement to the royalists.

Bolívar moved to newly independent Haiti, having first avoided an assassination attempt. There, he met Alexandre Pétion, leader of the country and enlisted his help.

Accompanied by Haitian soldiers Bolívar landed in Venezuaela in 1817. He took Carúpano, on 2 June granting liberty to the slaves held there. The expedition advanced to the port of Ocumare de la Costa where Bolívar was accidentally separated from his army and was forced to return to Haiti. Undaunted, he put together a second force and arrived on the island of Margarita, off the Venezuelan coast.

Crossing to the mainland, his objective was to capture Guayana Province and use it as a base for the liberation of the remainder of the country. He took the capital, Angostura and organised the state, creating all the apparatus to enable it to be run properly. He encouraged sympathy for his cause when he issued the decree, 'The law of Distribution of National Property'. In 1818 he set out to complete the liberation of Venezuela, surprising the royalist force under General Morillo in the city of Calabozo. Then his troops were defeated near Semen and he narrowly escaped death at the hands of the royalists. He returned to Angostura on 5 June. By now his force was being bolstered by European volunteers, eager to seize a chance to to fight for liberty, and he also enjoyed the tacit support of the United States. He was elected president of the Second Republic of Venezuela.

At the Second Venezuelan Congress, held in Angostura on 15 February 1819, he delivered a famous speech in which he said: 'We are not Europeans; we are not Indians; we are but a mixed species of aborigines and Spaniards. Americans by birth and Europeans by law, we find ourselves engaged in a dual conflict: we are disputing with the natives for titles of ownership, and at the same time we are struggling to maintain ourselves in the country that gave us birth against the opposition of the invaders.'

This conference also created the federation of Gran Colombia, comprising territory covered by modern-day Venezuela, Colombia, Ecuador and Panama. Símon Bolívar was named president of that, too. On 7 August 1819, Bolívar won an important victory at the Battle of Boyacá. New Granada was now liberated and the federation of Gran Colombia was confirmed, Now, all of the northern part of South America was free of Spanish rule.

His next target was Peru which had been partially liberated from the Spanish by the Argentine General José de San Martín. Bolívar marched his army of the revolution across the Andes and set about freeing the remainder of the country. San Martin returned to Argentina while Bolívar prepared for the fight against the Spanish in their last Latin American stronghold. In September 1823, he arrived in Lima and began his preparations. He was named Dictator of Peru on 10 February 1824, giving him the power to reorganise the country's political system and its army. In August, he defeated the Spaniards at Junín and they also lost heavily at Ayacucho in December. Spain's centuries-long grip on South America was over.

The following August, the Congress of Upper Peru announced the founding of the Republic of Bolivia, named in honour of its liberator,

Símon Bolívar. He became one of the few men in history to have a country named after him.

In the meantime, he was finding it very difficult to maintain control of the unwieldy Gran Colombia federation. Personal rivalry amongst the generals coupled with civil wars eroded the unity for which Bolívar had worked so hard. There was a growing sense of dissatisfaction and there were uprisings in a number of places. He hoped to put it right at a constitutional convention held in Ocaña in 1828.

In order to preserve and strengthen his dream of a federation based on the one created by the American Revolution where the liberty of the individual was paramount, he had to develop a different mode of government. The conference failed to resolve the problems, however, and Bolívar, struggling with illness, had no option but to proclaim himself dictator on 27 August 1828, a measure he hoped would be merely temporary while he re-established his authority. It was unpopular, however, causing anger amongst his opponents, one of whom tried to assassinate him towards the end of September.

Things did not improve and in the next two years there were uprisings in New Granada, Venezuela and Ecuador. Eventually, it proved too much and he resigned on 27 April 1830. His plan was to travel to Europe and possibly live in France but he would not live long enough to set sail. The tuberculosis from which he had been suffering, killed him on 17 December in the Quinta de San Pedro Alejandrino in Santa Marta, Gran Colombia. He was buried in Santa Marta, but in 1842 his remains were moved to a monument in the Pantéon Nacional in Caracas.

QUEEN VICTORIA

THEY CALLED HER the 'Grandmother of Europe' because she arranged the marriages of her nine children and forty-two grandchildren across the continent, stitching together the royal families of the continent. More than that, though, she was queen of a United Kingdom that really did rule the world. The Industrial Revolution – with its astonishing social, economic and technological advances – had begun in Britain and during Victoria's time on the throne, it reached its zenith, the nation reaping the financial rewards gained from being the 'workshop of the world'.

In 1817, on the death of the heir to the throne, George III's only legitimate grandchild, Princess Charlotte Augusta of Wales, there was a scramble amongst the king's twelve surviving children to marry and father children to secure the succession to the throne. George's younger sons had thought that they had little chance of making an appearance in the line of succession and had, consequently, shown little interest in marriage until then.

One of them, the Duke of Kent was fifty years old, but swiftly married a widow, Princess Victoria of Saxe-Coburg-Saalfeld and just as swiftly, she gave birth to a daughter, Alexandrine Victoria, born in Kensington Palace on 24 May 1819. She became fifth in line to the throne of Britain behind her father's three older brothers and her father.

Baptised in June of that year, she had illustrious godparents – the Prince Regent, her paternal uncle, her fourth cousin, Tsar Alexander I, whose name George III had insisted she be given as her first, 'Alexandrine', and the Dowager Duchess of Saxe-Coburg-Saalfeld, who was her maternal grandmother. Formally titled Princess Victoria of Kent, she was known at home as 'Drina'.

254

The choice of the name 'Victoria' was made by the Prince Regent who would later become George IV. 'Elizabeth' had been suggested by the future William IV and there was criticism of the name 'Victoria', that it was not English enough for a future queen. However, the Duchess of Kent dug her heels in and refused to change the name. By now, anyway, it had become popular in the press.

Her background was entirely German and German was her first language. However, she also learned English and French and could speak equally as well in any of the three languages.

Eight months after her birth, her father died following a short illness. Six days later, King George III, her grandfather died. The Prince Regent took the throne as King George IV.

In 1830 George IV's heavy drinking and indulgent lifestyle finally caught up with him. Having no surviving children, the throne should have passed to his brother, Prince Frederick, Duke of York and Albany, but he had died, leaving no children and yet another brother, Prince William, Duke of Clarence became King William IV. Incredibly, King William had ten surviving children with his mistress, the actress Dorothy Jordan, but none with his wife. Suddenly, the young Queen Victoria found herself heir presumptive to the British throne.

Following the death of Victoria's father, her mother, the Duchess of Kent, had formed a close relationship with Sir John Conroy, an Irish soldier and adventurer who served as Comptroller for the Duchess's household. Some even suggested that he was actually Victoria's natural father, but this is now thought to be highly unlikely. Victoria, nonetheless, had a very bad relationship with Conroy who treated her as his daughter. Her principle concern about him was that she believed that he wished to become the power behind the throne if she were to become queen before she turned eighteen, when her mother would have to act as regent. Fortunately, however, William IV died aged seventy-one of heart failure, twenty-seven weeks after she had reached her majority at which point she banished Conroy from the court although she could not, of course, banish him from her mother's household. She did award him a baronetcy and a pension a few months after she assumed the throne, however. Ungrateful to the end, he was disappointed, believing that he should have been given an earldom.

Victoria was crowned Queen at Westminster Abbey on 18 May 1837 and she became the first monarch to take up residence at Buckingham Palace in London. Interestingly, although she could inherit the throne of the United Kingdom, in Hanover Salic law it stated that no woman could ever be monarch. The throne of Hanover passed, therefore, to her uncle, the Duke of Cumberland and Teviotdale, the eighth child of George III, who reigned as Ernest Augustus I.

Victoria would have ten Prime Ministers during her time on the throne, but there is little doubt that the one she liked best was the first, the Whig, Lord Melbourne. Fifty-eight years of age and a widower, he and Victoria got on very well, to the extent that there were rumours that she was even considering marriage to him. He became a close political adviser and it was estimated that he often spent six hours a day with the young queen. He even had an apartment at Windsor Castle. It was considered unseemly in some quarters and sometimes when she was on a royal visit she would hear some members of the crowd shouting out 'Mrs. Melbourne'.

Melbourne would, however, not remain in office for long. He was having difficulties with the British colonies and was forced to resign in 1839 when the Tories and the Radicals opposed him on a bill to suspend the Jamaican Constitution.

Victoria asked the Tory, Sir Robert Peel to form a government, but a farcical row blew up that would become known as the Bedchamber Crisis. It was the custom of the time for the Prime Minister to appoint members of the Royal Household and, naturally, people would be employed purely on their party loyalties. Victoria's Ladies of the Bedchamber were, of course, all the wives of prominent Whigs and Peel wanted to replace them with the wives of prominent Tories.

QUEEN BOUDICCA (or BOUDICEA)

A statue of Queen Boudicca of the Iceni, standing on her chariot in Hyde Park, London. Today, Boudicca is revered as a great leader, a hero of ancient Britain.

ALFRED THE GREAT

Alfred the Great, (c.849–901), was King of Wessex from 871.
Alfred was given the title 'Great' because not only was he a great
military leader but an able administrator and a ruler with foresight.

SIR FRANCIS DRAKE

Sir Francis Drake (1540–1596) was an English admiral and the first English sailor to reach the Pacific Ocean. He circumnavigated the globe and preyed successfully on Spanish shipping. Sir Francis Drake definitely comes under the classification of a great leader, as he frequently inspired his men to face great difficulties.

GEORGE WASHINGTON

George Washington was such a monumental figure that his name is still everywhere. His face adorns the dollar bill and the 25 cents coin. He has twenty-six mountains named after him, as well as 740 schools, a dozen colleges and universities, 155 towns and counties, various bridges, parks and forts; not to mention an entire state of the union and the very capital of the country he did so much to found. Above is his bust in Mount Rushmore National Memorial in South Dakota, USA.

KARL MARX

Karl Marx was considered to be the father of the communist revolution. He was an enormously influential revolutionary thinker and philosopher, but unfortunately did not live to see his ideas carried out.

EMMELINE PANKHURST

Emmeline Pankhurst was founder of the Women's Political and Social Union and England's most famous suffrage leader. Pankhurst and her three daughters, Christabel, Sylvia and Adela, gained the adulation of Edwardian society in their direction of the militant suffragette campaigns of 1905–1914.

EVA PERÓN

Eva Perón was the second wife and political partner of President Juan Perón of Argentina. She was also an important political figure in her own right, and is remembered for her campaign for female suffrage, her support of organised labour groups and her organisation of a vast social welfare programme that benefitted and gained the support of the lower classes.

HO CHI MINH

Ho Chi Minh worked single-mindedly for more than fifty years to realise the end of a French colonialism and built up a Vietnamese national state. It was his determination, rather than his genius, that was this man's hallmark as a leader.

Victoria, however, baulked at this idea and forbade him to do it. These ladies had become her friends. Ridiculously, Peel resigned over the matter, returning Melbourne to office.

Victoria first met her future husband, Prince Albert of Saxe-Coburg and Gotha in 1836 when she was aged seventeen. When she met him again a year later, she was much taken with him. '…dear Albert…' she wrote, 'He is so sensible, so kind, and so good, and so amiable too. He has besides, the most pleasing and delightful exterior and appearance you can possibly see.' He was, in fact, her first cousin, his father being her mother's brother.

Being a monarch, she had to propose to him and they were married on 10 February 1840 in the Chapel Royal of St James's Palace. Albert would become an important adviser to her as well as her husband replacing, somewhat, the influence of Melbourne. They would have nine children over the course of the next eighteen years.

Melbourne had been reluctant to involve Victoria in social matters, even instructing her not to read Charles Dickens' Oliver Twist to spare her blushes about the deprivations of modern British life endured by many of her subjects. Albert, was different, however, inviting, for instance, the Earl of Shaftesbury, the English politician and philanthropist, one of whose chief interests was the welfare of children, to come to Buckingham Palace to discuss his findings about child labour in Britain.

While she was pregnant for the first time, in 1840, Victoria experienced the first of a number of attempts on her life. Eighteen-year-old Edward Oxford tried to shoot her while she drove in a carriage with Prince Albert. Neither she nor Albert was injured and their first child, a daughter also named Victoria, was born in November 1840. However, this assassination attempt was merely the first of a number. On 29 May 1842, John Francis fired a gun at her and missed as she again rode in a carriage and just over a month later, John William bean tried to shoot her but was found to be using a gun filled with paper and tobacco. Although all of the assassins' sentences were commuted, the punishment for attempting to assassinate the monarch was death. Albert felt that this was too harsh, especially in the case of Bean's pathetic attempt and he lobbied Parliament to reduce the mandatory sentence to seven years imprisonment and flogging.

In the meantime, he and the Queen had made their first journey by train in a special carriage created by the Great Western Railway from Slough, near Windsor Castle to Bishop's Bridge in London. Accompanying them was the engineer of the Great Western Line, none other than Isambard Kingdom Brunel. However, both the Queen and her husband complained that the train was travelling too fast when it achieved a speed of twenty miles per hour and feared that it would be derailed.

Victoria fared better with Sir Robert Peel during his second term as Prime Minister and she also enjoyed a good relationship with Lord John Russell who succeeded Peel. However, she disliked intensely the fourth Prime Minister of her reign, Lord Palmerston. The two disagreed about British foreign policy, Palmerston believing that the main objective for a British government should be to increase Britain's power in the world. Victoria and Albert, on the other hand, did not believe that foreign governments should be humiliated or weakened to achieve this. His habit of sending official dispatches to foreign governments without her knowledge also greatly irritated her. Furthermore, she also found some of Palmerston's behaviour distasteful, especially when he attempted to seduce one of her ladies-in-waiting, Lady Dacre, while staying as a guest at Windsor Castle. She would have had him thrown out of office had Melbourne not intervened to save him.

In 1850, however, she did ask Lord John Russell to dismiss Palmerston, a request that Russell informed her he could not comply with as Palmerston was very popular with Members of Parliament. When Palmerston congratulated Louis Napoleon Bonaparte on his coup in France, however, Russell finally accepted Victoria's advice and dismissed him from office.

In 1855, Palmerston was back in power and this time Victoria tried to co-exist with him. It was not easy. 'We had,' she wrote, 'God knows! Terrible trouble with him about foreign affairs. Still, as Prime Minister he managed affairs at home well, and behaved to me well. But I never liked him.'

Potential assassins had been on the streets of London again and in 1849, an unemployed Irishman fired at her carriage on Constitution Hill, while in 1850, she was slightly injured when she was assaulted by an ex-army officer, Robert Pate. Pate struck her on the head with his cane as her carriage passed him.

Although Victoria loved Ireland and donated £2,000 for the relief of Irish people starving as a result of the potato famine, she refused to establish a royal residence there and then would not visit Ireland because the Dublin Corporation had refused to congratulate her son, the Prince of Wales on his marriage and the birth of his son. It did no good to the British or the monarchy's cause in Ireland and her appeal there diminished greatly as her reign progressed.

When Prince Albert tragically died of typhoid on 14 December 1861, Victoria was devastated. A widow at forty-three, she responded by withdrawing entirely from public view, spending the majority of her time at her beloved Scottish retreat, Balmoral, in the company of a Scottish servant, John Brown. There were even rumours that she had secretly married Brown. People became angry at such rumours and also at the fact that she declined all public appearances and would not even come south to open Parliament. Radical MPs in the House of Commons asked whether the British people were getting their money's worth out of the Queen and began to speak in favour of abolishing the monarchy and making Britain a republic.

Victoria disliked William Gladstone's liberalising politics when he became Prime Minister in 1868. She was much happier with the more conservative policies of the Tory, Benjamin Disraeli, who came to power in 1874, and considered him to be a much more charming man. Disaraeli would later say, however, 'Everyone likes flattery, and when you come to royalty, you should lay it on with a trowel.'

When Gladstone returned to office in 1880, she was disappointed and was opposed to his foreign policy, especially his failure to take action to relieve general Gordon at Khartoum. The relationship between the two became even frostier when he discovered that she had been passing confidential government documents to the leader of the Conservatives, the Marquess of Salisbury who would be the final Prime Minister of her reign.

Queen Victoria celebrated her Diamond Jubilee in 1897, having surpassed George III as the longest-reigning monarch in British history on 22 September 1896. The entire British Empire celebrated her achievement and the procession included troops from every colony and dominion. A service of thanksgiving was held outside St Paul's Cathedral but the Queen did not emerge from her carriage throughout, dressed in her customary mourning dress, trimmed with white lace.

On Tuesday 22 January 1901, she died, aged eighty-one, of a cerebral hemorrhage at Osborne House on the Isle of Wight where she had spent every Christmas since the death of Prince Albert. Around her were her son, the future King Edward VII and her eldest grandson, the German Emperor, Wilhelm II.

Strangely for someone who dressed in the black of mourning for some forty years, she hated black funerals and, consequently, London was dressed up in purple and white to mark her passing. She was laid to rest beside her beloved Prince Albert in Frogmore Mausoleum in Windsor Great Park and had reigned for a staggering sixty-three years and seven months.

JESSE JAMES

As is usually the case with outlaws, there are two opposing camps when the career of Jesse Woodson James is discussed. To some he is a handsome folk-hero who represented the pioneering values of the Old West against the growing industrialisation of the late 19th century that was threatening the old farming way of life. To others, he was a champion of the last vestiges of the Confederate states who had lost the American Civil War. Many, however, would describe him as a ruthless killer and bank robber; an uneducated, unprincipled hoodlum who killed at least half-a-dozen men in his lifetime and created mayhem and fear wherever he and his gang of equally vicious associates went. He led his men in dozens of daring robberies during a thrill-packed sixteen-year period before dying at the hands of a member of his own gang, the cowardly Robert Ford.

Was he the Robin Hood figure he is often portrayed to have been? He is said to have always been prepared to help out another cowboy down on his luck and only rarely did he rob the passengers on the trains he was robbing. Even when he resorted to that, it was said to be only because the spoils were so poor in the safes they blew up. However, it is reported he always checked the hands of the people he was robbing. If they displayed the calluses of a working man, he would leave them and their wallets alone.

It is easy to see why his reputation is different to almost any other outlaw of those times. Newspapers found in him a hero of the little man, ground down by the stiff mortgages he had to pay the banks for his property. Crowds would turn up at his robberies as if they were attending a festival or an event and James and his gang would ride in and leave the scene like a rock band leaving a stadium where they have just played a rousing gig.

Born in Clay County, Missouri in 1847, Jesse James had a good start in life in spite of the fact that his father, Robert, a farmer and a Baptist minister died when Jesse was only three years old. His mother, Zerelda remarried twice, the second time to a doctor, Reuben Samuel, in 1855.

America was devastated by the outbreak of civil war in 1861 following the attempt by the southern, Confederate states to secede from the Union. In Jesse's native Missouri, pro- and anti-slavery factions stalked the land, committing atrocities in the name of their beliefs. Jesse's older brother, eighteen-year-old Frank was caught up in the fever and joined the Confederate army, riding with Quantrill's Raiders, a loosely organised Confederate gang.

Jesse, just fourteen at the outbreak of hostilities, remained at home, working on his step-father's farm. In 1863, however, the farm was raided by a group of Union troops who set fire to all of its buildings because they had heard that Frank was fighting on the other side. Jesse protested, but received a savage beating for his trouble. They tried to hang Dr. Samuels, but he survived their attack.

As soon as he reached the age of seventeen, Jesse went to war, signing up with the notorious guerrilla unit led by 'Bloody Bill' Anderson. Anderson was the most-feared Confederate leader, renowned for the brutality and lack of mercy he displayed towards captured and defeated Union soldiers. Jesse himself suffered some brutal treatment at the end of the war when he was shot and badly wounded as he tried to surrender. The woman who nursed him back to health – his cousin, named Zerelda after his mother – would later become his wife but only after a nine-year courtship.

The end of the war left many former combatants finding it difficult to adjust to civilian life. Often, criminality was their only option in a country that had been torn apart by terrible strife for four years. Jesse and Frank teamed up with a gang of men led by Archie Clement, another ruthless former Confederate guerrilla leader, described by one Union soldier as Bill Anderson's 'scalper and head devil'. At a little over five feet tall, Clement was known as 'Little Arch' and had taken over from Bloody Bill when he had been killed in an ambush. Just over a year after the end of the Civil War, Clement led Jesse and Frank James and others in the first post-war bank robbery at the Clay County Savings Association in Liberty, Missouri. They got away with a massive $58,000 in cash and bonds. During the robbery, however, Jesse shot and killed an innocent bystander. He claimed afterwards that the only reason he had taken part was to get back the deeds to his family's land, held at the Clay County Savings Association.

Shortly after, they hit the Alexander Mitchell Bank in Lexington and many more followed. However, it would be an 1868 robbery that would make Jesse's reputation.

They hit a bank in 1869 in Gallatin, Missouri, where they believed that Bloody Bill's killer, a man named Cox worked as a cashier. It transpired that they were wrong, but, unaware of this, Jesse shot the man dead. This episode was written about by the editor of the Kansas City Times, John Newman Edwards, who was a Confederate sympathiser and who would continue to write supportive articles about him and publish letters from him throughout his career. He became the catalyst for Jesse's fame.

The Younger brothers – Cole, Bob and Jim – had also fought on the Confederate side in the war. Cole Younger had signed up after his father had been murdered by Union troops under a commanding officer who claimed he owed him money. He had ridden with Quantrill and participated in the massacre of 200 men and boys at Lawrence, Kansas. Along with his brothers, he had joined up with Little Arch after the war. Frank and Jesse joined forces with the Youngers and the James-Younger Gang robbed its way across the West. They began with stagecoaches and banks before graduating to trains in 1873. Crowds often gathered to watch these spectacles and the outlaws hammed it up as they carried out their robberies. On 9

April 1874, they robbed a stagecoach near Lexington with a huge crowd of hundreds of spectators watching the action from across the Missouri river.

Even the strongest force for law and order, the Pinkerton Detective Agency could not tame the James-Younger boys. Founded in 1850, by a Scottish immigrant, Allan Pinkerton, the Pinkertons had made their name when they foiled a plot to assassinate President Lincoln. Lincoln subsequently employed Pinkerton's agents as his personal bodyguards during the Civil War when his life was constantly under threat. The agency's motto was 'We Never Sleep'. However, agents sent to infiltrate the James-Younger Gang or follow their movements, inevitably turned up dead. John Younger was fatally wounded in a gunfight with them in March 1874.

Missouri Governor, Silas Woodson was seriously embarrassed by the inability of even the Pinkerton agency to stop the gang and put a massive reward of $2,000 on their heads. He also persuaded the state legislature to give him $10,000 to fund a hunt for the gang. Meanwhile, Jesse and the boys were undaunted, netting $30,000 from a train they held up near Muncie in Kansas.

Allen Pinkerton took the loss of his agents personally, leading a raid on the James family farm in January 1875. An incendiary device was thrown into the farmhouse, killing Jesse and Frank's nine-year-old brother and blowing off their mother's arm. The Pinkertons were too late, however. The gang had left the farm earlier that day. Several months later, Daniel Askew, a neighbour who had let the Pinkertons use his farm as a base for the raid, was gunned down by an unknown gunman. Jesse and Frank moved to Nashville in order to ensure their mother's future safety and from there, Jesse wrote numerous letters to the newspapers, making his political views clear.

The Northfield, Minnesota bank robbery, although the most famous in the James-Younger Gang's career and one of the most famous in US criminal history would also set the scene for the demise of the gang. Once again it had political overtones, the

Northfield Bank having connections with two prominent Union generals and politicians – Benjamin Butler and Adelbert Ames.

The gang, consisting at the time of Frank and Jesse, accompanied by Cole, Jim and Bob Younger, Charlie Pitts, Clell Miller and Bill Chadwell travelled by train to Minneapolis at the beginning of September 1876. On arrival, they split into two groups, one going to the town of Mankato on one side of Northfield, the other heading for Red Wing on the other side. They bought horses and began to plan the robbery, scouting out the land around the town.

At two in the afternoon of 7 September, three of them entered the bank, the remaining five standing guard on the street outside. Word quickly spread that a robbery was in progress and a number of armed local men gathered and opened fire on the outlaws in the street. Miller and Chadwell were killed and the Youngers were wounded. One of the local men was also shot dead. Meanwhile, inside the bank, cashier Joseph Lee Haywood, having refused to open the safe, was gunned down.

The remnants of the gang fled on horseback, hiding themselves in nearby woods. After several days of dodging posses and road blocks, they had only succeeded in getting a few miles away from Northfield and they decided to split up. The Younger brothers failed to make it, though, and were eventually captured near Madelia, Minnesota. Jesse and Frank, however, succeeded in getting back to Missouri. It was the end of the road for the James-Younger Gang.

For the next three years, Jesse and Frank lived quietly in Nashville, Frank adapting easily to his new life, but Jesse finding it more difficult. By 1879, he was ready to return to his old life, assembling a new gang and launching a wave of robberies in Alabama, Kentucky and Missouri. In October 1879, they held up the Chicago and Alton Railroad, getting away with $40,000. In September 1880, they robbed a Wells Fargo Stagecoach in Kentucky and, shortly afterwards, a paymaster's office in Muscle Shoals, Alabama. The Seton Bank in Riverton, Iowa, brought them a $5,000 haul.

Jesse's fame spread and dime novels took it even further, telling amazing stories about him. The newspapers, meanwhile, lionised him and were in awe of his audacity. He grew a beard to enhance his image. One day in 1881, when they yet again hit the Chicago and Alton train, the safe yielded only a paltry amount of cash. For only the second time in his outlaw career, Jesse ordered his men to rob the passengers of their jewellery and wallets. Meanwhile, he walked through the train, the only member of the gang not concealing his identity with a mask and introduced himself to the astonished passengers.

There was a new Governor of Missouri, Thomas T. Crittendon, and he was determined to bring Jesse James's reign of terror to an end. He persuaded the railroads to stump up a reward of $10,000 – an unheard of amount – for the capture, dead or alive, of the James brothers. The law started to close in on them and various members of the gang were arrested or shot until, by 1882, there were only three of them left; Jesse and two brothers, twenty-year-old Robert and twenty-five-year-old Charley Ford. Jesse was not to know, however, that there was a traitor in their midst. Robert Ford had arranged a meeting with Governor Crittendon at which he had made a deal to kill Jesse in exchange for immunity and the $10,000 reward.

On April 3 that year, the two brothers were visiting Jesse who was living in Virginia under the name of Howard. While Jesse's wife was busy in the kitchen and his children played outside, the three men made plans for the robbery of the Platte County Bank. Jesse had removed his jacket because it was a hot day and had also taken off his gun belt in order not to arouse suspicion.

Suddenly, he noticed that a picture on the wall of the house was not straight. He pulled up a stool and stood on it in order to straighten it. As he did so, Robert Ford seized his chance, jumping to his feet, pulling out his revolver and shooting Jesse from a range of about four feet. The first bullet hit him in the neck, just below his ear, and he was hit by another three that Ford fired, to make sure. The stool toppled over and Jesse James crashed to the ground, dead.

Five months after his brother's death, Frank James, tired of being on the run, surrendered to Governor Crittendon. They tried him but found him not guilty and he lived the rest of his life a free man, working in a variety of jobs; he was a shoe salesman and then a theater guard in St. Louis; he was an AT&T Telegraph operator in St Joseph, Missouri, and he worked the lecture circuit with his old comrade, Cole Younger. In 1902, he became betting commissioner at the Fair Grounds Race Track in New Orleans and towards the end of his life, he lived on the James Farm, giving tours for twenty-five cents. He died in 1915, aged seventy-two.

The Ford brothers did not live such happy lives. Charley shot himself several years later while Robert bought a saloon in Colorado. He had to live with the words of a popular song ringing in his ears. It described him as 'The dirty little coward who shot Mister Howard'. Eventually he was shot dead in 1892 by Edward O'Kelley who gained notoriety as 'the man who shot the man who shot Jesse James'.

BUTCH CASSIDY

ROBERT LEROY PARKER, alias Butch Cassidy has become one of the best-known figures of the Old West, mainly because of the sympathetic way he has been portrayed on film, principally by Robert Newman in the much-loved film *Butch Cassidy and the Sundance Kid.* Cassidy became famous as the leader of one of the most notorious of all the outlaw gangs of the time, the Hole-in-the-Wall Gang – also known as the Wild Bunch – a group of murderous cut-throats who cut a bloody swathe through several states of the Union, robbing trains and banks and taking out anyone who got in the way.

Butch was born into a Mormon family in April 1866 in Beaver, Utah and his pioneer parents brought him up on a ranch near Circleville. He changed his surname in honour of a rustler he started riding with, Mike Cassidy; Cassidy would ultimately kill a rancher and disappear. He got his Christian name from time spent working as a butcher in Rock Springs in Wyoming It was almost an honest living, except that the cattle he butchered had all been rustled.

After working for a while as a ranch-hand, in 1887, he met Matthew Warner and the two of them raced a horse, earning a good living from their winnings. At about this time, he made the acquaintance of the young Billy the Kid, still going by the name of Henry McCarty, and his brother Tom. The Kid and his brothers were by this time veteran bank robbers, despite their youth, and it is probable that they taught Butch the strategies required for robbing banks and trains. Together they robbed a number of trains, on one occasion, at Grand Junction in Colorado, getting away with a mere

$50. However, other occasions, such as an 1889 bank robbery, when they escaped with $21,000, proved more lucrative.

Butch was arrested for the first time in 1894 for horse-theft and extortion but only served eighteen months of a two-year sentence, being offered the remission on condition that he did not offend in the state of Wyoming again. Needless to say, it was a promise he failed to keep.

When he came out of prison, he hooked up with the gang of men who became known as the Wild Bunch. The members were Harry Longabaugh, known as the Sundance Kid, with whom he would have a lifetime friendship, Kid Curry, Ben Kilpatrick, known as the Tall Texan, Harry Tracy and Elzy Lay, Butch's best friend. Although the gang was loosely organised and different members would take part in robberies depending how busy, drunk or rich they were at the time, it developed into one of the most successful gangs of robbers of its time, putting together the longest sequence of robberies in the history of the Wild West.

They based themselves at the legendary Hole-in-the-Wall, a remote hideaway in the Big Horn Mountains of Northern Wyoming where Butch masterminded their robberies. His natural charm and courage meant that others were more than happy to take part, believing that if he was involved they would be successful. For the robbery of the San Miguel Bank in Telluride, Butch introduced the tactic that became the trademark of the gang. They would station fresh horses along their escape route, leaving whoever was pursuing them trailing in their wake on tired animals.

The name 'the Wild Bunch' was coined by the Pinkerton National Detective Agency. However, by the time the name stuck, around the start of the twentieth century, a number of its members were either dead or in jail. The survivors carried on robbing, nonetheless. In September 1900, they snatched $32,000 from a Winnemucca bank and a phenomenal $60,000 from a train near Wagner in Montana.

In between these heists, the gang posed for a photograph in Fort

269

Worth. The famous Fort Worth Five photo shows Butch, Sundance, Kid Curry, Ben Kilpatrick and Will Carver suited and booted and wearing smart bowler hats. Unfortunately, the Pinkerton Agency got their hands on a copy and it was used on a 'Wanted' poster for the gang.

Following the Wagner train robbery, the gang split up as usual, heading in separate directions but the forces of law and order were hot on their heels. One gang-member, Will Carver, was killed by a pursuing posse and Butch and Sundance decided they stood a better chance back east. They fled to New York. Then, on 2 February 1901, feeling the hot breath of their pursuers still on their necks, they embarked for South America, accompanied by Sundance's girlfriend, Etta Place. They travelled on the British steamship, *Herminus*, destination Argentina.

At the time, the Argentinean government was trying to persuade Americans to settle on their vast swathes of unoccupied territory. Butch and Sundance had plenty of money and on their arrival, they purchased a 15,000 acre ranch near the town of Cholila in west-central Argentina where they began raising cattle, sheep and horses, registering their brands and joining in with the efforts of their neighbours to have more land freed up for farming. They had gone legitimate.

The Pinkertons, however, had not given up and learned that the two outlaws were in South America. A veteran agent, Frank Dimaio had been working on a case in Brazil and after it was finished, travelled to Buenos Aires to see if he could discover their whereabouts. He discovered they were living in Cholila and, returning to the United States tried to raise funds from the railroads and banks that the Wild Bunch had robbed, but no one was interested. All they could do was distribute 'Wanted' posters and warn the Argentinean police of the danger in their midst. 'It is our firm belief that it is only a question of time until these men commit some desperate robbery in the Argentine Republic. They are all thorough plainsmen and horsemen, riding from 600 to 1,000 miles after committing a robbery. If there are reported to you any bank or train hold up robberies or any other similar crimes, you will find that they were undoubtedly committed by these men.'

Sure enough, when a bank in Rio Gallegas, was robbed in February 1905, reportedly by 'two Yankees', Butch and Sundance were presumed to be the perpetrators, even though the town was 700 miles from their ranch and the descriptions of the robbers were nothing like them. They also had alibis for the time of the robbery but the authorities still moved in to arrest them and only a tip-off from a friend saved them. They fled with little option but to return to their old ways.

Later that year, they were back in Argentina with a friend, robbing a bank at Villa Mercedes de San Luis. They fled with their ill-gotten gains across the border into Chile, hotly pursued by a number of heavily armed posses.

They spent some time in the northern Chilean coastal town of Antofagasta before Etta decided that she had had enough of life on the run and sailed back to the United States. Meanwhile, Butch and Sundance decided to try their luck in another country and travelled north to Bolivia, using the aliases of James 'Santiago' Maxwell and H.A. Brown, respectively. They found work at the Concordia Tin Mine as, of all things, payroll guards. The mine's manager was aware of their criminal past, however, but experienced no problems with them.

Leaving their jobs with Concordia in 1908, they arrived in the southern Bolivian town of Tupiza. Butch was now going by the name of James 'Santiago' Lowe while Sundance was Frank Smith. They planned to rob the town's bank before heading south to Santa Cruz, a town on Bolivia's eastern border that Butch had taken a liking for.

However, as they waited to carry out the robbery, a platoon of cavalry arrived in town and they had to change their planes, opting instead to rob the Aramayo, Francke Mining Company which was in the habit of sending its weekly payroll overland from Tupiza to Quechisla without any protection.

The money was always transported by the manager of the mine and on 3 November 1908 they followed him as he set out. When he stopped to rest on the first night, they circled around him and waited along the trail for him to pass. The next morning they ambushed him at a place called Huaca Huañusca (Dead Cow Hill), relieving him of the money and his mule. Unharmed, he rushed back to town to raise the alarm.

Posses set out in pursuit of the robbers but Butch and Sundance headed south to stay at the camp of an English gold miner they had encountered while waiting in Tupiza. They forced him to guide them on a tortuous escape route through the mountains which he knew well, releasing him after a day before riding on alone, in a northerly direction, possibly headed for Oruro, a town that Butch knew.

At sundown on 6 November they rode into the small mining town of San Vicente. With the help of the town's mayor, they found lodgings in the adobe house of one of the villagers but the mayor's suspicions had been roused by the two gringos and he set off to alert a posse consisting of an army captain, two soldiers and a policeman that had arrived in the village earlier that afternoon. They came to investigate, minus the captain, who could not be found, but as they entered the house and approached the room in which the two robbers were staying, Butch suddenly appeared in the doorway and opened fire, hitting the leading soldier who fired back with his rifle, but died a few minutes afterwards following their retreat to a nearby house. The other two positioned themselves outside the patio door of the house occupied by Butch and Sundance and started to fire into the room occupied by the outlaws.

When the captain of the platoon eventually turned up, he ordered the mayor to tell the villagers to surround the building to prevent the Americans from escaping, but as the mayor began to do so, there were three desperate screams from inside the house. By the time the villagers had encircled the building, the firing from inside had ceased.

When they finally went inside, they found Butch's body stretched out on the floor. He had a bullet wound in his temple and another in the arm. The Sundance Kid lay behind the door, shot in the forehead and had also suffered several bullet wounds to his arm. It looked very much as if Butch had put his friend out of his misery with the bullet to the head, before ending his own life with one in the temple. They found the stolen money in the room along with a map showing their movements since they had arrived in Bolivia. The bodies were identified by the man they had robbed, but they were never named and were buried as 'desconocidos' (unknowns).

The news of their deaths soon spread to Chile but it took a while to filter back to the United States. A wire service story in Buenos Aires was the first to link the deaths at San Vicente with the famous Butch Cassidy and the Sundance Kid.

Of course, their legend grew in the years following their deaths. The force that stood against them at San Vicente was exaggerated out of all proportion, some accounts claiming that they were up against 100 Bolivian soldiers at the end.

Robin Hood or ruthless killer and outlaw, Butch Cassidy was outstanding in his field, masterminding countless robberies and carving a special place in the history of the Old West as the leader of one of its greatest outlaw bands.

GUISEPPE GARIBALDI

It was a fortuitous meeting in a seaport inn in Taganrog in Russia that changed Guiseppe Garibaldi's life, leading to the unification of Italy and the recognition of Garibaldi as one of the country's great heroes.

In April 1833, he was a captain in the merchant marine and his schooner Clorinda was moored in Taganrog on the Russian coast with a cargo of oranges on board. Enjoying a drink in an inn, he bumped into another Italian a long way from his home-town of Oneglia – Giovanni Battista Cuneo. Cuneo had been forced to leave Italy because of his membership of *La Giovine Italia* (Young Italy), a political movement led by Guiseppe Mazzini, a philosopher, patriot and politician, dedicated to creating a united Italian republic through promoting an insurrection in all the lands of Italy, including those in the north occupied by the Austrian Empire. Members of Young Italy had been ruthlessly suppressed, many having been arrested and executed after a plot was foiled in Savoy and Piedmont. Following his conversation with Cuneo, on his return to Italy, Garibaldi joined Young Italy, swearing an oath to dedicate his life to the struggle for the liberation of his country from Austrian dominance. He threw himself into the movement enthusiastically and was sentenced to death *in absentia* for his role in an 1834 plot. He fled to Marseille in France, before sailing to Tunisia.

He next turned up in Brazil where he began a career as a privateer, or mercenary, joining up with the people engaged in the struggle for the independence of Rio Grande do Sul, the gaucho rebels known as *farrapos* (ragamuffins) who were fighting against the newly independent Brazil. The War of Tatters or Farroupilha Revolution was one of the bloodiest episodes in Brazil's history. During this time, however, Garibaldi met an extraordinary woman, Ana Ribeiro da Silva – known as 'Anita' – a courageous and skilled horsewoman who fought alongside him in several battles.

In 1841, the couple travelled to Montevideo in Uruguay where he found work as a trader and schoolteacher. They married there and had four children between 1840 and 1847. In 1842 Garibaldi was given command of the Uruguyan fleet and became involved in the Uruguyan Civil War, taking the side of the Uruguayan Colorados of Fructosa Rivera and Argentine Unitarios. They were fighting with the support of Britain and France against the forces of former conservative President Manuel Oribe – the Blancos – and the Argentine Federales headed by the authoritarian Juan Manuel de Rosas.

Garibaldi raised an Italian Legion that fought under a black flag with a volcano at its centre, the colour being chosen to represent Italy in mourning and the volcano representing the occupied territory's dormant power. It was here that Garibladi first sported the red shirt that was to become the uniform of his movement. From 1842 until 1847, he fought for the defence of Montevideo against Oribe's troops, using skilful guerrilla tactics to win two famous victories – at Cerro and San Antonio del Santo in 1846.

Meanwhile, in Italy, the liberal Pope Pius IX had been elected in 1846, exciting revolutionaries, especially when his first act was to declare an amnesty for political prisoners who picked up where they had left off in the struggle for unification. Garibaldi was especially optimistic and wrote to Pius in October 1847: 'If these hands, used to fighting, would be acceptable to His Holiness, we most thankfully dedicate them to the service of him who deserves so well of the Church and of the fatherland. Joyful indeed shall we and our companions in whose name we speak be, if we may be allowed to shed our blood in defence of Pius IX's work of redemption.' That same year, Garibaldi met the papal envoy in Rio de Janeiro and offered the services of his Italian Legion in the liberation of the peninsula.

1848 was a year of revolution across Europe, workers and students rebelling in France, Berlin, Hungary, Sweden and Austria. At Palermo in Sicily, a popular revolt took place on 12 January, birthday of King Ferdinand II of the Two Sicilies. It would result in sixteen months of virtual independence for Sicily, but would ultimately be crushed after sixteen months. When Garibaldi heard about the rebellion, he decided the time was right and, accompanied by sixty members of his Italian Legion, sailed for his homeland.

He immediately presented himself to King Charles Albert of Piedmont-Sardinia who had been favourable to the idea of a united Italy and who had also demonstrated some liberal tendencies. But Charles Albert rejected his offer, distrusting Garibaldi. Undaunted, Garibaldi travelled north with his followers to Lombardy to offer help to the city of Milan which, along with Venice and the main cities of the Kingdom of Lombardy-Venetia, had rebelled against the Austrians and established a provisional government.

When the First War of Independence erupted in 1848, between the Kingdom of Sardinia – allied with the Papal States and the Kingdom of the Two Sicilies – and the Austrian Empire, Garibaldi took part, winning a couple of minor victories at Luino and Morazzone. However, a crushing defeat in the Battle of Novarra for the Piemontese forced him to move to Rome where he supported the republic that had been proclaimed in the Papal States. It was being threatened by a French force sent by Louis Napoleon, President of the Second Republic. Guiseppe Mazzini, the founder of Young Italy, recommended that Garibaldi be given command of the defence of Rome.

The siege of Rome began on 1 June 1848 and despite Garibaldi's resolute stance, the French captured the city on 29 June. The options were stark – whether to continue the fighting on the streets of Rome, a course destined to fail and cause thousands of casualties and much destruction, or for Garibaldi and his men to retreat to the mountains to fight another day. He decided on retreat and a truce was negotiated before the French marched into Rome.

Garibaldi, pursued by Austria and the forces of its allies – Spain, France and the Kingdom of Naples, fled northwards with 250 men, hoping to reach Venice where the Venetians were being besieged by the Austrians. Tragically, in San Marino Anita, carrying the couple's fifth child, became ill and died.

With his enemies on his heels, he was forced once more to emigrate, heading for Tangier, from where he embarked on a ship for New York, arriving there on 30 July 1850. In New York, he stayed for two years with the Italian inventor Antonio Meucci, working in Meucci's factory as a candlemaker before returning to the sea as a captain, making long voyages across the Pacific.

He left New York in 1853 as master of the sailing vessel *Commonwealth*, arriving in South Shields in north-east England to unload a cargo in March 1854. Garibaldi was very well known on Tyneside and was welcomed as a hero by the workers of the area, being presented with an inscribed sword that was paid for by public subscriptions.

After around a month on Tyneside, he left for Italy, buying half of the small island of Caprera in northern Sardinia with a legacy left to him by his brother. He became a farmer, but on the outbreak of the Second Italian War of Independence in 1859, he returned to the fray, being appointed major general. He assembled a unit he called *Cacciatori delle Alpe* (Hunters of the Alps) but was now convinced that Mazzini's vision of a republican solution to Italy's future was no longer feasible; the only way Italy would be unified, he believed, was under the leadership of the Piemontese monarchy.

It started well and he won at Como, Varese and elsewhere. Meanwhile, he married a Lombard noblewoman, Guiseppina Raimondi, but left her immediately after the ceremony on learning that she had been unfaithful to him.

In April 1860, there were rebellions in the towns of Messina and Palermo in the Kingdom of the Two Sicilies. Garibaldi saw his chance and embarked for Sicily with a thousand men, known popularly as *I Mille* (the Thousand) or *Camicie Rossi* (the Redshirts) due to the uniform they wore. They landed at Marsala on Sicily's west coast on 11 May and swelled their ranks with local rebels. At Catafimi four days later, he defeated a force twice the size of his own using the innovative tactic of an uphill bayonet charge. Cleverly, he realised that the terraced slopes offered an opportunity for his men to be sheltered from the Neapolitan forces above them. It was a critical defeat in that it established Garibaldi's power on Sicily and laid the foundations for the remainder of his campaign.

On 16 May, he declared himself dictator of Sicily in the name of King Victor Emmanuel II of Italy before laying siege to Palermo, the capital on 27 May. The Neapolitans abandoned the city following an armistice brokered by the British.

As Garibaldi's name rang around the world and adulation grew throughout Italy, he marched on Messina and, following a ferocious battle at Milazzo, he won, leaving only the citadel to be captured.

The British Navy helped him to cross the Strait of Messina to the mainland where he marched northwards. Resistance en route was minimal with people celebrating as his army passed through their towns and villages. He entered Naples on 7 September and finally faced the Neapolitan Bourbon army on 30 September at the Battle of Volturno in northern Campania. The two armies were evenly matched in size – Garibaldi had 24,000 troops, Naples 25,000 – but the Neapolitan force was better organised, having been rebuilt in Capua under Marshal Giosuè Ritucci. However, the arrival of Piedmontese reinforcements swung the battle – the largest in which Garibaldi had ever commanded – in his favour.

His next objective was Rome, where he wanted to proclaim the Kingdom of Italy, but he faced opposition from the Piedmontese who, even though they had captured most of the Papal States on their march south, had skirted Rome, wanting to avoid a confrontation with its French occupying force. Pope Pius saw Garibaldi's desire as a threat to papal power and threatened excommunication for anyone who supported such an effort. Catholics around the world sent money and volunteers to the papal army to protect the Holy City.

The decision as to how matters would proceed now lay with French ruler, Louis Napoleon. He could choose to end the Pope's temporal authority and allow Garibaldi to proclaim Rome the capital of Italy or let the Sardinian king take control of the rest of Italy, but leave Rome intact. However, Garibaldi decided at that point to call a halt. On 26 October, he met Victor Emmanuel at Teano in Campano and with the famous 'Handshake of Teano', he hailed him as King of Italy, dashing the hopes of republicans everywhere. He handed over all his southern conquests to Victor Emmanuel and retired once more to Caprera, leaving the king to proceed with the unification.

His retirement did not prevent him, however, from contacting United States President, Abraham Lincoln to offer his services. When he was offered the rank of major general in the Union army, he replied that he would only serve if the President could confirm that slavery would definitely be abolished in the event of a Union victory and if he was given full command of the army. The offer was quietly withdrawn.

Victor Emmanuel was wary of the international reaction to an attack on the Papal States, but Garibaldi was certain that the government would support him if he attacked Rome. Frustrated by Victor Emmanuel's indecision, he organised a new expedition and in June 1862, he landed at Palermo where he mobilised support for a march on Rome, with the slogan Roma o Morte (Rome or Death). With 2,000 men, he set sail from Catania, landing on the mainland on 14 August.

The Italian government was not supportive and, in fact, sent troops against Garibladi's force, the two meeting in Aspromonte in Reggio Calabria. But, Garibaldi would not permit his men to fire on fellow Italians. During the skirmish, a number of the volunteer force were wounded and Garibaldi himself was shot in the foot. Many were arrested, including Garibaldi who was briefly imprisoned before being released to return to Caprera.

Victor Emmanuel, meanwhile, negotiated a treaty with the French for the removal of French troops from Rome in September 1864. By December 1866, the last French troops left the capital and Italy was free of foreign soldiers for the first time in a thousand years.

Garibaldi, on his island, never gave up dreams of liberation and had plans to liberate occupied nations such as Croatia, Greece and Hungary, but they came to nothing.

Nonetheless, he did go to war one more time in 1866. Italy had sided with Prussia against Austria-Hungary in the Austro-Prussian War. The government hoped to take Venetia from the Austrians and, thus, the war is sometimes known as the Third Italian War of Independence. With a force of 40,000, Garibaldi defeated the Austrians at Bezzecca and headed for Trento. It would be the sole Italian victory in the conflict but, due to Prussian successes in the north, Austria did cede Venetia to Italy in the peace treaty at the war's conclusion. When Garibaldi was ordered to stop his advance towards Trento, he replied in a telegram with the famous motto: 'Obbedisco!' (I obey!).

He never gave up on Rome and agitated constantly for its absorption into Italy. In 1867, he marched north again but his volunteers were badly equipped and no match for the Papal army. Garibaldi was again wounded, with a bullet in the leg, and taken prisoner before being sent back to Caprera.

In 1870, when the Franco-Prussian War broke out, the French garrison in Rome was recalled to France and the Italian army at last captured the Papal States, but without Garibaldi who was on his way to France to fight for the newly declared French Republic. His army of volunteers remained undefeated in the conflict.

Garibaldi spent his last years on Caprera. In 1897, he founded a political party, the League of Democracy that advocated universal suffrage, the abolition of ecclesiastical property and a provision for a standing army. In 1880, he married for a third time, to Francesca Armosino, with whom he already had three children.

He died on 4 July 1807, aged seventy-five, and Italy went into mourning for one of its greatest sons and an extraordinary human being.

ABRAHAM LINCOLN

EVEN AS A boy, Abraham Lincoln, the future President of the United States, was tall and rangy and by the age of twenty-one he would have reached his full height – a towering six feet four inches.

He was born on 12 February 1809, in a log cabin consisting of one room on the Sinking Spring Farm in Hardin County in Kentucky, a smallholding that his father, Thomas Lincoln had bought the previous year for a cash payment of £200. However, in 1816, the family was forced to move to Indiana, partly because of difficulties with Kentucky land ownership that made it difficult for farmers to prove that the land they farmed actually belonged to them.

When Lincoln was nine years old, his thirty-four-year-old mother died and his father re-married. Fortunately, Lincoln and his siblings got on well with their stepmother, even though his relationship with his father was never entirely satisfactory. More land-right issues led the family to uproot once again in 1830, moving to Macon County, Illinois, but their first winter there was overwhelmingly harsh and they re-located again the following year, returning to Illinois.

Lincoln, now aged twenty-two, decided it was time to make his own way in the world, travelling down the Sangamon River to the village of New Salem in Sangamon County where he found a job transporting goods from New Salem to New Orleans on a flatboat.

Lincoln had only gone to school for eighteen months, and so had little in the way of formal education. However, he had taught himself to read and became a voracious reader. Aged twenty-three, he made his first foray into politics when he ran unsuccessfully for the Illinois General Assembly, representing the Whig Party, and arguing for navigational improvements to the Sagamon River, of which, of course, he had direct personal experience. He hoped that the improvements he supported would provide economic benefit to the poorer areas along the river.

In 1832, he was first able to test his leadership ability when he was elected captain of a militia company fighting in the Black Hawk War. This frontier war was named after war chief of the Sauk, Fox, and Kickapoo Native Americans and was fought over land in Illinois and the Michigan Territory of present-day Wisconsin. Lincoln was just one of a number of men whose political careers were given a boost by their involvement and in 1834 he was finally elected to serve in the state legislature. Meanwhile he began to teach himself law and was admitted to the bar in 1837, moving to Springfield, and practising with John T. Stewart. He became a formidable and successful lawyer, dealing with more than 5,000 cases in his twenty-three-year legal career and appearing before the Illinois State Supreme Court more than 400 times.

In 1837, Lincoln completed his fourth term in the Illinois House of Representatives and that year he also met his close friend Joshua Fry Speed who was a confidant and supporter for the rest of his life. In 1842, Lincoln married Mary Todd, daughter of a slave-owning family and two years later started his own law practice with William Herndon, a fellow Whig.

The year 1846 saw Lincoln elected to the US House of Representatives but during his first term, he courted controversy by speaking out against the Mexican-American war that had broken out following the United States' 1845 annexation of Texas, a territory to which Mexico claimed ownership. Like most Whigs, Lincoln opposed the war and he was severely critical of President Polk, accusing him of seeking what Lincoln termed 'military glory'. His opposition to the war damaged his reputation, however, and he decided not to run for re-election. The new Whig President, Zachary Taylor, offered Lincoln the governorship of Oregon but Lincoln was not prepared to give up his career in Illinois in exchange for a posting to such a remote territory. Therefore he declined and for several years devoted himself to his law practice, having little to do with politics.

Eventually, it was slavery and his opposition to its extension that brought him back to politics. The Kansas-Nebraska act of 1854 expressly repealed the limits on slavery that had been laid down by the Missouri Compromise of 1820. It had, effectively, regulated slavery in the western territories and prohibited it in the Great Plains while allowing it in Missouri and Arkansas.

Influential Illinois Senator Stephen A Douglas argued that in a democracy people should have the right to decide locally whether or not slavery should be permitted in their area. Such a decision, he believed, should not be imposed on them by Congress. Lincoln, by now a member of the Republican Party that he had helped to found, was offered a Senate seat when the Republicans won Illinois in 1854. He declined, however, and then came second in the 1856 contest to be the Republican candidate in the Presidential election of that year. He finally became a Senator in 1858, delivering a famous speech about the divisions in the country about slavery: 'A house divided against itself cannot stand. I believe this government cannot endure permanently half slave and half free. I do not expect the house to fall but I do expect it will cease to be divided. It will become all one thing, or all the other.' It provided a rallying call for Republicans across the North.

The 1858 campaign became a debate on slavery, Lincoln arguing that it was contrary to the spirit of Republicanism, while Douglas spoke of democracy or, as he called it, popular democracy whereby if people wanted the continuation of slavery in their area, they could vote to do so. Douglas won re-election, but Lincoln had now become a national figure as a result of his campaigning.

The Republicans nominated him as their candidate for the 1860 Presidential election. He was an attractive candidate for several reasons. Firstly his views on slavery were more moderate than some other Republicans. Secondly, his western origins made him more attractive to new states. No man born outside the original thirteen states had ever been elected President. Therefore, they thought he could win in the West. Others claimed, however, that his election would encourage secession by the slave states of the South.

In the run-up to the election Lincoln neither campaigned nor gave speeches. His campaign was handled locally by state and county Republican officials. There was virtually no campaigning in the South but in the North the publicity campaign was massive with posters, leaflets and marches. A vital element of the campaign was Lincoln's own story, the poverty of his childhood, his pioneer upbringing, his lack of education and the fact that he had come from nowhere. They called him 'Honest Abe' and most people marvelled that a farm boy could be standing for president.

On 6 November 1860 Abraham Lincoln was elected the 16th president of the United States and the first from the new Republican Party. Of course, his victory relied entirely on the North; he did not even appear on the ballot in nine southern states. He gained 1,865,908 votes (39.9%) and 180 electoral votes with his nearest rival winning just seventy-two electoral votes.

The rise of the Republicans and of Lincoln was a serious rebuff to southern secessionists who realised that their power in national politics in America was weakening as the Democrats had been more pro-southern. During the election, they had, in fact, made it clear that should Lincoln win, they would leave the union. The first to do so was South Carolina on 20 December 1860. Within two months, six other southern states had done likewise and these seven states proclaimed themselves a new nation, the Confederate States of America. Both incumbent President Buchanan and President-elect Lincoln refused to recognise the Confederacy.

President Lincoln's inauguration took place on 4 March 1861, after he had travelled to Washington D. C. in disguise in case of a possible assassination attempt. In his inaugural speech he made a final attempt to save the union and prevent war, supporting the Corwin amendment to the Constitution that provided a guarantee that slavery would be protected where it already existed. But, it was already too late and none of the breakaway states wanted to rejoin the union on any terms. Nonetheless, Lincoln refused to act against the South unless the South attacked first.

War broke out in April 1861, when Confederate troops fired on union troops at Fort Sumter in Charleston, South Carolina as Lincoln tried to reinforce the garrison there. The union troops were forced to surrender and Lincoln called on the governors of every state to send reinforcements to protect the capital and preserve the union as well as recapture the forts lost to the Confederates. The action in South Carolina encouraged four other states to secede from the union – North Carolina, Virginia Tennessee and Arkansas. At the same time Lincoln held negotiations with the leaders of the slave states of Missouri, Kentucky, Maryland and Delaware, stopping them from breaking away.

On the outbreak of war, Lincoln ordered the arrest of rebel leaders in border areas. Over 18,000 were arrested and incarcerated in military prisons without trial. None were executed, however.

In July 1862, he oversaw the passing of the Second Confiscation Act which freed slaves. Lincoln hoped that this act would weaken the rebellion which was largely led by slave owners. It permitted the legal institution of slavery to remain intact but that would be abolished by the introduction in December 1865 of the Thirteenth Amendment to the American Constitution. The first section of the Thirteenth Amendment says: 'Neither slavery nor involuntary servitude, except as a punishment for crime where of the party shall have been duly convicted, shall exist within the United States, or any place subject to their jurisdiction.'

On 22 September 1862, the important Emancipation Proclamation was announced, consisting of two executive orders, the first declaring the freedom of all slaves in any Confederate state that did not return to the Union by 1 January 1863 and the second naming the specific states to which it applied.

Meanwhile Union armies advanced deeper into the South, liberating slaves as they went. Over three million were freed.

However, Union casualties were heavy and Lincoln's efforts to reinforce them using the draft were proving unpopular, especially among immigrants who rioted in New York on just this issue in July 1863. By the autumn of that year, it was becoming clear that his people were beginning to turn against him and the war but, undeterred, he delivered one of his most famous speeches – the Gettysburg Address – while dedicating a cemetery in Gettysburg, Pennsylvania. The ceremony should not be just a dedication, he proclaimed, it should also consecrate the living, declaring that 'government of the people, by the people, for the people, shall not perish from the earth.'

Confederate defeats at Gettysburg, Vicksburg and Chattanooga had, by this time, turned the tide of the war in the Union direction and victory seemed certain. Lincoln promoted Ulysses S. Grant to General-in-Command of the Union army and supported him in a strategy of wearing down the Confederates in a bloody campaign known as the Overland Campaign. It was a war of attrition and delivered heavy Union casualties although Confederate losses were proportionally greater. Lincoln provided Grant with more men and galvanised both party and people behind the war effort.

As the war continued, another Presidential election was held, with many of his supporters fearing that Lincoln would not win a second term. Cleverly, however, he chose as his running mate, the War Democrat, Andrew Johnson. War Democrats had split with the main body of the Democratic Party to support President Lincoln. Together, they ran on the Union Party ticket, hoping to form a broad coalition, uniting Republican and Democrat.

He won the election with a landslide, gaining 212 of the 233 electoral votes available. By the time of his inauguration on 4 March

1865, slavery was abolished and the war was almost won. In 1864-1865, Grant trapped Confederate General Robert E. Lee in the Siege of Petersburg, ten months of brutal trench warfare, taking Richmond and, shortly after, bringing the American Civil War to an end.

Lincoln ordered Grant to destroy the South's morale and economy by attacking civilians and the infrastructure of the region. Farms and towns were attacked in Georgia and South Carolina as General Sherman marched his army southwards to the sea, from Atlanta to the port of Savannah.

Lincoln's approach to the reintegration of the Southern states into the Union was considered and moderate, aimed at not alienating them. He offered pardons to all who had not held a Confederate civil office and who had not mistreated Union prisoners of war. They also had to sign an oath of allegiance to the Union.

Lincoln's PR skills were sharply honed by this time and when he visited General Grant's headquarters at City Point, Virginia, he made a point of being seen seated at the desk of Jefferson Davies who had been President of the Confederate States from 1861 to 1865. In this way, he re-affirmed his authority over the entire country. Meanwhile, freed slaves welcomed him as a conquering hero.

Apart from the abolition of slavery and the winning of the Civil War, Lincoln's Presidency introduced many important pieces of legislation to the United States. The Homestead Act of 1862 made millions of acres in the West available cheaply; his government gave financial support for the construction of the USA's first intercontinental railway which was completed in 1869; he introduced the first income tax to the United States and his government created the system of national banks.

His death, at the hand of the actor and Confederate sympathiser, John Wilkes Booth, on 14 April, shocked the nation. Wilkes Booth had been outraged when Lincoln delivered a speech advocating voting rights for blacks and decided to kill him.

On the night in question, Lincoln and his wife were attending a performance of the play *Our American Cousin* at Ford's Theatre in Washington. Seated in his box, Lincoln was unaware that his guard for the night had remained in the saloon across the road from the theatre after the interval. Booth leapt into the box and shot Lincoln in the head with a single shot from a .44 calibre pistol. One of Lincoln's guests in the box had his arm slashed with a knife as he grappled with the assassin who freed himself and jumped from the box onto the stage, shouting '*Sic semper tyrannis!*' (Thus always to tyrants!). He managed to flee despite breaking his leg on landing but, after a twelve-day manhunt, he was shot to death after being tracked down to a Virginia barn.

Meanwhile, Lincoln had been carried out of the theatre and taken to the Petersen boarding house across 10th Street. There, as the house filled with people, he lingered for a number of hours without regaining consciousness. At 7.22 the following morning, the greatest President America has ever had, died, aged fifty-six.

KARL MARX

'THE HISTORY OF all hitherto existing society is the history of class struggles'. So, went the opening line of the first chapter of Karl Marx's book, *The Communist Manifesto*. It was a line that summarised all that he believed and was the basis of a political and economic system that would sweep the world in the 20th century before collapsing as the century drew to a close.

Marx was born in Trier in Germany in 1818, the son of a Jewish lawyer, Hirschel Marx and his wife Henrietta. Confronted by the anti-Semitism that was rampant at the time, Hirschel abandoned his Jewish faith while Karl was still a child to become a Protestant, even though most of the population of Trier was Catholic. At the same time, he did away with his Jewish Christian name, changing it to Heinrich.

Karl was a very able pupil at school and enrolled at Bonn University in 1835 to study law. Like many young men, freed for the first time from parental restraints, he got himself into trouble, running up debts and spending more time socialising than studying. When he was wounded in a duel, his father decided to pay his debts and move him to the more sedate surroundings of Berlin University.

Karl knuckled down at Berlin, throwing himself into his studies. One reason for his new commitment was the influence of a lecturer at the university, Bruno Bauer. Bauer was a radical thinker, an atheistic theologian, philosopher and historian who argued that Jesus Christ was a myth and that early Christianity owed more to the Greek philosophy of Stoicism than to Judaism. Unsurprisingly, he was constantly in trouble with the university authorities. However, he introduced Marx to the work of the former professor of philosophy at the university, Georg Wilhelm Friedrich Hegel and Hegel's work became vital to Marx, especially his theory that a thing or a thought could not be separated from its opposite. According to him, a slave could not exist without his master, and the opposite also applied. Unity would eventually be achieved, Hegel, argued, by the synthesis of all opposites.

Marx's life was turned upside down when his father, who had been funding his studies, died. Suddenly, he had to earn a living and decided to become a teacher. Unfortunately, however, his old teacher, Bauer, who he had hoped would be able to help him find a position, had made one outrageous atheistic comment too many for the authorities and had been dismissed.

He turned his hand to journalism but most editors found his views too radical for their readers. In Cologne, however, there was a liberal-thinking group, known as the Cologne Group, that published its own newspaper, the *Rhenisch Gazette*. In his first article for them, he defended the freedom of the press, drawing no doubt on what he believed to be the suppression of his writings by frightened newspaper and magazine editors. His piece went down so well that he was appointed editor of the newspaper.

In the company of another radical, Moses Hess, Marx began attending meetings where the new thinking of socialism was discussed. At these meetings he first learned of the desperate conditions in which the German working class lived and worked. Only socialism, the meetings argued, could bring an end to their suffering. Then, in January 1934, Marx wrote an article that described the plight of wine-farmers on the Mosel and was highly critical of the Prussian government. The Prussian authorities banned the newspaper soon after.

Now in grave danger of being arrested, he decided to flee to France, accompanied by his new wife, Jenny von Wesphalen. He found work as editor of a new political publication, *Franco-German Annals* and was in good company; on its pages were his old mentor

Bruno Bauer, the Russian anarchist, Michael Bakunin and a man who would become an essential part of the story of Karl Marx and his philosophy – Friedrich Engels.

The eldest son of a wealthy German industrialist, Engels had been shocked by the poverty he witnessed in Manchester when sent there by his father to help manage a cotton factory he owned. He had written about it in *Condition of the Working Class in England* and had also met with leaders of the Chartist movement, the movement for social reform and possibly the first mass working class labour movement in the world. He and Marx became close friends and began to work together.

It was while he was in Paris that Marx began mixing for the first time with members of the working class. Their poverty shocked him but, at the same time, he was impressed by their spirit and camaraderie. His thinking was developed in an article he wrote for *Franco-German Annals* in which he applied Hegel's dialectic theory to what he had observed. He wrote that the working class would be the emancipators of society and now began to describe himself as a communist. The magazine was immediately banned in Germany and he had antagonised its owner, Arnold Ruge, by attacking capitalism.

That same year, Marx wrote a series of notes between April and August called *Economic & Philosophical Manuscripts* in which he covered a wide range of topics including private ownership, communism and money. They are best known for his descriptions of alienation in a capitalist society. The worker is alienated from what he produces; he is also alienated from himself and it is only when he is not working that he feels truly himself. People are alienated from each other, competing in a capitalist society against each other. The only solution, he argued, was communism.

Marx and Engels complemented each other perfectly. Marx was a brilliantly complex thinker, while Engels brought the ability to communicate those ideas to a mass audience. However, as they began work on their first piece of joint work – an article entitled *The*

Holy Family – Marx was deported from France after the Prussian government pressured the French government about his activities. He went to Belgium and Engels soon joined him in Brussels. At that time Belgium permitted the greatest degree of freedom of expression in Europe and for that reason there were a large number of political exiles, a community into which Marx and Engels fitted perfectly.

Being from a wealthy family, Engels was able to provide financial support for Marx and his family. He even donated to Marx the royalties of his book about the English working class. Furthermore, he solicited donations from like-minded people to enable Marx to spend all his time on his work.

In July 1845, the two men visited England, studying books in Manchester library and meeting the Chartist leader, George Julian Harney. Marx then returned to Brussels to work on his book, *The German Ideology* in which he re-stated his theory of history, the theory he was beginning to describe as the 'materialist conception of history'.

In January 1846, Marx tried to establish a network of socialist leaders from different parts of Europe that he called the Communist Correspondence Committee. A conference was held in London and a new organisation, the Communist League, was founded. Marx launched the Brussels branch on his return and then later in the year returned to London to attend a meeting of the Communist League Central Committee. At this meeting they described the organisation's objective as 'the overthrow of the bourgeoisie, the domination of the proletariat, the abolition of the old bourgeois society based on class antagonisms, and the establishment of a new society without classes and without private property'.

Returning to Brussels, he started work on *The Communist Manifesto,* working from a first draft that Engels had produced that was entitled the Principles of Communism. It was 12,000 words long and was completed in six weeks. It would be one of the most important documents in history, accessible, and intended for a mass audience.

It described the imminent revolution and the communist society that the proletariat would create afterwards. The most important classes in the 19th century, he wrote, were the proletariat and the bourgeoisie, the owners of the means of production and the products made. The proletariat, he argued, owned very little apart from their labour which they were forced to sell to the capitalists. The conflict between these two classes, he said, could lead only to revolution and the triumph of the workers, the proletariat. The bourgeoisie would be wiped out as a class and a classless society would be the end-result. 'The state is not abolished,' Engels later wrote, 'it withers away.'

It was published in February 1848, causing uproar, even in Belgium. The Belgian government expelled Marx and he and Engels re-located back to Cologne where they launched a radical newspaper, *The New Rhenish Gazette* with the intention of creating some of the revolutionary atmosphere they had encountered in a visit to Paris en route to Cologne.

Marx helped to establish a Committee of Public Safety following examples of police brutality in the city and, meanwhile, their newspaper published reports of revolutionary activity all over Europe. It was, indeed, an exciting year for Marx and Engels, one in which they must have thought all their dreams were coming true. A wave of revolutions broke out all over the continent. In France, Louis Philippe abdicated and Napoleon's nephew, Louis Napoleon became president and there were revolutions in Milan, Naples, Venice, Rome, Berlin, Vienna, Prague, Budapest and Austria where the Democrats seized power. Best of all, the Emperor was forced to flee the country.

Marx's euphoria at the prospect of world revolution was short-lived, however. The Emperor returned with the support of the army and uprisings in Dresden, Baden and the Ruhr were swiftly suppressed. Worse came when he was informed that he was about to be expelled from the country. He published the last edition of *The Rhenish Gazette*, printed entirely in red and defiantly stating that although they were forcing him to leave, he would continue his work until 'the emancipation of the working class'.

He travelled to France, fully anticipating a socialist revolution at any moment, but was once again shown the door shortly after arriving. The only country that would have him, it seemed, was Great Britain, although the Prussians tried to persuade the British government to expel him. Prime Minister, Lord John Russell, an ardent believer in freedom of speech, refused their entreaties.

Life was hard for Marx and his family. He was surviving only on what money Engels sent him and they were ejected from a two-roomed flat in Chelsea in 1850 for failing to pay the rent. They moved into cheaper accommodation at 26 Dean Street in Soho in London and remained there for six years. Their fifth child was born there but she died at one year old. In 1855, Eleanor Marx was born, but their third child, Edgar died, the third child Marx and Jenny had lost.

Marx now famously spent much of his time in the Reading Room of the British Museum, reading old copies of *The Economist* and numerous books, in his efforts to analyse capitalist society. Engels, meanwhile, was forced to return to work for his father in Germany in order to be able to send money to Marx to help him carry on with his work. It arrived as postal orders for £1 or £5, cut in half and sent in separate envelopes to avoid theft. The family's only treat during the week was a family picnic every Sunday on Hampstead Heath.

His luck took a turn for the better in 1852 when Charles Dana, the socialist editor of the *New York Daily Tribune* offered Marx the opportunity to write regularly for his newspaper. He was also commissioned to write for *The New American Cyclopaedia* by another radical, George Ripley. Then Jenny inherited £120 from her mother. With things suddenly looking up, they re-located to 9 Grafton Terrace, Kentish Town.

His wife's health started failing after she gave birth to a stillborn baby at the age of 42 and then contracted smallpox. Marx, too, was ill but, even in the face of such misery, he retained a sense of humour; when he wrote to Engels about a bad bout of boils from which he had suffered, he said that the only consolation was that 'it was a truly proletarian disease.'

When the work for the *New York Daily Tribune* came to an end, Marx was back where he had started. He was receiving £5 a month from Engels but was spiralling deeper and deeper into debt. He was sent money by Ferdinand Lascelle, a rich socialist from Berlin who also offered him the opportunity to edit a radical new newspaper he was planning to launch in Germany, but Marx refused to go back to his homeland.

In 1867, the first volume of his masterpiece, *Das Kapital*, was published. It provided a detailed analysis of capitalism, and discusses revolution, claiming that capitalism will eventually bring about its own destruction. While competition will bring about a diminishing number of capitalists, the misery and oppression of the proletariat will increase. They will ultimately unite and overthrow the system that is at the root of their suffering. He immediately started work on the second volume, helped by his sixteen-year-old daughter, Eleanor, who would later go on to play an important part in the British labour movement.

The formation of the Paris Commune in March 1871 filled him with optimism but he was dismayed by its collapse in May of that year and the slaughter of around 30,000 communards by troops.

It seemed to be the last straw for Karl Marx and he began to lose his momentum. Work was very slow on the second volume, particularly when Eleanor left home to become a teacher in Brighton.

By 1881, both he and Jenny were so ill that Eleanor had to return home to nurse them. Jenny died in December of that year but Marx lived on for another couple of years. His oldest daughter died of cancer in January 1883 and Marx, devastated by her loss, died two months later, on 14 March 1883, aged sixty-five.

OTTO VON BISMARCK

OTTO VON BISMARCK was not known as the 'Iron Chancellor' for nothing. Under his leadership, Prussia would become one of the great powers of Europe and he would achieve his objective of politically unifying Germany under Prussian domination. He was also a skilful diplomat whose carefully crafted alliances preserved peace in Europe. By the time he left office in 1890, the map of the continent had changed immeasurably.

Bismarck was born in 1771 on his family's estate in Prussia. His father was a landowner and former officer in the Prussian army, his mother the daughter of a politician. After school, he studied law at the University of Göttingen before going to the University of Berlin.

He had intended to make diplomacy his career but, instead, underwent training to be a lawyer in Aachen and Potsdam. He then joined the army for a year, becoming an officer in the reserve, before returning home to the family estate when his mother died. In 1847, he married a noblewoman, Johanna von Puttkamer and the couple had two sons and a daughter

The year he got married, Bismarck was selected to represent the new Prussian legislature, the Vereinigter Landtag (United Diet). His entry into politics was arranged by Ernst von Gerlach and his brother, Ludwig, founders of the ultra-conservative Kreuzzeitung organisation – on the cover of whose newspaper featured an Iron Cross. Like them, he was a committed royalist, which immediately became obvious to others in the Diet. He believed in the divine right of monarchs to rule and supported his reactionary opinions with razor-sharp rhetoric.

The year 1848 saw revolutions across Europe. Uprisings against the status quo broke out in numerous countries and Prussia was no exception. To the great disgust of the Prussian military and conservative politicians like von Bismarck, the King, Frederick William IV, gave concessions to the rebellious liberals, donned the red, yellow and black revolutionary colours, promised a constitution and agreed that all the German states should unify to make one nation. Finally, he appointed the liberal, Ludolf Cam to the post of Minister-President, head of government.

Bismarck was outraged. He attempted to persuade the peasants on his estate to march on Berlin and then travelled there in disguise to offer help against the forces of liberalism. Frederick William's brother, the future Wilhelm I, had fled to England when trouble broke out, and Bismarck tried to persuade his wife Augusta to put their son, the future Wilhelm III on the throne, but she refused and disliked Bismarck for even suggesting it.

Within the year, however, the liberal momentum had waned and the conservatives regained control of both Berlin and the King.

In 1849, Bismarck was elected to the lower house of the new Prussian parliament. He was, at this time, opposed to German unification and represented these views at the Erfurt parliament, a conference of German states convened to create a union of German states. The union failed due to the opposition of Prussia and Austria.

In 1851 he was appointed Prussian envoy to the Diet of the German Confederation in Frankfurt, a role for which he had to give up his seat in the Diet. He famously fought for equal treatment to the Austrian Count Thun, insisting on the same privileges, copying the count when he smoked or removed his jacket. Nevertheless, his eight years in Frankfurt changed him. Removed from the influence of his ultra-conservative cronies in Berlin, he became less reactionary and more pragmatic in his political opinions. He also became more supportive of a united Germany, realising that it was probably the only way in which the growing power of Austria could be dealt with.

He also came to believe in retaining a good relationship with the Russians and the French, a position that would have horrified his friends in Berlin. But he saw a much bigger picture. He wanted to counter-balance Austrian power and ensure at the same time that France did not form an alliance with Russia.

In 1858, Frederick William IV became incapacited both physically and mentally and Wilhelm took over the government as regent. He was a friend to liberal Britain – his son, the future Frederick III, had just married Queen Victoria's oldest daughter – and he introduced moderate conservatives, known as the 'Wochenblatt' after their newspaper, into his government.

Wilhelm made Bismarck Prussia's ambassador to the Russian Empire. It was a promotion, but Bismarck felt he was being isolated from the cut-and-thrust of Prussian politics. When France expelled Austria from Lombardy, he recognised an opportunity for Prussia to push its borders south, but Prussia, instead, went on the defensive against the French in the Rhineland. He felt frustrated, a feeling not helped by the fact that the Regent had refused to promote him to major-general, as was customary for the ambassador to Russia. He remained in St Petersberg for four years, returning to Prussia with only one leg, having lost the other due to a medical error.

June 1862 saw him being sent to Paris, as ambassador to France and he also crossed the Channel to England during his stay. He met Napoleon III, and the British Prime Minister, Lord Palmerston, as well as Foreign Secretary, Earl Russell and British Conservative, Benjamin Disraeli. Disraeli said of Bismarck: 'Be careful of that man – he means what he says.'

When Frederick William IV died in 1861, his regent became Wilhelm I and he immediately went to war with his parliament, threatening to abdicate when they refused funding for a re-organisation of the army. An impasse was reached and Wilhelm believed that the only man capable of breaking the deadlock was Bismarck.

On 23 September 1862, Otto von Bismarck became Minister-President and Foreign Minister of Prussia. The King and he would soon become powerful allies, especially when he solved the budget crisis by merely applying the previous year's budget. However, he would remain in conflict with the Diet until the King dissolved it. Bismarck then issued an edict restricting press freedom, making himself even more unpopular. There were repeated calls for his dismissal and the liberals routed his supporters in the 1863 election, taking two-thirds of the seats.

In 1863, Frederick VII of Denmark died and succession to the German-speaking duchies of Schleswig and Holstein, which were claimed by Frederick's successor, Christian IX, became an issue when Christian completely annexed Schleswig. Bismarck issued an ultimatum to Christian to return Schleswig to its status before his predecessor's death. He refused and Prussia and Austria invaded and forced Christian to cede both duchies. Britain, unwilling to commit ground troops to help Denmark, was humiliated in this incident. Bismarck engineered things so that Prussia received Schleswig and Austria gained control of Holstein. As a reward, Bismarck was created a count as Graf von Bismarck-Schönhausen. However, in 1866, the Austrians reneged on the agreement they had made with Bismarck, insisting now that the Diet decide the Schleswig-Holstein issue. It was all that Bismarck needed and he declared war on Austria and invaded Holstein. The two armies were virtually equal in size, but the entry of Italy into the war on the Prussian side, stretched the Austrian army over two fronts. This intervention, coupled with the tactical genius of Fieldmarshal General, Helmuth von Moltke the Elder, won the decisive Battle of Königgrätz, which was the largest battle fought in Europe up to that time.

Buoyed with this victory, the King was anxious to continue the war, but Bismarck was more cautious and negotiated the Peace of Prague in which Prussia gained territory and Austria agreed to stay out of German affairs. The North German Confederation came into being, with Wilhelm as President and Bismarck taking the role of Chancellor. Bismarck, who normally dressed in a uniform anyway, even though he never commanded troops in a battle situation, finally obtained his promotion to major general. Better still, his popularity ensured the defeat of the liberals in parliament and the approval of the last four years' budgets.

Bismarck acted very much like a modern politician, placing stories in newspapers and 'spinning'. To bribe people, he had a slush fund and he used it for spying and discrediting his political rivals. He also took a great interest in the upbringing of the future Wilhelm II, distancing him from his parents and teaching him to be insolent towards them.

The French were becoming increasingly wary of Prussian power and Bismarck waited for his chance to go to war again. It came in 1870 in a dispute over the succession to the Spanish throne which had been vacant ever since a revolution in 1868 had overthrown Queen Isabella II. The new government offered the crown to a German prince, Leopold of Hohenzollern-Sigmaringen and Bismarck, unsurprisingly, was supportive of his candidacy. France, fearful of a German on the Spanish throne, protested about him and Bismarck published a heavily edited version of a conversation between Wilhelm I and Count Benedetti, French ambassador to Prussia. The Ems Dispatch, as it came to be known, gave an account of an unplanned meeting of the two men in a park in Ems, during which the ambassador demanded the King should never approve of the Prince's candidacy. Bismarck edited the piece masterfully, making it appear that the King had insulted the Count. At the same time, however, he also made it look like the Count was insulting the King. It was masterful and worthy of a modern spin-doctor. It was released to the press and caused outrage in Paris.

France declared war five days later, on 19 July, and was, consequently, seen as the aggressor, as Bismarck had intended. The German states rose up in support of Prussia and the Prussians, again guided by the military genius of Moltke the Elder, proved unbeatable. The Franco-Prussian War lasted until May 1871 and during it Napoleon III was taken prisoner. The French suffered the indignity of having Paris besieged but world opinion was alienated by the Prussians when they bombarded the capital.

Taking advantage of the success of victory in the war, Bismarck made moves to unify Germany under Wilhelm. The Prussian king was proclaimed German Emperor on 18 January 1871 in the Hall of Mirrors in the Château of Versailles. He was not sovereign over the German states, however. The new Germany was more like a federation of 25 states.

In the settlement after the war, Prussia gained Alsace and part of Lorraine which was demanded by Prussian generals like Moltke, but it was against Bismarck's wishes. He did not want to make France any more of an enemy than it already was.

He, too, was rewarded, being given the title of Fürst (Prince) von Bismarck. He was appointed Imperial Chancellor of the German Empire, while still retaining his Prussian offices, and was promoted to lieutenant general. He became extremely wealthy when he was given an estate. His concerns were now the Catholic Church whose influence in Germany he tried to reduce, and the different nationalities in the German state, especially the Poles whom he considered a great threat – 'One shoots the wolves if one can,' he wrote. The rising tide of socialism also occupied him and to mitigate it, he introduced a number of social reforms, including health insurance, accident insurance and old age pensions. The workers still distrusted his conservative government, however.

He also worked at maintaining peace in Europe, ensuring that the German Empire was secure. He isolated France and maintained good relations with everyone else. He made alliances such as the Triple Alliance with Austria and Italy against the Russian threat. In the early 1880s Germany took part in the 'Scramble for Africa' and created a colonial empire.

In 1888 Wilhelm I died, closely followed by his successor, Frederick III. Wilhelm II became Emperor and he had a more expansionist policy than Bismarck. The Chancellor's anti-Socialist legislation brought the final difference of opinion. It also took Bismarck's party out of power. After a great deal of political manoeuvring, Bismarck had little option but to resign, in 1890, at Wilhelm's insistence. He was promoted to Colonel General with the Dignity of Field Marshal and given the title of Duke of Lauenberg.

Resentful and aged seventy-five, he retired to his estates at Varzin in modern-day Poland. Following the death of his wife just a month later, he moved to Friedrichsruh, close to Frankfurt. All the while he waited, hoping he would be asked for advice on the weighty matters of the day.

He died in 1898, aged eighty-three. On his gravestone is inscribed: 'Loyal German Servant of Kaiser Wilhelm I'.

CHIEF SITTING BULL

IT WAS 1872, and a battle was in progress between the Lakota Indians and soldiers protecting railroad workers laying track close to the Yellowstone River. In the midst of it five braves strolled out between the lines, sat down and lit up a pipe which they calmly passed amongst each other. As the bullets whizzed around them, the Indians finished their smoke, carefully knocked the ashes out of the pipe, stood up, stretched and walked casually back to their side. The leader of the group was one of the greatest Native American leaders of them all, the great warrior Chief Sitting Bull.

He was born around 1831 and given the temporary name Hoka-Psice (Jumping Badger). He would actually adopt his father's name, Thathanjka Iyothanjka, meaning Sitting Bull. As a child he was a fast runner and became an expert horseman and a good shot with a bow. He earned his first white eagle feather – the symbol of his first action – at the age of fourteen when he was part of a war party that encountered a party of Crow Indians. As the Lakota chased the Crow, Sitting Bull managed to knock one of them off his horse. As a result of his courage, he earned the right to use the name of his father.

In 1863, he had his first encounter with the American military when he took part in action against a US Army force that was engaged in a campaign following a Native American uprising in Minnesota.

He married in 1851 and had a son, but his wife died during the birth. When his son died at the age of eight, he adopted his nephew, One Bull, and then another boy who took the name Jumping Bull.

Sitting Bull is reputed to have been an intensely spiritual man, given to having visions and in his twenties he became a Sioux holy man. He learned about the complicated rituals and beliefs of the

Sioux and attempted to gain an understanding of the universe and how he could use it to bring benefits to his people. Healing was also an important part of the holy man's duties and he learned about medicinal herbs and techniques for curing people of ailments.

Trouble had been brewing with white settlements and traders and the Sioux for some time and in 1862 these came to a head. The United States had been violating treaties and Indian agents had been making late or incorrect annuity payments that were causing starvation and hardship amongst the tribe. On 17 August a skirmish between a Dakota hunting party and white settlers persuaded the Dakota that it was finally time to go to war. They attacked white settlers across southern Minnesota but in late 1862 were forced to surrender and were expelled to Nebraska and South Dakota. Their reservations were abolished.

Sitting Bull's people were largely unaffected by the Dakota War, as it came to be called, but some Dakota refugees arrived in their territory, pursued by Minnesota troops. There were a couple of engagements in which Lakota took part, at Dead Buffalo Lake and Stony Lake and it is almost certain that amongst the Lakota braves was Sitting Bull. The Dakota/Lakota alliance was defeated, and 100 Sioux died.

The war continued in 1864 when General Alfred Sully led a force out from Fort Sully. Several thousand Lakota and Dakota Sioux, including Sitting Bull, awaited them in the foothills of the Killdeer Mountains. The 28 July Battle of Killdeer Mountain was another overwhelming defeat for the Sioux, unable to withstand the might of Sully's artillery and rifles. The Sioux retreated, attacking again from 7 to 9 August. They lost again and Sitting Bull persuaded the chiefs to resist making another attack and to withdraw. Sitting Bull travelled southeast with a band of Hunkpapa Indians.

On 2 September, his band attacked a wagon train and Sitting Bull was wounded in the hip and back. Eventually, the Indians withdrew. Sitting Bull, however, had hardened in his attitude to the white man and he spent the next three years leading raiding parties against various forts – Fort Berthold, Fort Stevenson and Fort Buford – and engaged in guerrilla warfare against smaller forts and wagon trains throughout the upper Missouri River area. These initiatives supported the war being fought by Oglala Sioux Chief, Red Cloud. When a treaty was signed to bring this war to an end, Sitting Bull rejected it and his attacks continued during the late 1860s and early 1870s. In 1868, he had become head chief of the Lakota nation.

The railroad was the next problem. The Northern Pacific Railway conducted a survey that meant a route would be constructed that passed directly through Hunkpapa land. The surveyors were attacked in 1871 and by 1872 they were being escorted by soldiers as they carried out their work. Sitting Bull forced them to abandon the work. They abandoned it again in 1873, even though the accompanying force was even larger.

The next threat to the Native American lands and way of life, however, was even greater. It had long been rumoured that there was gold in the Black Hills of Dakota, an area that was regarded by many Native American tribes as sacred. Because of this, it had been rendered off-limits to white settlers by the Fort Laramie Treaty of 1868. When an expedition led by the flamboyant Lieutenant Colonel George Armstrong Custer confirmed that there was, indeed gold in the Black Hills, to the Indians' horror prospectors began a gold rush in the Black Hills, flooding into the area. When the Indians rejected the government's offer to buy the land, the government set aside the Fort Laramie Treaty and the commissioner of Indian Affairs announced that all Lakota not on their reservations by the end of January 1876 would be considered hostile and hunted down.

Needless to say, Sitting Bull paid no heed to the commissioner's warning and, instead, launched the campaign that would make him famous.

Lieutenant Colonel Custer was a decorated veteran of the American Civil War with presidential ambitions. By the 1870s he was a well-known figure among both Native Americans and whites, having distinguished himself and added to his fame with a number of battles against Native Americans, most of them controversial dawn attacks on their camps.

Sitting Bull, too, was by now very well known amongst his people for his stand against the white man and even wielded influence amongst other tribes such as the Northern Cheyenne and the Northern Arapaho. In March he convened a meeting of the Laota, Cheyenne and Arapaho at his camp on Rosebud Creek in Montana. They performed the Sun Dance Ritual, prayed to Wakan Tanka, the Great Spirit, and Sitting Bull slashed his arms a hundred times as a sign of sacrifice. He claimed to have had a vision during the ceremony, in which soldiers fell into the Lakota camp like grass-hoppers dropping out of the sky.

On 25 June 1876, Custer's 7th Cavalry advance party employed his usual surprise tactics at a camp on the Little Big Horn River in eastern Montana. However, unknown to Custer, 3,000 Indians had rallied to Sitting Bull, leaving their reservations to join him. This time, the Indians were ready and they fought back. Custer called the retreat as the numerical strength of the force he faced dawned on him. The counter-attack by the Indians when it came was terrible. Five of his companies were annihilated and amongst the 210 dead were Custer, two of his brothers and a brother-in-law.

The Indians were elated by their victory but their celebrations were short-lived. Thousands of US soldiers were ordered into the area and in the course of the next year they hunted the Lakota. Many surrendered, but Sitting Bull, stubborn to the end, refused, leading his band into Saskatchewan in Canada. He would remain there for many years, even after he had been granted a full pardon by the US government.

But life was hard for him, his family and the 200 Sioux who had accompanied him on the journey northwards. They were hungry and the winters were extremely cold. They decided to return across the border and give themselves up. On 19 July 1881, aged fifty,

Sitting Bull and his son Crow Foot rode into Fort Buford situated where the Missouri and Yellowstone Rivers met in the state of North Dakota. Sitting Bull surrendered his rifle to the commander of the fort and said that he wanted to look upon the soldiers and the white man as friends. Two weeks later, he and his band were moved to Fort Yates, close to the Standing Rock Indian Agency.

When Sitting Bull and his party of one hundred and eighty-five arrived, they were kept apart from the other Native Americans. The authorities still feared the great chief's ability to cause trouble and worried that he would incite the others gathered there to rise up again. So, he and his band were moved yet again, to Fort Randall, on the south side of the Missouri River in South Dakota. This time, however, they were held as prisoners of war. After almost two years, they were returned to the Standing Rock Agency.

Two years later, in 1885, Sitting Bull's life took a bizarre turn. William Frederick 'Buffalo Bill' Cody was one of the Wild West's most colourful characters. A decorated soldier, he had earned his nickname when he had killed 4,280 buffalo in just eighteen months in the late 1860s. As the West became more civilised, Buffalo Bill joined up with some friends, including gunfighter and scout, Wild Bill Hickock, in a hugely successful travelling Wild West show. In 1885, Sitting Bull was permitted to leave the Standing Rock reservation to join the show, earning $50 a week for merely making one lap of the arena on horseback. He was unhappy, however, often reported to have cursed his audiences in his native tongue, but also making speeches asking for education for the young people of his tribe.

He left after just four months but was by now being celebrated as a freedom fighter. He had also made a lot of money by charging for autographs and to have pictures taken with him, money he is said to have often given to homeless people and beggars. Critically, his travels in the white man's world made him finally realise how futile it would be to continue to fight with these people. They were too numerous and too powerful.

He returned to Standing Rock, living, with his family in a cabin on the Grand River. He rejected Christianity, refusing to give up the old ways and living with two wives. He did believe in the need for education, however, and sent his children to a nearby Christian school where they would learn to read and write, skills he was convinced were essential to the success of the next generation of Lakota.

Around this time, he is said to have had a vision in which a meadowlark landed on a hillock beside him and said 'Your own people, Lakotas, will kill you'.

A Northern Paiute leader, Wovoka, who went by the name of Jack Wilson, and who had gained a reputation as a powerful shaman, had a prophetic vision on 1 January 1889. In the vision he saw the resurrection of the Paiute dead and the removal of the white man from North America. He taught that to make this vision come true, Native Americans must live a good life and perform a traditional dance, the Ghost Dance, in a series of five-day gatherings. The Ghost Dance Movement, as it became known, spread rapidly amongst the tribes on their reservations, especially the Lakota Sioux. The Ghost Dance frightened federal officials and made them defensive in their dealings with the Indians, a feeling exacerbated by the focus of some Indians on the part of Wilson's vision dealing with the eradication of the white man.

The authorities feared that Sitting Bull, still revered as a spiritual leader, would support the Ghost Dance Movement. The Lakota on a couple of other reservations had already adopted the dance and troops had been called in to bring the movement under control. They sent forty-three police officers to arrest Sitting Bull and before dawn on 15 December 1890, they burst into his cabin and dragged him outside where his followers, hearing a commotion, had gathered to protect him. Gunshots rang out and the great chief was killed by a shot fired by a policeman into the side of his head.

He was initially buried at Fort Yates, but in 1953 his remains were exhumed and taken to a site near Mobridge, South Dakota by his fellow Sioux who wanted him to be buried close to his birthplace on Sioux lands. A granite shaft marks the grave of one of the most inspirational leaders in the history of the Unites States.

LILI'UOKALANI
QUEEN OF HAWAII

LILI'UOKALANI WAS BORN on 2 September, 1838 in a grass hut near Honolulu. Her parents were Hawaiian royalty – High Chiefess Analea Keohokalole and High Chief Caesar Kaluaiku Kapa'akea. She would be the last monarch and only queen regnant of the Kingdom of Hawaii.

It was the custom in Hawaiian culture – known as *hanai* – to give up your child to a close friend or relative, in order to strengthen family ties and the concept of the extended family, the *ohana*. Lydia, as Lili'uokalani was known, was, therefore, adopted at birth by Abner Paki, and his wife, Laura Konia. Abner was a Hawaiian nobleman, politician and close friend of the king and Lydia grew up at his residence on King Street, Hawaii, a house he had built himself from the grass hut that had originally been located there.

Lydia's full name was Lydia Lili'u Loloku Walania Wewehi Kamaka'eha, a name that was was given to her because her mother had been suffering from an eye infection when she was born. Therefore, her name means 'Lydia Smarting Tearful Anguish the Sore Eyes'. When she was named Crown Princess by her brother, King David, he changed it to the name by which she is more commonly known – Lili'uokalani, which means 'the smarting of the royal ones'.

She was well educated from the age of four, with her two brothers, David Kalakaua and James Kaliokalani, at the Royal School for the children of chiefs, learning to speak English fluently. Her other siblings were Anna Ka'iulani, Ka'imina'auao, Miriam Likelike and William Pitt

311

Leleiohoku. When she was ten, however, the school was closed by a measles epidemic that killed around 1,000 people on Hawaii, some of whom were children attending the Royal School. Sadly, Lili'uokalani's three-year-old sister, Ka'imina'auao, died in the epidemic.

On 16 September 1862, at the age of twenty-four, Lili'uokalani married the American-born John Owen Dominis who would go on to become Governor of the Hawaiian islands of O'ahu and Maui. She had three hanai children – Lili'uokalani Ka'onohiponiponiokalani Aholo; Kaiponohea Ae'a, the son of a retainer; and John Dominis Aimoku, John Dominis's son by another woman.

The popular Hawaiian King, Kamehameha V, never married, dying in 1872 without issue and without having named an heir to the throne. In such a situation, according to the Hawaiian Constitution, the choice of a new king fell to the Hawaiian parliament. They decided to hold an open election and the late king's cousin, William Charles Lunalilo won. Within two years, however, he was dead and once again there was a constitutional crisis as he also left no heir. Another election was held and Lili'uokalani's brother Davis Kalakaua stood against King Kamehameha IV's widow, Queen Emma. The election was bitterly fought and arguments raged about the claims to the throne of the respective parties. However, David Kalakaua won and was crowned King of Hawaii. He named his brother William Pitt Lelei hoku as heir apparent and gave his sisters, Lili'uokalani and Likelike royal titles.

In 1876, heir apparent, William, died and the question arose as to who would take his place. Princess Ruth Keelikolani offered to take his place – he was her hanai son. The cabinet rejected her offer, however, because the next in line after her would then be her cousin, Bernice Pauahi Bishop who was reputedly offered the crown by King Kamehameha V, but had turned his offer down. Instead, on 10 April 1877, they offered the position to Lili'uokalani. The new Crown Princess toured the island of O'ahu with her brother the king and her sister and her husband.

In April 1887, Lili'uokalani travelled to England to attend the Golden Jubilee of Queen Victoria's ascension to the throne. The Hawaiian royal party was largely treated on an equal footing to the great royal families of Europe and the world who attended the celebrations, in marked contrast to the manner in which the Americans had treated King Kamehameha IV when he had visited the United States in the 1860s. He had been treated with prejudice because of the colour of his skin. It later emerged in Queen Victoria's journals, however, that the King of the Belgians and the King of Saxony had both refused to accompany Princess Lili'uokalani because she was 'coloured'. Victoria had been outraged by this, apparently, and had commanded her son, Albert, to accompany the Hawaiian princesses.

While they were in Europe, however, constitutional trouble broke out at home and they were forced to cut short their tour and hurry back. A new constitution had suddenly been introduced by wealthy businessmen and plantation owners that turned Hawaii into a constitutional monarchy, divesting the monarchy of much of its power and placing it in the hands of American, European and native Hawaiian elites. It also removed voting rights from native Hawaiians and Asians. It was called the 'Bayonet Constitution' because it had been forced upon King David by armed militia who ordered him to sign it or be killed or deposed.

There was nothing to be done until January 1891 when King David Kalakaua died and Lili'uokalani ascended the throne. She responded to petitions from political parties and the people to abrogate the Bayonet Constitution, remove power from the hands of the wealthy few and restore voting rights. The response of the people behind the Bayonet Constitution was to announce that by not supporting the 1887 Constitution, Queen Lili'uokalani was, in effect, abdicating. They began actively seeking annexation by the United States, especially after Lili'uokalani had made it clear that she was against the Reciprocity Treaty of 1887 that her brother had signed, giving privileged concessions to the United States and ceding Pearl Harbour to them. This alienated foreign – particularly American – businessmen who actively began to work against her. There was also little doubt, however, that many of the American businessmen in Hawaii also objected to the fact that there was a woman on the throne.

The rebellious businessmen formed a Committee of Safety, claiming to speak for Americans living in Honolulu and expressed their fears about the safety of themselves, their families and their property. John L. Stevens, US Department of State's representative in Hawaii called on a company of US Marines from USS Boston and two companies of US sailors to protect the United States legation and Consulate.

Lili'uokalani was forced to relinquish her throne on 17 January 1893 – temporarily, she hoped – to 'the superior military forces of the United States', as she termed it, rather than to the Provisional Government that had been established. In a statement, she said she was doing so to avoid loss of life. She called upon the United States to restore her to the throne 'upon facts being presented to it.' However, on 1 February, the US representative, Stevens, declared Hawaii to be a protectorate of the USA.

US President Grover Cleveland ordered a report into the affair that concluded that the overthrow of Lili'uokalani was, in fact, illegal and that Stevens had acted 'inappropriately'. The President offered to restore Lili'uokalani to her throne if she granted an amnesty to everyone involved in the coup. Initially, she was outraged and insisted that she would have them all beheaded. She then relented and on 18 December, her reinstatement was demanded by a senior US representative. The Provisional Government would not back down, however, and the United States responded by commissioning another report, the Morgan Report, that found everyone involved innocent of responsibility for the overthrow of the government. Everyone, that is, except Queen Lili'uokalani.

On 4 July of the next year, Sanford B. Dole, one of the first of the opponents to Lili'uokalani's monarchy, was declared president of the Republic of Hawaii. The United States recognised the new republic as a protectorate.

Robert Wilcox, nicknamed the 'Iron Duke of Hawaii', was a native-born revolutionary, soldier and politician. He was very much against Dole's Republic of Hawaii and was brought in to organise a counter-revolution to restore Queen Lili'uokalani to the throne. In this, he was assisted by Sam Nowlein, the head of the Queen's guard, Charles T. Gulick, advisor to both King David Kalakaua and Lili'uokalani and a planter of British origin, William L. Rickard. Wilcox's force met the republican army at the foot of Diamond Head Mountain on 6 January 1895 and at Mo'ili'ili the following day. One man was killed in the skirmishes, a member of a prominent Hawaiian family. However, the royalists were easily beaten and the leaders were all in custody by 16 January. That day, Queen Lili'uokalani was herself arrested and imprisoned in the Iolani Palace in Honolulu. Guns had been found in the gardens of her home, but she denied all knowledge of their existence.

The queen was sentenced to five years hard labour in prison and fined $5,000, the sentence eventually being commuted to incarceration in an upstairs room of the palace, a time she used well, composing many well-known songs.

She abdicated her throne after eight months, in exchange for her release and the commuting of all the death sentences on her collaborators including Wilcox who had been charged with treason. She insisted that in reality it had been the Committee of Safety who had committed treason and they, not her associates should be under sentence of death.

When they asked her to sign a document in her married and not her royal name she was furious. 'Before ascending the throne, for fourteen years, or since the date of my proclamation as heir apparent, my official title had been simply Lili'uokalani. Thus I was proclaimed both Princess Royal and Queen. Thus it is recorded in the archives of the government to this day. The Provisional Government nor any other had enacted any change in my name. All my official acts, as well as my private letters, were issued over the signature of Liliuokalani. But when my jailers required me to sign ('Liliuokalani Dominis,') I did as they commanded. Their motive in this as in other actions was plainly to humiliate me before my people and before the world. I saw in a moment, what they did not, that, even were I not complying under the most severe and exacting duress, by this demand they had overreached themselves. There is not, and never was, within the range of my knowledge, any such a person as Liliuokalani Dominis.'

She worked as head of the Oni pa'a (Stand Firm) movement, the motto of which was 'Hawaii for the Hawaiians,' fighting bitterly against the annexation of the islands by the United States. It was inevitable, however, occurring in July 1898. Hawaii subsequently became America's 50th state in 1959.

Queen Lili'uokalani sued the United States government for $450,000 to cover her loss of property and for other losses. Eventually, the legislature of Hawaii allowed her a pension of $4,000 a year and gave her the income from a large sugar plantation. She returned home to Washington Place and on her sixtieth birthday, large numbers of her loyal subjects visited her at there. Many brought gifts and a large number kneeled in her presence in her presence and backed out the same way they entered. She was still their queen.

The last reigning monarch of Hawaii died of a stroke in November 1917 at the age of seventy-nine.

CRAZY HORSE

THERE WERE NEVER any photographs taken of him. It would be contrary to the spirit and culture of his people, the Lakota, who lived in North and South Dakota and, indeed, he fought – ferociously, by all accounts – against the white man for most of his life, struggling to protect and preserve the Lakota way of life and their culture.

Born on the South Cheyenne River around 1840 into the Ogala, one of the tribes of the Lakota, Crazy Horse was initially given the name In the Wilderness and enjoyed the nickname amongst his family and friends of Curly due to the light, curly hair he had inherited from his mother, Rattling Blanket Woman. His father passed his own name of Crazy Horse to his son and adopted the name Wagula, meaning 'Worm'.

Crazy Horse came from famous antecedents; Rattling Blanket Woman's father was Black Buffalo, a Lakota who had stopped the expedition of Lewis and Clark on the Bad River. Wagula was, himself, a bold warrior. Leading a small hunting party in the summer of 1844, he came across a Lakota village under attack from enemy Crow warriors. Wagula led his band to victory over the numerically superior Crow and saved the village. The village chief, Corn, gave Wagula his three daughters in gratitude, but when they returned to his village, his wife Rattling Blanket Woman was upset that he had taken other wives. She hanged herself from a cottonwood tree and Crazy Horse would from then on be brought up by his aunts, Good Looking Woman and They Are Afraid of Her.

Crazy Horse grew up as leader of the Hoksi Hakakta or 'Last Child Society,' which numbered 40 members and who were the last-born males of specially chosen families. While still young, the camp

Crazy Horse lived in was attacked by a contingent of United States cavalry, led by a Lieutenant Grattan. Following the attack, in which the Lakota leader, Conquering Bear, was killed, Crazy Horse began to have trance visions. He underwent *hemblecha* – vision quest – with his father and was given a medicine bundle that would protect him during his life. He was also shown his face paint – a yellow lightning bolt down the left side of his face. He was given a sacred song and it was made known to him that he would be a protector of his people.

A medicine man also gave him a black stone to protect his horse, a black and white pony called Inyan, meaning 'rock'. He placed the stone behind the horse's ear, believing it would protect him and Inyan in battle.

Crazy Horse's reputation as a great warrior started when he was still very young. Aged just thirteen, he was part of a raiding party stealing horses from the rival Crow Indians and he led his first war party before the age of twenty. His first kill was a Shoshone raider who had killed a Lakota woman and he took part in numerous battles with his tribe's enemies, amongst whom were the Shoshone, the Crow, the Blackfeet, the Pawnee and the Arikara.

It all changed in 1864, however, following the massacre of 400 Cheyenne and Arapaho – men, women and children – by the Colorado Territory militia in a village at Sand Creek in Colorado. The Lakota allied with the Cheyenne and began to focus their attention on the US army, rather than on neighbouring tribes. By now, Crazy Horse's ability as a warrior was becoming well known and he took part in the Battle of Red Buttes and the Platte River Station Battles in July 1865. He became known as 'Ogle Tanka Un' – 'War Leader'.

In December 1866, Crazy Horse, leading just six braves, lured Lieutenant William Fetterman's attachment of fifty-three infantrymen from Fort Phil Kearny, in Wyoming, up a hill now known as Massacre Hill. Meanwhile, six other braves led the twenty-seven cavalrymen in the attachment towards Peno Creek. Lakota warriors poured over the brow of Massacre Hill and threw themselves at the infantry. The cavalry were surrounded and were unable to get back to help their colleagues. Every soldier died, killed by a force of around a thousand Cheyenne and Lakota in an action that became known as Red Cloud's War, even though Red Cloud was not present on the battlefield that day. It was, until that time, the worst defeat suffered by the Army on the Great Plains.

Again close to Fort Phil Kearny, Crazy Horse was part of the Lakota band that attacked a wood-cutting crew that ran for cover behind a circle of wheel-less wagon boxes. The soldiers were using a particularly effective new rifle, the Second Allin breech-loader that could fire ten bullets in a minute and the Lakota suffered huge casualties as they charged, expecting the soldiers to re-charge their weapons as they had done with the older weapons they had used.

Crazy Horse was almost killed by one of his own when he took as a wife, Black Buffalo Woman. She had been married to No Water, a Lakota who could often be found drinking whisky, like many others, near army forts. She had divorced him on account of his lifestyle and was on a buffalo hunt with Crazy Horse, when No Water found them in a tipi in the Slim Buttes area. He drew his pistol and aimed it at Crazy Horse's heart from the tipi entrance. Just as he was about to fire, Touch the Clouds, a cousin of Crazy Horse ran across knocking the pistol upwards as No Water pulled the trigger. The bullet hit Crazy Horse in the jaw and No Water took off for his own village, Crazy Horse's braves in pursuit. Eventually, the two men were persuaded by the elders to come to an agreement so that no more blood would be spilt and No Water gave Crazy Horse three Horses as compensation. A woman the elders sent to help heal Crazy Horse, Black Shawl, became another of his wives and bore him a daughter who died, aged just two in 1872.

The No Water incident had led to Crazy Horse being stripped of his title of War Leader but in August 1872, he accompanied the powerful Lakota Chief Sitting Bull at the inconclusive Battle of Arrow Creek where the Lakota attacked a Pacific Railroad crew.

The Battle of Little Big Horn was a defining moment for both the Lakota and the US Army. It arose out of the US government's 1876 demand that all Indian tribes return to their reservations. Native Americans rebelled against the order and Crazy Horse led the resistance in an alliance with the Cheyennes, to whom he was related through marriage – his first wife was a Cheyenne. In June 1876, he rode at the head of a force of around 1,500 Lakota and Cheyenne that surprised 1,000 soldiers led by Brigadier General George Crook, that was marching to join up with General George Custer's 7th Cavalry. Crook was held up for a sufficient amount of time to ensure that Custer lost his last, famous battle. On 25 June, Crazy Horse joined forces with Sitting Bull and led his band in the attack that destroyed the 7th Cavalry, flanking the Americans from the north and west as Hunkpapa warriors led by chief Gall charged from the south and east. It was reported that during the battle, Crazy Horse charged repeatedly into Custer's men, succeeding in splitting them in half, causing them to panic and waste bullets. His courage enabled his braves – many without rifles – to attack and overcome the cavalrymen who had already fired their one-shot rifles and who were desperately trying to re-load. Following the battle, he was highly praised by both Lakota and Cheyenne as the bravest warrior in the Battle of the Little Big Horn.

His next contact with the army came in September when, accompanied by his band of braves, he unsuccessfully attempted to rescue a Miniconjou village that had been attacked by Captain Anston Mills and two battalions of the 3rd Cavalry. The village headman, American Horse and many members of his family were killed after hiding in a cave for a number of hours.

On 8 January, the following year, Crazy Horse fought his last major battle against the US Cavalry, at Wolf Mountain in Montana. By 5 May, with his people freezing and starving due to the decline in the buffalo population, he knew that his time was up. He and other Ogala chiefs arrived at the Red Cloud Agency near Camp

Robinson in Nebraska and formally surrendered to First Lieutenant William P Clark.

The Ogala Lakota set up a village close to the agency but after four months rumours began to spread that Crazy Horse was unhappy and wanted to return to the old ways. Other tribes were also unhappy. In August 1877, Chief Joseph had led his Nez Perce tribe out of its reservation in Idaho and made for Canada, by way of Montana. Lieutenant Clark and the Miniconjou leader, Touch Clouds, were asked to join the Army in hunting down the Nez Perce, but the two men refused, saying that they had promised to be peaceful when they had surrendered. Tension mounted at the agency as mistranslated words seemed to suggest that Crazy Horse would either go north and fight until all the Nez Perce were killed or would go north and fight until not a white man was left alive. No one was sure what he meant.

They summoned General Crook to meet him, but the meeting had to be cancelled when it emerged that Crazy Horse had said that he was going to kill the general during the meeting. Crook ordered that the Indian chief be arrested and then left the agency under the command of Lieutenant Colonel Luther P. Bradley. Reinforcements were sent to Camp Robinson and they moved against Crazy Horse's village on the morning of 4 September.

They were too late, though. Crazy Horse had fled. Taking his sick and the other members of the tribe with him, he had gone to the nearby Spotted Tail Agency but after meeting officials there, he agreed to return to his village.

The next morning, 5 September, accompanied by the Indian agent at Spotted Tail, Lieutenant Jesse M. Lee, and Touch the Clouds, he left for Camp Robinson. That evening, Lee was ordered to hand Crazy Horse over to the officer of the day. Lee protested, but to no avail and learned that Crazy Horse was to be taken to Division Headquarters. He handed the Lakota chief over to Captain James Kennington who was in charge of the guard at the post. He led Crazy Horse and another Lakota, Little Big Man, to the guardhouse.

Arriving there, Crazy Horse became uneasy about what awaited him and in a struggle with his escort was stabbed with a bayonet by one of the guards. With blood pouring from his wound, he was rushed to the office of the adjutant, but the post's assistant surgeon, Dr. Valentine McGillicuddy was unable to save him. He died later that night, aged just thirty-seven.

An alternative version of the incident was later provided by Little Big Man who claimed that as Crazy Horse was being led to the guardhouse, he pulled out two knives from beneath his blanket, one of them fashioned from an army bayonet. Little Big Man was immediately behind him and, not wanting the soldiers to be given an excuse to kill the Lakota leader, grabbed both his elbows, pulling his arms behind his back. As Crazy Horse struggled to release himself from Little Big Man's grip, one of his arms jerked free and the bayonet-knife penetrated deep into his lower back. The guard had at the same time thrust with his bayonet, but his lunge had missed. Little Big Man said that the post commander had invented the story that the guard had in fact killed Crazy Horse to avoid a vendetta against him when Crazy Horse's tribe found out. The truth will probably never be known.

The great warrior's body was handed over to his elderly parents who took it to Camp Sheridan where, in accordance to Lakota custom, it was put on a scaffold. A month later, when the Spotted Tail Agency moved to the Missouri River, his parents transported the body to an undisclosed location and buried it.

As he lay dying, Crazy Horse spoke to the commander: 'My friend, I do not blame you for this. Had I listened to you this trouble would not have happened to me. I was not hostile to the white men…We preferred hunting to a life of idleness on the reservation, where we were driven against our will. At times we did not get enough to eat and we were not allowed to leave the reservation to hunt. We preferred our own way of living. We were no expense to the government. All we wanted was peace and to be left alone.'

V
THE MODERN WORLD

CHARLES 'LUCKY' LUCIANO

BORN SALVATORE LUCANIA in 1897 outside Palermo in Sicily, Lucky Luciano invented organised crime as we know it today and masterminded the postwar international heroin trade that has made billions for criminals around the world. So great has been his influence on the modern world that *Time* magazine named him as one of the top twenty most influential builders and titans of the 20th century.

Luciano arrived in New York in 1906 with his family in search of a better life, like hundreds of thousands of other immigrants from the Old World. But by 1907, ten-year-old Salvatore was already in trouble with the police, arrested for shoplifting. But that was small-time stuff for Lucky. He had started his first racket, offering protection to younger Jewish kids on the way to school. If they refused to pay, he beat them up anyway.

It all went fine and he was making good money until he found one boy who simply would not pay. Meyer Lansky was from Poland and he was tough. So tough, in fact, that Lucky found it hard to beat him and Lansky actually fought back. Lucky was so impressed he suggested to Lansky that they join forces. Lansky, seeing an opportunity to earn some easy money, readily accepted.

Aged 14, Lucky was again in trouble with the law, doing four months in a youth correctional facility for playing truant from school. Then, aged eighteen, he spent six months in a reformatory for selling heroin and morphine.

In 1915, Lucky met Frank Costello, known then as Frank Castiglia, who would go on to become not only a friend, but also a business partner and by 1920, like many other hoodlums taking advantage of Prohibition, they had set up a bootlegging operation with a legitimate trucking company as the front for their activities.

Vito Genovese, another early friend of Luciano's who would go on to become a big noise in the Mafia, introduced Luciano to a heroin dealer, Charlie 'Big Nose' Lagaipa who persuaded him to invest in his drugs business. It would prove to be a bad decision; Luciano was arrested by the police with a large quantity of heroin in his possession. He faced a long prison stretch and not even judiciously placed bribes had worked. He offered the authorities a deal. In exchange for showing them where a huge stash of heroin was hidden, he would be allowed to walk free. He then instructed his men to plant the heroin where he had said they would find it. They found it alright but Lucky noticed that not all of it made its way back to police headquarters.

He had joined the crime family run by Joe 'the Boss' Masseria, the largest in the country. Luciano was now associating with some of the biggest gangsters of the time – Joe Adonis, 'Big Bill' Dwyer, Arnold Rothenstein, Dutch Schultz and 'Dandy' Phil Kastel. However, Masseria disagreed with Luciano on the way the business should be conducted. Luciano admired the way that his friend Frank Costello bribed corrupt city officials and the police to obtain protection for his rackets but Masseria, was very much of the old school, the Mafia men known as 'Moustache Petes', and he trusted no one who was not Sicilian. Costello was Italian, but not from Sicily and was, therefore, not welcome. Masseria, to Luciano's mind, was becoming a major obstacle to his vision of what organised crime could actually become.

One day in the late 1920s, Luciano was abducted at gunpoint by three men as he was standing on Sixth Avenue in New York. They beat him – giving him the distinctive scar that made his eye droop – stabbed him and left him for dead on a beach in New York Bay. When he asked around to find out who had been behind the attack, his friend Meyer Lansky provided him with the answer – Masseria.

Lucky was furious. So furious, in fact, that he decided to throw in his lot with Masseria's rival, Sal Maranzano, another crime leader who had ambitions to become the boss of bosses. He met secretly with his erstwhile rival and agreed to betray Masseria.

In 1928 one of the most destructive of all Mafia wars broke out on the streets of New York. The Castellammarese War would last for two years and would define organised crime for the remainder of the 20th century. Luciano, however, kept out of it. Instead, he spent time with the younger mafiosi from both sides, learning how they felt about the way things were going. He discovered that no one was particularly happy and that everyone was hoping that one of the two old bosses would kill the other so that the remaining boss could himself be killed and there could be changes in the way the gangs operated, something that would never happen while the two 'Moustache Petes' were still at the head of their respective operations. As he moved amongst these factions, Luciano began to be seen as their leader.

By 1931, the war was still raging with Maranzano winning, but Masseria still wielding a lot of power. Luciano decided it was time to make his move. He requested a meeting with Masseria and then, in one of the most famous Mafia hits of all time, had four men mow him down at the meeting place – Scarpato's Restaurant on Coney Island.

Thus, Lucky had ensured victory for Maranzano in the Castellammarese War and the boss was, naturally, very grateful, promoting him to number two in the huge criminal empire he now controlled. But Lucky Luciano had not put in all that work for the past two years to end up number two to a man for whose methods he had no respect.

Maranzano was no fool, and was quite aware that Luciano was after him. He set plans in motion for the murder of not only Lucky, but also many of his associates including Genovese and Costello. Unfortunately for him, he failed to move swiftly enough. Lucky hired

Samuel 'Red' Levine and three other hitmen to pay Maranzano a visit at his offices on the 9th floor of the Hemsley Building on 10 September 1931. They got in posing as police officers, disarmed Maranzano's gurds and stabbed the old boss to death.

That night became known in the annals of Mafia history as 'The Night of the Sicilian Vespers'. Dozens of mobsters met their end – as many as ninety, according to some sources – assassinated on the orders of Luciano or Lansky. Lucky was cleaning out the dead wood, ready for a fresh start for organised crime.

Charles 'Lucky' Luciano was now, aged thirty-four, top of the heap – he immediately got to work reorganising. Johnny Torrio urged him to establish an overall governing body for the Mafia. Luciano established the Commission – also known as the National Crime Syndicate – which involved all the top men from each family and at the very top of which sat Luciano. Like the Supreme Court, it was there as the last voice in all disputes. It also divided up territories and rackets. Before someone could become a 'made man', a fully paid-up member of the organisation – his boss had to appear before the Commission to obtain permission for the new man to be accepted. Murder Inc., the Mob's murderous enforcement arm, also reported to it.

The Commission was composed of men from New York's Five Families, the Buffalo Crime Family and Al Capone's Chicago operation. The Detroit Family was also part of it, as were the wiseguys from Los Angeles and Kansas. Everyone had an equal say, each family possessing one vote on any matter under discussion. In reality, however, it was controlled by one man – Lucky Luciano.

At this time, he made his famous statement about the way the Mafia should do business: 'We only kill each other'. It was a stricture to which mafiosi adhered surprisingly well. In fact, when Dutch Schultz tried to kill the Mafia's great enemy, US attorney and future Republican presidential candidate, Thomas Dewey, it was Shultz who found himself dead.

Luciano was at his zenith. The crime family at the head of which he sat, and which now bore his name, was the largest and most powerful in the country. Money flooded in from illegal bookmaking, loansharking, extortion, numbers rackets and fortunes were gleaned from labour and union activities. He controlled the New York waterfront and was involved in construction, garbage disposal, the clothing industry and trucking.

Apart from Meyer Lansky who was his top adviser and whose advice Lucky always listened to, other men who had been with him on the way up benefited, too. Vito Genovese was appointed his Underboss, former Chicago boss, Johnny Torrio, became a Senior Adviser, and his capos, the men who supervised what went on on the streets included a veritable Who's Who of the mafia for the next few years – Frank Costello, Joe Adonis, Michael 'Trigger Mike' Coppola, Anthony 'Tony Bender' Strollo, Generoso Del Duca, Thomas 'Tommy Palmer' Greco, Louis 'Louie the Gimp' Avitabile, John 'Duke' DeNoia, Gaetano Ricci, Rocco 'The Old Man' Pelligrino, John 'Footo' Biello, Guarino 'Willie Moore' Moretti, Angelo 'Gyp' DeCarlo and Ruggero 'Ritchie the Boot' Bioardo in New Jersey, Salvatore 'Big Nose Sam' Cufari in Connecticut and Anthony 'Little Augie Pisano' Carfano in Florida.

Luciano, wealthy and always exquisitely dressed, was having a ball. He liked to be seen around town, dining at all the right places and enjoying himself with a different woman on his arm every night at exclusive nightspots such as the Stork Club or the Copacabana.

Ironically, however, the very man whose life he had saved from Dutch Schultz's murderous intentions in 1935, had now set his sights on him. Thomas Dewey was targeting him as a leader of organised crime and succeeded in prosecuting him on what were trumped-up prostitution charges after raiding eighty brothels and taking into custody almost a hundred madams and girls who provided huge amounts of information about their businesses and Luciano's involvement in their business. It was ironic really, as Luciano famously believed prostitution to be despicable. Of course, that did not prevent him from enjoying the vast amounts of money his organisation generated from it. He had even, at one point said of the brothels he ran – 'We'll run them like chain stores.'

He was sentenced to thirty to fifty years in prison but tried to carry on running the business from his prison cell at the notorious Dannemora Prison, using his trusted men, Costello and Lansky.

It seemed as if he was doomed to spend the rest of his life behind bars until the wily Lansky saw opportunity in America's entry into World War Two. Luciano was, of course, connected with Sicily where the Allies planned to launch an invasion of Europe and could help smooth the way amongst the locals and even enlist the help of the local mafiosi in ensuring safe passage for Allied forces as they moved up through the Italian peninsula. Through his Italian Mafia connections he was also able to provide information about communist influence amongst resistance groups and local governments. Furthermore, he knew the New York docks inside out, having controlled them for so many years and the authorities believed them to be in serious danger from Nazi saboteurs; an attack on the docks could seriously hamper the war effort. Lansky approached Naval intelligence and offered Lucky's help. In May 1942, they moved him to the more secure Great Meadow Prison in Comstock, New York which was like a country club compared to the harsh regime that prevailed in Dannemora.

Having given them all the help they had asked for, Luciano believed that at the end of the war he deserved to be set free. The only man who could authorise his release, however, was none other than Thomas Dewey, now Governor of New York. In January 1946, he commuted Lucky Luciano's sentence, setting him free on condition that he be deported back to Italy. At 8.50 on the morning of Sunday 10 February 1946, Lucky found himself standing at the rails of the SS *Laura Keene*, looking back at the Statue of Liberty as he set sail for Italy.

Although deeply hurt at being forced to leave the land that he called his own, Luciano threw himself back into his old activities. Although the Italian government had provided strict guidelines for him – he was not allowed to travel more than a few miles from Naples, for instance, and had to provide information to them about any visitors – in 1947 he flew to Cuba for the famous Havana Conference attended by all the Mob's main players. It was at that meeting that he gave the order for the execution of Bugsy Siegel who was believed to be pocketing cash from a loan given to him by the Mafia to build the Flamingo Hotel and Casino complex at Las Vegas. When the Americans discovered Luciano was in Cuba, however, he was forced to return to Italy.

He continued to earn large sums of money but in the late 1950s it would begin to affect his friendship with his old colleague, Meyer Lansky, who believed that Lucky was taking too much out of the business and also believed him to be cutting him out of some lucrative business deals.

On 26 January 1962, Lucky was due to meet a scriptwriter who was going to write about him for a film about his life. When Luciano met him at Naples airport, however, the gangster suddenly clutched his chest and collapsed to the ground. His increasingly weak heart had finally given in and he succumbed to a major heart attack.

They finally allowed his body to be returned to the United States in 1972, ten years after his death and he was buried at St John's cemetery in New York.

AL CAPONE

AL CAPONE'S FATHER, Gabriele, arrived in America in 1894, from the village of Castellmare di Stabia, sixteen miles south of Naples. Gabriele was a barber who had the advantage of being able to read and write Italian and with him he brought his pregnant twenty-seven-year-old wife, Teresa, two-year-old son, Vincenzo and baby son, Raffaele.

The family began their life in America in an apartment in a slum area of Brooklyn, but Gabriele's literacy got him a job in a grocery store, while Teresa took in sewing work. Her third son, Salvatore, was born in 1895 and her fourth on 17 January 1899. He was named Alphonse Gabriel Capone and he would grow up to be leader of a powerful criminal empire and, possibly, the most infamous gangster of them all.

Gabriele achieved his ambition when he opened his own barbershop in Brooklyn, and moved his family into the aprtment above it. This area was more cosmopolitan than the one in which they had previously been staying and young Al, as he called himself, played with Irish, German, Swedish and Chinese children. It was an experience that would benefit him later in life.

Al attended school from the age of five, but, when he was fourteen, he was hit by a woman teacher and, possessed of a quick temper, he retaliated. Expulsion from school followed, bringing his formal education to an abrupt end. Crucially, however, around this time, the family moved to Garfield Place where Capone would meet some formative influences – an Irish girl called Mae who would become his wife, and the mobster, Johnny Torrio.

Torrio was a new breed of hoodlum, something of a criminal visionary, and Capone noted carefully how he ran his affairs – numbers racketeering, brothels and prostitution – like a business enterprise. It was Torrio, in fact, who would invent the concept of the National Crime Syndicate in the 1930s. He was a role model for local boys, including Capone who earned pocket money running errands for him. He won Torrio's trust and was given more to do. Meanwhile, Capone learned the art of appearing, like Torrio, to be respectable to the outside world while involved in the world of organised criminality.

When Torrio moved to Chicago in 1909, to provide protection for Chicago crime boss and old-time gangster Giacomo 'Big Jim' Colosimo, who was married to his aunt, the ten-year-old Capone came under other influences. He started running with street gangs, the South Brooklyn Rippers, the Forty Thieves Juniors and the Five Point Juniors. There was still no sign, however, of the criminal mastermind he would become in years to come. He lived at home and worked diligently to help the family, first in a munitions factory and then as a paper cutter. He was a quiet boy who did not stand out.

It was when he met Frankie Yale, a young man of Calabrian origin, that Capone really began to change. Frankie was a tough nut who saw violence as the only way to get ahead in life. He had opened a bar on Coney Island and, on Johnny Torrio's advice, took Capone on as a bartender.

Yale was ambitious and had his eyes on the Chicago criminal empire run by, Colosimo. In May 1920, he made his move, shooting Colosimo dead in his own restaurant, but he lost out to Johnny Torrio who took control of Colosimo's business affairs. It was lucrative, too. Prohibition was adding a huge boost to criminal earnings and Torrio could add income from speakeasies to what he was already earning from thousands of brothels and gambling joints.

It was to this world that Torrio introduced the twenty-two-year-old Al Capone and, before long, Capone had become his partner rather than his employee. He ran the Four Deuces, a combination speakeasy, gambling joint and whorehouse and his brother, Ralph arrived from New York to work with him. Meanwhile, Al made friends with Jake 'Greasy Thumb' Guzik who would become a lifelong friend. From a Jewish Orthodox family that earned its living through prostitution, Guzik was like a big brother to Al.

Married now to Mae, with a boy called Sonny, Capone was going up in the world. He bought a house for his family in a respectable neighbourhood and to his neighbours, he was a second-hand furniture dealer.

But things changed when Chicago's corrupt mayor, 'Big Bill' Thompson was succeeded by the earnest reformer, William E. Dever. Graft became more difficult, forcing Torrio to the conclusion that they should move their operations out of Chicago. The suburb of Cicero seemed ideal. There they could easily buy up the entire city government and police department. Capone was put in charge of establishing the operation in Cicero and managed it with little opposition. His older brother, Frank handled the city government, Ralph managed the opening of a working-class brothel called the Stockade and Al put his energies into the gambling side of the business, investing in a new gambling joint, the Ship. At the same time he took control of Hawthorne Race Track.

On municipal election day in 1924, Capone's men did what they could to stop opposition candidates having any chance of success, kidnapping workers, stealing ballot boxes and threatening voters with violence. News spread of their activities and the Chicago Police Chief decided to intervene. He sent seventy-nine armed police officers in plain clothes and driving unmarked cars to Cicero. Frank Capone was approached by this convoy as he walked down the street. They recognised him and opened fire on him, riddling his body with bullets. They called it self-defence since Frank pulled a gun when he saw the cops approach carrying guns.

Al was furious but, in spite of the best efforts of the authorities, the day was won and Cicero was his. He threw the most lavish funeral ever seen in the town for his brother, the flowers alone costing $20,000.

For five weeks, Capone exercised restraint, but after Joe Howard, a small-time thug, assaulted his friend, Jake Guzik, after Guzik had refused him a loan, Capone tracked Howard down in a bar. Howard was stupid enough to call Al a 'dago pimp' and Al, in a rage, shot him dead. William H. McSwiggin, known as 'the hanging prosecutor', went after Capone for the murder but witnesses seemed to develop memory loss as soon as the name Capone was mentioned. He got away with it, but the case gave him a notoriety very different a million miles from the discreet anonymity sought by Johnny Torrio and his ilk.

Al Capone was now twenty-five and a powerful and wealthy man. He was also acutely aware that he was in the sights not just of the law, but also of rival mobsters who wanted a piece of his action.

Dion O'Bannion was one such. He had a growing florist and bootlegging business but was a dangerously unstable individual who killed on a whim. Torrio and Capone often had to make peace amongst rival gangs who were their allies and when O'Bannion went to war with the Genna brothers, O'Bannion provided Torrio with a solution. He said he would retire if Torrio would buy his brewery from him. Knowing that there was going to be a raid at the brewery, O'Bannion arranged a meeting there with Torrio. During the raid, Torrio was arrested and O'Bannion refused to give back the money Torrio had paid him for the brewery. A big mistake.

Not long after Torrio's arrest, a large funeral was taking place for the head of the Unione Siciliana in Chicago, Mike Merlo. When three gangsters walked into his florist shop, O'Bannion thought they had merely come to collect a wreath. He reached out his hand to shake theirs and one of the men, knowing that the florist always kept one hand free to grab one of the guns he kept in three special pockets tailored into his suits, grabbed his free arm. Six gunshots later, O'Bannion lay on the floor in a pool of blood. No one was ever charged with his murder.

However, a couple of O'Bannion's associates, 'Hymie' Weiss and 'Bugs' Moran, were convinced they knew who was ultimately responsible and from then on, Johnny Torrio and Al Capone had to take careful precautions. Torrio even left Chicago for a while which was not a bad idea as, during the next two years, there were a dozen attempts on Capone's life, in spite of the two bodyguards who accompanied him everywhere he went and the fact that he travelled only at night.

When Torrio returned to the city in January 1925, Moran and Weiss struck. As he left his car to walk to the door of his apartment building, they attacked, shooting him in the chest, neck, right arm and groin. Moran then put his gun to Torrio's head and pulled the trigger to finish him off. But the gun was empty and all Torrio heard was the click of the hammer. He was rushed to hospital where Capone organised security for him, even sleeping on a cot in his room to ensure his old friend was safe.

The incident understandably made a deep impression on Torrio and he was never the same man again. While serving a nine-month sentence for the brewery arrest, he made the decision to get out of organised crime. He called Capone to the prison and handed over all his assets – brothels, nightclubs, gambling joints, breweries and speakeasies – to him and his brothers.

Capone was now a force to be reckoned with and a very wealthy one, at that. He moved his headquarters into a suite at the Metropole Hotel in Chicago at a cost of $1,500 a day and was suddenly famous. He was advised by friend and newspaper editor, Harry Read, to cultivate political connections and become more visible. He was seen at the opera, he attended sporting events and charitable functions. He became almost respectable. After all, he was only a bootlegger and everybody drank.

He was still no angel, though. In December, 1925, Frankie Yale invited him to a Christmas Day party at one of his speakeasies, the Adonis Club. He told Capone that he had learned that a rival,

Richard 'Peg-Leg' Lonergan, planned to gatecrash the party with his men and suggested cancelling. Capone told him to let the party go ahead and organised a surprise Christmas present for Lonergan. When the gatecrashers burst into the club at around 3 am, Capone calmly gave a signal and Lonergan's men did not even have time to pull their guns out before being peppered with bullets.

By early 1926, Capone was on top of his game. In the *New Yorker* magazine, he had been described as 'the greatest gang leader in history' and he had done a deal with Yale that would completely change the interstate transportation of bootleg whiskey. In April of that year, however, he made his first mistake. He heard that a rival bootlegger, Jim Doherty, was drinking in Cicero. This represented a territorial insult to Capone. What he did not know, however, was that Doherty was in the company of the young 'hanging prosecutor', Billy McSwiggin who had tried to get Capone for the murder of Joe Howard in 1924.

Capone and his men waited for Doherty outside the bar in which he was carousing and when he staggered out in the company of others, they opened fire with machine guns. Doherty and McSwiggin were both killed, creating a huge outcry against gangster violence and especially against Al Capone. It was widely suspected that he had been behind the killings. But there was no evidence to implicate him and officials and police could do nothing as he still walked the streets. The police took revenge, launching a series of raids on his establishments and forcing Capone into hiding while detectives scoured the country for him, their searches stretching as far as Canada and Italy. All the time, he was with friends in Michigan, re-considering his life, thinking of giving up his criminal activities, of using his fortune to pursue legitimate business enterprises.

As a first step, he negotiated a surrender to Chicago police, returning, in July, 1926 to Chicago to face the murder charges that were stacked up against him. Amazingly, however, the authorities failed to establish enough evidence to bring him to trial and they had to set him free.

Back in business, Al sought to make his peace with Hymie Weiss who still smarted over Dion O'Bannion's demise. Capone offered him a favourable business deal, but Weiss turned it down. The following day Hymie Weiss was gunned down.

As people became more and more disgusted by the violence on their streets, Capone held a bizarre, highly publicised press conference, at which he appealed to fellow bootleggers to end the violence. 'There is enough business for all of us without killing each other like animals in the streets. I don't want to die in the street punctured by machine-gun fire,' he said. An amnesty was negotiated whereby it was agreed there would be no further murders or beatings and for two months it held. Then, in January 1927, a friend of Capone, Theodore 'Tony the Greek' Anton, was killed and the bullets started flying again.

May 1927 saw the return to power of the corrupt 'Big Bill' Thompson but a decision in the Supreme Court put new pressure on bootleggers and especially on Capone. It stated that income tax should be paid even on illegally-derived revenues. This meant that the Internal Revenue Service were now in a position to pursue Capone and his money. He was unconcerned, however, and carried on much as before, becoming a jazz impresario with the opening of his famous Cotton Club. He seemed to have no prejudices, either racial or social and helped the careers of many black musicians, including Louis Armstrong.

But, they were closing in on him and wherever he went, the police were not far away. When he travelled, he found police at every station en route. They surrounded his house and repeatedly arrested him for the smallest things. He was hounded. Meanwhile, the IRS was making a detailed investigation of his income and expenditure – no easy task, as all his business was conducted through third parties and every transaction he made was conducted with cash.

Frankie Yale was becoming a problem to Capone. Their whiskey deal was not working as envisaged and there were numerous hijackings, for which Capone thought Yale was probably responsible. On Sunday, 1 July 1928, Yale was drinking in a Brooklyn speakeasy when he was called to the telephone. Whatever he was told on the phone sent him running out to his car. He drove off, but minutes later, as he drove along Forty-fourth Street, he was pushed to the kerb by a black sedan which sprayed his car with bullets from several different types of gun – revolvers, sawn-off shotguns and machine guns. Problem solved.

Capone moved from the Metropole to a special suite with its own kitchen at the Lexington Hotel. He had secret doors installed, in case he needed to make a swift exit. Now, seeing the approach of the end of Prohibition, he was beginning to invest in other rackets such as unions and protection.

There was still a blot on Capone's landscape, however – Bugs Moran. Moran had twice tried to kill a friend of Capone's – Jack 'Machine Gun' McGurn. Capone decided that Moran should be assassinated and gave the task to McGurn who put together a crew consisting of some top out-of-town mobsters – Fred 'Killer' Burke, James Ray, John Scalise, Albert Anselmi, Joseph Lolordo and, from Detroit's notorious Purple Gang, murderous brothers Harry and Phil Keywell. They would take part in the most famous incident in gangster history.

The date for the hit was to be Thursday 14 February, Valentine's Day. Moran and his henchmen were to be lured to a garage to buy whiskey. Four of McGurn's men would be waiting for them there, dressed in stolen police uniforms and trench coats in order to look as if they were raiding the place.

A man who resembled Moran was spotted by the Keywells and four of the phoney cops went into the garage where they found seven men. They took the men's guns and lined them up against the wall before opening fire with two machine guns. All were killed apart from a man called Frank Gutenberg who was still breathing.

Two of the killers were then marched at gunpoint out of the garage in their trench coats as if they had been arrested by the other two. They got into a stolen police car and drove off.

There was one small problem. Bugs Moran was not amongst the dead men. Bugs had been late for the meeting and, seeing the stolen police car outside the garage, had driven past the scene. When police arrived, they found Frank Gutenberg still alive and asked him who had shot him. He replied: 'No one. Nobody shot me.' He died shortly after.

Everyone knew that Moran had been the intended target and that Capone was behind it, but there was nothing to connect him to the killings. He had been in Florida, after all. The Valentine's Day Massacre received massive publicity on a national scale and Capone became the subject of countless books and newspaper articles. He loved the notoriety, employing noted journalist and short story writer, Damon Runyan, as his press agent. President Herbert Hoover announced that the Federal agencies were focusing all their efforts on Capone and his associates.

But, Capone had other fish to fry. Three men – Albert Anselmi, Giuseppe 'Joseph Hop Toad' Giunta and John Scalise – were causing him problems. So, he arranged a meeting with them over a lavish dinner. They ate and drank until midnight, but when Capone pushed his chair away from the table, they realised, as he began to speak of their disloyalty, that they were in big trouble. They had forgotten the old Sicilian tradition of hospitality before execution and, worst of all, they had stupidly left their guns in the cloakroom.

Capone's bodyguards jumped on them, tying them to their chairs with wire and gagging them. Capone picked up a baseball bat, walked the length of the table and stood behind one of the men. He swung the bat, smashing the man's shoulders, arms and chest. He then did the same to each of his other guests, reducing them to a pulp. One of his bodyguards then shot each of the three in the back of the head.

The Valentine's Day Massacre and the subsequent publicity forced the US government to launch a plan to attack Capone on two fronts.

Firstly, through Treasury agents searching for evidence of tax evasion and secondly to gather evidence of breaches of the Prohibition laws. Prohibition Agent, Eliot Ness was the man charged with the second task and he put together a team of young agents to carry it out known as 'the Untouchables' because they were impervious to bribery.

Meanwhile, at a conference in Atlantic City, in May 1929, the Mob was reorganising in an effort to stop the territorial battles that had become the norm. As part of this, Capone was ordered to hand over his interests to Johnny Torrio to divide up. Capone, of course, had no intention of doing anything of the kind.

After the conference he went to a movie but, on leaving the cinema, he was approached by two detectives who arrested him for carrying a concealed weapon. He was convicted and sent to prison where he remained until the following March. On his release, he was enraged to find that he had been made Public Enemy Number One on a new list compiled by the Chicago Crime Commission, adapted by J. Edgar Hoover, head of the FBI, as a list of the Most Wanted criminals in America.

Things became increasingly difficult. His brother, Ralph, was convicted on tax evasion charges in October 1930 and Ness and his 'Untouchables' began raiding and closing down Capone breweries at will.

By now, the Government had succeeded in infiltrating Capone's organisation and one agent, working undercover, discovered that when one of the establishments had been raided years previously, a ledger had been taken that contained information that could bring Capone's empire tumbling down. Miraculously, Capone had not killed the two bookkeepers responsible for the ledgers after the raid had taken place and the man on the inside learned their names. When they were tracked down, both agreed to cooperate.

Ness, for his part, was out to humiliate Capone. During their raids on Capone's breweries, the Untouchables had captured dozens of

Capone's trucks which were to be auctioned. Ness called the Lexington and managed to be put through to Capone. 'Well, Snorkey,' he sneered, using a nickname only the gangster's close friends dared use, 'I just wanted to tell you that if you look out your front windows down onto Michigan Avenue at exactly eleven o'clock you'll see something that should interest you.' Capone was puzzled and slammed the phone down, but was incandescent with rage when at eleven, all his trucks slowly drove past the hotel, in convoy.

In spring 1931, the US Government started to move. An indictment was returned against Capone for a tax liability of $32,488.81. In June, a second indictment was returned on twenty-two counts of tax evasion totalling over $200,000. A third arrived a week later. Ness and his team provided evidence that charged Capone and sixty-eight of his gang with 5,000 separate violations of the Volstead Act, the law that had introduced Prohibition.

On the day the trial started, the judge was full of surprises. Realising that there had been efforts to bribe jurors, he arrived in court and ordered that the jury that was to deliberate on the Capone case should be swapped with a jury in another courtroom. Capone was horrified. Worse still, he had pleaded guilty, believing he and his lawyers had a deal with the authorities that would get him a light sentence but the judge was having none of it. Instead of the two year sentence had had been expecting, he was sentenced to eleven years, fined $50,000 and ordered to pay costs of $30,000. To add insult to injury, as he left the court, an IRS official slapped papers on him announcing that the government was seizing property belonging to him, in lieu of tax. Capone tried to attack the official, but was restrained.

He went to Atlanta Prison, a tough federal facility, where he enjoyed special privileges. But, in August 1934, he was sent to the new Alcatraz Prison in San Francisco Bay where his privileges ended. He seemed to bear up well, but his health did not. He had contracted syphilis as a young man and it developed into neurosyphilis. By 1938, dementia had set in and the man who had once commanded a huge crime empire went into serious decline.

He was released in November 1939, spending his first six months of freedom in hospital. His health slowly got worse and he was cared for by his wife, Mae. Finally, Al Capone, the most famous gangster of all, died of cardiac arrest, aged forty-eight, on 25 January 1947 with his family at his bedside.

EMMELINE PANKHURST

'DEEDS, NOT WORDS' she stipulated when she founded the Women's Social and Political Union (WSPU) in 1898. Under her indomitable leadership, it became the militant wing of the movement for women's suffrage, notoriously smashing windows, assaulting policemen and inciting arson. 'The condition of our sex is so deplorable that it is our duty to break the law in order to call attention to the reasons why we do,' she reasoned.

She was born Emmeline Goulden in July 1858 in Moss Side in Manchester. Her family was politically active and had been for generations. Her mother, Sophia Jane Craine, was from an Isle of Man family that had been involved in social unrest there and it is this heritage that she drew on in her struggle to obtain votes for women. The fact that the Isle of Man was the first place to give women the vote in 1881 must also have galvanised her thinking. On her father Robert's side, his mother had worked with the Anti-Corn Law League and his father had been present at the Peterloo Massacre when a cavalry charge was made on a crowd demanding parliamentary reform. Robert Goulden was involved in local politics, serving for a number of years on Salford Town Council.

Emmeline was a voracious reader and a bright, intelligent girl, but, as was the custom in those days, she was not provided with the educational opportunities afforded to her brothers. Instead, she and her sisters were trained in the domestic arts and were expected to marry young and well so that they did not have to work for a living.

Nonetheless, her parents were interested in women's suffrage and it was through their interest that she was given her introduction to the subject. Her mother subscribed to *Women's Suffrage Journal*, the organ of the growing movement. When she was just fourteen, her mother took her to a meeting featuring the magazine's editor, Lydia Beecher, a woman that Emmeline greatly admired. From that day on, she later wrote, she was a 'confirmed suffragist'.

At fifteen, she was sent to Paris to attend the École Normale de Neuilly where she studied chemistry and bookkeeping as well as learning domestic arts such as embroidery. There, she became acquainted with Noémie Rochefort whose father had been sent to prison in New Caledonia for the part he played in the Paris Commune, the attempted uprising that had taken place in 1871. She would remain friends with Noémie for a number of years, and almost married a Swiss painter that Noémie found for her. However, her father refused to pay the dowry expected of him and the painter swiftly withdrew his offer of marriage.

In 1878, she met Richard Pankhurst at a public meeting. He was a barrister who supported women's suffrage and was an ardent advocate of freedom of speech and educational reform. Richard, forty-four when they first met, had resolved to remain a bachelor because he felt that way he could more easily devote his life to serving the public. After debating whether they could openly live together out of wedlock – he said her political life would be over if they did – the couple married in Eccles in 1879.

She had five children in ten years but still found time, while looking after her husband and children, to be politically active. They hired a servant to help and she gave more of her time to the establishment of the WSPU.

They were living in Emmeline's parents' house and Robert Goulden did not appreciate Richard's increasingly radical views. They moved out in 1885 and their daughter Adela was born soon after. The following year, they moved to London and Richard failed in an attempt to become an MP. He launched a fabric shop called Emerson & Co.

Their son, Francis, died of diphtheria in 1888 and Emmeline was naturally devastated. A poor drainage system at the back of their house was blamed for his illness and they moved to the more affluent Russell Square. In 1889, she gave birth to another son, named Henry Francis.

Their home became a meeting house and was a destination for activists of all kinds. Visitors such as the American abolitionist, William Lloyd Garrison, Indian MP Dadabhai Naoroji, socialists Herbert Burrows and Annie Besant and French anarchist Louise Michel would sit and debate in the midst of her sumptuously decorated home.

Until 1888, the movement for women's suffrage had been fairly apolitical, not aligning itself with any particular political parties. The National Society for Women's Suffrage, the country's first national coalition of women's suffrage groups, decided that year, however, to admit into its membership organisations with political affiliations. There was a split and an alternative organisation was formed by Lydia Becker and Millicent Fawcett, the Great College Street Society. The group set up in opposition to it was called the Parliament Street Society (PSS) and Emmeline Pankhurst aligned herself with that group. They did not reject a step-by-step approach to winning the vote for women. Therefore, they were supportive of the idea of giving the vote to single women and widows on the principle that Married women's husbands voted for them. Pankhurst rejected this view and decided to form another group dedicated to winning the vote for all women, regardless of whether they were married or not.

The Women's Franchise League met for the first time in July 1889 and William Lloyd Garrison spoke at the first meeting. He advised the meeting against caution and moderation, telling the attendees that the slavery abolition movement in the United States had been hampered by such an approach.

So, the WFL became a radical organisation. It reached beyond suffrage in the scope of its desire for women's rights, into the areas of divorce and inheritance. It fraternised with socialists and supported the trade union movement. Its brief became the wider issue of social equality. However, it lost members as a result, especially when it disrupted a meeting organised by Lydia Becker who was leading the opposition group. In 1893 the WFL collapsed.

By now the Pankhursts were experiencing financial problems. The shop had never succeeded and Richard was having difficulty in attracting business. As a result, in 1893 they closed the shop and moved back to the northwest, living for a while in Southport and then in the village of Disley. Eventually, they settled in Manchester's Victoria Park. Emmeline returned to the political fray, working with several political groups and gaining respect in her community for her work. She continued to campaign for women's suffrage, of course, but she also became involved with the Women's Liberal Federation, an organisation with ties to the Liberal Party. It was too moderate for her, however. More to her taste was the Independent Labour Party, founded by a Scottish socialist, Keir Hardie, whom Emmeline had met and befriended in 1888. Hardie had been elected to parliament in 1891 and his new party followed two years later. She joined the ILP, believing it to be the answer to her political prayers.

On behalf of the party, she distributed food to the poor through the Committee for the Relief of the Unemployed. She became more active in this area when she was elected as Poor Law Guardian in Chorlton-on-Medlock. The conditions she found people living in appalled her, especially in the Manchester workhouse. She later wrote: 'The first time I went into the place I was horrified to see little girls seven and eight years old on their knees scrubbing the cold stones of the long corridors . . . bronchitis was epidemic among them most of the time . . . I found that there were pregnant women in that workhouse, scrubbing floors, doing the hardest kind of work, almost until their babies came into the world . . . Of course the babies are very badly protected . . . These poor, unprotected mothers and their babies I am sure were potent factors in my education as a militant.'

After helping her husband in another unsuccessful election campaign, she found herself in trouble when she breached a court order banning meetings of the ILP. The two men accused with her spent two months in prison, but she was let off, the judge possibly fearing the outrage if a woman so highly thought of in the community had been sent to prison. But the episode put a strain on the couple's finances and on Richard's health. Having suffered from a gastric ulcer, he died in 1898. Tragically, Emmeline read about his death in a newspaper she was reading on a train on her way back from Switzerland where she had been visiting her old friend, Noémie.

She was left with a considerable amount of debt and moved the family to a smaller, more affordable house. She also had to find a job and resigned from the Board of Guardians, taking a position as Registrar of Births and Deaths in Chorlton. This position, however, helped to increase her experience of the conditions in which women had to live. She was told sometimes horrific stories of what they had to endure in conditions of abject squalour and poverty. She became even more convinced that women's voting rights would help women to live better, more fulfilled lives. Then, in 1900, her election to the Manchester School Board widened her experience still further, providing her with many more examples of unfair treatment. She also hoped to bring in more money by re-opening the shop.

Emmeline's children had taken up their mother's cause enthusiastically. Christabel, in particular, became a fervent advocate for women's suffrage, speaking at meetings and campaigning. But, years of speeches and debates had really achieved very little. MPs had consistently rejected suffrage bills brought before them and Emmeline began to despair. At this point, she came to the conclusion that only militant action would raise women's suffrage up the political agenda and bring results. She and several others founded the Women's Social and Political Union (WSPU), an organisation dedicated to direct action. 'Deeds, not words'.

To begin with, the WSPU gathered signatures for a petition and published a newsletter, *Votes for Women*. It also organised a series of Women's Parliaments. Another bill demanding votes for women came before Parliament in 1905 and the WSPU was there in

Westminster loudly demonstrating and being moved on by police. The bill was yet again rejected, but the WSPU gained a huge amount of publicity and Emmeline was convinced that finally this was the correct route to take. She was the leader of 'a political force' as she described it in 1906.

It became a family affair. Christabel was arrested for spitting at a policeman during a Liberal Party meeting in October 1905 and Adela and Sylvia were arrested a year later while protesting outside the Houses of Parliament. Emmeline was arrested in 1908 as she tried to enter Parliament to deliver a petition to the Prime Minister, Herbert Asquith. She went to prison for six weeks but, of course, protested about the conditions. She now viewed imprisonment as a sure way to gain publicity for the cause and in 1909 hit a policeman twice in the face just so that she would be arrested. She would be arrested seven times in all.

The WSPU remained aloof from the political parties, especially those who opposed their cause. This caused problems with the Liberal Party, many of whose members were supporters of votes for women. They were often accused of losing elections for Liberal candidates. On one occasion Emmeline and a colleague were attacked by a crowd of Liberals who blamed the WSPU for the loss of a by-election to a Conservative candidate. They threw rotten eggs and stones packed in snow at the women and they were beaten.

The strength of women's feeling could be gauged by the fact that 500,000 turned out at Hyde Park in June 1908 to demand votes for women. Still, nothing changed, however, and some members of the WSPU decided to increase the militancy of their activities. When twelve of them tried to speak in Parliament Square, they found themselves being pushed by police into a crowd of their opponents. Frustrated and angry, two members made their way to Downing Street where they proceeded to throw stones at the windows of Number Ten, the Prime Minister's residence. They were sentenced to two months' imprisonment. Emmeline stood up in court and reminded the judge that men had broken windows since their invention while demanding their rights. The hunger strike became another weapon in their armoury in 1909. June Marion Dunlop had been jailed for writing an extract from the 1689 Bill of Rights on a wall in the House of Commons. In prison, she began a hunger strike and fourteen other imprisoned women joined her, being occasionally and painfully force-fed by the authorities. Other organisations felt that the hunger strike and the condoning of damage to property were a step too far, in particular the National Union of Women's Suffrage Societies which refused to take part in a march of women's suffrage groups in protest at the activities of the WSPU.

Emmeline was now constantly on the road, having sold her house. She toured Britain and the United States giving speeches and taking part in debates. She was often separated from her family, but the tours were highly lucrative and she needed the money, especially when her son, Harry, was taken ill. A week after he died in January 1910, she was due to give a speech in front of an audience of 5,000 in Manchester which would be filled with the customary hecklers and opponents. The crowd sat in respectful silence as she talked.

In 1910 it looked as if a bill going through Parliament might finally achieve their goals and the WSPU agreed to suspend its activities while it was being debated. When, like all the others, it was defeated, Emmeline led a march of 300 women to Parliament Square on 18 November on what became known as Black Friday. They were met by an aggressive police force. Women were beaten and injured and although Emmeline was allowed to enter the Palace of Westminster, Asquith refused to meet her.

By March 1912, further bills had been defeated and Emmeline found herself in court yet again on charges of property damage. The police had this time raided the offices of the WSPU and she and Emmeline Pethick-Lawrence were charged with 'conspiracy to commit property damage'. Christabel, also wanted by the police, fled into exile in Paris from where she continued to direct WSPU activity.

In Holloway Prison, Emmeline began her first hunger strike and underwent the agony of being force-fed until she threatened violence. She was arrested and imprisoned frequently in the next few years, but was often released due to her poor health. The government even introduced a bill known as the Cat and Mouse Act which allowed for prisoners to be released if their health was in danger. They wanted no more of the bad publicity engendered by force-feeding. Emmeline, meanwhile, began to use disguises to prevent police officers from arresting and harassing her and hired a female bodyguard proficient in jujitsu.

Arson was the next tactic to be adopted by the WSPU. The Theatre Royal in Dublin was set on fire after a visit by Asquith in 1912. A refreshments building in Regents Park, an orchid house at Kew Gardens, pillar boxes and a railway carriage were all set alight by WSPU members in the next few years. Emmeline stated that neither she nor Christabel had given the orders for these acts, but they certainly supported them.

As the violence escalated, some members became disaffected and a number of prominent women left the WSPU or were dismissed following disputes. Even Emmeline's daughter Adela left the group, appalled at the instances of property destruction. Meanwhile, Sylvia, her other daughter was dismissed following a dispute.

On the outbreak of World War I, Emmeline abandoned her campaigning to throw her considerable energy into the war effort, supporting the government although her daughters, both pacifists were horrified by their mother's attitudes and wanted to continue the struggle. Emmeline organised rallies and toured constantly, speaking at meetings and lobbying the government to help women enter the work force while their men were overseas fighting. She opened an adoption home and was criticised for looking after children born out of wedlock. She adopted four children and for the first time in many years bought a house in which they could be looked after.

She travelled in the United States rallying people in support of the USA entering the war and in 1917 she was sent to Russia by Prime Minister David Lloyd George to put pressure on the Russian people not to accept the peace terms they had been offered by Germany. Returning from Russia, she learned that at last her dream was about to become reality. The Representation of the People Act granted the vote to women over thirty years of age.

GOLDA MEIR

ISRAELI PRESIDENT DAVID Ben Gurion used to call her 'the best man in the cabinet'. She was stubborn, indomitable and straight-talking and with her steely-grey hair done up in a bun and her lined face, she was instantly recognisable around the world.

She was born Golda Mabovitch in Kiev in the Russian Empire in 1898. Her father was a carpenter and she had two sisters. Her parents, Moshe and Blume had five other children who died in childhood. Resolved to escape the rigours of life in Kiev, Moshe boarded a ship for America in 1903 and in 1906, sent for his family. They settled in Milwaukee in Wisconsin where Moshe worked as a carpenter while Golda's mother ran a grocery shop.

School in America was a great opportunity for Golda and she grabbed it with both hands. Arriving there with not a word of English, by the time she left she was fluent and received distinctions in the subject. Her leadership qualities were evident early in her life. She organised a fundraising event to pay for her school's books and founded the American Young Sisters Society for which she organised public events, hiring halls and soliciting audiences.

Aged fourteen, however, she ran away from home and from the marriage her mother was trying to arrange for her, going to stay with her sister, Sheyna Korngold, in Denver. It was an exciting and stimulating time for the young Golda. Her sister and her husband held meetings at their home where the great issues of the day were discussed – women's suffrage, trade unionism, socialism and so on and her convictions began to form in this ferment of intellectual stimulus. She did return to high school, however, graduating in 1915 and beginning to teach in public schools. She had begun to be politically active, too, joing the Zionist movement Young Poale Zion which would later become the labour Zionist youth movement, Habonim.

Her private life, too, changed in Denver when she met Morris Meyerson, a sign painter whom she married. She was nineteen years old and it was 1917. Her one condition for accepting Morris's proposal of marriage was that they would leave the United States and settle in Palestine. However, the First World War had curtailed all transatlantic passenger services and she had to postpone her move to the Middle East. Instead, she threw herself enthusiastically into her Poale Zion activities, embarking on a fundraising campaign that had her crossing the United States. Around this time, she fell pregnant, but had an abortion as she did not feel that it would be right to have a child when she was so occupied with her Zionist duties.

Finally, in 1921, Golda and Morris made the journey to Palestine, accompanied by her sister, Sheyna. They joined a kibbutz where they picked almonds, planted trees, worked in the chicken coops and in the kitchen.

Golda, however, stood out and recognising her leadership qualities, her colleagues in the kibbutz selected her as their representative to the Histadrut, the General Federation of Labour. In 1924 she went to live in Tel Aviv and then in Jerusalem where she and Morris had two children, Menachem and Sarah.

In 1928, she was elected secretary of the Working Women's Council – Moetzet HaPoalot for whom she had to spend two years in the United States, taking her children with her, but leaving Morris in Palestine. She and her husband began to grow apart – perhaps no one could take the place of her political convictions – and they would eventually divorce in 1951.

Returning from America in 1934, she was elected onto the Executive Committee of the Histadrut, and was then further promoted to the position of head of the organisation's Political Department.

In July 1938, a conference was convened by US President Franklyn D. Roosevelt at Evian in France to discuss the issue of

Jewish refugees who were fleeing from Nazi persecution in Adolf Hitler's Germany. Golda was sent as Jewish observer. She listened as the thirty-two countries present at the conference persistently expressed their sympathy for the plight of the European Jews, but resolutely refused to do anything to help the situation. It was a disappointing and depressing moment for Golda Meyerson. 'There is only one thing I hope to see before I die,' she said to journalists reporting the conference, 'and that is that my people should not need expressions of sympathy anymore.'

In 1946, in Palestine, paramilitary Zionist movements were causing a great deal of trouble for the British forces based there to police their mandate of the territory. In response to bobings, they arrested many leaders of the Jewish settlements in the Holy Land. Amongst these was Moshe Sharett, who was head of the Political Department of the Jewish Agency. Golda took over his role while he was incarcerated and, as such, she became the main negotiator between the Palestinian Jews and the British Mandatory authorities. She remained in the role until Israel was founded in 1948.

The new state was in need of funds to buy arms, given the likelihood that as soon as it was established, the hostile Arab countries surrounding it would launch an attack. Golda was chosen to travel to the United States to try to raise the necessary funds. It was thought that she would probably be able to raise no more than around $8 million. She in fact returned with $50 million, an astonishing amount. Israel's first president, David Ben Gurion, described her as the 'Jewish woman who got the money which made the state possible.'

Four days before the establishment of the new state, she travelled to Amman in Transjordan, disguised as an Arab woman to try to persuade King Abdullah not to join in the Arab attack on Israel. When he urged her not to hurry to proclaim the new state, she replied, 'We've been waiting for two hundred years. Is that hurrying?'

Four days later, on 14 May 1948, she became one of the twenty-four signatories to the Israeli Declaration of Independence. The following day, the Israeli War of Independence broke out when the armies of Egypt, Syria, Lebanon, Transjordan and Iraq attacked the fledgling state.

Golda Meyerson was issued with the very first Israeli passport in order to travel to Moscow. She had been appointed Israel's ambassador to the Soviet Union but remained there for only a brief period, returning home in 1949. While there, however, she was mobbed by thousands of Russian Jews when she attended services at a synagogue in Moscow. It was a scene that would be commemorated thirty-five years later on the Israeli ten thousand shekel banknote. On the other side of the note would be a portrait of Golda.

Back in Israel, she was elected to the Israeli Parliament, the Knesset, representing the Mapai party. She would serve until 1974 as a member of parliament. She took the role of Minister of Labour until 1956 at a time when Israel was embarking on major projects to modernise its infrastructure. Then, in 1956, Gurion appointed her as his Foreign Secretary. By now, she had changed her name to the more Hebrew-sounding Meir.

One facet of her time as Foreign Minister was her attempt to gain allies in the international community. She turned to the newly independent states of Africa, believing that there was much that Israel could teach these liberated states about nation-building. 'Like them,' she later wrote, 'we had shaken off foreign rule; like them, we had to learn for ourselves how to reclaim the land, how to increase the yields of our crops, how to irrigate, how to raise poultry, how to live together, and how to defend ourselves.'

In January 1966, Golda retired from the Foreign Ministry, aged sixty-eight. She was exhausted and unwell – her doctors had diagnosed her with lymphoma several years previously. She was not gone for long, however, returning as Secretary General of Mapai, supporting Prime Minister Levi Eshkol.

When Eshkol died suddenly in February 1969, the only person

who seemed qualified to replace him and who was acceptable to all parties in the ruling coalition, was Golda Meir. She took office as Prime Minister on 17 March, maintaining Eshkol's coalition.

Golda Meir worked tirelessly to maintain peace while not giving up any Israeli gains. In August 1970, she accepted a US peace initiative calling for an end to Egypt's War of Attrition and an Israeli promise to withdraw to secure any recognisable boundaries.

Following the murder of eleven Israeli athletes at the Munich Olympics in 1972, she authorised Mossad, the Israeli secret service to hunt down and kill the members of the terrorist groups Black September and the Palestinian Liberation PFLP who carried out the murders.

The biggest test in Golda Meir's life came in October 1973 when she was informed that Syrian troops were massing on the Golan Heights. It was the beginning of the conflict known as the Yom Kippur war. It had been thought unlikely that the Arabs would attack again following their defeat in the Six-Day war in 1967, but she felt that things were moving the same way they had just prior to that conflict. She was granted special powers to order a full-scale mobilisation, but held off on making the decision. She was advised by Israeli war hero and Minister of Defense that war was unlikely while a high-ranking officer, General David Elazar, urged her to consider a pre-emptive strike on the Syrians. Wisely, she decided to reject Elazar's advice, reckoning that if Israel were to strike first, initiating hostilities, other countries, in particular the United States, would be reluctant to provide the aid she badly needed to defeat the Arabs. She was later proved right when the US Secretary of State Henry Kissinger said that if Israel had attacked first she would not have received 'so much as a nail'.

After the war, Israel was in anguish about the nation's apparent lack of readiness for it. The Agranat Commission was established to investigate the war and cleared Golda Meir of responsibility and her party won the general election of December 1973. On 11 April the following year, however, she resigned, feeling that she no longer had the support of the people of Israel. She was succeeded by Yitzhak Rabin.

On 8 December 1978, the grey-haired grandmother of the Israeli people died of cancer at the age of eighty. Few people had been as dedicated to their people as she was.

MAHATMA GANDHI

HE WAS ASSASSINATED sixty years ago, but his disciples are now everywhere. The struggle for freedom from apartheid in South Africa was led by men – Nelson Mandela and Archbishop Desmond Tutu – who subscribed to his concept of non-violent protest. In Burma, Aung San Suu Kyi leads her pro-democracy activists in the spirit of Gandhi. In the recent past, Martin Luther King Jr led the fight for equal rights for African-American in the United States without resorting to the gun or the bomb and union leader, Lech Walesa, led Poland to democracy without a shot being fired.

Political and spiritual leader of India, as it fought for independence following centuries of British rule, Gandhi's use of non-violent civil disobedience began not in India, but in South Africa, where he was working as a lawyer. He had been born in the coastal town of Porbander in modern-day Gujurat in Western India in 1869 to a father who was Prime Minister of Porbander state and was brought up in the Jainist religion of which his mother was a devout follower. Jainism introduced him to a great many of the guiding principles of his later life such as vegetarianism, fasting to purify the self, compassion to sentient beings and tolerance of different people and beliefs.

It was the custom in the area for people to marry very young and Gandhi was married at the age of thirteen to a fourteen-year-old girl, Kasturbai Makhanji, known as 'Ba'. In 1885, the young couple's first child was born but died after a few days – Gandhi was fifteen.

He graduated from school and passed the entrance exam for Samaldas College at Bhavnagar and then, in September 1888, travelled to London to study to be a barrister at University College, London. While in London, he joined the Vegetarian Society and was elected to its executive committee, founding a local chapter, an experience he found invaluable in learning organisational skills. He also read extensively about the world's religions during this time.

Returning to India after completing his studies, he had only limited success establishing himself in Mumbai. He went home to Gujurat where he drafted petitions for litigants but was forced to close down his practice after he had a disagreement with a British officer. Running out of options in the legal profession in India, in 1893 he signed a year-long contract to work on behalf of an Indian law firm in Natal in South Africa.

At that time, discrimination was as rife in South Africa as it would later be in apartheid times and Gandhi experienced it first-hand. He was thrown off a train for refusing to move to a third-class carriage from a first-class carriage for which he had a valid ticket. On the same journey, he received a beating from a stagecoach driver for refusing to travel on the footboard to allow space for a European passenger to travel inside the coach. He also found it difficult to locate a hotel that would give him a room. Even in court, he encountered problems. A judge at one point ordered him to remove his turban. He stubbornly, and characteristically, refused.

These events helped to galvanise his thinking about his own and his people's place in the British Empire.

He decided to stay in South Africa in order to help the Indians living there in their fight against legislation that would deny them the right to vote. The bill was passed, but he founded the Natal Indian Congress which helped draw attention to the plight of South Africa's Indians. His political activity was not without danger, however, and in 1897, he was attacked and almost lynched by a white mob. He characteristically refused to press charges.

In 1906 he led a mass protest against a new law in the Transvaal requiring its Indian population to register. He was now developing the style of protest that would make him famous – *satyagraha* or non-violent protest. He recommended that it be applied to this particular protest and in the seven years during which the protest continued, thousands of South African Indians were imprisoned, flogged or shot for engaging in peaceful resistance that included striking and refusing to register, amongst other methods. Public outrage finally persuaded South African segregationist General Jan Smuts to negotiate a settlement to the matter.

In 1906 when the Zulu War broke out, Gandhi, in his columns in the *Indian Opinion* newspaper, encouraged the British army to recruit Indians to fight the Zulus in an effort to legitimise their claims for full citizenship. They were not keen, but let him command a squad of Indian stretcher-bearers.

He returned to India in 1915 and became politically active. He fought on behalf of impoverished and oppressed Indians in Champaran, establishing an ashram and coordinating the cleaning up of villages previously blighted by alcoholism, famine and extreme poverty. When the police arrested him and charged him with creating unrest, he was ordered to leave the province. The charges had to be dropped, however, when hundreds of thousands of people began protesting outside the court. Continuing his work, he obtained compensation for farmers and more control for them of their farms. Planned tax rises were also postponed.

At this time, people began to address him as *Bapu* (Father) and *Mahatma* (Great Soul). He became famous and Indians everywhere began to realise that a very special human being walked amongst them.

It was a massacre at Jallianwala Bagh in the Punjab that made him decide that India should control its own destiny. In the Amritsar Massacre, as it is also known, 379 Indians were shot dead and more than 1,000 injured by British soldiers in just ten minutes and the entire nation was both horrified and outraged. There were protests and some violence, but Gandhi criticised both sides – the military authorities and the Indians who had retaliated violently. To him, all violence was evil for whatever reason it was perpetrated.

In 1921, he was appointed leader of the political party, the Indian National Congress and directed all of its efforts at achieving independence for India. He advocated the boycotting of foreign-made – particularly British – goods. He recommended that all Indians should wear home-spun clothing and that they should spend time each day spinning the material to make their clothes. He also asked people to boycott British institutions such as schools, colleges and law courts and to resign from government jobs.

Indians embraced his policy of non-cooperation wholeheartedly, but it all came to a halt in 1922 when a mob, fired by nationalist sentiments, set the police station on fire in Chauri Chara, killing twenty-two policemen. Gandhi feared matters were spinning out of his control and could only lead to violence and many deaths, both Indian and British. Consequently, he called of the campaign of mass-disobedience. The authorities arrested him for sedition and sentenced him to six years' imprisonment, of which he served two.

On his release, he found an Indian Congress Party split into two factions and tried to reconcile the opposing views, but even a three-week fast in 1924 failed.

For a number of years, he stayed out of active politics, working to heal the rifts in his party and also establishing programmes to fight against the scourges of untouchability, ignorance and poverty.

In December 1928, he called on the British to grant India dominion status, as had been given to Canada in 1867 and Australia in 1901 or face a fresh campaign of civil disobedience. There was no response and the flag of India was unfurled in Lahore on 31 December 1929. The Congress Party declared 26 January 1930 as Indian Independence Day.

Gandhi launched a campaign in March 1930 against the tax on salt, walking 248 miles, accompanied by thousands of Indians, in the famous Salt March that lasted from 12 March to 6 April. When he arrived in Gujarat, he himself made salt. The British put 60,000 people in prison.

At last, however, the government in London was beginning to take notice and they asked for a meeting with Gandhi. The result was the Gandhi-Irwin Pact, signed in March 1931with Lord Edward Irwin, the British Viceroy of India. The British agreed to release all political prisoners in exchange for the end of any civil disobedience. Gandhi was invited to London to discuss India at a conference, but it was disappointing and did not focus on independence.

Back in India, there was further suppression of the nationalists and Gandhi found himself arrested again.

In September 1932 he embarked on a six-day fast in protest at low caste Untouchables – or Dalits – being given separate electorates in the new constitution, the beginning of a new campaign by Gandhi on behalf of this excluded section of Indian society. He called them harijans – the children of God. May 1933 brought another fast, for twenty-one days this time.

Not all the Dalits supported him and he certainly did have many enemies. In 1934, there were several attempts to assassinate him.

More internal wrangling in the Congress Party followed and at one point Gandhi withdrew for two years. He continued to want to focus all the party's efforts and activities on independence, although he did not stand in its way as it adopted a socialist agenda. By 1938, the party under the presidency of Subhas Bose had begun to move away from Gandhi's commitment to non-violence and democracy. Bose won a second term as president but was forced to resign when leaders began to resign in protest at his abandonment of Gandhi's approach.

When World War II broke out, India was unilaterally taken into the war by the British. All Indian Congressmen resigned in protest and Gandhi eloquently protested that India could not be expected to fight for democracy when that very principle was being denied to its own people. Of course, his response to tyranny – even of the kind espoused by Hitler and Mussolini – was non-violence.

In July 1942, the Indian National Congress passed a resolution demanding complete independence, promising that if the demand was not met, the British would face a massive civil disobedience campaign. It was a defining moment and many leaders and politicians were uneasy about it but men such as Jawaharlal Nehru and Maulana Azad supported Gandhi's leadership. Others, especially the younger members of Congress and students were openly enthusiastic. On 8 August the Quit India Resolution was passed in a meeting of the All-India Congress while in Bombay Gandhi launched the Quit India movement, urging supporters to maintain the principles of non-violence and to act as an independent nation, ignoring the orders of the British. Hundreds of thousands of Indians took part.

The British were already concerned by the advance of the Japanese army to the Indian-Burmese border and their response was to arrest Gandhi and all the other leaders of the movement the following day and imprison them. The Congress Party was later proscribed. However, even in the absence of real leadership, the movement took off, workers failing to turn up at their places of work and strikes breaking out across the country. There were sporadic outbreaks of violence with bombs being exploded, power lines cut and transport seriously disrupted.

There were mass detentions with more than 100,000 people being arrested by the British. Public floggings were carried out and hundreds died in volleys of gunfire by police and soldiers.

Gandhi and the other leaders were kept in isolation for three years, during which the Mahatma suffered personal loss when his wife, Kasturbai died after being imprisoned for eighteen months, followed shortly after by the death of his personal secretary. Frequent twenty-one-day protest fasts were also taking a toll on his health and following a serious malaria attack, he was released from his incarceration in early May 1944. His death in prison would have represented a serious embarrassment to the authorities. In spite of this, he carried on campaigning for the release of all the Congress leaders.

By this time, however, the Quit India campaign had lost a great deal of its initial momentum – partly because of ruthless suppression by the British – and the country was once again relatively peaceful. However, as other politicians, communists and Hindu extremists became highly critical of Gandhi and the perceived failure of Quit India, it began to become clear that British resistance to the idea of independence was wilting in the face of the cost of the war and the fact that the only way it could remain in control of the sub-continent would be through repression. Britain, like the rest of Europe had been devastated by the war and the British people and its army had little stomach for a struggle four thousand miles away. 100,000 political prisoners were freed and for the first time the British indicated that a transfer of power was at hand.

The trouble was not yet over, however, as Indian political factions fought for power amongst themselves and between 1946 and 1948, more than 5,000 people died in violence. Gandhi was himself opposed to the British independence proposal, believing that it would only lead to partition of the country – the separation of the Muslim states from the remainder – but he lost this particular argument. Congress feared that not to accept the proposal would allow control of the government to pass to the Muslim league. Partition was approved by Congress leaders with the stated aim of preventing a Hindu-Muslim war but, given Gandhi's support throughout the nation, they needed his assent. Eventually, he was persuaded to accept the plan, but only with extreme reluctance and disappointment.

There had been five failed assassination attempts on Gandhi since 1934 and there was little doubt that antagonism to him remained strong in some quarters. It erupted violently on 30 January 1948. He was on his way to a meeting in the grounds of the Birla House where he was staying in New Delhi. As he walked, his assistants on either side, he was approached by Nathuram Godse, a hindu radical who had links with the Hindu extremist group, Mahasabha. Godse pulled out a pistol and shot the Mahatma three times in his chest at point-blank range. The holy man fell to the ground uttering the words 'Hai Ram' (Oh God) three times.

On 13 February 1948, almost a million people accompanied Mahatma Gandhi's funeral procession to the cremation grounds by the holy waters of the Yamuna, near New Delhi. A funeral pyre of stone, brick and earth had been built at Rajghat, close to the river. The Mahatma's body was placed on it and at 4.45 pm, Ramdas, Gandhi's third son, set the pyre alight, accompanied by a huge groan from the crowd. Ramdas then consigned the ashes to the Ganges. Later, in similar ceremonies at sacred sites along rivers and seashores at some fifty places in India and Pakistan, portions of Gandhi's ashes were ceremoniously committed to the waters in the presence of millions of mourners. Millions more, in towns and villages with community wireless sets, listened to a three-hour commentary on the Allahabad ceremony, broadcast in English and Hindu by All-India Radio.

All work throughout the country stopped that day, the last of a thirteen-day period of State mourning in which the nation paid its respects to the little man who had achieved the seemingly impossible – independence for his country without the use of violence.

WINSTON CHURCHILL

HE IS ONE of only six people to be granted Honorary American citizenship and one of only three of those to be granted it during their own lifetime. He was awarded the Nobel Prize for Literature, notably for his six-volume *The Second World War*. In a BBC2 poll to find the 100 Greatest Britons, he was voted the greatest of them all and *Time* magazine named him as one of the most influential leaders of all time.

Winston Churchill had already led an extraordinary life long before he was called upon to inspire Britain and her Allies to victory in their 'darkest hour' – World War II. He had been a soldier, a journalist, a novelist, a historian, an artist and had held very senior positions in government, including Chancellor of the Exchequer and First Lord of the Admiralty. It was this exceptional curriculum vitae and a noble heritage stretching back to his ancestor, the great 18th century general, the Duke of Marlborough, that prepared him for the ardours of war leadership.

Winston's father, Lord Randolph Churchill, was the third son of the 7th Duke of Marlborough and a Conservative politician. His mother, Jennie, was the daughter of an American millionaire. Their son, Winston, was born two months early on 30 November 1874 at Blenheim Palace in Oxfordshire and he was willful from the start, a trait which did not serve him well in his schooling and for which he was regularly punished. In 1888, he went to Harrow, one of England's great public schools.

His relationship with his parents was difficult. From school, he wrote regularly to his mother, pleading with her to visit him, but she never did and his relationship with Lord Randolph was distant. The early death of his father in 1895, persuaded the young Winston that life could, indeed, be short and that if he wanted to achieve anything, he had better get on with it.

Leaving school in 1893, Churchill applied for the Royal Military Academy at Sandhurst in Surrey, signing up for the cavalry as the entrance requirements were less than for the infantry. He had failed the entrance exam three times but graduated from Sandhurst in December 1894 with distinction – coming eighth out of one hundred and fifty students. In February 1895, he joined the 4th Queen's Own Hussars as a Second Lieutenant.

Churchill's army pay was not sufficient and he decided to supplement it with work as a war correspondent. To that end, he sought postings, using all the influence of his family, to active campaigns. He began to make a name for himself as a journalist for several London newspapers and also began to write books describing the campaigns he took part in.

The year 1895 saw him in Cuba on behalf of a London paper, observing the struggle for independence being fought by Cuban guerrillas against the Spanish. Whilst there, not only did he come under fire for the first time, he also began a lifelong love affair with good Havana cigars and the large cigar would become one of his trademarks during World War II. Then in 1896, he was transferred to India and while there, read avidly, forming a dislike of religion and a survival of the fittest view of the world. While in India, he started work on the only novel he ever wrote, *Savrola; A Tale of the Revolution in Laurania*. It was published in 1900.

In 1897, he volunteered to join the fight against a Pashtun tribe in Malakand in an area now in Pakistan. His commander, General Jeffery sent him with a party of fifteen scouts to explore the Mamund Valley and they were engaged by an enemy tribe. Fighting continued for an hour before reinforcements arrived. However, hundreds of tribesmen now attacked and Churchill was ordered to get his men to safety. He alerted the brigade who attacked. So fierce was the fighting that it was two weeks before the dead could be recovered. He wrote about this encounter in *The Story of the Malakand Field Force*, being paid a handsome £600 for his account.

In 1898, he was transferred to Sudan, serving with the 21st Lancers under General Herbert Kitchener. Coincidentally, other figures whose names will be forever associated with World War I were also there – Douglas Haig, at the time a captain, but later a Field Marshal as the First Lord Haig, senior commander of British forces during some of the Great War's biggest battles and John Jellicoe, a gunboat lieutenant at the time, but by 1916 admiral and First Sea Lord. In the Sudan, Churchill took part in the last British cavalry charge during the Battle of Omdurman in September 1898. Meanwhile, he continued sending back reports to British newspapers. On his return to England, he wrote his account of the war in which he had just fought – the two-volume *The River War*. In May 1899, he resigned his commission and left the British Army.

His next move was an attempt to follow his late father into politics. He stood as a Conservative in the Oldham by-election of 1899, but came third. Seeing the door close on that career-path, he decided to further his work as a war correspondent. The Second Boer War had broken out in South Africa between Britain and the Boer Republics and Churchill obtained a job reporting on the war for the conservative newspaper, the *Morning Post*.

After several weeks in South Africa, Churchill was taken prisoner while accompanying a scouting expedition on an armoured train and incarcerated in a prisoner of war camp in Pretoria. Within a short while, however, his indomitable spirit came to the fore and he escaped, travelling 300 miles to the Portuguese colony of Lourenço Marques from where he filed his story and became something of a celebrity back in England. Returning to South Africa, he was present at the relief of the Siege of Ladysmith and when Pretoria was taken. He was there as a commissioned officer in the South African Light Horse which he had joined.

Returning home in 1900, he wrote *London to Ladysmith* and *Ian Hamilton's March*, a second volume of Boer War memories. He stood for Parliament again in Oldham and won this time before embarking on a series of lucrative speaking tours in both Britain and the United States.

In 1904, Churchill changed his political allegiance, crossing the floor of the House to become a member of the Liberal Party and when the Liberals took office in 1905, he became Under-Secretary of State for the Colonies. He became MP for Manchester Northwest in 1905 and in 1908 was made President of the Board of Trade. By now, he was representing Dundee. In 1908, he was responsible for introducing the first minimum wage regulations in Britain and set up the country's first labour exchanges in 1909 to help the unemployed find work. He helped draft the National Insurance Act of 1911, introducing unemployment pension. In 1910, he became Home Secretary and by the start of the First World War, in 1914, he was First Lord of the Admiralty. However, following the catastrophic eight-month long Battle of Gallipoli, a joint British Empire and French venture to capture the Ottoman capital, Constantinople, in which many lives were lost and which he championed, he resigned from the war cabinet. He returned to the army, hoping to rehabilitate his career, obtaining a commission in January 1916 as Lieutenant-Colonel with the 6th Battalion, the Royal Scots Fusiliers. He commanded his battalion on the Western Front with characteristic bravery and daring before being recalled to the government in 1917 as Minister of Munitions and then, in 1919, Secretary of State for War and Secretary of State for Air. He became Secretary of State for the Colonies in 1921 and that same year was one of the signatories of the Anglo-Irish Treaty that established the Irish Free State.

In the general election of 1922, he lost his parliamentary seat of Dundee, eventually returning to parliament in 1924 as an independent, representing Epping. He returned to the Conservative Party and became Chancellor of the Exchequer in Stanley Baldwin's government, controlling the nation's finances during a very difficult time. He controversially reintroduced the Gold Standard, a decision that resulted in deflation, unemployment and the General Strike of 1926. He would consider it to be the greatest mistake of his life. Although the fact that during this time he is reported to have advocated using machine guns on striking miners and called Mussolini 'the Roman genius . . . the greatest lawgiver among men', may also be regarded as huge errors of judgement.

Following the defeat of the Conservative government in 1929, he became increasingly distanced from the mainstream of Conservative politics, and in 1931, when Ramsay MacDonald formed a coalition National Government, Churchill was not offered a post. He entered a period in his career known as 'the wilderness years'.

Instead of concentrating on political matters, he wrote – *Marlborough: His Life and Times*, a biography of his ancestor John Churchill, 1st Duke of Marlborough; *A History of the English Speaking Peoples* (not published until after World War II); *Great Contemporaries* (newspaper articles and collections of speeches). He became one of the highest-paid writers of his time.

Meanwhile, he gave speeches, often controversial ones, and on several occasions, antagonised his Conservative Party. His views on India and German rearmament stirred up trouble and increased his isolation. For some time, he was a lone voice on the rearmament issue, warning that Britain should be strengthening its armaments in order to counter the German threat. In 1934, he urged Britain to strengthen its air force and introduce a Ministry of Defence. He also advocated a renewed role for the League of Nations.

When Germany invaded the Rhineland in 1936, Churchill made what was described as a constructive speech, but he was passed over for the position of Minister for Co-ordination of Defence. He continued his efforts to make the government act to prepare Britain for war, at one point leading a delegation of senior Conservatives to see Baldwin, Chamberlain and Halifax.

Churchill's actions during the Abdication Crisis of 1936 further damaged his standing. He publicly supported King Edward VIII, trying to delay the King's abdication announcement. When he pleaded in the House of Commons for a delay, he was heckled and shouted down by members of all political persuasions. At that point, he really did believe his political career was at an end.

When war was eventually declared against Germany on 3 September 1939, Churchill was appointed to his old post, First Lord of the Admiralty, and became a member of the war cabinet. During the so-called Phoney War, the only real action took place at sea and he, consequently, became a very visible member of the cabinet. He was hawkish from the beginning, but was faced by the more considered and cautious approach of Prime Minister, Neville Chamberlain and the rest of his cabinet.

When Chamberlain resigned in May 1940, as Hitler's tanks rolled into France, it was decided that his successor should be someone who would receive the support of all political parties in the House of Commons. Lord Halifax had been the first candidate, but had turned it down because he believed he could not carry out his duties as an unelected member of the House of Lords. On 10 May, King George VI asked Winston Churchill to form a coalition government.

The political maverick was now in charge of Britain at one of the most difficult times in its entire history.

On 4 June, he gave the first of many memorable speeches that became a stirring part of the war effort and are recognised as some of the finest examples of oratory in history. In the Commons he said: 'We shall go on to the end, we shall fight in France, we shall fight on the seas and oceans, we shall fight with growing confidence and growing strength in the air, we shall defend our Island, whatever the cost may be, we shall fight on the beaches, we shall fight on the landing grounds, we shall fight in the fields and in the streets, we shall fight in the hills; we shall never surrender...'

Then, just a fortnight later, he said, again in the Commons: 'I expect that the Battle of Britain is about to begin...' and that '...if the British Empire and its Commonwealth last for a thousand years, men will still say, 'This was their finest hour.'' With such speeches he galvanised the people of Britain and the Empire into committing themselves to the war effort, even when it looked like all might be lost, which was perhaps when Churchill was, after all, at his most effective.

He immediately put his friend, the newspaper tycoon, Lord Beaverbrook in charge of Britain's aircraft production and, using all the experience and persuasive skills learned in the commercial world, Beaverbrook geared up the production of planes, production that would prove vital to the eventual Allied victory.

Churchill also used his friendship with American President, Franklin D. Roosevelt, to secure oil, munitions and military hardware for Britain on credit – a system known as Lend-Lease. When the Japanese bombed Pearl Harbor in December 1941 and the United States entered the war, Churchill knew it might take time, but was certain now that the Allies would ultimately be victorious.

Nontheless, the stress was showing and Churchill at sixty-seven years old, was no longer a young man. In December 1941, he suffered a mild heart attack while at the White House and in 1943 he had pneumonia. His stamina, however, was extraordinary for a man of his age. Throughout the war his journeys to meet other leaders covered some 100,000 miles. These conferences gradually began to prepare for a world after the war, re-drawing European boundaries and establishing how to treat the defeated nations – Germany in particular – so that they would not want to go to war again within a few years.

There is little doubt that it is often the case that to be great also means to be ruthless and Winston Churchill was no exception. The carpet bombing of the German city of Dresden is a case in point. Between 13 and 15 February 1945, thirteen square miles of the beautiful baroque capital of Saxony were destroyed and up to 40,000 civilians were killed, many in a firestorm that swept through the city centre. In the same way that the American atomic bomb dropped on Hiroshima and Nagasaki hastened the end of the war in Asia, so, the destruction of Dresden was intended to hasten the defeat of Germany. There are critics, however, who describe the action as a war crime.

In June 1944 the Allies invaded Normandy and the push for Berlin began on three fronts. On 7 May 1945, the German surrender was accepted in Rheims and the following day Britain celebrated VE – Victory in Europe Day. Churchill broadcast to the nation and told a crowd gathered in Whitehall: 'This is your victory.'

He did not celebrate for long. Instead, he began to warn of the dangers that the Soviet Union offered. He ordered the development of a plan – Operation Unthinkable – by which Britain and the United States would go to war with the Russians. It was rejected as militarily unfeasible.

The man who had led the country so gloriously and so effectively during the war was evidently not seen by the British people as the right man to lead them during the peace. In the general election of 1945, they rejected him, looking, instead, for a Prime Minister who would lead post-war reform.

Churchill served as leader of Her Majesty's Opposition for six years, but his status was undiminished as he travelled the world, making his customary impact on world affairs. In 1946, for instance, speaking in the United States about the division of Europe, he made another of his famous, definitive speeches: 'From Stettin in the Baltic to Trieste in the Adriatic, an Iron Curtain has descended across the continent. Behind that line lie all the capitals of the ancient states of Central and Eastern Europe. Warsaw, Berlin, Prague, Vienna, Budapest, Belgrade, Bucharest and Sofia, all these famous cities and the populations around them lie in what I must call the Soviet sphere.'

He argued against Britain's involvement in Europe, viewing the British Isles as something apart from the continent and believing that it should align itself with the Commonwealth and the United States rather than the French and the Germans.

Another general election, in 1951 restored him to Downing Street with a majority of sixteen seats at the age of seventy-seven. It was a time of foreign crises as British influence abroad began to wane and Churchill's approach was direct and abrasive – as when he sent British troops to Kenya to put down the Mau Mau rebellion – still a firm believer in Britain as an international power. Other crises he inherited, such as the Malayan Emergency when he again chose to send in the troops.

In June 1953, his health began to fail and he suffered a stroke in Downing Street. Parliament and the British people were told he was simply suffering from exhaustion and he recuperated at his country home, Chartwell. He did return to speak at the Conservative Party Conference in Margate in October, but eventually it was evident that he was slowing down and simply getting too old. He retired as Prime Minister in 1955.

He remained an MP until 1964, on the unfamiliar back benches that he had not occupied since the 'wilderness years' of the 1930s. He lived out his remaining years either at Chartwell or in his London home, at Hyde Park gate, painting and fighting what he termed the 'black dog' of depression that had hovered over him during his life.

On 24 January 1965, he suffered another stroke, much more serious this time and it left him gravely ill. Nine days later, at the age of ninety, he died.

As a measure of his greatness, Winston Churchill was one of only four people in the 20th century, not members of the Royal Family, who were accorded a state funeral. His body lay in state for three days and the funeral service was held at St Paul's Cathedral. As his coffin was carried down the Thames on the launch, the Havengore, dockers lowered the jibs of their cranes in respect. There was a nineteen-gun salute and a fly-past of sixteen fighter planes. It was also the largest gathering of world leaders in history. Thousands stood in silence along the funeral route on roads and at stations as the train carrying the coffin of the greatest Briton passed on its way to his last resting place in the family plot at St Martin's Church, Bladon, close to his birthplace at Blenheim Palace.

FIDEL CASTRO

DIFFICULT THOUGH IT is to believe, Cuban intelligence estimates that the CIA made 638 unsuccessful attempts on Fidel Castro's life during the time he was President of Cuba. The Marxist former revolutionary has been a thorn in American flesh for almost fifty years, sitting just ninety miles off the Florida coast, leading a socialist outpost that has stuck resolutely to communist principles even as the rest of the communist world has collapsed around it.

Those principles have brought much that is good to Cuba. Castro has been credited with bringing 10,000 new schools to the island and the system of universal health care that he introduced has drastically reduced infant mortality. Of course, it has been at a price. Civil liberties have been eroded; there is no right to strike or criticise the government in the media and Castro abolished democratic elections many years ago. There is little tolerance for religion and enforced emigration and executions and imprisonment have taken care of countless enemies of the Castro regime as well as thousands of undesirables over the decades.

It is estimated that more than 120,000 Cubans have fled from Cuba to the United States, many in small boats inadequate to cope with the dangerous waters of the Straits of Florida. Often these excursions were added to by people with mental health problems, criminals and homosexuals.

He was born Fidel Alejandro Castro Ruz in Oriente, in the east of Cuba in 1926, the illegitimate son of a servant, Lina Ruz Gonzalez. His father was Angel Castro, a wealthy sugar plantation owner of Spanish origins for whose wife his mother worked. When Fidel was fifteen, however, his father divorced his wife to marry his mother. He was able to take his father's name and enjoy a life of wealth and privilege while around him the Cuban people laboured in poverty under a series of corrupt regimes.

Castro attended Jesuit schools as a boarder before enrolling in 1945 at the University of Havana to study law. At university, he began to become involved in politics, supporting Cuban nationalism, rejecting what he perceived to be the imperialism of the United States and developing a passion for socialism. It was a time of turmoil in student politics and university elections were violent affairs. He has been said to have been involved in several shootings at the time and even to have made an attempt on the life of his bitter rival, Rolando Masferrer, leader of MSR Action, even though the two men participated in a plot to overthrow the tyrannical Dominican Republic President, Rafael Trujillo in 1947.

Edouard Chibás, leader of the Partido Ortodoxo, was a charismatic anti-communist politician but he had a great influence on Castro. Chibás believed corruption to be the greatest threat that Cuba faced in the 1940s and 1950s and Castro joined his party, working fervently for him, even after Chibás lost the presidential election. In 1951 Chibás shot himself during a radio broadcast and Castro accompanied him to hospital where he died.

Violence was rife in Cuban politics and in 1948 there were three political assassinations, with Fidel Castro linked to all of them, in one case being identified by witnesses as the assassin. He was never arrested or charged for them, however. That same year, funded by Argentinean president, Juan Perón, he travelled to Bogotá, capital of Colombia, where he took part in anti-American demonstrations.

It was also the year in which he married Mirta Diaz Balart, a fellow student who came from a wealthy family. His honeymoon, a lavish three-month stay in New York, was paid for by Mirta's father.

He graduated in 1950 and began practising law in Havana. Meanwhile, in speeches he voiced his Cuban nationalism and fervid opposition to the United States and its involvement in the Korean

War. When Batista staged a *coup d'état* in 1952, cancelling the imminent elections in which Castro was standing as a prospective member of the Cuban parliament, he was furious. He accused Batista of violating the Cuban constitution but was denied a hearing in the courts. This denial persuaded him finally that revolution was the only way he would get rid of the Batista government and banish corruption from his homeland. He abandoned his law practice and went underground.

He and his followers, who included his brother Raul, started to assemble a collection of weapons and ammunition in preparation for their first action, an assault on the Moncada barracks. It was a disaster. Of the 135 insurgents who attacked the barracks, more than sixty were killed. The survivors, including Castro, escaped into the mountains but were discovered and arrested. Many were executed, but Castro and Raul were allowed to live and stand trial, mainly, it is said, because an officer in the government forces recognised Castro from his university days. He was sent to prison for fifteen years but not before he gave an impassioned speech in court, known as History Will Absolve Me. In it he said, '. . . my voice will not be stifled – it will rise from my breast even when I feel most alone, and my heart will give it all the fire that callous cowards deny it . . . Condemn me. It does not matter. History will absolve me.'

Prison gave him the opportunity to make plans for the overthrow of Batista and he decided that he would reorganise and train his men in Mexico.

Released early, in 1955, as part of an amnesty, he headed for Mexico with a group of supporters. He called the movement he founded the 26 July Movement, in tribute to those who had fallen at the Moncada barracks on 26 July 1952 and he resolved to make it into an effective guerrilla movement. This notion was helped by his meeting with a fervent revolutionary and passionate advocate of guerrilla warfare – Ernesto 'Che' Guevara. Guevara would become fundamental to Castro's movement and helped to develop his political thinking.

Funding for weapons and supplies was obtained from wealthy Cuban opponents to the Batista regime living in the United States, ousted Cuban president, Carlos Prio Socarras amongst them while training was carried out by a Cuban-born veteran of the Spanish Civil war, Alberto Bayo. By late 1956 they were ready. On 26 November, eighty-two of them set sail on the yacht Granma for Cuba.

Once again it went badly and most of them were killed or captured within weeks of their landing close to the eastern city of Manzanilla. The twenty men who remained fled into the mountains to regroup and launch a guerrilla war against Batista from their mountain stronghold. Meanwhile, throughout Cuba, the President's unpopularity was leading to the formation of underground groups working against him and his supporters. By mid-1957, Castro had more than 800 men at his disposal and was being lionised by the world's media as a charismatic, bearded revolutionary, appearing on the covers of magazines and on the front page of the *New York Times*. In 1957, when he signed an undertaking to hold elections within eighteen months of taking power, the Cuban people rallied to him even more.

Batista took action against this dangerous new force, launching Operation Verano, an offensive aimed at wiping out the 26 July Movement once and for all. The plan failed, however, with Castro and other rebels winning a series of victories against poorly trained government forces. Operation Verano having failed, Castro launched a full-blooded attack, ordering his men into central Cuba, capturing a number of towns on the Cauto Plains.

His advance continued and men began to desert from the Cuban army in droves. Eventually, in the early hours of 1 January 1959, Batista resigned as head of the government and fled the country, possibly taking as much as $700 million with him in art treasures and cash. The jubilant people of Havana took to the streets rejoicing at the news and waving the black and red flag of the 26 July Movement. Thirty-two-year-old Fidel Castro and his victorious army marched into the capital, through streets lined with celebrating Cubans, to take power.

Initially, Jose Miro Cardona who had taken over from Batista was prime minister, with Castro as commander-in-chief of the military, but Cardona resigned the following month, and Castro was sworn in as leader, swearing to hold elections in two months.

He wasted no time, nationalising farms and factories and threatening United States financial interests in Cuba. He penalised them by paying them compensation based on the artificially low prices they had paid past Cuban governments for land. He did visit the United States around this time, but President Eisenhower, viewing Castro's acts as those of a communist – although Castro at the time denied it – refused to meet him.

Before the year was out, he had reformed Cuban agriculture, limiting the amount of land a person could own and banning foreign ownership of property. He also purged his army of opponents and began to censor the media.

Critically, however, he began to build a relationship with the USSR, signing trade agreements with them. He nationalised US oil refineries and they retaliated with restrictions on Cuban sugar imports to the United States.

Cuba and Castro landed firmly on the world stage in 1961 during what has become known as the Cuban Missile Crisis. It began with a failed invasion of the island by 1,400 Cuban exiles who had actually been trained and armed by the CIA and had the tacit approval of the US government for their action. The Bay of Pigs fiasco was a severe embarrassment for the Americans and especially for the new president John F. Kennedy who had reluctantly inherited the plan from Eisenhower. Hundreds died and Castro's forces captured almost 1,000.

Castro responded by declaring Cuba officially to be a socialist state, banning democratic elections, declaring himself a Marxist-Leninist and beginning half a century of denunciation of the United States. The Americans imposed an embargo on trade with Cuba.

Castro solidified his country's relationship with the USSR and accepted a plan from Soviet premier, Nikita Khrushchev to base Russian missiles, aimed at the United States, on Cuban soil. When the bases were spotted by a US U-2 reconnaissance flight, the Americans were outraged, demanding their immediate removal. For several days the world stood on the brink of war as Soviet ships, carrying what were thought to be missiles, steamed towards Cuba and an exclusion zone imposed by President Kennedy. Finally Kennedy won the war of brinksmanship when Khrushchev agreed to remove the missiles.

For Castro, however, it had been an embarrassing experience. He had not been involved in any of the negotiations between the two superpowers. Cuba also became more isolated in the world, being expelled from the Organisation of American States and being treated like a pariah by most of the rest of the world.

Castro directed his energy at revolution, founding organisations to promote revolution in South and Central America as well as in Africa. He became a spokesperson for Third World countries and supported his Russian allies in their struggles in Yemen, Angola and Ethiopia.

The 1991 collapse of the Soviet Union was disastrous for Cuba, so long reliant on aid from its communist cousins. After forty years, the US embargo remained firmly in place, further inhibiting economic progress. Castro was forced to initiate change. He adopted a type of free market economy, encouraged foreign investors and promoted tourism. He even invited Cuban emigrés to return to their native land from America.

In the late 1990s, now in his mid-seventies, his health went into decline and questions began to be asked about the succession. In 2006, he underwent surgery for gastrointestinal bleeding following which he dramatically announced that he was stepping down temporarily and that his brother Raul, another survivor of the revolution, who had been his deputy for many years, would take his place.

On 19 February 2008, forty-nine years after he had marched triumphantly into Havana, a frail, eighty-one-year-old Fidel Castro resigned the Cuban Presidency because of ill health. Seventy-six-year-old Raul Castro was officially elected President by the Cuban National Assembly.

It seems that after surviving vicious guerrilla warfare, poison pills, exploding cigars and Mafia hitmen, it will, after all, be old age and ill health that will finally bring to an end the life of one of the greatest and most charismatic leaders the Americas have ever seen.

LECH WALESA

Born in Popowo in Poland in 1943, to a carpenter and his wife, Lech Walensa, a shop steward in the Gdansk shipyards, created a popular movement that brought down the Polish government, bringing an end to communism in Poland and igniting the spark that would lead to similar government changes across communist Eastern Europe in the 'velvet revolutions' of 1989. The efforts of this feisty, mustachioed electrician changed the direction of 20th century history, creating a genuine workers' revolution and leading to his name being etched in history as one of its greatest and most determined leaders.

A devout Roman Catholic, like most Poles, Walesa began his working life as a mechanic before spending two years in the Polish army. He found work in the vast Lenin shipyard in Gdansk on Poland's Baltic coast in 1970 as an electrical technician. A year earlier he married Danuta Golos and the couple would go on to have eight children.

Walesa was horrified by the conditions under which Polish shipyard workers had to work and shocked by the brutal repression of workers' protests by the government. He became involved with opposition groups but in 1976, his militant union activities led to him being sacked from his job in the Lenin Shipyard after he had led the workers in a confrontation with the government. For two years he had little work and was forced to do odd jobs to support his family.

Nonetheless, he persevered with his union activities, in 1978 joining the non-communist and, therefore, illegal Wolne Zwiazki Zawodowe Wybrzeza (Free Trade Unions of the Coast). The government, meanwhile, had put him under surveillance and his every move was followed and recorded by state security officers. In 1980, when a strike was called in the Gdansk shipyards in support of better conditions and rights for workers, Walesa climbed the perimeter wall of the shipyard to join the sit-in. Soon his passion, ready wit and great oratory led to him being elected leader. He worked to move his fellow workers away from complaining only about wages towards a much more dangerous demand – the demand for free trade unions.

The government was forced to concede to their demands and the Gdansk Agreement was signed in September 1981, giving workers the right to strike and to organise independent unions, although they would not, of course, be entirely free. It was the first time since 1917 that workers in a communist state were free to organise themselves in trade unions. The strike committee immediately formalised itself as the National Coordination Committee of Solidarność, known in English as Solidarity. Walesa was elected Chairman of an organisation that immediately had ten million members and found himself to be famous and in demand around the world. The International Labour Organisation took him to Italy, Japan, Sweden, Switzerland and France.

The situation in Poland remained tense for the next sixteen months. The government and Solidarity struggled to coexist and it all went on against the backdrop of the threat of invasion by the Soviet Union, just as had happened in Hungary in 1956 and Czechoslovakia in 1968 when there was a danger of liberalisation.

Walesa was in his element. Cunning and sometimes infuriatingly unpredictable, he began to display an uncanny knack for politics. He was loved by the people and was able to read the popular mood at any given moment, often guiding it with his innate powers of oratory.

Concerned about the rising tide of unrest in Poland, Prime Minister General Jaruzelski felt he had no option but to declare martial law on 13 December 1981, arresting Walesa and interning him in a country house near the Soviet border in southeastern

Poland for eleven months. He was released on 14 November 1982 and in 1983 applied to return to work at the Gdansk shipyard as an electrician. Later that year, this simple electrician was awarded the Nobel Peace Prize, remaining under strict surveillance by the Polish security service even after this.

Even while Solidarity was being repressed by the government, Walesa and his supporters worked hard to keep it alive, encouraged to do so by the Pope, John Paul II, also Polish, and the United States as well as other governments around the world. He led the semi-illegal Temporary Executive Committee of Solidarity Trade Union from 1987 until 1990. But things were changing in the communist world. When Mikhail Gorbachev became leader of the Soviet Union with his policies of *glasnost* (openness) and *perestroika* (re-structuring), there at last seemed to be some light at the end of the tunnel.

In 1988, Walesa organised another occupation of the Lenin Shipyard. The workers were this time demanding the restoration to legality of Solidarity After a few months, the government entered into negotiations with them. Incredibly, the government gave in and conceded to the re-legalising of Solidarity and to allowing elections to the Polish parliament that, although not entirely free, were a step in the right direction. Solidarity became a political party and, naturally, enjoyed a great deal of success in the elections. The opposition to the government won all the seats in the Sejm, the lower house of the parliament that were subject to free elections and all but one of the seats in the newly re-established Senate. Only Communist Party members and their allies were allowed to stand in sixty-four per cent of the Sejm seats.

Walesa's political cunning now came into play as he succeeded in persuading the formerly communist ally parties to form a non-communist coalition government. It would be the first non-communist government in one of the nations of the Eastern Bloc and Tadeusz Mazowiecki became the first non-communist prime minister of Poland in over forty years.

Walesa was still not happy, however, seeing Poland being run by his former advisers in collaboration with former communists. He launched his own campaign to be President of Poland in 1990, running against his own former adviser. He won, becoming the country's first non-communist president. He had come a long way from clambering over a shipyard wall to join a strike just ten years earlier.

He remained the same man he had always been – outspoken and ordinary but some found him uncouth and undignified as head of state. Long, formal speeches were a problem to this firebrand more used to gauging the mood of the crowd and extemporising when delivering speeches.

In foreign policy, too, he made gaffes such as when Poland was waiting to be admitted to NATO, he suggested a 'NATO bis', a kind of second-tier NATO for those awaiting admittance to the organisation. He also surprised many by making his chauffeur his closest adviser and by developing close links with the military and the security services who had reported his every move for so many years. His style was criticised as being authoritarian.

He lost the 1995 presidential election to a former communist, Aleksander Kwasniewski and returned to live in Gdansk with his family. Reluctant to retire completely and still young enough to believe his political life was far from over, he made efforts to establish his own political party and lent his support to a new party, Solidarity Electoral Action which won the parliamentary elections in 1997. However, he was not a high profile member of the party whose organiser was the new Solidarity Trade Union leader, Marian Krzaklewski.

In 2000, against the wishes of many Poles, Walesa put himself forward once more for the presidential election, but made a poor showing, disappointingly winning a mere 1 per cent of the votes.

At last, he declared that he was retiring from politics and has since then spent his time giving lectures on the history and politics of Central Europe at foreign universities.

In 2006, he announced that he had quit Solidarity, citing differences with the party's support of the Law and Justice party, and the rise to power of Lech and Jarosław Kaczyński.

Lech Walesa was the right man at the right time for the Polish people. He was the architect of their freedom from the communist chains, but, a good man in a fight, he was found, perhaps, to be less able once that fight had been won and it was time for stable government.

Undoubtedly, however, it was his sheer doggedness, his hunger for the fight and his determination to win that enabled Solidarity to survive martial law and illegality. Without that, the peoples of Eastern Europe might never have thought it possible that they too could be free of the Soviet yoke. It is for that reason that Lech Walesa's name will forever occupy an important position in the rollcall of great European leaders.

FRANKLIN D. ROOSEVELT

ON 3 JANUARY 2000, Franklin Delano Roosevelt was named runner-up – behind Albert Einstein – as *Time* magazine's Man of the Century. Elected to four terms in office – the only US president to be elected more than twice – his terms in, lasting from 1933 until 1945, coincided with some of the biggest crises America, and the world have ever faced – the global depression, the rise of dictatorships and the Second World War.

Franklin Roosevelt – FDR for short – was a fifth cousin of Theodore Roosevelt, President from 1901 until 1909. The Roosevelts were an old and wealthy family from New York State and were successful in fields other than politics. FDR's first cousin, Ellen for instance was a tennis champion and his family was related to many illustrious Americans such as Elizabeth Monroe, wife of the fifth President of the United States, James Monroe. Amongst his ancestors were Bendict Arnold and Joseph Smith Dr, founder of the Church of the Latter day Saints.

Franklin was born on 30 January 1882 in the upmarket Hyde Park in New York State, the only child of James and Sara Roosevelt. His father was old – fifty-four when he was born – and fairly distant, leaving his mother as the major influence on his early life which was one of undoubted privilege. He made frequent trips to Europe as a child, learning to speak German and French as well as becoming proficient, as was the way of wealthy young men of his time, in riding, shooting, rowing, polo and tennis.

The headmaster of his school, Endicott Peabody, was another formative influence on the young Roosevelt. He particularly urged his students to enter public life at the end of their education and Roosevelt listened carefully to him.

He was admitted to Harvard where he became editor of the *Harvard Crimson* newspaper and, meanwhile, he idolised his cousin Teddy who had just been elected President of the United States, admiring his vigorous presidential style and his reforming zeal. In fact, his future wife, Anna Eleanor Roosevelt, was Teddy Roosevelt's niece and he first met her at a White House reception.

FDR entered law school in 1905, but never graduated, having already passed the New York State Bar Exam. He began his work as a lawyer with a prestigious Wall Street firm – Carter Ledyard & Milburn.

His mother seriously opposed his union with Eleanor, but on 17 March 1905, the couple were married with President Theodore Roosevelt giving the bride away in place of her deceased father. They had six children between 1906 and 1916 but Roosevelt was unfaithful on occasion. He had an affair with his wife's social secretary, Lucy Mercer, after she was employed in 1914, a liaison that Eleanor discovered in 1918 when she offered FDR a divorce. His mistress, however, was a Roman Catholic and refused to marry a divorced father of five children. Although FDR and Eleanor reconciled, their marriage was, from then on, merely a marriage of convenience and she lived in a separate house in Hyde Park.

Roosevelt launched his political career in 1910, when he was elected by a landslide to the New York State Senate, the first Democrat to be elected from his district since 1884. Soon, he was a well-known and highly respected member of the Democratic Party.

He resigned from the Senate in 1913 when he was appointed Assistant Secretary of the Navy by then President, Woodrow Wilson. Running for the United States Senate the following year, he lost, but continued in his post, expanding the US Navy and founding the

United States Naval Reserve. During this time, he showed his lack of fear at getting the United States involved in foreign adventures and he was responsible for some US interventions in Central America and the Caribbean. However, his work at this time was vital in building US defences in the lead-up to the Second World War. He enthusiastically encouraged the development of the submarine as a vital element of modern warfare and a critical means of stopping the German submarine threat in the Atlantic. He also proposed a barrier of mines across the North Sea, stretching from Norway to Scotland.

In 1920, the Democratic Party Convention chose Roosevelt as its Vice-Presidential candidate on the ticket of Ohio Governor James M. Cox and FDR resigned from his position as Assistant Secretary of the Navy to fight the campaign. It was to no avail. The Republican candidate, Warren Harding, swept all before him and the Cox-Roosevelt candidacy was heavily defeated that November. Roosevelt returned to his legal practice, but not for long.

His political future and his very life were threatened around this time. In August 1921, he was on holiday with his family on the Canadian island of Campobello Island. Roosevelt suddenly became very ill with an illness that was thought to be polio. He became paralysed from the waist down although for the remainder of his life he refused to concede that he was in fact so debilitated. Naturally, he tried everything in search of a cure but none was forthcoming, although he did found a hydrotherapy centre at Warm Strings, Georgia that still operates under his name. From then on, he used leg and hip braces and a cane to get around in public, supported on each side by his sons or aides. In private, he used a wheelchair but he was never seen in it beyond the confines of his own domain.

He had remained in touch with Democratic politics and in 1928 was narrowly elected Governor of New York on a platform of reform. It was necessary; the Democratic Party machine, known as Tammany Hall, that had controlled politics in New York City since the 1790s, had become corrupt over the years and Roosevelt fought against this corruption, especially when it became an election issue when he ran for a second term as Governor in 1930. His investigations into such matters as the sale of judicial office earned him a healthy 700,000 majority.

His success in New York made Roosevelt the perfect candidate in the 1932 Presidential election. With support from men such as the newspaper magnate, William Randolph Hearst and the leader of Irish Americans, Joseph P. Kennedy, he won the hotly contested Democratic nomination, famously declaring in his acceptance speech, 'Throughout the nation men and women, forgotten in the political philosophy of the Government, look to us here for guidance and for more equitable opportunity to share in the distribution of national wealth ... I pledge you, I pledge myself to a new deal for the American people ... This is more than a political campaign. It is a call to arms.'

The blight of the Depression cast a shadow over the election campaign. Millions of Americans were out of work or had lost their homes and businesses. Roosevelt and the Democratic Party reached out to the nation's poverty-stricken, advocating the mobilisation of the poor into organised labour to create great projects. His use of the phrase 'New Deal' in his acceptance speech would become the clarion call for the early years of his presidency.

Uncharacteristically for a Democrat, FDR campaigned on a platform of public expenditure cuts, 'abolishing useless commissions and offices, consolidating bureaus and eliminating extravagances.' He popularly advocated the repeal of the Prohibition that had kept America more or less sober for over a decade, realising the useful revenue the renewed sale of alcohol would bring to government coffers.

American politics were transformed and energised by one of the most important elections in the country's history and he won fifty-seven per cent of the vote, taking all but six of the States of the Union.

Things were getting worse, however. In the last months of the term of office of the previous President, Herbert Hoover, the economy collapsed completely and then, in 1933, Roosevelt narrowly escaped an assassination attempt that killed the man sitting next to him.

As he swore the oath of office in March 1933, declaring to Americans that 'the only thing we have to fear is fear itself', a quarter of America's workforce was out of work. Agricultural prices had fallen by sixty per cent and industrial production was half what it had been in 1929. Two million people were homeless and thirty-two of the forty-eight states had closed their banks. As with the recent 21st century economic crisis, Roosevelt attributed the collapse of the banking system to the greed of bankers and financiers.

He embarked upon a programme of 'Relief, Recovery and Reform', presenting his ideas to the people of America in radio broadcasts that became known as 'Fireside Chats'. He hired 250,000 young men to work on local projects, under the heading of the Civilian Conservation Corps and under his aegis, mortgage relief was provided for millions of farmers and home owners.

In 1933, the Securities and Exchange Commission was founded to regulate Wall Street and to prevent a crisis such as the Depression in the future. Joseph P. Kennedy, father of President John F. Kennedy, was put in charge.

Roosevelt created the biggest government-owned industrial enterprise in US history, the Tennessee Valley Authority, to build dams and power stations as well as to modernise agriculture and living conditions for American people.

He did succeed in cutting the federal budget, and repealed Prohibition in April 1933. In 1936, he was re-elected with a landslide. Now, though, he had bigger concerns than the US economy.

Adolf Hitler's rise to power in Germany and other issues such as Mussolini's invasion of Ethiopia in 1935, created fears of a global war. In the United States, Congress passed the Neutrality Act which banned the shipment of arms from America to a nation at war. Roosevelt opposed it, reasoning that it penalised the victims of aggression, such as Italy's against Ethiopia, but he signed it in the face of overwhelming public support for it. In a 1937 speech he made his feelings clear when he said that warrior states should be 'quarantined'. Meanwhile, in the background, he had resumed his interest in naval affairs, secretly speeding up a programme of submarine-building in the face of the threat from Japan. However, he steadfastly denied that America would become involved in a coalition of nations attempting to prevent Hitler from expanding his country at the expense of others, particularly Czechoslovakia, at which the Nazis were casting hungry glances. America would remain neutral, he insisted.

On the outbreak of war in Europe in September 1939, following Germany's invasion and annexation of Poland, Roosevelt immediately began to help the beleaguered European Allies. He established regular communications with British Prime Minister, Winston Churchill, and passed the Lend-Lease Act in March 1941, when British financial resources were running dry. This allowed the USA to give Britain, Russia, China and others more than $50 billion of military supplies, with no repayment after the war.

As the countries of Europe fell one by one to the Nazis, Roosevelt was determined that Britain would not fall. He had begun increasing American military spending but when Paris was captured, American isolationist sentiment began to decline in strength and FDR began to use his own personal powers of communication to win the country round to his view that the USA should help the Allies. In 1940, in defiance of the Neutrality Act, he gave fifty destroyers to Britain in return for the right to establish military bases in the Caribbean and in Canada.

It had been traditional for American Presidents to stay in office for a maximum of only two terms and any who had suggested doing otherwise, such as Theodore Roosevelt and Ulysses S. Grant, had been criticised for it. After Roosevelt's death, the 22nd Amendment to the United States Constitution would formalise the notion of a maximum two-term presidency. However, in 1940, he was made the Democratic candidate by popular acclaim and was elected to a third term in office by taking fifty-five per cent of the popular vote and thirty-eight of the forty-eight states. His third term would be entirely dominated by the Second World War and the stress of it would damage his health beyond repair.

1. He delivered a number of 'Fireside Chats' that had isolationists calling him a war mongerer – the 'Arsenal of Democracy' talk and the 'Four Freedoms' broadcast notable amongst these. In the Four Freedoms talk in January 1941, he listed the basic inalienable freedoms that all human beings should have by right: Freedom of speech and expression, freedom of religion, freedom from want and freedom from fear.

2. Meanwhile, the American economy had been given a boost by the construction of weapons, tanks, planes and ships with the number of unemployed falling below a million.

3. US ships began escorting Allied convoys in the Atlantic and could fire upon German aggressors if needed. He was now supporting the Allies with 'all aid short of war' and ordered his Secretary of War, Henry Stimson, to prepare for America's inevitable entry into the conflict. He expected to put ten million men into arms in 1943, but the US entry into the war came rather sooner.

4. On 7 December 1941, the Japanese attacked the US Pacific Fleet at Pearl Harbor, destroying or damaging sixteen battleships and killing more than 2,400 US military personnel and civilians. The isolationists were silenced and the American people rallied for war. The day following the attack, Roosevelt delivered one of the most famous speeches in American history, the 'Infamy Speech', declaring the date of the previous day's attack to be 'a date which will live in infamy'. He ended the speech by asking for Congress's endorsement for a declaration of war between the United States and Japan. Three days later, Germany and Italy declared war on America.

5. FDR met with Churchill in late December and they planned the prosecution of the war with the aim of stopping the Axis forces in the Soviet Union and North Africa. At the same time, there would be an invasion of Western Europe and in the east, Japan would be defeated. Meetings would be held on several occasions during the war, involving Roosevelt, Churchill and Joseph Stalin and towards the end of the war, they laid out a vision of how Europe should be after hostilities had ended.

6. Roosevelt put General Dwight D. Eisenhower in charge of the Allied invasion of Europe – Operation Overlord – in preference to General George Marshall and the Allied forces began their march on Berlin.

7. On the afternoon of 12 April 1945, as Allied troops closed in on the German capital, Roosevelt, resting at Warm Springs, complained of 'a terrific headache' and collapsed. He was carried into his bedroom where he died of a massive cerebral hemorrhage.

8. America was shocked as radio transmissions were interrupted to give the news of their leader's death. Eighteen days later, Adolf Hitler committed suicide in his bunker in Berlin and a week later, the Allies accepted the surrender of Nazi Germany.

INDIRA GANDHI

EIGHT MINUTES AFTER nine in the morning of 31 October 1984, sixty-six-year-old Indira Priyadarshini Gandhi, Prime Minister of India, clasped her hands in front of her face, smiled at the two turbaned and bearded Sikh guards who protected her route from her office and uttered 'Namaste', the Indian greeting. It was the last word she ever said.

She was in good spirits, attempting to secure a fifth term as prime minister of India. That morning she was on her way to be interviewed by distinguished British actor, Peter Ustinov, for an Irish television documentary. He had been following her for a few days as she campaigned through the eastern state of Orissa.

The guards were Satwant Singh and Beant Singh. She had known the latter man for ten years and he had become a favourite of the Prime Minister. As she greeted them, about seven feet from them, Beant Singh drew a .38 revolver and before anyone could react, pumped three shots into her stomach. As she collapsed to the ground, Satwant Singh fired repeatedly into her body with the Sten automatic he was carrying. Tragically, she had stubbornly always refused to wear a bullet-proof vest and received a total of seven bullets in her abdomen, three in her chest and one in her heart. As she lay dead, the two Sikhs calmly dropped their weapons and Beant said, 'I've done what I had to do. You do what you have to do.'

The security men took them to a guardhouse where Beant made a lunge for a gun being carried by one of the guards while Satwant drew a dagger from his turban. They were both shot, Beant dying almost at once and Satwant being critically wounded.

Meanwhile, Indira Gandhi's body, wrapped in its blood-soaked sari, was carried to her Ambassador car and rushed to the All-India Institute of Medical Sciences Hospital where, even though she was dead, they operated, praying for a miracle. It was not until 1.45 pm that the announcement was made. The Indian news service screamed, 'GANDHI IS DEAD'.

The previous night, she had delivered a speech in which she had proudly declared, 'I am not interested in a long life. I am not afraid of these things. I don't mind if my life goes in the service of this nation. If I die today, every drop of my blood will invigorate the nation.'

Her death had been precipitated by her reaction to problems in the Punjab region of India and especially to the seizure of the Golden temple in Amritsar the previous September by a militant group of Sikh separatists led by Jarnail Singh Bhindranwale. The Golden Temple is the Sikh religion's holiest shrine and a symbol of Sikhism to the world. There were thousands visiting it as the separatists took up their positions in the carefully planned operation, but, in spite of the danger to innocent bystanders, the stubborn and determined Indira Gandhi ordered the army in with orders to clear the building and the area of attackers at any cost. The result was a huge number of casualties. Estimates differ; some say that as many as 500 or more troops and 3,000 others died, including many pilgrims.

Her assassination was revenge for the carnage at the Golden Temple and it brought to an end the life not only of one of India's most remarkable politicians, but also one of the world's great leaders.

She had been born into politics in 1917. Her father was Pandit Jawaharlal Nehru, a lawyer who would become independent India's first prime minister and her grandfather, Motilal Nehru, was one of the most prominent members of the Indian national Congress, the political movement founded by Mahatma Gandhi that would later become India's principal political party.

From the outset, Indira was a loner. Her father and grandfather were absent much of the time, engaged on political matters while she was cared for solely by her mother, Kamala. The engagement of her family in independence politics also made it difficult for the young Indira to enjoy normal friendships with her peers.

Through time, she, too, became involved, launching the Vanara Sena movement for girls and boys and she helped to distribute sensitive publications and materials banned by the British. She attended good schools in both India and Britain and went to Oxford University, but academic work was not her forte and she failed to graduate.

During her sojourn in Europe, she had met Feroze Gandhi – no relation to the Mahatma – and the couple married when she was twenty-five years old in March 1942. Their two sons, Rajiv and Sanjay would be born in 1944 and 1946, respectively.

It was an exciting time in India. Gandhi and his Congress Party had just launched the Quit India movement, the final determined initiative to push the British out. The occupiers, however, came down hard on Gandhi and his supporters and Indira and her husband were arrested by the authorities and imprisoned without charge. She spent eight months in prison before being finally released on 13 May 1943.

India was finally given independence in 1947, with her father being appointed prime minister, but had to endure a difficult partition, the division of the country into two separate entities, India and the Muslim-dominated Pakistan. During this chaotic time when ten million refugees migrated into India from Pakistan, Indira worked in the organisation of refugee camps and the provision of much-needed medical care.

With the couple now living in Allahabad, Feroze worked for the Congress party newspaper as well as for an insurance company. But his relationship with his wife was becoming difficult, especially when she and her sons moved in with her father so that she could help him. Through time, she and Feroze separated while remaining married.

She managed the campaigns of her father and her husband in India's first elections in 1951. Both won, but even though Feroze was now living in Delhi, where she was, the couple remained apart. They would be reconciled in 1958 after he suffered a heart attack, but he died in 1960. Ironically, when he died she was abroad with her father.

In 1960, she was elected President of the Congress Party, performing her duties while still working as chief of staff for her father who remained Prime Minister until 1964. However, she did not run for political office out of respect to her father's views on nepotism, a practice that he abhorred.

Following his death, however, she felt no such constraint and, in 1964, at the urging of new Prime Minister, Lal Bahadur Shastri – Gulzarilal Nanda had held the position temporarily – she was elected to parliament, immediately being appointed Minister for Information and Broadcasting.

At the time there had been rioting in the non-Hindi speaking southern Indian states over the decision to make Hindi the national language of India. Indira travelled to Madras and dealt with the situation brilliantly, calming local officials and supervising the reconstruction effort where damage had been done. Her prompt action embarrassed Shastri and other government officials who had done nothing to help the region.

She also did her reputation no harm during the Indo-Pakistani War of 1965. She had been on holiday in the border region of Srinigar when hostilities broke out. As insurgents approached the city, she refused to be evacuated, remaining there to rally local government officials and the people. When Shastri died a few hours after signing a peace agreement with Pakistan, it was inevitable that she would be named as a candidate for the office of Prime Minister. In the party election, she defeated the conservative candidate, Morarji Desai, by 355 to 169 to become the fourth Prime Minister of India and the first woman to hold that position.

The party she inherited was in disarray, split into two factions –

her socialists and Desai's conservatives. In the 1967 election, the discontent showed and Congress lost sixty seats, although she retained a majority. For a while, she co-existed with Desai while he served as Deputy Prime Minister and Finance Minister, but in 1969, the party split. She was forced to solicit the support of the Socialist and Communist Parties to remain in power.

She nationalised Indian banks in July 1969 and in 1971, declared war on Pakistan in an effort to solve the problem being created with refugees from East Pakistan which was fighting for independence and with whom she sided. It was a war that set the two superpowers, the United States and the USSR against each other. US President Nixon threatened India with the Seventh Fleet, warning her to stay away from East Pakistan. Undaunted, however, she turned to America's enemy for help. The Russians provided the political and military support that helped India to defeat the Pakistanis and led to the founding of the new country of Bangladesh. Her relations with Nixon would continue to deteriorate – he called her 'the old witch' – while India and the Soviet Union developed even closer relations.

Indira Gandhi made many important reforms in India and put a great deal of effort into dragging the country into the modern age, encouraging the introduction of technology and working towards making a nation that historically had suffered from chronic food shortages in which many millions had died into one that was self-sufficient and even able to export.

In response to the nuclear threat from her eastern neighbour, China, she initiated a nuclear programme in 1967. Her first underground nuclear test – codenamed 'The Smiling Buddha' – was successfully carried out in 1974, near the village of Pokhran in Rajasthan.

She launched a programme to reform food production in India known that has become known as the Green Revolution. It was designed to remove India's reliance on food aid from countries such as the United States. As a result, milk and rice production were increased and wheat production went up threefold.

The Green Revolution, combating malnutrition, especially amongst children, and improving the lot of India's peasant class, secured for her a second term as Prime Minister in 1971 with a massive majority. It was a majority, however, that led to accusations of authoritarianism being levelled against her. She had amended the constitution, tilting the balance of power away from the States towards the centre. There was also a growing resentment at the interference of her son, Sanjay, who was now her political adviser and right-hand man. Even former fighters for independence who had struggled alongside her father, spoke out against her.

On 12 June 1975, the growing dislike for Indira Gandhi's methods found its expression when the High Court in Allahabad declared her election in her constituency of Rae Bareli illegal on the grounds of malpractice. She was removed from her seat and banned from standing for election for six years. As the Prime Minister of India must be a member of either the Lok Sabha – India's lower house – or the Rajya Sabha – its upper house – she was effectively removed from office. She appealed but the opposition screamed for her resignation. India was paralysed by strikes and huge crowds surrounded the parliament building, calling for her to resign.

Indira responded by ordering the arrest of members of the opposition parties and a state of emergency was declared by President Fakhruddin Ali Ahmed. Police were granted special powers to impose curfews and to detain people, newspapers were censored and legislative elections that were due to be held were cancelled. Furthermore, all opposition state governments were removed from office. She took on extraordinary powers and was accused of ruling by decree. Thousands were arrested and many more were left homeless or dead in Delhi when her son Sanjay undertook the clearing of the slums.

It could not go on forever, of course, and she finally called elections in 1977, fearing probably that if she did not, the armed forces might intervene, remove her from office and call elections. She underestimated the public mood, however, and both she and Sanjay lost their seats. Congress was left with only 153 seats and Desai became Prime Minister.

She eventually won a by-election in 1978 but was expelled again from parliament when she was arrested, along with Sanjay. Her long-running trial, however, elicited sympathy from many and her star began to rise once more. She gave speeches apologising for mistakes and in the election of 1979 Congress was returned to power in a landslide victory. She was Indian Prime Minister for a fourth term.

Following Indira Gandhi's assassination, her son Rajiv became Prime Minister, reluctantly leaving his job as a pilot to follow what was his destiny as a Nehru-Gandhi. Sanjay had been her first choice as a successor but he had died in a flying accident in June 1980. In May 1991, Rajiv, too, would be assassinated by Tamil Eelam militants. The dynasty continued, however, when his wife, Sonia, Italian by birth, led the United Progressive Alliance to power in 2004, although she declined the opportunity to become Prime Minister, a role from which her Italian origins probably precluded her, anyway.

Indira Gandhi was loved and hated in equal measure by the warring factions of Indian politics but there can be no denying her astonishing achievements as a woman, as a politician and as a leader of the world's most populous democracy.

EVA PERÓN

FEW WOMEN HAVE enjoyed the type of worship lavished on Eva Perón by the people of Argentina. So powerful, in fact, was her hold on the Argentine people that even in death she seemed to terrify the government to the extent they that they did not even permit her body to be buried on Argentinean soil for twenty-four years after her death. Her mummified corpse was buried anonymously in Italy and then spent time in the attic of her exiled husband's home in Madrid, before the emotional return to her native country and burial in her family tomb in Buenos Aires.

She was born Maria Eva Duarte in rural Argentina in 1919. Her mother and father were unmarried and Eva spent her early years in the Buenos Aires province of Junin. Her father, Juan Darte, was already married and returned to his first family in 1920 when Eva was a year old, leaving Eva, her four brothers and sisters and their mother in extreme poverty, her mother having to take in sewing to feed her children. Eva spent as much time as she could at the cinema and dreamed of becoming a famous actress. Meanwhile, her mother dreamed of marrying her off to a local man.

At the age of fifteen, she moved to Buenos Aires with her belongings in a cardboard suitcase in pursuit of her dream and to escape the misery of her upbringing. She had not escaped her mother entirely, however – she travelled on the train with her and accompanied her to an audition at a radio station. Eva moved in with the Bustamontes family who were friends of her father.

With no formal education and few connections in the city or the entertainment business, she immediately found life in the capital difficult. Getting noticed was especially difficult as the city was thronged with people who had been force to move there by the Depression that was ravaging the country and the world. Nonetheless, on 28 March 1935, she made her professional debut, appearing onstage at the Comedias Theatre in a play called *The Perezes Misses.*

Gradually, she began to find more work – she toured with a theatre company, did some modelling and was cast in small parts in a few low-budget films. In 1942, she began to make a name for herself on the radio, starring in a daily soap on Argentina's biggest radio station at the time, Radio El Mundo, and she also signed a five-year contract with Radio Belgrano. By 1943 she was earning good money as one of the highest-paid radio actresses in Argentina and had moved into her own apartment in an exclusive neighbourhood.

Juan Perón had been born in 1895 and entered the Argentinean Military Academy at sixteen, joining the army in 1915. He was a captain in 1930 when he played a minor role in the coup of that year. In 1936, he became military attaché to Chile and just before the outbreak of the Second World War he was sent to Europe where he travelled extensively. He returned in 1942 and in 1944 was involved in raising money to help the victims of a major earthquake when he met the beautiful young Eva Duarte at a gala. The forty-eight-year-old soldier-politician and the twenty-four-year-old actress fell head-over-heels in love and are reported to have left the event together at around two in the morning. Not long after, to the horror of Buenos Aires society, they moved in together. People were scandalised firstly because Argentinean society was very class-driven and entertainers and politicians were viewed as coming from entirely different strata. Secondly, it was still seen as improper for an unmarried couple to be living together. Perón cared little for what others thought, however, introducing Eva to his circle of friends and associates and also beginning to involve her in all aspects of his political career, seeing something very special in his beautiful girlfriend. She would sit in on meetings with advisers and other members of the government and would just sit quietly, taking it all in.

A few months later, when it was announced that all broadcast performers had to organise themselves into a union, Eva achieved her first public office when she was elected its first president. Of course, it seems likely that Perón was behind the idea of the union which would have made it seem politic to elect his mistress as their president. Not long after, she launched a daily radio programme, *Towards a Better Future* that dramatised the achievements of Juan Perón, often featuring his own speeches.

On 24 February 1945, President Pedro Pablo Ramirez resigned his office and Edelmiro Julian Farrell – a friend of Perón – took his place. However, such was Perón's influence within the government that the new president and members of the government feared the workers would rise up in his favour and install him as president. Perón was arrested on 9 October 1945.

The president was right to fear Perón's popularity. A few days later a huge crowd of around quarter of a million people gathered in front of Argentina's government house demanding his release. The government had little option but to let him go and at eleven o'clock that night, Perón stepped onto the balcony of government house to deliver a rousing speech. It was an evening that has been described as being almost religious in nature, so much did the people worship the man on the balcony.

Eva and Perón were married thirteen days later on 22 October.

Perón campaigned in the 1946 presidential election as the candidate of the Labour Party, and Eva used her weekly radio broadcast to fervently support his candidacy. She spoke directly and powerfully to the poor and the disenfranchised urging them to vote for Juan Perón, using her humble background to show that she was one of them. She travelled the length and breadth of the country with him, her appearance on the podium irritating the rich, the military and other politicians. But the public, familiar with her radio shows and films, loved her. They began to call her 'Evita' – Little Eva.

Perón defeated the rival Radical Civil Union Party candidate by around 11 per cent to became President of Argentina.

In 1947, Perón was invited to visit the Spanish dictator, Francisco Franco but as Argentina had only just gained membership of the United Nations, it was felt dangerous for him to visit the head of Europe's only remaining fascist state. Therefore, it was decided that Eva should go instead and that she should visit as many other countries as possible. Her 'Rainbow Tour' as it was called, was seen as a goodwill tour and after visiting Franco, she went to Rome to meet the Pope, followed by France where she met President Charles de Gaulle. She cancelled her trip to England on hearing that she would not be meeting the royal family, although she publicly cited exhaustion as the reason. In Switzerland, someone threw stones at her car and protestors threw tomatoes at her as she met with the country's Foreign Minister. After two months on the road, she decided to go home.

The tour had done no harm to Eva's reputation – she was the first and only South American first lady to appear on the cover of *Time* magazine. However, the magazine mentioned the fact that she had been born out of wedlock and was, consequently, banned in Argentina for a time. Her style changed too as a result of the trip. She changed the colour of her hair, subduing it from its previous brilliant gold and began to wear it pulled back into the simple chignon that became her trademark. Her dress style became more sober and simple to reflect the serious political persona that she was trying to cultivate.

On her return, she threw herself into charitable work. In one case, however, the old prejudices arose. It was customary for the wife of the president to be invited to be head of the influential Sociedad de Benefencia charity that was made up of eighty-seven of society's leading women. In Evita's case, however, the ladies did not extend an invitation because of her background. Evita was furious, ordering the charity's government funding to be diverted to her own charitable institution, the Eva Perón Foundation. Within a few years the foundation was huge, employing 14,000 people and with assets of some $200 million. It distributed annually 400,000 pairs of shoes, 500,000 sewing machines and 200,000 cooking pots. It gave scholarships and built homes, hospitals and schools for poor people. Entire communities were built using its funds. Evita immersed herself in the foundation, often working twenty-hour days there.

She became idealised and some poor Argentineans even began to regard her as a saint. She spent a great deal of her time meeting the poor and is said to have been seen placing her hands on wounds as if she could heal them. Like Princess Diana many years later, she was unafraid to be in the company of people with very serious and often contagious diseases.

She also threw a great deal of energy into gaining the right to vote for Argentinean women, broadcasting on the radio and writing articles in the newspapers about it. Women's suffrage was eventually obtained in 1947. As a result, she created the Female Perónist Party, Argentina's first large female political party, with 500,000 members and thousands of offices across the country. It was a decisive moment for women in Argentina and many entered politics because of her actions. The Female Perónist party also greatly contributed to Juan Perón retaining the presidency in 1951.

In that election, Evita had set her sights on being named as vice-presidential candidate. She received intense support in this from the working class, the unions and, of course, her own party and in August of that year, she was acclaimed as the candidate by a crowd of two million in the Avenida Nueve de Julio in Buenos Aires. But the idea was anathema to the Argentinean military, reluctant, in the event of Perón's death in office, to take orders from a woman. Nine days after declaring her candidacy, she was forced to withdraw for fear that the army would stage a coup if she did not. Of course, she did not go quietly. She renounced her candidacy at a huge rally in Buenos Aires, her husband delivering a eulogy to her. She gave a speech that day that tore at the heartstrings of the watching audience and the listening radio audience. Her words 'I have left the shreds of my life on the road' resonated with the Argentinean people. At its conclusion, she collapsed into the arms of her husband.

Evita had been ill since 1950. After she had fainted while opening a building in Buenos Aires, they had removed her appendix. However, they discovered the real cause of her constant exhaustion and ill health – she was suffering from ovarian cancer, ironically, the illness that had killed Perón's first wife.

She was never told what her illness was – they printed special newspapers for her to read that made no mention of it – and the story was kept from an outside world which became increasingly worried by her drastic weight loss. By Christmas 1951, she was beginning to resume her full schedule of duties, meeting workers, opening clinics and working at the foundation. By February 1952, however, she was unwell again. The cancer had spread and Perón was told that his wife had no more than a month to live.

She was still alive in April and strong-willed enough to attend the funeral of Perón's vice-president, Hortensio Quijano. Skeleton thin, she made her final speech on 1 May, held up by her husband. By 4 June, she weighed a mere eighty-two pounds and was barely able to stand. Nonetheless, when Perón had to travel through Buenos Aires in an open-topped car, she stood beside him, waving and smiling, but numbed by a huge dose of morphine and kept on her feet by a large plaster support.

Perón found her last days difficult and was unable to visit her and she finally died on Saturday 26 June. However, although her extraordinary life may have ended, the legend of Evita was merely beginning.

Her corpse was embalmed and her body was restored to its former glamorous self, her hair coloured and styled and her nails manicured. She was placed in a glass casket, rosary beads – a gift from the Pope – in her hands. The queues to view her body stretched for miles and for thirteen days they shuffled past the coffin, kissing it or touching it as they passed. For three days, the entire population had to wear black armbands. Two million lined the streets of the capital as her body was then taken to the Argentinean Labour Federation building to await the construction of a huge mausoleum.

Plans for the mausoleum were shelved in 1955, however, when Juan Perón was overthrown and forced into exile in Spain, as a guest of General Franco. Evita's body, meanwhile, was flown secretly to Milan in Italy where, it was buried with another woman's name on the headstone. Only a few people knew where she was and a letter containing her location was given to the new President, Pedro Aramburu who refused to open it.

When in 1970, he was kidnapped by Perónists, he was forced to divulge where her body was buried. It was found and taken in the back of a bakery truck to Perón in Spain where he put the coffin in the attic of his Madrid home.

Astonishingly, Perón was returned to power in October 1973 on a wave of Perónist nostalgia. By now remarried, his new wife appeared on election posters with him. But a third figure also appeared on the posters – Evita.

Juan Perón died nine months later of a heart attack but his wife, Isabel, achieved what Evita might have, had she lived – she became President of Argentina.

Evita, meanwhile, finally returned to Argentina on 17 November 1974. During the overthrow of Isabel Perón by a military coup in 1976, however, her casket was ejected from Perón's Olivos Residence where it had been kept and was returned to her family. She was finally laid to rest in the family vault in Buenos Aires' Recoleta cemetery, twenty-four years after her death.

VLADIMIR
ILYCH LENIN

BORN VLADIMIR ILYCH Ulyanov in 1870 in Simbirsk, close to the Volga River, Lenin, as he later styled himself, led the October Revolution that brought the communists to power and became in 1917 the first head of the Russian Soviet Socialist Republic and then in 1922, the first leader of the Soviet Union. He was undoubtedly one of the greatest and most important leaders of the 20th century, taking part in and often instigating changes that irredeemably changed his country and cut its ties with its monarchist past forever.

He was the son of a conservative Russian school inspector who was a devout churchgoer and Lenin was baptised into the Russian Orthodox Church. His father died of a cerebral hemorrhage in January 1886 and Lenin came increasingly under the influence of his radical older brother, Alexander who introduced him to the writings of the philosopher and political theorist, Karl Marx.

In 1887, Alexander, by now a member of the revolutionary group, People's Will, took part in a failed attempt to assassinate Tsar Alexander III and was executed as a result. His execution put his younger brother's future in some doubt as the brother of a state criminal. He had been doing well at school, although frustrated and angered by the conservative views of his teachers, and did expect to go to university. After attempts had been made to prevent him furthering his education, he succeeded in gaining admittance to Kazan University to study law.

It was inevitable that this highly politicised young man would become involved in politics and he was arrested after one demonstration. Finally, his political fervour eventually irritated the university authorities sufficiently to expel him. In order to continue his studies, he moved to St Petersburg where he enrolled as an external student, qualifying as a lawyer in 1891 and practising law in Samara, a city on the eastern bank of the Volga River. By 1893, however, he was back in St Petersburg where he renewed his interest in politics. In 1895, he travelled to Switzerland where he met with members of the Liberation of Labour group that argued that it would be impossible to overthrow Russia's authoritarian government and replace it with peasant communes.

Returning to Russia, Lenin and other like-minded individuals founded the Union for Struggle for the Emancipation of the Working Class. His activities had come to the notice of the authorities, however, and, arrested in 1896, he was sentenced to three years internal exile in Siberia where he wrote several books and had articles printed in journals. In Shushenskoye, in 1898, he married a woman he had met several years previously, Nadezhda Krupskaya, the daughter of a Russian military officer and, like him, a committed radical and Marxist.

When he was released from his term of exile in 1900, Lenin decided it would be best to leave Russia and, accompanied by his wife and an associate, Jules Martov, he moved to Geneva to hook up with the Liberation of Labour and to publish a newspaper supporting their aims, *Iskra*. Amongst those involved were George Plekhanov, Pavel Axelrod, Gregory Zinoviev and Leon Trotsky.

Iskra became the official journal of the Social Democratic Labour Party whose aims were to unite all the disparate socialist groups who were seeking the overthrow of the autocratic regime that ruled Russia.

In a 1902 pamphlet, *What Is To Be Done?*, Lenin argued for a party of professional revolutionaries devoted to the socialist cause and the overthrow of the Tsar. It was an idea he promoted at the Second Congress of the Social Democratic Labour Party in London in 1903.

He was opposed in this thinking by his old friend, Jules Martov, who argued that more could be achieved by a large party of activists. Lenin lost the argument by twenty-eight votes to twenty-three but refused to give up the idea. He founded a faction within the group known as Bolsheviks while those who followed Martov's thinking came to be known as Mensheviks.

In 1905, there was a violent wave of political terrorism, strikes, peasant unrest, and military mutinies directed at the Russian government. This 1905 revolution failed to bring down the government or the monarchy, but it led to a number of concessions, such as a new Russian constitution, the multi-party political system and the establishment of the State Duma of the Russian Empire, a parliament. Although Lenin did return home when the revolution broke out, unlike Leon Trotsky and the Mensheviks, he played little part in its development. Finally, despairing of there ever being the armed uprising in Russia that he so desired, he instructed Bolsheviks to participate in the elections for the Third Duma in 1907.

Meanwhile, he was fund-raising for the party. The Moscow millionaire, Sava Morozov and the writer, Maxime Gorky, were major donors but armed robbery proved much more lucrative. One such raid, on a post office, netted 250,000 roubles, a considerable sum. However, bombs were used during the robbery and several people died in the blasts. The Mensheviks were disgusted when they heard that their rivals had been behind the incident and George Plekhov called for his side to break off relations with the Bolsheviks. The money came in useful, however, to print revolutionary literature and newspapers. They were also able to use it to gain control of a number of the trade unions that were emerging in Russia's cities.

In 1911, Lenin, Zinoviev and Lev Kamenev moved to France, setting up a Bolshevik Party School in a village just outside Paris. There, they would train agents before sending them back to Russia. In 1912, they tried and failed to seize control of the Social Democratic Labour Party, during its conference in Prague, an attempt that marked the end of the fragile union of the Bolsheviks and Mensheviks. The party split and they became two distinctly separate entities.

Lenin moved to Galicia in Austria in 1913 and hosted a conference of Bolshevik leaders in August 1913. Five of the twenty-two leaders who attended were later discovered to be agents of Okhrana, the Russian secret police.

At the outbreak of the First World War in 1914, the Austrian authorities arrested Lenin as a Russian spy, but they only imprisoned him for a short while before allowing him to leave for Switzerland where he declared the war to be imperialist and accused socialists who supported the war of betraying the proletariat. He directed all his efforts at turning the 'imperialist war into a civil war', distributing propaganda urging Allied troops to turn their rifles on their officers and to launch a socialist revolution.

The war was not going well for Russia by 1917. Tsar Nicholas II had assumed command of the Russian Army fighting on the eastern front and failures to supply troops with the necessary equipment and the high death toll – 1,300,000 men killed in battle – added to his unpopularity and that of his government. Furthermore, there were serious food shortages while prices for what there was were sky-high. Workers came out on strike and people protested in the streets, demanding food. The Tsar tried to close down the Duma on 26 February 1917, but the members refused, continuing to meet to discuss the escalating situation. The President of the Duma wrote to the Tsar suggesting that the best course of action would be to appoint a new government led by someone that the people could trust and in whom they would have confidence. Prince George Lvov was asked to head a provisional government.

Meanwhile, the High Command of the Russian Army feared revolution and told the Tsar that to head it off, he should abdicate and let a more popular member of the royal family take the throne. Grand Duke Michael Alexandrovich, the younger brother of the

Tsar was asked but refused, leaving the Tsar left with no option but to abdicate, which he did on 1 March.

Lenin was helped to return to Russia by the German Foreign Ministry who believed that his presence on Russian soil would hasten the end to the war on the Eastern Front. He and twenty-seven fellow Bolsheviks were provided with a special train to transport them back to St Petersburg.

On his return, in a speech, he announced the April Theses, a set of directives for the members of the Bolshevik Party. In these, he criticised party members for supporting the provisional government, telling them they had betrayed socialism and should leave the party, and instructed those who remained to tell the Russian people that they should be using this opportunity to seize control of their country. The peasants should be grabbing the land from rich land-owners, he said, and factory workers should seize control of the factories in which they worked.

Joseph Stalin, listening to Lenin, realised that he was being presented with a dilemma. As one of the editors of the newspaper *Pravda*, which had supported the provisional government, he could be accused of being one of those who had betrayed socialism. Therefore, he was left with a stark choice – he could oppose Lenin and challenge him for leadership of the Bolshevik Party or he could recant on his views and show his loyalty to Lenin.

He thought long and hard for ten days and then issued an edition of the newspaper in which he disdained any thought of working with the provisional government, denouncing left-wing members of the government such as Alexander Kerensky and Victor Chernov. Like his leader, he urged the peasants and factory workers to seize the initiative.

Moderate socialist, Kerensky, became leader of the government, but even though he was seen as a champion of the working class, he refused to withdraw Russia from the war. A new summer offensive was announced and soldiers at the front, disappointed by the news, mutinied, as many as two million deserting by the autumn of 1917. A great number returned home, using their weapons to do just as Lenin and Stalin had asked – they seized by force the land belonging to the nobility.

Kerensky, realising the threat that Lenin and his Bolsheviks posed to the government, issued orders for his arrest and the arrest of others such as Zinoviev and Kamenev. Lenin, however, was tipped off before troops raided Bolshevik headquarters and managed to escape to Finland where the Helsinki chief of police, who was a closet socialist, hid him. While hiding out in Helsinki, he completed his book *State and Revolution*, describing in it the role that the state plays in society as well as promoting the necessity of proletarian revolution.

When the failure of the July Offensive on the Eastern Front, Kerensky replaced his military commander General Alexei Brusilov with General Lavr Kornilov. But, before long, Kerensky and his new Supreme Commander were disagreeing about the conduct of the war and about military policy. Kornilov sent troops to take control of St Petersburg, leaving Kerensky little option but to ask the Bolsheviks to help protect the city. Lenin agreed to help, but made it very clear that he would be fighting against Kornilov and not for Kerensky.

He recruited 25,000 armed men for the defence of St Petersburg. The city was fortified, but as they were doing so, Lenin sent men out to talk to Kornilov's troops, waiting to attack outside the city, persuading them not to attack. One general, Krymov, killed himself and Kornilov was arrested.

In late September, Kerensky formed a new coalition that included more Mensheviks and Socialist Revolutionaries but he feared the growing power of the Bolsheviks, especially as Lenin now had 25,000 armed men under his command.

The Bolsheviks established their headquarters in the Smolny Institute and Kerensky finally had to take action. On 22 October, he issued orders for the arrest of the Bolshevik Military Revolutionary Committee. He also closed down the Bolshevik newspapers and cut the telephone wires stopping communication into and out of the Bolshevik headquarters.

Trotsky called for the government to be brought down and Lenin was in agreement. He ordered Bolsheviks to occupy the railway stations, the telephone exchange and the State bank on 24 October. On 25 October Red Guards surrounded the Winter palace with the cabinet inside, although Kerensky had already fled. When the ship the Aurora and St Petersburg's fortresses began shelling the palace, its defenders surrendered and the Red Guards arrested the members of the cabinet.

The All-Russian Congress of Soviets handed power to the Soviet Council of people's Commissars and Lenin was, as expected, appointed Chairman with Trotsky being given responsibilities for foreign affairs and Stalin for nationalities.

Lenin immediately abolished the private ownership of land and re-distributed it amongst the peasants. Banks were nationalised and workers were given control of the factories in which they worked. Political parties were banned, including the Mensheviks. He also created the notorious secret police force, the Cheka, to protect the new government from counter-revolutionaries and political opponents.

He wanted to end Russian participation in the war as swiftly as possible, but, after weeks of stalemate in negotiations, Trotsky was ordered by Lenin to accept the Central Powers' terms for an armistice. Russia handed over the Ukraine, Finland, the Baltic Provinces, Poland and the Caucasus, an unpopular move that resulted in General Kornilov being able to raise a Volunteer Army. He was supported by other groups opposed to the Bolsheviks and the soldiers who fought against the Soviet Army became known as the Whites.

The Civil War that lasted until late 1920 was a very difficult time for Russians, with social distress, more food shortages and riots and demonstrations. Lenin had his own problems. On 30 August 1918, Lenin had been shot by Dora Kaplan, a member of the rival Social Revolutionaries who described him as a 'traitor to the revolution'. He had been speaking at a meeting and was just getting into his car, one foot on the running board, when a woman's voice called out to him. When he turned, she had fired three bullets, hitting him with two of them. One bullet fairly harmlessly struck him in the arm; the other was far more serious, entering his body at the juncture of the neck and jaw. He had declined the chance to go to hospital as he was certain that the assassins would be waiting for him. The bullet remained in him as he recovered. Ever since, his health had been poor and he complained often of headaches, dizziness and insomnia. He realised that he needed to find a trustworthy lieutenant and decided on Joseph Stalin who had been a staunch supporter. Others saw him as no more than a mouthpiece for Lenin, not realising that in the new position of General Secretary of the party, Stalin was positioning himself perfectly to succeed Lenin.

Lenin was hospitalised for the removal of Dora Kaplan's bullet from his body. However, a blood vessel burst in his brain, leaving him paralysed down his right side and unable to speak. To his rivals' chagrin, Stalin took control, purging from the party thousands of supporters of Trotsky, his main rival for the leadership.

He began to disagree with Lenin on matters of policy and Lenin, fearing that he was about to be usurped as leader, wrote to Trotsky, asking for support. Stalin discovered the content of Lenin's letter and quickly realised that his political future was in danger. Following an abusive telephone call that Stalin made to Lenin's wife, ranting at her for allowing her husband to write such letters while he was ill, Lenin decided that Stalin was not the man to succeed him. He dictated to his secretary a letter containing his thoughts on the senior members of the party. Of Stalin he wrote, '[I] propose to our comrades to consider a means of removing Stalin from this post and appointing someone else who differs from Stalin in one weighty respect: being more tolerant, more loyal, more polite, more considerate of his comrades.'

Three days later he suffered a third stroke and entirely lost the power of speech and the ability to write. He died in Gorki on 21 January 1924 and more than 900,000 people walked past his coffin as it lay in state for four days in the Hall of Columns. The city of St Petersburg was renamed Leningrad in his honour three days after he died and statues were erected throughout the Soviet Union; many of these remain standing, even after the fall of communism. His body has been on permanent display in a mausoleum in Red Square in Moscow since January 1924.

JOSEPH STALIN

A NATIONAL POLL held recently suggested that, if he was still alive today, more than a third of Russians would vote for him. Incredibly, in another poll to find the most popular person in Russian history and culture, he occupied the top position. Considering the fact that he was probably responsible for the deaths of up to sixty million of his people and for the incarceration of millions in the gulags of Siberia, these findings are extraordinary. What was it about this trainee priest, weatherman, newspaper editor, bank robber and fervent revolutionary that still gives him such appeal to the Russian people?

Born Josif Dzhugashvili in Georgia in 1878, he was the son of an alcoholic Ossetian cobbler whose drinking brought an end to his marriage when Stalin was still young. In 1894, he won a scholarship to the Georgian Orthodox seminary at Tiflis where the teachers imposed Russian language and culture on students – Stalin had spoken Georgian for the first years eight or nine years of his life. He was drawn to Georgian nationalism at this period and also became a well-known poet, his work appearing in local newspapers and periodicals.

Already, he was providing the authorities with problems, being punished at the seminary several times for reading banned materials – foreign literature and the work of the socialist thinker, Karl Marx. He was forced to leave the seminary in 1899 for other reasons, however. They put up the fees and his mother simply could no longer afford them. It mattered little to the young Stalin, however. By this time, he had been introduced to the revolutionary thinking of Vladimir Lenin. The course of his life was decided from that moment on – he would be a revolutionary.

He still had to live, however, and found a job at the Tiflis meteorological observatory that allowed him time to indulge his political activities. He wrote, gave speeches, organised strikes and took part in demonstrations and protests. Soon, he came to the attention of the government and was being sought by the dreaded secret police of the Tsar, the Okhrana. They had arrested many of his colleagues and sympathizers and Stalin decided to go underground, living off money given to him by friends and associates.

Under an assumed name, he found work at an oil refinery at Batumi but was soon embroiled in a labour dispute when a fire broke out at the refinery. The workers put the fire out and believed they were due to be paid a bonus. Management, believing that the fire had been started deliberately, refused to pay. A bloody and violent strike broke out and Cossack soldiers were brought in to restore order, but not before thirteen strikers had been killed. Stalin played a prominent part in the organisation of the strike – some suggest he even started the fire – and was arrested and sent to Siberia for three years.

He did not remain there for long, however, escaping after just five weeks and making his way back to Tiflis. Once again, he launched himself into socialist politics, backing Lenin's Bolsheviks, one of the two factions into which the Social Democrats had split, the other being the Mensheviks. He founded the Georgian Social Democratic party and began to come to the notice of the leaders of the national party.

They were heady times in Russia. People were pressing for greater freedoms and the Tsar had ruthlessly repressed any efforts to liberalise the country. A failed revolution in January 1905 gave a hint of things to come. Two hundred workers were brutally slaughtered in Baku and people took to the streets in protest. Stalin used the upheaval to lead a group of armed Bolsheviks who functioned like gangsters to raise funds for their political activities, running protection rackets and robbing businesses and banks.

After 1905, however, the Tsar was still in power but Stalin continued his illegal activities, as well as railing against the Mensheviks from stages and platforms across the country.

In 1906, he was elected one of three representatives from the Caucasus to be sent to the Bolshevik Conference of that year held in Finland. He met Vladimir Lenin for the first time and the two men hit it off, Stalin making a good impression on Lenin. He attended the Fourth Conference of the Russian Social Democratic Labour party in April 1906 where he was angered by the decision of the conference to ban bank robbery as a means of raising party funds. In 1907, with Lenin he attended the Fifth Congress of the Russian Social Democratic Labour Party which confirmed the Bolshevik supremacy in the party and discussed communist revolution in Russia. Stalin also encountered the man who would become his great rival, Leon Trotsky, at this conference.

It was a defining time for Stalin who began to realise that if he was going to make progress in the party, he needed to pay less attention to the more parochial atmosphere of Georgia and become more involved in Russian politics. He even began to write in Russian. He also staged a huge robbery around this time – 250,000 roubles, worth around £1.5 million in today's terms. He and his gang ambushed a convoy carrying the money and in the ensuing gunfire and explosion of home-made bombs around forty people died. He took account of the party's ruling that there should be no more bank robberies by considerately resigning temporarily from the party shortly before the robbery.

In July 1906, he found time to get married, to Ekaterina Svanidze and she would give birth to their son, Yakov, the following March. But she became ill in 1907 and died. According to friends and associates, Stalin was devastated by her death. It was feared by some that he might commit suicide and they took his pistol away from him.

Murder had been added to his crimes and he had taken part in the assassination of a general as well as many right-wing supporters of the Tsar. He was now a powerful figure in the party but continued to annoy many by persisting with his illegal activities of robbery and extortion. Once again, however, the Okhrana tracked him down. In April 1908 he was arrested and spent seven months in prison before being sentenced to a further two years in Siberia. Again, he escaped, dressed in women's clothes. A few months later, he was back in Georgia and engaged in his old activities.

Arrested again in 1910, they banned him from the Caucasus for five years and once again sent him into exile. This time he was released after a year.

The Bolsheviks were now a political grouping outside the Social Democratic Party and Stalin became a member of its central committee. They gave him the important job of editing the party newspaper, *Pravda*. Before long, however, he was arrested again, and sent into exile. Naturally, he escaped as soon as he could, after just thirty-eight days. He returned to St Petersburg where he made efforts to unite the Bolsheviks and the Mensheviks into one powerful political force, using *Pravda* to promote this idea. Lenin disapproved, however, and removed him from the role of editor, appointing him as leader of the Russian Bureau of the Bolshevik Party. At this time he used the name 'Stalin' for the first time, as author of a tract entitled *Marxism and the National Question*. He had used countless *nommes de guerre* until this time, including 'Koba', the name of a Robin Hood-type hero in a novel by Alexander Kazbegi. However, it was Stalin that stuck and became the name by which the world came to know him.

He faced exile again following the betrayal to the authorities of the entire central committee by a spy and informant. They were all arrested and Stalin was sent to the isolated Siberian province of Turukhansk where he spent six months. The authorities learned, however, that he was about to escape and sent him even further away, to a hamlet on the edge of the Arctic Circle where he had to live by fishing and hunting. He also enjoyed an affair during his two years there with a thirteen-year-old girl with whom he fathered two children.

When the Russian Revolution broke out in February 1917, Stalin was released from exile and was back in St Petersburg. Most of the party leadership remained in exile, and he seized the opportunity to take control of *Pravda*. To begin with he supported the government of Alexander Kerensky in its pages, but Lenin's return brought a change in party thinking and the paper began to call for the downfall of Kerensky's regime.

Fighting broke out between the Bolsheviks and Kerensky's men and when Lenin had to be smuggled out of the country to Finland, Stalin took control, taking the position of editor-in-chief of the party press and being re-elected to the all-important central committee.

Kerensky turned to the Bolshevik militias in September 1917 when he faced a threat from inside his own party. He armed the Bolsheviks and allowed them to recruit. It was a fatal error, however, as he discovered when he found himself confronted by an armed and militant Bolshevik army in November of that year. Kerensky and his cabinet were arrested and the Bolsheviks formed the Council of People's Commissars. Stalin was given the job of People's Commissar for Nationalities' Affairs, with the objective of winning over the myriad non-Russian ethnic groupings of the Russian Empire.

Not long after, civil war had broken out. The opposing sides were Lenin's Red Army and the anti-Bolshevik White Army. Stalin led the Red Army in his native Caucasus, showing no mercy to counter-revolutionaries and destroying countless villages in order to force the peasants into submission. He staged public executions of dissenters and deserters. The civil war was won and Lenin headed the new government of the Soviet Union.

When Lenin died in January 1924, the party was headed by three men - Stalin, Lev Kamenev and Grigori Zinoviev. Stalin was well aware that whoever took over the party would have to show loyalty to the heritage of Lenin and he organised his funeral and made speeches displaying undying loyalty to the ideas of the late leader.

His first move was to eliminate Trotsky from the leadership and then he forced out Zinoviev and Kamanev, allying himself with other senior members of the party against them.

By 1927, Russia was tired. Years of factionalism and fighting had exhausted the country and the people gladly accepted Stalin's philosophy of building *Socialism in One Country*. He created a one-party state that brooked no opposition or dissent and any that arose was ruthlessly dealt with by a merciless secret police. By 1928, Trotsky had been exiled in Mexico where he would be assassinated on Stalin's orders in 1940. Stalin was now unchallenged as leader of his party and his country.

He established an intelligence network the like of which the world had never seen with spies in every major country as well as at home.

The way forward for the Soviet economy, he decided, lay in a series of Five-Year Plans. He aimed with these plans to change the Soviet economy from an agrarian economy to an industrial one, collectivising farms but in the process signalling a noticeable drop in living standards for millions of his countrymen. He brought in foreign experts to improve manufacturing processes and to teach the Russians about modern industry.

The first two plans proved to be successful, radically modernising the previously backward Soviet economy. There was a huge cost, however. It is estimated that around five million Ukrainian peasants died in famines caused by failed harvests and the excessive demands of the state which took much of their produce. Stalin stubbornly refused to release grain reserves to the starving peasants.

Stalin's vice-like grip on his country became even stronger as the years passed. In the 1930s he consistently purged members of the party and disposed of opponents, assassinating them or sending them to the gulags. It began with the killing of the popular Leningrad party leader, Sergei Kirov, Stalin claiming that he was part of a conspiracy against him led by his hated rival, Trotsky. Other supposed conspirators, Zinoviev, Kamenev and fourteen other senior members of the party were assassinated in 1936. Those who did not die were featured in show trials in which many politicians and military leaders were convicted of treason. On the outbreak of the Second World War he realised how misguided he had been to eliminate experienced military men. But no section of society was left untouched by the great purge and people would inform on others simply to deflect blame from themselves. It took very little to be named an 'enemy of the people'. Around 700,000 were executed during this period, the majority peasants and workers. By the end of it, only three of the 'Old Bolsheviks' were left intact – Stalin, Mikhail Kalinin and Vyacheslav Molotov. Naturally, history was re-written to remove the names of those who had been purged.

When Stalin signed a non-aggression pact with Adolf Hitler in 1939, the world was surprised but Stalin had his eyes on the eastern part of Poland and Hitler offered it to him on a plate. On the day Hitler invaded from the west, 1 September 1939, Stalin ordered his troops into Poland from the west. Two months later Soviet troops invaded another neighbour, Finland, anticipating an easy victory. They found a resolute Finnish people who stood their ground and ceded only a small part of their territory. The cost to the Soviet army was high – over 400,000 casualties.

Stalin exported his callous brutality to the regions he occupied. In March 1940, in an incident known as the Katyn Massacre, Stalin approved the order for the execution of 25,700 Polish nationalists and 'counter-revolutionaries' in the sections of the Ukraine and Belarus that had been annexed from Poland.

Of course, it would only be a matter of time before Hitler cast his eyes to the east and in June 1941, having failed to submit Britain to Nazi control, he launched Operation Barbarossa, the invasion of Russia. It was the beginning of what the Russians call the 'Great Patriotic War' and by its end many millions of them would have died.

The Germans benefitted from the element of surprise and the Germans made initial gains, taking prisoner and killing many Soviet troops. Stalin, paranoid as ever, meanwhile ordered the killing of all the political prisoners held in the gulags. He feared they would rise up and help the Germans. Around 100,000 were bayonetted to death or had grenades tossed into their crowded prison cells.

The Russians began to fight back, however, turning the Germans back at Moscow in late 1941.

Stalin, meanwhile, had become a world figure, appearing at the meetings the Allied leaders held at Tehran, Yalta, Moscow and Potsdam, helping Roosevelt and Churchill to win the war and organise the post-war world. Back home, deserters and troops who had retreated were sent to the gulags, 3.5 million of them never to return home.

The post-war world was very different to the world that had existed in 1939. Stalin created a Communist empire, surrounding the Soviet Union with satellite states and riding on a wave of nationalism. The Cold War began, the world's two great super-powers, the USA and the USSR often coming close to armed conflict but being retrained by the threat of a nuclear holocaust.

He tested the patience of the Americans on many occasions – the blockade of Berlin in 1948 as well as during the Korean War in which he supported the North Koreans against the American-backed South Koreans.

He finally died on 1 March 1953, failing to emerge from his bedroom after a late night spent in the company of his lieutenants, Lavrentiy Beria, Georgy Malenkov, Nicolai Bulganin and Nikita Khrushchev. 'Uncle Joe' had died in the night of a stroke and lay for a long time on the floor of his room because everyone was too afraid to disturb him.

Some suggest that he was assassinated and in 2003, a group of Russian and American scientists announced that he had swallowed warfarin, a flavourless, powerful rat poison. But it is unlikely that the truth will ever be known.

His body was originally placed in Lenin's Mausoleum in Red Square in Moscow but was later moved to a position by the Kremlin walls, another step in a rigorous programme of de-Stalinisation that began after his death, as the Soviet Union breathed a sigh of relief.

GENERAL GEORGE C. MARSHALL

GENERAL GEORGE C. Marshall was America's chief of staff during the Second World War, from 1939 to 1945. As such, he built and commanded the largest army in history. At the end of the war, he became a diplomat, excelling at that and devising in 1947 what became known as the Marshall Plan, a programme of aid given by the United States to Europe to help re-build the nations of a continent devastated and made bankrupt by six years of war.

George Catlett Marshall Jr was born in 1880 in Uniontown, Pennsylvania, into a middle-class family descended on both sides from settlers who had arrived in the American colonies in the 17th century.

His father owned a prosperous coal and coke business when he was born, but by the time the young George Marshall decided on a military career, enrolling at the Virginia Military Institute in Lexington, the business was struggling. After a poor start at the institute, he gradually improved, graduating in 1901 as senior first captain in the corps of cadets.

He received a commission as second lieutenant of infantry in February 1802 and before embarking on eighteen months in the Philippines, married a Lexington girl, Elizabeth Carter Coles. He would re-marry in 1927 following the early death of his first wife.

At the institute, Marshall had focused on leadership, working hard to develop his skills and many spoke of the quiet self-confidence with which he commanded men. He was a man of rigid self-discipline and an unassuming quality who was able to make his case to both his men and to civilians, persuasive skills that would serve him well throughout his career as both a soldier and a diplomat.

Leaving the Philippines in 1903, Marshall was posted to various places and performed a variety of roles. In 1907, he graduated with honours from the Infantry-Cavalry School at Fort Leavenworth and from the Army Staff College the following year. He was thoroughly trained in modern warfare.

Having distinguished himself wherever he was sent, when the United States entered the First World War in 1917, he sailed to France with the First Division, the first American attachment to fight in the war, having been appointed to the General Staff. He served as Chief of Operations and his role in the Battles of Cantigny, Aisne-Marne, St. Mihiel and Meuse-Argonne earned him fame and promotion. He was Chief of Operations during the critical Meuse-Argonne Offensive in 1918, personally responsible for the design and coordination of an action that was a major contributor to the defeat of the Germans on the Western Front.

In 1918, he was promoted to American Expeditionary Forces Headquarters where he worked until 1924 as aide de camp to the famous American General, John J. Persching.

Marshall again performed a variety of roles, to a large extent focused on training the techniques of modern warfare. For five years, he was assistant commandant in charge of instruction at the Infantry School in Fort Benning in Georgia where he taught many of the officers who would become outstanding commanders in World War Two. He spent three years in China and taught at the Army War College. From 1932 to 1933, he was commanding officer at Fort Screven in Georgia, and like General de Gaulle in France, committed his thoughts about modern warfare and the lessons learned in World War One to book form. *Infantry in Battle* is still used as an officer's training manual in the US Infantry Officers' Course and it would also have been read and used by most of the infantry officers who fought in World War II.

In 1936, he was promoted to brigadier general, commanding the Vancouver barracks in Washington until 1938. On 1 September 1939, the day that Germany invaded Poland, making war inevitable, he was promoted to full general. He also became, on President Franklin Roosevelt's recommendation, Army Chief of Staff.

Prior to Japan's bombing of Pearl Harbour and America's entry into the war, Marshall had, with little success, been urging the government to put more money into the army. Therefore, the army of 200,000 men that he inherited was out-of-date, badly trained and inadequately equipped. His first task was to bring it up-to-date and expand it. Incredibly, by 1942, it numbered 8,300,000 men. He had built the largest ground and air force in the history of the United States, for which Winston Churchill dubbed him 'the organiser of victory'.

He had also hand-picked his generals and amongst them were such men as Omar Bradley and future president of the United States, Dwight D. Eisenhower. He would not be so popular with Churchill and his generals, however, in the conferences at Casablanca, Washington, Quebec, Cairo and Teheran, when he argued stubbornly for an all-out Allied offensive against the Germans across the English Channel, rather than the Mediterranean strategy proposed by the British.

On 16 December 1944, Marshall attained the highest rank ever by an American general, being promoted to the new position of Five-Star General, roughly the equivalent of a British Field-Marshall.

Ever the organiser, Marshall wrote the document that would be used as the central strategy for the Allied Forces in Europe. Meanwhile, he re-organised the American army, making it ready for combat. There was surprise, however, when he was passed over for supreme command of Operation Overlord, the invasion of Europe by the Allies. When Eisenhower was given the role, Roosevelt made it clear to Marshall that he was not given the job because of his success in working with the US Congress to make things happen at home. Also, interestingly, Marshall had refused to lobby for the position. But quite simply, Roosevelt could not rest easy if Marshall was not in Washington. It would also have meant that he would have had to give up his role as overall head of the army and the American people were horrified by the notion that he would effectively be receiving a demotion.

He spent the remainder of the war coordinating operations in the main theatres of the war, Europe and the Pacific. In 1944, he was named Man of the Year by *Time* Magazine.

He resigned his post as Chief-of-Staff in 1945, but did not retire – US generals are not permitted to retire. The new president, Truman, sent him to China in a futile attempt to broker an agreement between the two sides in the Chinese Civil War – Mao Zedong's Communists and Chiang Kai-shek's Nationalists. His suggestion of a coalition government was rejected out of hand by both sides who had, after all, been fighting each other for almost twenty years.

Marshall returned to the United States in 1947 and was appointed Secretary of State, taking on special responsibilities for the State Department's ambitious plans for the re-construction of Europe following the war. On 5 June 1947, he delivered a speech at Harvard University, in which he outlined his plan for Europe, known at that time as the European Recovery Program. It became known as the Marshall Plan after it was suggested by White House Counsel Clark Clifford that it be known as the Truman Plan and he rejected the idea, naming it for the general.

It was a momentous time and Marshall was in the thick of it, providing aid to Greece and Turkey, recognising the new state of Israel – although Marshall was opposed to it and argued vehemently with Truman about it – and establishing the North Atlantic Treat Organisation (NATO).

In 1949, he was again named *Time* Magazine's Man of the year, and in 1953, he was awarded the Nobel peace Prize for his work on re-building Europe. He had resigned from the State Department in

1949 due to ill health and had become President of the American National Red Cross.

He did not stay out of government for very long. In 1950, when the United States went to war in Korea, it soon became evident how badly prepared the US army was. President Truman fired his Secretary of Defense and brought in the seventy-year-old Marshall to reorganise and restore confidence, just as he had done at the start of the Second World War. He served for less than a year, however, before retiring from politics entirely, although he was the American representative at the coronation of Queen Elizabeth II.

ADOLF HITLER

IT WAS APRIL 1945 and Soviet troops were closing in. They had reached the outskirts of Berlin and fierce fighting had been taking place, the capital defended by a hard core of Hitler's fanatics, reluctant to believe that the Thousand-Year Reich was coming to an end after only a dozen or so years.

The Führer was in hiding in his bunker beneath the Reich Chancellery, surrounded by his lieutenants and in the company of his mistress, Eva Braun. Everyone had urged him to flee, run to the mountains and make a stand there. The Führer, however, resolved to remain in Berlin, knowing full well that it was there that he would meet his end.

To make matters worse, there were those who were plotting against him, opportunists who saw their chance to make some capital out of Nazi Germany's death throes. Hermann Göring, Commander-in-Chief of the Luftwaffe and Hitler's former deputy, had argued that he should assume leadership of the country, with Hitler stranded in Berlin, unable to do anything. A furious Hitler had him stripped of his government positions and ordered his men to arrest him. They were preoccupied with other things, however, and Göring would survive long enough to commit suicide in prison, robbing the Allies of the chance to hang him along with the other leaders of the Nazi regime. Heinrich Himmler, too, had tried to negotiate with the Allies. He was arrested under Hitler's orders.

Towards the end of April, it was all over. Hitler dictated his last will and testament to his secretary and married Eva Braun. He heard of the death of his ally, Benito Mussolini, on 28 April, shot by a group of Partisans in northern Italy and strung up by his feet like a piece of meat. That, the Führer resolved was not going to happen to him. On 29 April, the Russians were only a few hundred metres away and he knew that they would show him no mercy if they got their hands on him. He took no chances, shooting himself in the mouth as well as biting on a capsule of cyanide. Eva Braun already lay dead by his side. They were carried out and their bodies placed in one of the hundreds of bomb craters that pock-marked the centre of the city. Petrol was poured over them and they were set on fire, until no trace was left of them.

At last Nazi Germany, embodied in the personage of this man, was no more.

He had stumbled into the philosophy that would irrevocably change his country and decimate the world almost by accident. He was working for the *Aufklärungskommando* (Intelligence Commando) after the end of the First World War with responsibility for influencing his fellow soldiers and for infiltrating the anti-Semitic, anti-Communist and nationalistic German Workers' Party that had been founded by Anton Drexler. The party immediately appealed to Hitler. Germany's defeat in the war had been a great shock to him. He believed that the people had been stabbed in the back by German politicians and by Marxists. The Treaty of Versailles after the war had been a further betrayal. Germany was severely punished by the treaty with loss of territory and punitive reparations to be paid to the victors. Worse still, to his mind, the armed forces were demilitarised.

Anton Drexler was immediately impressed by the former lance-corporal. He asked him to become a member of the party and Adolf Hitler willingly accepted his invitation, becoming the 55th member. Another founder of the party became a formative influence on Hitler. Dietrich Eckhart exchanged ideas with him and gave him advice on everything, including how to speak and how to dress. Hitler, with Eckhart's help, began to mix with influential people. The Austrian with the little moustache and the hair swept across his forehead began to be noticed. Soon, the party changed its name to the *Nationalsozialistische Deutsche Arbeiterpartei* (the National Socialist German Workers Party).

Hitler had been born in the Austro-Hungarian Empire on 20 April 1889, fourth child in a family of six, only two of whom – Hitler and his sister – would survive into adulthood. His father had been a customs official and Hitler had a strict upbringing. His father was often violent towards him and to his mother to whom he was very attached.

His father's job had meant that the family moved frequently but the young Hitler proved an able pupil in spite of this until he was aged eleven when his school work slumped and he was forced to repeat a year. At the time, he claimed, he was rebelling against his father who insisted on his son following his footsteps and becoming a customs official. Hitler on the other hand was determined to become a painter. His father died in 1903 and a couple of years later, Hitler left school to follow his dream.

He moved to Vienna where he attempted to get into the Academy of Fine Arts. They rejected him twice, however, telling him his work made him better suited to be an architect than a painter. Entry into architectural school was an impossibility, however, as he did not have the requisite qualifications. Meanwhile, he tried to sell his paintings and make his living that way. He copied postcards and sold them to tourists, but it was tough and by 1910, he was living in a hostel.

His father's estate eventually provided some respite in 1913. He used the money to move to Munich in Germany, a move that also, handily, got him out of doing military service in Austria. When the Austrian authorities finally caught up with him, however, they found him to be unfit for service anyway.

Back in Munich, he enlisted in the Bavarian army at the outbreak of the First World War, serving in both Belgium and France. In the war, he was a runner, a dangerous position that exposed him regularly to enemy fire. He fought at Ypres, the Somme, the battle of Arras and at Passchendale and was twice decorated for bravery. His award of the Iron Cross, First Class, in 1918 was one rarely given to a soldier of his rank. He was wounded in the leg in 1916, but returned to the front in March 1917. He lacked the leadership qualities his superiors were looking for, however, and never made it further up the ranks than lance-corporal.

His war experiences made him feel the *Dolchstsslegende* (dagger-stab legend), the belief that Germany had been betrayed, all the more. The national Socialists were, therefore, exactly the vehicle for which he was searching to express his disappointment.

The party, too, was delighted to have found him. He had, they discovered, remarkable powers of oratory, the ability to enflame the passions of a crowd, to summon up feelings of nationalistic pride in them. He began to draw huge crowds. Six thousand people turned up at one of them to hear him rail against the Treaty of Versailles, Jews and Marxists.

It was not long before his overriding ambition took him to the top of the party hierarchy. In July 1921, he ousted Drexler and adopted the name by which he would become known to the world – Der Führer.

The national Socialist party began to increase its membership, attracted by Hitler's fiery oratory. Other names that would enter the Nazi pantheon of evil arrived on the scene - Rudolf Hess, Hermann Göring and Julius Streicher were all early members.

In Italy, Benito Mussolini had come to power in dramatic fashion, riding on a wave of anti-Communism and nationalism similar to that being espoused by Adolf Hitler. He had staged a coup by marching on Rome and Hitler resolved to emulate his success. He had already gained the support of important and influential people such as Gustav von Kahr, de facto ruler of Bavaria and General Erich Ludendorff. The army and police were also sympathetic towards him and he thought the time was right to make his move.

On 8 November 1923, Hitler and his *Sturmabteilung* (storm troopers) staged the 'Beer Hall Putsch'. They stormed a public meeting in a large beer hall outside Munich. He proclaimed the establishment of a new government and demanded support of von Kahr and the local military leaders. The following day as Hitler and his group marched from the beer hall to the Bavarian War ministry to overthrow the Bavarian government, they were attacked and dispersed by the police. Sixteen members of the National Socialist Party died in the fighting that ensued. The attempted coup was a complete failure.

Hitler was charged with high treason and sentenced to five years in Landsberg prison. However, the coup and the trial brought his name and his politics, expressed in a speech at his trial, to the attention of a national audience for the first time. He was released after only nine months but had put his time to good use, writing his political manifesto and biography, *Mein Kampf.* Published in two volumes, by the end of the Second World War, it would have sold around ten million copies.

Released from prison, he reorganized the party using the principle by which he ruled – the *Führerprinzip* (Leadership principle). According to this principle, leaders were appointed by their superiors and were accountable to them while enjoying absolute and unquestioning obedience from those beneath them.

The Depression plunged Germany into a deep financial crisis that Hitler manipulated for his own ends. The German people loathed the Weimar government that had ruled the country since the war and was desperate for change. The Depression only heightened this desire. In 1930, Chancellor Heinrich Brüning, leading a minority government, was forced to introduce emergency decrees to implement his measures. These lasted for several parliaments and paved the way for the authoritarian style of regime that Hitler would introduce just a few years later.

Hitler became a German citizen, finally in 1932, making it possible for him to stand in the elections for German President, against the incumbent, Paul von Hindenberg. He lost this election but in the July 1932 elections for the German parliament, the Nazi Party won 230 seats, making them the largest party in the Reichstag, the German parliament. Hitler was offered the position of vice-Chancellor by Fritz von Papen, but refused it, willing only to accept the position of Chancellor. When von Papen's minority government collapsed, fresh elections once again left the Nazis as the largest party in parliament.

After several more attempts to form a minority government had failed, President von Hindenberg had no option but to appoint Hitler Chancellor of a coalition government, but with politicians from other parties taking the key roles in the cabinet. On 30 January1933, Adolf Hitler took the oath of office in von Hindenberg's office.

Again, as no party had a majority, the Reichstag was dissolved in readiness for new elections in March 1933, but on 27 February, everything changed when the Reichstag building was burned down in an arson attack which Hitler and his cohorts immediately blamed on the communists. The government reacted by suspending basic civil liberties and by banning the German Communist Party. Communists were rounded up, fled or, in some cases, were murdered.

The Nazis using anti-Communist hysteria, increased their share of the vote from thirty-three per cent to forty-three per cent. Again, however, they had to form a coalition government. Hitler now introduced the Enabling Act which allowed the cabinet to introduce measures without first gaining the approval of the Reichstag. It was to last for four years and represented his first step on his road to total power. On 14 July 1933, the Nazi party was declared the only legal political party in Germany and the power of the state government was abolished.

Hitler now turned on his own organisation, ruthlessly turning it into the viciously effective machine that would control Germany and much of Europe. He purged his stormtroopers, killing around 90 –

although possibly many more – of them during the 'Night of the Long Knives' between 30 June and 2 July 1934.

The death of President von Hindenberg in August 1934 provided him with another opportunity. He declared the position of president to be redundant and took on the role himself as Führer and Reichskanzler. He made the armed forces swear an oath of loyalty to him personally, as commander of the military. He was now unchallenged as dictator of Germany.

He launched a massive campaign of industrial renewal in Germany and began work on the improvement of the country's infrastructure, building new roads, dams, and railways. He showed off the new Germany to the world with the 1936 Olympic Games, demonstrating what the Nazis considered to be the superiority of the Aryan race. Black American sprinter, Jesse Owens, dented his plans somewhat, however, by winning no fewer than four gold medals. Hitler was furious.

His real ambition now began to emerge. He had written about his notion of *Lebensraum* for the German people in *Mein Kampf* and this idea began to appear in his speeches. He also advocated *Anschluss* (merger) with Austria, restoration of the pre-First World War frontiers, abolition of the restrictions on the German armed forces, return of Germany's former African colonies and a German zone of influence in eastern Europe.

He saw Britain as an ideal ally and attempted to forge an alliance with her that would help him to defeat his sworn enemies, the Communist Russians. The British government refused to support him as he agitated to be given permission for an increase in the size of the German army. He went ahead with it anyway, increasing the army to 600,000 in 1935, six times the number that had been allowed by the Treaty of Versailles. He also signed a pact with Mussolini's Italy in October 1936, an Axis that was joined by the Japanese, also enjoying an upsurge of nationalism, later that same year.

At home, too, he was making dramatic moves. The 1935

Nuremberg Rally brought a speech from him in which he introduced the Nuremberg laws, draconian laws that banned sex and marriage between Aryan Germans and Jewish Germans. Non-Aryans were also prohibited from being German citizens.

The systematic extermination of the Jews in death camps began in 1939. He had already made efforts in the direction of the purification of the race by killing mentally or physically disabled children in a heinous programme known as T4. His killing took place on a scale unheard of even in the bloody annals of European history. Between 1939 and 1945, somewhere between eleven and fourteen million people, including six million Jews, died in the death camps, in ghettoes and in mass executions, killed by poison gas, starvation and disease while working as slave labourers.

He achieved his desired merger with Austria in 1938. Next was the Sudetenland, a German-speaking region governed by Czechoslovakia. In September 1938, as Europe became alarmed, a meeting attended by Hitler, British Prime Minister, Neville Chamberlain, French premier, Daladier, and Mussolini, arrived at the Munich Agreement. Hitler was given the Sudetenland in this agreement and promised he would not make any more such moves. Chamberlain naively believed him, returning to Britain claiming to have secured 'peace in our time'. How wrong he was. A little over six months later, Hitler's army had invaded Czechoslovakia.

Poland was the final straw for the European policy of appeasing Hitler. His tanks rolled in on 1 September 1939, supported by the Russians from the east who had agreed with Hitler to divide the country between them. Britain had guaranteed Polish independence and Chamberlain had little option but to declare war on 3 September.

After a period in which little happened, the 'phony war', Denmark and Norway fell in April 1940. Belgium and the Netherlands were under the Nazi jackboot by may and France surrendered on 22 June. By now, Italy was fighting on the side of its German ally.

Britain was next, but Hitler and Hermann Göring, head of his air force, underestimated the resolve of the new British leader, Winston Churchill and the British people. Britain won the battle of Britain, fought in the air above the country.

Meanwhile, however, Germany and Italy had been bolstered by support from Hungary, Romania and Bulgaria.

On 11 December, he launched his attack on Russia, Operation Barbarossa, ripping up the pact that he had signed with the Soviet government in 1939. He immediately made huge gains – the Baltic States, Belarus and the Ukraine amongst them.

On 11 December, however, as his troops bore down on Moscow, he faced a new and more potent threat. The Japanese bombed Pearl Harbour and the United States entered the war. Things were not going well elsewhere. He lost at the second Battle of El Alamein, the German 6th Army was wiped out at Stalingrad and he lost in the huge Battle of Kursk.

His behaviour was becoming erratic and his once sure touch seemed to be deserting him on the battlefield. The economy at home was in a dangerously unstable condition. He was not a well man, some suggesting that he suffered from Parkinson's Disease or even syphilis.

By June 1944, the Allies were pushing his forces back towards Germany from every direction and a group of officers tried to assassinate their leader and bring what was becoming a disastrous war to a conclusion. They failed to blow him up in his Wolf's Lair at Rastenberg and Hitler's reprisals were awful, with almost 5,000 people being killed.

Just under a year later, the Russians stood beside a smoking bomb crater outside the Reich Chancellery, the remains of the object of their relentless push to Berlin smouldering in front of them.

The Thousand Year Reich dreamed up by an Austrian painter was over.

CHARLES DE GAULLE

CHARLES DE GAULLE'S father, Henri, came from a long line of Norman and Burgundian aristocrats, while his mother Jeanne's family were rich entrepreneurs from the industrial region of Lille in northern France. The de Gaulle family were Roman Catholic, patriotic and middle class. Henri was a teacher of philosophy and literature and there had been historians and writers in the family.

The young Charles, however, was fascinated by military matters and it was a career in the army that he chose after being educated at the prestigious private Catholic school, College Stanislas, in Paris, and then briefly in Belgium. He attended the elite École Spéciale Militaire de Saint-Cyr, France's foremost military academy, located in Brittany. Graduating in 1912, he joined the 33rd Infantry Regiment of the French Army, based in Arras, as a second lieutenant. His regiment was commanded by Colonel Philippe Pétain whose name would arise again during World War II, but in a much less glorious context.

De Gaulle was conscientious and hardworking and, as a soldier, courageous and self-assured. World War I saw him fighting in the great Battle of Verdun, being wounded three times and mentioned in dispatches three times for conspicuous bravery. He was captured by the Germans and was held prisoner for two-and-a-half years, during which he made no less than five attempts to escape. Between escape attempts, he used his time well, co-authoring a book about the German Empire, *The Enemy and the True Enemy*.

Following the war he spent some time in Poland as part of a military mission, instructing Polish infantry forces during that country's war with the Soviet Union, a conflict during which he won the highest Polish military honour, the Virtuti Militari for distinguishing himself in an operation near the River Zbrucz. He returned to Saint-Cyr for a year to teach before undergoing a two year course in strategy and tactics at the French École Supérieure de Guerre (War College). In 1925, Pétain promoted him to the staff of the Supreme War Council.

In the late 1920s, de Gaulle served as a major in the French army occupying the Rhineland. It was an interesting time for this deep military thinker. He could see for himself the dangers a powerful and well-equipped German military machine presented to what he believed to be inadequate French defences. This tour of duty was followed by two years in the Middle East and then, promoted to lieutenant colonel, four years as a member of the secreteriat of the national Defence Council.

Meanwhile, he wrote books and articles on military matters, showing him to be a brilliant and progressive military thinker. He urged the creation of a mechanised army with armoured divisions manned by professional specialist soldiers in contrast to the prevalent theories that championed such outmoded defensive systems as the Maginot Line – concrete fortifications, tank obstacles, artillery emplacements, machine gun posts, and other defenses – that France had constructed along its borders with Germany and Italy. Despite the acceptance of such views by senior military men such as the United States' Dwight D. Eisenhower and General Wladislav Sikorski of Poland, French politicians, worried about the political reliability of a professional army, and de Gaulle's colleagues, including Pétain, rejected his ideas. Relations became strained as a result.

When war with Germany finally arrived in autumn 1939, de Gaulle was in command of a tank brigade attached to the French Fifth Army. Following the German breakthrough at Sedan in May 1940, he was promoted to brigadier general, commanding the 4th Armoured Division. At last he had the opportunity to try out his theories. On 17 May, he attacked the Germans at Montcornet with

200 tanks and no air support; on 28 May, he forced the German infantry to retreat to Caumont, but these were amongst the very few military successes the Germans enjoyed during this very difficult period. Again, he demonstrated his brilliant leadership skills as he fought the advancing Germans. He was asked to join the government of a fervent supporter of his work, Paul Reynaud, as Undersecretary of State for Defence and War, with responsibility for co-ordinating with Britain, but just ten days after his appointment, the Reynaud government fell, to be replaced by a government headed by Marshal Pétain who was bent on seeking an armistice with Hitler. De Gaulle had suggested that, instead of seeking peace, the French government should go to North Africa and govern in exile but this plan was rejected. When Pétain took office, de Gaulle left immediately for England with 100,000 gold francs and on 18 June made a radio broadcast to France, denouncing Pétain's Vichy government and exhorting his countrymen to continue the fight with him as leader of the Free French Forces, the French troops who had fled France or were stationed in its colonies.

De Gaulle launched his political career at a serious disadvantage – namely that he was virtually unknown in France and Great Britain. He also had very few people on his staff. What he did have, however, was strength of character – or stubbornness, as it often seemed to the British – and a strong conviction that his leadership qualities were sufficient to save the country he loved. His speech galvanised the French resistance movement and earned him a great deal of respect and popularity.

Meanwhile, in July, at a court martial in Toulouse, the Vichy regime sentenced him, *in absentia*, to four years imprisonment; a second trial a month later found him guilty of treason and sentenced him to death.

Based in Berkhamsted, north of London, de Gaulle set about organising the Free French. He worked closely with the British and the Americans, but at all times insisted on retaining full freedom of action on behalf of France which often irritated the Allies. He held a particular distrust of the British whom he suspected of intending to appropriate France's considerable colonial possessions in North Africa. The Americans, for their part, did not actually recognise de Gaulle's position as head of the Free French for some time after he arrived in London, preferring, instead, to deal with representatives of the Vichy government. Even a lot of French people were suspicious of this staunch Catholic military man, especially those on the left. Meanwhile, the right saw Pétain as a genuine military hero and distrusted de Gaulle's rebellion against him.

In May 1943, following the Allied invasion of North Africa the previous November, he moved the Free French headquarters to Algiers, assuming the role of chairman of the French Committee of National Liberation.

Cleverly, following Operation Overlord in 1944, when the Allies invaded France and began their push to Berlin, de Gaulle succeeded in manoeuvering affairs so that there was no Allied Military Government for France and he established the Free French as the principal authority in the country. Several days prior to the liberation of Paris on 19 August 1944, he flew into France, visiting the liberating forces at the front and then driving into the city itself. He made a famous, rousing speech from the Hotel de Ville, in which he credited the French people with liberating the capital. He then went back to work in his old office in the Ministry of War.

He was appointed President of the Provisional Government of the Third Republic in September and immediately sent French troops to Indochina to re-establish control there in the face of nationalist uprisings. He assembled a force of Free French and colonial troops – the French First Army – that fought on the western front, liberating much of France. It also succeeded in capturing a large section of German territory which meant that France was able to play a role in the signing of the German surrender and in the settlement at the end of the war. A French occupied zone was established in Germany, much against the wishes of the Russians.

On 20 January 1946, de Gaulle suddenly resigned from the government, citing the disagreements between the various political factions who made up the governing coalition. He also did not approve of the newly-drafted constitution of the Fourth Republic, believing it gave too much power to the French National Assembly.

De Gaulle would persist in his opposition to the constitution for many years and his opposition to the French political parties led many to express the suspicion that he really wanted to form a 'bonapartist' style of government, with all power vested in one man. That man would, of course, be de Gaulle.

In 1947, he formed the Rassemblement du Peuple Francaise (the Rally of the French People), known as the RPF, initially as a mass movement, but by 1951 a political party, gaining 120 seats in the National Assembly. De Gaulle directed his hostility at the other political parties, the constitution and, in particular, French Communists. In 1953, however, he severed his connections with the party as in-fighting broke out and members started to defect. It was dissolved in 1955 and de Gaulle retired from public life, spending his time quietly at his home at Colombey-les-Deux-Eglises, working on his memoirs.

In May 1958, he was called upon as France once more faced another dangerous and volatile situation. Political instability at home, failures in Indochina and the crisis in Algeria had led to the collapse of the government. On 13 May, settlers attacked government buildings in the Algerian capital, Algiers, enraged by what they believed to be French government weakness in the face of Algerian Arabs' demands for independence. French General Jacques Massu formed a Committee of Civil and Public Security, while General Raoul Salan, Commander-in-Chief of the French Army in Algeria declared the country had been provisionally taken over by the army. Massu, a Gaullist sympathiser, persuaded Salan to proclaim 'Vive de Gaulle!' from the balcony of the government building on 15 May and de Gaulle responded two days later with a statement that he was prepared 'to assume the powers of the Republic.'

Many worried that he would violate civil liberties if he returned with the support of the army, but his response was direct: 'Have I ever done that? Au contraire, I have re-established them when they had disappeared. Who honestly believes that, aged sixty-seven, I would start a career as a dictator?' He also confirmed that he would only accept power if offered by a legally constituted authority.

Meanwhile, the crisis deepened and France tottered on the brink of a military takeover. French paratroops flew in from Algeria and seized Corsica and a landing near Paris was discussed. In the midst of the confusion, political leaders from all sides – apart from the Communists, of course – agreed that de Gaulle was the man to save France for a second time. On 29 May, French President René Coty invited him to become President of the Fourth Republic.

He agreed to do so, but only on condition that he could have emergency powers for six months and that a new constitution be created and presented to the people of France. The National Assembly agreed to his terms and on 28 September in a referendum the French voted overwhelmingly for the new constitution. The Fifth republic came into being. Two months later, he won a large majority in the general election. He was inaugurated as president of France in January 1959.

He made sweeping reforms, introducing tough economic measures, issuing a new franc, worth 100 old francs and pushed for France to become an independent power with its own nuclear deterrent. Franco-German cooperation led to the creation of the European Economic Community (EEC). His words 'Yes, it is Europe, from the Atlantic to the Urals, it is Europe, it is the whole of Europe, that will decide the destiny of the world,' became a clarion call, although this Europe would exclude Britain for a time. He persistently vetoed Britain's applications to join the EEC.

The Algerian question remained and although he certainly believed France could defeat the rebels, he knew that it would be indefensible in the eyes of the world. So, Algerian independence was only a matter of time. Meanwhile, he quashed several rebellions and covered up a shameful massacre of up to 400 Algerians in Paris by the police in 1961. The Organisation Armée Sécrète, a right-wing terrorist group made several attempts on his life. Eventually, following a referendum on Algerian independence in 1961, he organised a cease-fire in Algeria, followed by the 1962 Evian Accords that allowed for Algerian independence in July that year. 900,000 French settlers fled the country.

His next battle was over the election of the French President. He obtained an amendment to the constitution that allowed the president to be directly elected by the votes of the French people. He then concentrated on the economy and serving French interests in Europe.

He was re-elected President in the election of 1965 but remained in office only until 1969. His style of government had become repressive and, often, heavy-handed. Eventually people had had enough and France erupted in May 1968, initially with student demonstrations and then with workers joining in and challenging de Gaulle's legitimacy. He briefly fled to Germany where, it is said, in discussions with General Massu, the possibility of army intervention was discussed. Instead, however, he agreed to introduce some reforms, dissolved the National Assembly and held elections. He won a stunning majority, the country rallying once again to his cause.

The following year, however, a referendum on changes to the upper house of the French parliament, rejected his recommendation. He resigned the Presidency on 28 April, reluctant to stay in power without widespread support. Some claimed that he no longer had the heart for politics following the events of 1968, that the referendum was, in fact, an act of political suicide.

Once again, he retired to Colombeuy-les-Deux-Eglises where, as he watched television on the night of 9 November, he suddenly pointed to his neck and said: 'I feel a pain here'. He fell unconscious and died of an aneurismal rupture. It was just two weeks before his eightieth birthday.

MIKHAIL GORBACHEV

IT IS A CURIOUS fact that the man who brought the Soviet Union to an end in 1991 was the first person to lead the Soviet Union who was born after the October Revolution of 1917 that brought the communists to power. With the curious, identifying birthmark on his forehead, Mikhail Gorbachev stands as one of the most significant people of the 20th century and one of the most important in the history of the continent of Europe. His policies of reform and openness not only changed the lives of millions living in the USSR and the satellite countries of Eastern Europe, but made a huge contribution to the end of the Cold War that had threatened the peace of the world on several occasions following the Second World War.

Mikhail Gorbachev was born in 1931 in Stavropol Krai, in southern Russia, at a tough time for anyone living in the Soviet Union. Joseph Stalin was ruling with an iron fist and Gorbachev's grandfather felt the full force of it when he was sent to the gulag – the Soviet Union's harsh penal labour camps – for nine years for hording grain instead of giving it to the local collective. In 1942, the local area was occupied by German troops resulting in extreme hardship and cruelty for the entire population that left its mark on the young Gorbachev.

Following the end of the war in 1946, he spent four summers working as an assistant combine harvester operator, learning a great deal about the life of the Russian peasant and coming to the conclusion that under communism there was little difference in the way of life to that of the serfs who had struggled under the Tsars that the communists had replaced.

He excelled at school and began to make a name for himself in 1947 when he was awarded the Order of the Red banner of Labour after helping his father to harvest a record crop at the collective farm. Aged just sixteen at the time, he was one of the youngest-ever recipients of the honour.

He enrolled at Moscow University in 1950, studying law, but seems to have been determined from an early age that his education was merely a means of obtaining a position with the Communist Party of the Soviet Union. He succeeded, becoming a candidate member of the Party that year.

In 1953, he married a girl he had met at university – Raisa Maksimovna Titarenko – before moving back to Stavropol, graduating there in June 1955. He worked for a while in the Prokuratura, a state legal department, before being transferred to the Komsomol, the Communist Union of Youth. In 1956 he became the First Secretary of the Stavropol City Komosol Committee, later being promoted to the regional committee for which he was First Secretary from 1961. 1963 brought promotion to Head of the Department of Party Organs in the Stavropol Agricultural Kraikom and in 1966, aged thirty-five, he obtained a correspondence degree as an agronomist-economist.

Promotions followed rapidly and in 1970 he became one of the youngest provincial party chiefs in the country, when he became head of the Stavropol Communist Party. He threw himself enthusiastically into re-organising collective farms, improving living conditions and giving workers a greater voice in issues that involved them. His good work led to him being made a member of the Central Committee of the CPSU, the Communist Party of the Soviet Union. He had really arrived in the corridors of power with this appointment because the Central Committee not only directed government activities between party Congresses, it also elected the Politburo – the party's executive committee – and the General Secretary of the CPSU.

In 1980, Gorbachev was, himself, appointed to the Politburo as a candidate member, having enjoyed the consistent support of his mentor, Mikhail Suslov, the powerful chief theoretician for the CPSU. Suslov had led the 1964 coup that had replaced premier Nikita Khrustchev with Leonid Brezhnev and was responsible for the promotion of future Russian leader, Yuri Andropov, as well as Gorbachev, to top party positions. Head of the Russian security service, the KGB, Andropov, was, in fact, also from Stavropol and he also ensured Gorbachev's rise through the ranks.

Working with Andropov, Gorbachev had responsibilities for personnel, overseeing the replacement of a great many of the old guard of Soviet communism with younger blood. Also during this time, he made a number of foreign trips, visiting West Germany, Canada and Britain, where he met the British Prime Minister of the time, Margaret Thatcher. She liked him and famously said of him, 'we can do business together.'

Andropov was briefly General Secretary – from November 1982 until his death fifteen months later when he was replaced by Konstantin Chernenko who himself only held the position for eleven months before he, too, died.

Three hours after the death of Chernenko, on 11 March 1985, with the Politburo supporters of his principal rival, Grigory Romanov out of Moscow, Mikhail Gorbachev was elected General Secretary of the Communist Party of the Soviet Union.

At the 27th Congress of the CPSU in February 1986, he announced a number of new policies intended to reform the party and the Soviet Union's economy. He introduced the twin policies of *glasnost* (openness) and *perestroika* (restructuring), as well as *demokratizatsiya* (democratisation), and *uskoreniye* (acceleration of economic development).

The Soviet economy was stagnating but Gorbachev set about modernising, beginning with changes of government personnel. The highest profile change was the replacement of Foreign Minister,

Andrei Gromyko, by Eduard Shevardnadze who shared Gorbachev's vision. Gromyko was a hard-liner who had served in government for twenty-eight years, becoming known as 'Mr Nyet' (Mr No) by Western leaders because of his intransigence.

Gorbachev's first major reform programme was launched against alcohol which had become a scourge in the Soviet Union with rampant alcoholism damaging family life and creating an unacceptable level of absenteeism from work. Prices were increased and sales restricted. Drinking in public was banned and drunkenness at work was subject to prosecution. Even scenes of alcohol consumption in films were prohibited. It was not a successful policy, making little difference to alcoholism – people just bought it on the burgeoning black market. Moreover, the state coffers lost 100 billion roubles in revenue.

Conservatives were, of course, opposed to perestroika, a fact demonstrated nowhere more clearly than following the accident at the nuclear reactor at Chernobyl on 28 April 1986. Gorbachev and his supporters were misinformed about the extent of the catastrophe and were late in delivering an official response. The international community upon whom the incident also impacted, was furious with Gorbachev and the Soviet Union, but mainly placed the blame on Gorbachev.

Change continued, however. Dissident intellectual, Andrei Sakharov was brought back to Moscow after six years of internal exile and corruption began to be exposed and dealt with. Riots were breaking out, however, in the far-flung corners of the Soviet Union as nationalities began to agitate for self-determination.

In 1987, he put forward proposals for multi-candidate elections and promoted the idea of appointing non-Party members to government positions. The Russian military also experienced change, especially after a young West German piloted a plane into Moscow that landed close to Red Square, circumventing a supposedly impregnable defence system. This incident allowed Gorbachev to purge the military and speed up the pace of reform.

That year also saw publication of his book, *Perestroika: New Thinking for Our Country and the World*, describing his reformist ideas. In a symbolic act, he also rehabiltated many of Stalin's opponents, another act in the continuing process of De-Stalinisation.

In 1988, Gorbachev stepped up the progress of glasnost, giving people greater freedom of speech as well as other freedoms that had been lost under the old guard. The press worked under fewer constraints and countless political prisoners and dissidents were set free. He gambled on support for these popular policies from the people that he gambled would put greater pressure on his opponents to accept his reforms. When accused of stealing his liberalising policies from Czech Prime Minister Alexader Dubcek's idea of 'Socialism with a human face' and asked what the difference was, Gorbachev sardonically replied, 'Nineteen years.'

Critically, however, for the first time in Soviet history, private ownership of businesses in some sectors was permitted and cooperative restaurants, shops and factories began to appear. The Russian national airline, Aeroflot, was split up into a number of independent airlines. Foreign investment was permitted and encouraged.

That year Gorbachev also proposed a reduction in Party control of government departments, put forward a new presidential system and introduced a plan for a new legislative house to be known as the Congress of People's Deputies, elections for which were held the following spring, the first free elections to be held in the country since the 1917 October Revolution. He became Chairman of the Supreme Soviet and was elected unopposed by the Deputies as President of the Soviet Union on 15 March 1990.

He still faced criticism, however, much of it televised in live sessions of the Congress. One of his major critics, Boris Yeltsin, had been elected in Moscow and was particularly vocal in his condemnation of Gorbachev who was trying to maintain a balance between reformers who felt he was moving too slow and conservatives who believed he was doing too much.

Unrest also continued in the various ethnic regions of the USSR as ethnic groups continued to protest against the Soviets. In the Eastern Bloc, in East Germany, Hungary, Poland and Czechoslovakia communist governments began to fall and be replaced by non-communist governments. Gorbachev acquiesced in their fall, agreeing to withdraw Soviet troops from their territories. He had also begun the withdrawal of Soviet troops from Afghanistan where they had waged a long and unsuccessful campaign.

Serious civil unrest broke out in a number of the republics that made up the Soviet Union, such as Azerbaijan, Georgia and Uzbekistan. Others, such as Lithuania, made a play for full independence. Gorbachev was not reluctant to use military force to suppress brutal fighting between rival ethnic factions in the Central Asian republics during 1989 and 1990. Nonetheless, the constitutional mechanisms allowing the secession of a republic from the USSR were being designed.

With the abolition of the CPSU's constitutional grip of political power in the Soviet Union, the way was gradually becoming clear for the legalising of other political parties.

In the face of the unrest throughout the republics, Gorbachev began to draft plans for a new treaty of union that would create a truly voluntary federation. The Central Asian republics were supportive as they badly needed the economic power and access to the markets of the Soviet Union. Men such as Boris Yeltsin, however, advocated the rapid movement towards a market economy and were happy to sacrifice the Soviet Union to achieve this. Yeltsin would around this time be elected president of the Russian Federation.

However, Gorbachev had never been willing to go all the way in allowing free market mechanisms and some restrictions remained on private ownership. The economy continued to deteriorate and at the same time, as he failed to augment his powers, his authority began to decline. He made the mistake in the face of a loss of public confidence, of allying himself with Party conservatives. These same hard-liners, believing that reform had gone too far and that too much power had been devolved to the republics, staged a coup in 1991, placing him under house arrest at his dacha in the Crimea from 19 to 21 August.

The coup failed due to staunch resistance by Yeltsin and other reformers, reluctant to let go of their hard-won freedoms, but when Gorbachev returned to Moscow, he found that he had lost the initiative. Support had swung in the direction of his rival Yeltsin.

In the next month, Estonia, Lithuania, Ukraine, Belarus, Moldova, Georgia, Armenia, Azerbaijan, Kazakhstan, Kyrgyzstan, Uzbekistan, Tjikstan and Turkmenistan all declared independence from the Soviet Union. Bóris Yeltsin, meanwhile, had issued an order for the CPSU to cease its activities on Russian soil. The Russian flag now flew alongside the Soviet flag at the Kremlin in Moscow.

Gorbachev had little option but to resign as general Secretary of the CPSU on 24 August and advised the Central Committee to dissolve. The Congress of Deputies was dissolved on 5 September.

On 1 December the people of Ukraine voted in a referendum for independence and a week later, the Presidents of Russia, Belarus and Ukraine met to found the Commonwealth of Independent States, declaring the end of the Soviet Union. After meeting with his old rival, Yeltsin, Gorbachev resigned on 25 December and the Soviet Union was formally dissolved the following day.

MARTIN LUTHER KING

THERE CAN BE few people who have made as much of an impact on his country as the great American civil rights leader, Dr Martin Luther King Dr and as the first black US President, Barack Obama, swore the oath of office in January 2009, there can be few watching who did not have Dr King's immortal words of August, 1963, 'I have a dream', running through their heads.

King's legacy has been immense and, if anything, his legend and his message have grown since his death in 1968. Countless schools, public buildings and roads in the United States as well as around the world, bear his name and from 1986 America has enjoyed a national holiday in his honour, on the third Monday in January. Appositely, in 2009 Martin Luther King Day fell on the eve of President Obama's inauguration. There is a sculpture of Dr King in Westminster Abbey in London and there are plans to erect a Martin Luther King Dr memorial in Washington D.C. No private individual in America's history has been accorded such an honour.

Of course, with time comes controversy and sometimes criticism and Dr King has been accused of having communist tendencies, has been criticised for his often-expressed opposition to the Vietnam War and since his death, attempts have been made to besmirch his reputation with accusations of marital infidelities. The FBI, under the supervision of J. Edgar Hoover, certainly investigated the latter accusations while King was still alive.

Some in the civil rights movement say that King's elevation to a Messiah-like status has hindered rather than helped his work and his legacy, but it is undeniable that King's was the most important voice on one of the most critical issues at a certain point in America's history. He was adept at turning protest into a moral crusade that attracted nationwide interest and that could not be ignored. Although serious social problems remain, he was instrumental in achieving the abolition of cruel and divisive segregation laws and improving the lot of the people for whom he struggled and for whom he gave his life.

Born on 15 January 1929, his upbringing was comfortably middle-class. Both his father, Martin Luther King Sr., and his maternal grandfather were Baptist ministers and his parents had both gone to college. His father was the pastor of the Ebenezer Baptist church in Atlanta and the family lived in a prosperous black area, on Auburn Avenue, a street on which stood some of the country's most prosperous black businesses and black churches.

However, it was the South and racial prejudice was never far away, even from the lives of this fairly privileged young man. He experienced it first hand when the parents of some white friends forbade them to play with him when they began to attend a segregated school.

He was further shaken in 1944 by the death of his maternal grandmother, Jennie, in 1941. She had been a great influence on his early years and, in an emotional and unstable condition, the twelve-year-old is said to have attempted suicide by jumping from a second-floor window.

At fifteen, he spent a summer working on a tobacco farm in Connecticut, his first sojourn in the desegregated north and, consequently, an eye-opening experience for him. He was shocked and delighted at the way the races mixed freely and wrote to his parents how blacks and whites could worship in the same church and eat in the same restaurants. His view of race relations was beginning to formulate.

That same year, King enrolled in Morehouse College in Atlanta, gaining entry via a special programme to further the education of promising high school students such as him. Initially, he studied medicine and the law, but his father had long wanted him to follow the family tradition by entering the ministry and in his senior year he fulfilled his father's wish. At this time, he came under another formative influence, the college president, Benjamin Mays, a social activist possessed of rich oratorial skills and progressive ideas. Mays fought against the black church's refusal to confront the issues of the day, concentrating rather too much, in his opinion, on the hereafter. His ideas made an indelible impression on the teenage Martin Luther King and he took them with him when he graduated in 1948.

To further his religious studies, he spent the next three years at Crozer Theological Seminary in Chester, Pennsylvania. King was elected president of the student body during his time there, an extraordinary achievement in a college that was almost exclusively composed of white students, although it was undoubtedly a testament to his already renowned skills at oratory. Crucially, however, it was here that he first encountered the idea of non-violent protest in the philosophy of the Indian nationalist leader, Mahatma Gandhi. Like South African leader, Nelson Madela, Gandhi's teachings became one of the greatest influences on Martin Luther King. He left Crozer with a bachelor of Divinty degree in 1951.

He attended Boston University until 1955, obtaining a doctorate and while there he met the woman who would become his wife and bear him his four children, Coretta Scott. They married in 1953.

In the mid 1950s, a small group of Montgomery, Alabama, civil rights activists decided to test the city's approach to segregation on its public transport system. On 1 December 1955, African American Rosa Parks refused to give up her seat for a white passsenger as the law stated she should and was arrested for violation of the city's segregation laws. King, at the time, pastor of the Dexter Avenue Baptist church in Montgomery, was elected leader of a group, the Montgomery Improvement Association whose aims were to boycott the transport system in the city while such invidious laws applied.

They chose him because, new to Montgomery, he had not had time to make too many enemies. In his inaugural speech, he set the tone for the remainder of his life and also introduced America to a voice and philosophy with which it would become increasingly familiar in the years to come: 'We have no alternative but to protest. For many years we have shown an amazing patience. We have sometimes given our white brothers the feeling that we liked the way we were being treated. But we come here tonight to be saved from that patience that makes us patient with anything less than freedom and justice.'

King now found he had enemies in numbers when his house was bombed and the lives of his family threatened. Undeterred, he continued to lead the boycott of the city's buses until just over a year later, Montgomery's buses were desegregated.

King realised that the movement for civil rights reform needed a mass movement that would provide him and others with a national platform from which to speak. The already-existing Southern Christian Leadership Conference provided such a platform and he used it to give speeches and take part in debates all over the United States. An important meeting in India with Prime Minister Jawaharlal Nehru and followers of Gandhi persuaded him, as it had also persuaded another freedom fighter, Nelson Mandela, that non-violent protest and peaceful non-compliance would provide him and his movement with a an unbeatable moral authority. He also looked to Africa and its struggle for freedom from colonialism as an inspiration.

In 1960, he moved back to Atlanta and became co-preacher, with his father at the Ebenezer Baptist Church. Most of his time and energy, however, went into his work with the SCLC and the civil rights movement. In late October, he agreed to participate in a protest by thirty-three young blacks over segregation at a lunch counter in a department store in Atlanta. King was arrested and, although charges were dropped to save embarrassment to the authorities, there was outrage when he was sentenced to be sent to a prison farm due to a minor traffic violation he had committed some months previously. King's incarceration became national news, outrage increasing when President Eisenhower refused to intervene. He was eventually freed following the intervention of Democratic presidential candidate, John F. Kennedy, an intercession it is believed that contributed significantly to his election to the presidency eight days later.

For the next five years, Dr Martin Luther King Dr was at the height of his powers, both oratorially and politically. The new medium of television loved the drama and the wisdom of this handsome young man's speeches and he, in his turn, recognised the power of the new medium to communicate with a vast new audience of all social and economic classes. He used it to promote his sit-ins, marches and speeches.

In spring, 1963, police turned fire hoses and dogs on demonstrators protesting about segregation in lunch counters and racially restrictive employment practices in Birmingham, Alabama. Many were arrested and sent to jail, including Dr King. Support was not universal for his actions, however, with many black pastors opposing his methods and white clergy who urged black people not to support him. King, languishing in prison in Birmingham, delivered an eloquent response to his opponents: 'You may well ask: "Why direct action? Why sit-ins, marches and so forth? Isn't negotiation a better path?" You are quite right in calling for negotiation. Indeed, this is the very purpose of direct action. Non-violent direct action seeks to create such a crisis and foster such a tension that a community which has constantly refused to negotiate is forced to confront the issue.'

On 28 August 1963, King led one of America's most historic protest marches, the March on Washington for Jobs and Freedom. More than 200,000 blacks and whites gathered in the shadow of the Lincoln Memorial to hear King deliver one of the greatest and most moving speeches in history, his 'I Have a Dream' speech. All men, he declared with astonishing emotional power, would one day be brothers.

The barriers finally began to come down. In 1964, President Lyndon Johnson signed a Civil Rights Act, authorising the federal government to enforce desegregation of public accommodations and outlawing discrimination in publicly-owned facilities. It also made it illegal to discriminate in employment.

In November 1964, King's campaign was given global legitimacy when he was awarded the Nobel Peace Prize.

As time passed, opposition to Martin Luther King's non-violent methods increased. For some African Americans the speed of change was too slow, and they believed that blacks had to be more forceful in their pressure for change. A march in Selma about the need for legal support for federal voting rights for black Americans in the south was turned back from the state capital by tear gas and nightsticks. Dr King, not present at the first march, decided to lead the second, despite legal efforts to force him to cancel it. Just outside Selma, the marchers came up against a mass of state troopers. King led his followers in prayer before turning back. Young radicals smelled a rat, suspecting that he had arrived at some kind of agreement with federal and local officials before the march. But they already believed he was being too cautious. Nonetheless, 1965 saw the passing of the Voting Rights Act.

The non-violent approach was seriously held up for examination when the Los Angeles district, Watts, erupted in days of violence in August 1965. King persevered, however, and the following year was working against racial discrimination in Chicago. An agreement was reached with the authorities after a concerted campaign of boycotts, sit-ins and marches that lasted through the spring and summer of that year, but it never had the support of the city's all-powerful mayor, Richard Daley, and ultimately came to nothing. Its failure provided the young activists with more ammunition.

Black militancy was on the rise, especially in the ghetto areas of

America's cities where economic hardship was at its worst. They saw King as middle-class and, even, old, even though he was only in his mid-thirties. They were impatient for action and confrontation and his patient and passive stance was anathema to them.

He began to broaden the reach of his campaigning, being criticised for his stated opposition to the Vietnam War and talking about poverty, not just of the blacks. In 1968, he was planning a Poor People's march to Washington but first travelled to Memphis to lend his support to a strike by sanitation workers. By now, he was tired and many have suggested that he knew his time was fast approaching. On the night before his assassination he spoke at the Mason Temple Church in Memphis, declaring prophetically, 'I've seen the promised land. I may not get there with you. But I want you to know tonight that we, as a people, will get to the promised land.'

The next day, 3 April 1968, Dr Martin Luther King Dr was shot dead by a white assassin, James Earl Ray, while taking the air on the balcony of the Lorraine Motel in Memphis. News of his murder sparked riots in 100 cities across the United States.

HO CHI MINH

He was an unlikely leader – a gaunt, almost emaciated little old man with a goatee beard, usually dressed in a threadbare bush jacket. His army, too – a host of similarly stick-thin men, and women, dressed in tattered clothing and poorly armed – seemed an unlikely foe for the great western powers, France and the United States. What drove them, however, was what had driven people to achieve extraordinary feats throughout history – independence for their country. As 'Uncle Ho', as he liked to be called, said in 1946 as war with France approached: 'You can kill ten of my men for every one I kill of yours, yet even at those odds, you will lose and I will win.' Later, when asked how long he would have fought the United States, he replied: 'Twenty years, maybe 100 years – as long as it took to win, regardless of cost. And it was a huge cost. Around three million Vietnamese – North and South – lost their lives in the conflict. Against such leadership and with an unending supply of troops willing to throw down their lives for the cause, no one stood a chance.

Ho was born Nguyen Sinh Cung in a central Vietnamese village, Hoàng Trù, in 1890, moving to Kim Lien, the village where his father was born, in 1895 with his sister and two brothers. Ho's father was a Confucian scholar, teacher and magistrate. The French would later sack him for torturing a peasant to death while drunk, but it was a trumped-up charge made against him because of the nationalist anti-French activities of his sons at school.

Ho received a French education and at the end of his studies, became a teacher at the Duc Thanh school in Phan Thiet in southeastern Vietnam. In 1911, he decided to further his education

463

in France, paying his passage by working in the kitchen of a French ship en route for Marseille. Once there, he worked in various jobs – as a waiter, cleaner and film re-toucher – and tried and failed to obtain entrance to the French Colonial Administrative School. When not working, he could be found studying western culture through books and newspapers in public libraries.

His next port of call was New York, again working his way there on board a ship. He moved to Boston, working as a baker in a hotel and in a series of menial jobs. He stayed there until 1913 when he crossed the Atlantic to England, living in West Ealing in London and then in Crouch End, working as a chef.

In 1919, it was back to France for Ho, but by this time, aged twenty-nine, his political sensibilities were beginning to stir and he began to take an interest in the new doctrine that was sweeping Europe – communism. He petitioned the Versailles Peace Talks that ended the First World War about the way the French were treating Vietnamese people and, wearing a tailcoat, he also approached US President Woodrow Wilson, believing that he would find a sympathetic ear, given the President's doctrine of self-determination. But his efforts to try to raise interest in independence for Vietnam were ignored and he decided on a different approach. When the French Communist party was founded in 1921 at the Congress of Tours, Ho was there, becoming a founder member, under the name he had been using in France, Nguyen Ai Quoc, meaning Nguyen the Patriot. At the congress, he made a speech decrying France's exploitation of its colonies. From there, in 1923, he travelled to Moscow where he became the Asian expert for Comintern, the Soviet body that liaised between all of the communist parties around the world. It was at this point that he became Ho Chi Minh. He became a secret agent for Moscow, roaming the world disguised as a Chinese journalist or a Buddhist monk. He had a staggering array of identities and every now and then he would be reported dead, but would then pop up again somewhere else.

China was his next port of call in 1924 and for the next couple of years he organised 'Youth Education Classes' and lectured. He spent the summer of 1927 in the Crimea, recovering from tuberculosis before returning to Paris in the November of that year. After visiting Brussels, Berlin, Switzerland and Italy, he embarked on a ship bound for Thailand. Bangkok, Hong Kong and Shanghai were next on his extraordinary itinerary, his stay in Hong Kong lasting slightly longer than originally planned, after he was arrested by the British police due to his communist affiliations and jailed for two years. He was released in 1933.

His tuberculosis had been getting progressively worse and on his release he returned to the Soviet Union where he spent the next few years recovering from it. Eventually, in 1941, he slipped back into his native country, surreptitiously crossing the border from China, after spending three years there as an advisor to the Chinese armed forces. He had been away for thirty years.

Japan had invaded Indochina in 1940 and found collaborators in the French officials in Vietnam who were loyal to the pro-Hitler Vichy administration in France. Some nationalists in Vietnam welcomed the Japanese as liberators, but to Ho they were no different to the French. In Vietnam, he had soon founded an independence movement, known as the Viet Minh ('Bringer of Light') and launched a campaign of attacks on the Japanese, supported covertly by the American secret service organisation, the Office of Strategic Services (OSS), the forerunner of the CIA.

Returning briefly to China, he was arrested and imprisoned until 1943 when he again returned to Vietnam.

On 9 March 1945, the Japanese overthrew the Vichy French government of Vietnam, making Bao Dai puppet Emperor. He had served as king of Annam, the name the French had given to Vietnam, from 1926. Then, following the dropping of atomic bombs on Hiroshima and Nagasaki, Japan surrendered to the Americans on 15 August. In Indochina, the Japanese made life difficult for the Allies, providing support for Vietnamese nationalist groups such as Ho's Viet Minh. Finally, on 25 August, the Emperor abdicated and on 2 September, Ho Chi Minh proclaimed the Democratic Republic of Vietnam.

A few days later two forces began the occupation of Vietnam as agreed at the Potsdam Conference held just a few months previously. The Chinese occupied the north and the British occupied the south.

Negotiations with the French began in late 1945, Ho prepared to accept something less than full-blown independence and, anyway, the French were preferable to the Chinese who were casting covetous glances across the border. He had little option but to sign an agreement with the French that Vietnam would become an autonomous state in the Indochinese Federation and the French Union.

No sooner had the Chinese occupiers left the country than fighting erupted with the French. Then, at a crucial meeting in Moscow with Stalin and Mao Zedong, Ho agreed to a plan for China to back the Viet Minh in the struggle against the French with training and weaponry. The early years of the war had involved fairly low-level rural insurgencies, but gradually, with the support of the superpowers it escalated. It began to be called La Sale Guerre (The Dirty War) by French critics of the war.

Eventually, in 1953, the French lost the decisive battle of Dien Bien Phu and withdrew from Vietnam.

The 1954 Geneva Accords that followed the First Indochinese War, split Vietnam in two. The communists were given the northern part of the country and the non-communists the south. Ho established his government of the Democratic Republic of Vietnam in Hanoi and North Vietnam became a Communist single-party state. A provision in the Accords stated that in 1956 there would be free elections for the entire country in order to unify it again, but these elections were rejected by the South and by the United States which was taking an increasing interest in Vietnam.

Meanwhile, people re-located in order to be in the part of the country that was best for them, around a million people moving south from Ho's North Vietnam, a much smaller number heading in the opposite direction. Ho launched land reform, executing, torturing or imprisoning thousands of landowners.

Ho began to encourage Communists in the south – known as Vietcong – to destabilise the South Vietnamese regime, sending support and, in 1959, building, the Ho Chi Minh Trail, the complex 600-mile-long maze of roads, bicycle paths, rivers and footpaths that allowed aid to be sent to the south through Laos and Cambodia. Not for nothing has it been described as one of the greatest military engineering achievements of the 20th century.

American advisors had been in South Vietnam for years before the first combat troops began to arrive in 1965. The fighting very quickly escalated, watched by millions as it became the first war to be broadcast on a nightly basis into homes around the world on television news broadcasts and Ho became an instantly recognisable figure. The Americans began bombing North Vietnam but Ho, now in his seventies, carried on living in his simple house located behind the Presidential Palace in Hanoi. Throughout the conflict, he refused to enter into negotiations with the Americans, stating that he would accept nothing less than an unconditional withdrawal of all foreign troops from Vietnam. These also now included the Australians who had entered the war to support the USA.

Although the North Vietnamese conceded in private that things were not going well for them by 1967, they were reassured by the ineffectiveness of the South Vietnamese army as well as by the overwhelming lack of support for the war from some sections of the American public, a sentiment that expressed itself, often, in violent demonstrations and confrontations with the authorities.

On 23 January 1968 Ho launched the massive Tet Offensive in an attempt to take South Vietnam by force. The offensive would continue for eight months, the People's Army of Vietnam striking at strategic targets throughout South Vietnam with the aim of sparking a general uprising amongst the population of the south to bring down the US-backed government. Both north and south governments had announced a two-day cease-fire to celebrate the most important holiday in the Vietnamese calendar, Tet Nguyen Dan, New Year. Instead, however, the North Vietnamese launched a wave of attacks. More than 80,000 troops struck in 100 towns across the country. Most were pushed back but there was intense fighting at the old imperial capital, Hue, and the US base of Khe San was besieged by Vietcong for two months. It was, ultimately, a disaster for the North Vietnamese but struck a huge blow at American morale and the American public's trust in the men running the war who had denied that the enemy had the ability to mount an attack on such a massive scale. It undoubtedly played a major part in America's eventual withdrawal from Vietnam.

Tragically for him, Ho Chi Minh did not live to see the end of the war that finally drove foreign forces from his country. Aged seventy-nine, he died of heart failure in his house in Hanoi on 2 September 1969, coincidentally the anniversary of his proclamation of the Democratic Republic of Vietnam twenty-four years previously. This coincidence made the government, reluctant to announce the death on such an auspicious day, hold back the news for two days after he had actually passed away.

It took another six years, but in 1975, a victorious North Vietnamese tank rolled through the conquered South Vietnamese capital of Saigon with a poster displayed on its side reading: 'You are always marching with us, Uncle Ho.'

MAO ZEDONG

CHAIRMAN MAO WAS many things to many people. Leader of the country with the world's largest population from its founding in 1949 until his death in 1976, he is seen by some, particularly the people of mainland China, as a great revolutionary who made China a world power. To others he is an iconoclast who destroyed millennia of Chinese culture and society. Some see him as a mass-murderer, responsible for the deaths of tens of millions of Chinese people. No matter which camp you fall into, he is, without doubt, one of the most important leaders of the twentieth century, if not of all time.

For all his Marxist revolutionary zeal in later life, Mao was born in December 1893 into a fairly well-off family in the rocky upland village of Shaoshan in Hunan Province where almost everyone shares the surname Mao. He had two brothers and a sister and as a child received a good education, attending school from the age of eight until thirteen when his father made him return to work in the fields during the day and do the accounts at night. It was a life he hated so much that he ran away. He went to stay with his mother's brother who entered him into primary school even though he was six years older than the other pupils who made fun of his tattered clothing and country manners.

Aged seventeen, he took a steamer to Changsha, capital of Hunan, where he attended middle school and began to learn about the world around him by reading newspapers which he would later cite as providing his entire education.

In the summer and autumn of 1911, news was reaching Changsha of an unsuccessful rebellion in Canton – modern-day Guangzhou –

led by the revolutionary, Huang Xing. It coincided with unrest in Changsha because of a rice shortage and was followed by news of yet another uprising, in Wuchang. It had begun because a revolutionary bomb had gone off by mistake and when police investigated they discovered that members of the ruling Qing Dynasty's New Army were members of revolutionary organisations. The army staged a coup and contacted revolutionaries in other provinces. Within six weeks, fifteen Chinese provinces had seceded. China was in a ferment.

Mao and a friend ran off to join the army but he continued to devour any reading material he could get his hands on, including pamphlets on socialism. After the fall of the Qing Dynasty, Mao was released from the army and returned to school, graduating in 1918, having learned to write poetry and having developed a keen sense of nationalism. At night, he and his fellow students taught workers, believing an educated workforce would be of benefit to the nation.

In 1918, he travelled to Beijing with his teacher, Yang Changji. He worked for a Marxist thinker for a while before returning to Changsha on the outbreak of the May Fourth Movement which brought an upsurge of nationalist feeling in China and a re-evaluation of Chinese culture. Mao showcased the movement in the Xiang River Review and became a spokesman against old China, speaking out about warlords and imperialism. He continued in journalism until the collapse of a student strike in 1919 forced him to flee.

He returned in 1920 to teach and to marry Yang Changji's daughter, Yang Kaihui. In the meantime, he had become a Marxist although anarchism still played a big part in his political thinking. By 1921, however, he was a communist and led the Hunanese delegation to the Chinese Communist Party's first congress in Shanghai in July of that year. He was made secretary of the Hunan branch and began sending representatives out to recruit and organise workers – coalminers, steelworkers, carpenters and others. In 1923, the warlords came down heavily on the movement and it was banned.

Now living in Shanghai, he was elected to the Central Committee of the Chinese Communist Party and committed himself to creating an alliance with the rival Guomindang (the National Party). It was difficult and demanding work and he became ill in 1924. He went to Shaoshan in Hunan to recuperate but became involved in helping local peasants to organise themselves. When the army arrived to put a halt to his work in 1925, he fled to Canton where he became a member of the Peasant Movement Committee and taught students how to mobilise the peasants for a national revolution. He believed the peasants to be the major revolutionary force.

The Communists and Nationalists finally fell out in 1927, the Communists becoming wanted criminals. They took part in the Nanchang Uprising, seen as the first major Kuomintang-Communist engagement of the Chinese Civil War and regarded by Chinese Communists as the date of the founding of the Chinese People's Army.

At an emergency conference, attended by Mao that August, Chen Duxiu was replaced as party leader and rural uprisings were planned. Mao was given responsibility for the uprising in Hunan, but he was defeated and, once more, had to flee with around 1,000 men, to traditional bandit-country in the Jingganshan Mountains. Working ceaselessly, Mao formed alliances with bandit leaders and organised peasant uprisings and his force was bolstered in 1928, when Zhu De joined him with 10,000 men. Zhu, a brilliant tactician, became commander of the Fourth Red Army with Mao as his political commissar. Soon after, another 1,000 men arrived under the command of Peng Dehuai. Attacked throughout the winters of 1928 and 1929 by warlords allied to Chiang Kai-shek who had replaced Sun Yat-Sen as leader of the Nationalists and leader of the government, Mao and Zhu took their army to Jiangxi Province but lost half of their men in fighting. Nonetheless, they established the Chinese Soviet Republic near Ruijin.

Now aged thirty-seven, Mao began to use his knowledge of the peasants to build a power base. He wrote essays laying out his theories about leadership, political training and military discipline but the Central Committee in Shanghai still espoused urban rather than rural revolution and Mao opposed the orders in 1930 to attack cities in central China. He and Zhu were forced to retreat from Nanchang when they attacked and the entire campaign proved to be a disaster as the Communist forces had to retreat into hiding once again in the autumn. It was also a personal disaster for Mao. In his home province of Hunan, the warlords took their revenge on him, executing both his sister, Mao Zehong, and his wife, Yang Kaihui, torturing Yang in front of their young son before putting her to death.

Chiang Kai-shek now focused on trying to wipe out the Communist threat. Police searched everywhere for Communists, precious army resources being occupied with the campaign, even after the Japanese invasion of Manchuria in 1931. The Communists, meanwhile, carried out surprise attacks and argued amongst themselves about the best way forward – revolution in the cities or slower rural revolution. At the same time, Communists were fighting merely to survive as Chiang tightened the noose.

The Central Chinese Soviet government decided to break out and in October launched its troops on the epic test of human endurance known as the Long March. It took them 370 days and they covered 6,000 miles, fighting virtually non-stop en route. After trying to make for Hunan to establish a new soviet republic, they lost more than half of their 10,000 force crossing the Xiang River. Mao persuaded them to change their plans and make for Giuzhou to the west, instead. There, they captured the city of Zunyi and at a conference of the Communist leaders afterwards, Mao criticised the style of fighting. He recommended instead, guerrilla tactics and, with the support of Zhou Enlai, who would become one of his most trusted colleagues, was elected military leader. Although he would not take over leadership of the party until 1943, the stage was set.

From 1936 to 1947, Mao led his movement against a range of enemies, including the Nationalists, his generals leading the armies and Mao writing and creating the philosophy that would re-create China as a Marxist state. He led the Communist resistance against the Japanese in the Second Sino-Japanese War that was fought between 1937 and 1945 and, meanwhile, he purged rival members of the party. He also divorced his third wife, He Zizhen, marrying an actress, Jiang Qing, better known later as Madame Mao. She would remain at his side for thirty-eight years and would say after his death: 'I was Chairman Mao's dog. I bit whomever he asked me to bite.'

When World War II ended, the Nationalists and Communists focused on each other once again, the USA supporting Chiang and the Soviet Union providing arms for Mao, now undisputed leader of the Chinese Communists. Eventually, in January 1949, the Nationalists were decisively defeated and driven from mainland China to Formosa, now known as Taiwan. More than twenty years of non-stop war – civil as well as international – were finally at an end.

The People's Republic of China was established on 1 October 1949 and Mao – known to all as Chairman Mao or the Great Leader – was in control. The media was put under the control of the Communist leadership and the image of Mao and the party were relentlessly promoted. Enemies of the country were vilified and amongst these were not only Chiang's hated nationalists, across the water in Taiwan, but also countries such as the United States and Japan.

Mao moved into a compound adjacent to the Forbidden City in Beijing and set about reforming the country. He introduced land reform, and a ruthless justice system in which public executions were used to deal with counter-revolutionaries. These included former supporters of the Kuomintang and intellectuals whose thinking might have been considered damaging to the Party. Between 1949 and 1953, Mao himself estimated that this campaign accounted for around 800,000 executions. That is likely, however, to be but a modest estimate, given that several landlords in every village in China were publicly executed. The number is more likely to be somewhere around two and five million. Labour camps were

473

established for those who were not executed and more than a million people are believed to have been incarcerated in these. Mao considered these killings to be necessary for complete control of China to be established.

The Hundred Flowers Campaign was introduced in the period 1956 to 1957 ostensibly in order to give voice to different opinions about how China should be governed. Mao used it, however, to identify critics of the regime and around 500,000 people who had taken part in the campaign were persecuted. It is thought that millions probably died as a result of the Hundred Flowers Campaign.

As in the Soviet Union, the large population had to be galvanised into action and as had been done there, he introduced a Five-Year Plan. The objective was to reduce China's reliance on its rural economy, Mao and his colleagues reasoning that in order for China to be a major power it had to become industrialised. The Russians helped until the success of the plan meant that their support was no longer needed. The Second Five-Year Plan, also known as The Great Leap Forward was launched in 1958. Land was re-distributed, steps were taken to increase literacy and price control was brought in.

It was not a success, however. New and unproven agricultural methods resulted in a fifteen per cent drop in grain production in 1959 and further drops in the years following. As local Party officials exaggerated their production, grain was brought from the country-side to the cities and was even exported, leaving insufficient quantities to feed the peasants. This was compounded by flooding and led to up to 20 million starving to death in what was probably the largest famine in history.

Furthermore, many of the major projects initiated during this period to improve China's infrastructure were equally flawed. Mao had rejected the use of qualified engineers as ideologically unsound and consequently the dams, canals and roads were very badly constructed.

The relationship between China and the Soviet Union began to founder in the late 1950s over a series of border disputes and ideological disagreements. The Chinese denounced the Russians as 'revisionists' and the Soviet Union became yet another country to add to the list of China's enemies. She was becoming increasingly isolated.

As the 1960s began, the Party was tearing itself apart. At the Conference of the Seven Thousand in Beijing in 1962, there was a dispute about the Great Leap Forward and Mao and his Defence Minister, Lin Biao, were severely held to account by State President Liu Shaoqi and Deng Xiaoping. Lin and Deng set about the disbanding of people's communes and even introduced private ownership of smallholdings. They began importing grain to deal with the famine.

These two were now a major threat to Mao. They were in favour of removing him from power and retaining him in a purely ceremonial capacity. Mao responded with a new movement that ravaged China for years – the infamous Cultural Revolution.

He handed power to the Red Guards, groups of students and young people, clad in their Mao jackets and caps and waving their Little Red Books containing the thoughts of Chairman Mao. The Red Guards became the tools with which he purged the country. They roamed the countryside and towns and cities, rooting out anyone not loyal to the Great Leader. Schools and universities were shut down and teachers, professors and intellectuals were put to work in the countryside. Huge numbers were imprisoned and a great deal of China's rich cultural heritage was destroyed. Millions died or had their lives ruined and the country descended into chaos both economically and socially. Many were driven to suicide, but when Mao was informed of this, he replied callously: 'People who try to commit suicide – don't attempt to save them!...China is such a populous nation, it is not as if we cannot do without a few people.'

He declared the Cultural Revolution over in 1969 but by then he was seventy-six and the question of who would succeed him was becoming a pressing matter. With Liu Shaoqi purged in the Cultural

Revolution – he suffered from diabetes and Mao ensured that he received no medical attention – Lin Biao was named as Mao's successor. Within two years, however, he had been killed in a suspicious plane crash after a coup led by him had failed to unseat Chairman Mao.

Mao had led a tough life and his health was now in serious decline. He was suffering from either Parkinson's Disease or motor neurone disease and his lifelong smoking habit had seriously damaged his lungs. On 2 September 1976, he had a heart attack, his third. A week later, at a few minutes after midnight on 9 September, the life support machine keeping him alive was switched off and Chairman Mao was dead, aged eighty-one.

NELSON MANDELA

It was 2.15 pm on 11 February and Nelson Mandela emerged from prison, clad in a grey suit, his hair touched with grey, holding the hand of his wife Winnie. Half a million people had waited for hours in the hot sun for this moment, but millions both in South Africa and around the world had waited twenty-seven years for it.

It was not just his long imprisonment and dramatic release that made Mandela such a potent symbol. It was the manner in which he dealt with his freedom which could so easily have signalled a bloodbath in South Africa. He embarked upon a policy of reconciliation and negotiation designed to ensure a peaceful transition from the heinous system of apartheid to a multi-racial democracy in what another great fighter for democracy, Bishop Desmond Tutu, described as the 'Rainbow Nation' of South Africa.

It all began in the tiny village of Mvezo, near Umtata, the capital of the Transkei in South Africa's Cape Province where he was born Rolihlahla Mandela on 18 July 1918. His father was Gadla Henry Mphakanyiswa, chief of the town of Mvezo and his mother, the third of his father's four wives, was Nosekeni Fanny.

The family moved to Qunu after Mandela's father had annoyed the local authorities in Mvezo, but he remained active in tribal politics, helping Jongintaba Dalindyebo to become King of the Thembu people, a favour King Jogintaba repaid by adopting the young Mandela when his father died in 1928. The King groomed the boy for high office and, the first of his family to attend school, he attended good ones on account of his royal connections – Wesleyan Mission School, Clarkebury Boarding Institute, where he completed his Junior Certificate in two years instead of the customary three, and Wesleyan College.

Now re-named 'Nelson' because one of his teachers had found the name 'Rolihlala' difficult to pronounce, he went to study at Fort Hare University, becoming friends with Oliver Tambo who would become a lifelong friend and colleague. Mandela lasted only one year at Fort Hare. He was thrown out after becoming involved in a student boycott against university policies.

On returning home, he was horrified to learn that King Jogintaba had arranged a marriage for him as well as for his own son, Justice. The boys fled to Johannesburg where Mandela worked in a number of jobs, including as a security guard at a mine before his friend Walter Sisulu found him a position as an articled clerk at a law firm. Meanwhile, he completed his degree through a correspondence course and enrolled to study law at the University of Witwatersrand while living in the township of Alexandria, north of Johannesburg. It was there that he met three students who would not only become central to his life but would also help to change South African history – Joe Slovo, Harry Schwarz and Ruth First. In 1943, he joined the Youth League of the African National Congress. The ANC had been founded in 1912 to fight for Africans' lands, rights and freedom but the group of young Africans in the Youth League wanted to turn it into a mass movement with the support of the millions of black South Africans who had been deprived of their rights. They also wanted to change the strategy of the ANC which had until that point been an ineffective one of petitioning. This change of tactics became even more necessary when the National Party, a predominantly Afrikaner party, won the 1948 election on a manifesto of apartheid and racial segregation.

A year later, the ANC adopted the Youth League's methods of protest – boycotts, strikes, civil disobedience and non-cooperation. Amongst their goals were full citizenship for black Africans the redistribution of land, the right to form trade unions and free education for all children. Mandela and Oliver Tambo now had their own law firm, Mandela and Tambo, which provided free, cheap legal advice to unrepresented blacks. He was also becoming more heavily involved in the ANC, being prominent in a 1952 Defiance Campaign and at the Congress of the People in 1955 during which the ANC adopted the Freedom Charter laying out its core goals. The Congress, attended by 3,000 people, was broken up by police on the second day and Mandela, his movements and relationships already constrained by banning orders, escaped by disguising himself as a milkman.

He was heavily influenced by the way Mahatma Gandhi had won independence for India with non-violent resistance – *satyagraha*. Gandhi had begun using it while living in South Africa and experiencing discrimination because he was Indian. But the authorities were starting to take notice of the ANC and, on 5 December 1956, 150 ANC members, including Mandela, were arrested and charged with treason. They were put on trial for five years until 1961, but all were eventually acquitted.

But by now a new breed of more militant African activist was emerging that considered the non-violent approach to be ineffective. They broke away to form the Pan Africanist Congress.

Soon, however, Nelson Mandela was also becoming convinced that non-violence was unproductive and gained the conviction that armed struggle was the only way forward. In 1961, he co-founded and led the armed wing of the ANC – *Umkhonto we Sizwe* ('Spear of the Nation'), or MK, as it was known. He now embarked upon a campaign of sabotage against military and government targets and prepared for a guerilla war, if all else failed. He led a bombing campaign, striking at symbolic targets such as government offices, post offices and magistrates' courts, but always stipulated that the bombs should go off in such a way that no one would get hurt.

By 1962, Mandela, who had been in hiding for seventeen months, was finally arrested for organising a three-day strike and for leaving the country illegally. The American intelligence agency, the CIA, had tipped off the South African authorities as to his whereabouts. He was sentenced to five years in prison.

Two years later, however, police rounded up prominent ANC leaders at a farm in Rivonia, north of Johannesburg. They, and Mandela, were charged with a number of crimes, amongst which were four acts of sabotage which Mandela admitted, treason and planning a foreign invasion of South Africa which he did not admit to – crimes for which they could be executed.

Mandela made an eloquent statement from the dock at Pretoria Supreme Court at the opening of the defence case. He explained the background to the ANC's use of violence, how the Sharpeville Massacre, in which sixty-nine black protestors – including eight women and ten children – were shot dead by police, had been the catalyst for their decision. He also blamed the referendum establishing the Republic of South Africa, the declaration of a state of emergency and the banning of the ANC for forcing them down that route. He ended the statement with the famous lines: 'During my lifetime I have dedicated myself to the struggle of the African people. I have fought against white domination, and I have fought against black domination. I have cherished the ideal of a democratic and free society in which all persons live together in harmony and with equal opportunities. It is an ideal which I hope to live for and to achieve. But if needs be, it is an ideal for which I am prepared to die.'

All but one of the defendants was found guilty and, fortunate to avoid the gallows, they were sentenced to life imprisonment.

He was sent to Robben Island prison which is situated on an island in Table Bay, seven kilometers off the South African coast. It had been used since the 17th century to isolate certain people and had become a maximum security establishment in 1959. Between 1961 and 1991, more that 3,000 men were incarcerated there. Prisoners were segregated by race and black prisoners received less food than others while political prisoners were kept segregated and received fewer privileges. Visits from family were restricted normally to once every six months, for only half an hour, the only reading material permitted was the Bible and prisoners were only allowed two letters a year, those often delayed for long periods. Barbaric practices such as breaking rocks were still in operation.

As ever, however, Mandela did not waste his time, studying for and gaining a law degree through a correspondence course provided by the University of London.

He became an internationally famous figure and a vigorous campaign had been launched to try to obtain his release. He was becoming such an embarrassment to the South African government that it was later disclosed that in 1969 a plot was concocted for him to escape so that he could be shot as he fled. It was thanks to British Intelligence that the plot was foiled.

In 1982, Mandela and some other ANC leaders were transferred to Pollsmoor Prison, ostensibly to stop them influencing the new generation of young, black activists arriving on Robben Island. The truth was, however, that they were moved so that they could be involved in secret discussions with a South African government that was beginning to buckle under the pressure of sanctions and world-wide revulsion. Three years later, in 1985, South African President PW Botha offered to release Mandela from prison if he agreed to renounce the armed struggle. Mandela flatly refused, issuing a statement through his daughter that said: 'What freedom am I being offered while the organisation of the people remains banned? Only free men can negotiate. A prisoner cannot enter into contracts.'

Serious discussions began in 1985 when government minister, Kobie Coetsee met Mandela in Volks Hospital in Cape Town where he was being treated for prostate surgery. For four years similar, tentative meetings were held, but they bore little fruit.

Meanwhile, international pressure was mounting on the South African government to release Mandela. Concerts and protest marches were staged all over the world and a song *Free Nelson Mandela!* became an international anthem for freedom.

FW de Klerk, a senior member of the National party, had placed himself at the head of the *verligte* (enlightened) faction within his party. When former president, PW Botha had a stroke in 1989, de Klerk replaced him, and in his first speech after being made president, he called for a non-racist South Africa and for negotiations on the future of the country. He lifted the ban on the ANC as well as other anti-apartheid organisations and announced the release of Nelson Mandela. Apartheid was over and black Africans were to be given equal voting rights.

So, Mandela walked through the gates of Victor Verster Prison in Paarl and went immediately to work, his first speech on his release being broadcast live around the world. In it he urged other countries not to lessen the pressure for constitutional reform that they had been putting on the government. He proclaimed his desire for peace and reconciliation with South Africa's white minority, but reiterated that the armed struggle would not be over until a proper settlement was reached: 'Our resort to the armed struggle in 1960 with the formation of the military wing of the ANC was a purely defensive action against the violence of apartheid. The factors which necessitated the armed struggle still exist today. We have no option but to continue. We express the hope that a climate conducive to a negotiated settlement would be created soon, so that there may no longer be the need for the armed struggle.' He emphasised that the black majority had to have the right to vote in national and local elections.

He was elected President of the African National Congress in 1991, his old friend, Oliver Tambo who had led the ANC from exile while Mandela had been in prison, becoming National Chairman. Negotiations were held with PW de Klerk, leading to South Africa's first multi-racial elections. Relations between Mandela and de Klerk were often strained and several times Mandela led the ANC out of the talks following atrocities which still occurred. Senior ANC leader Chris Hani, for instance, was assassinated in 1993.

Elections were finally held on 27 April 1994 and the ANC won sixty-two per cent of the vote. On an astonishing day, 10 May 1994, Nelson Mandela was inaugurated as the country's first black president.

In this position, unthinkable a few short years previously, Mandela really showed his quality as a great man as well as a great leader. His policy of national and international reconciliation ensured a smooth and peaceful transition from apartheid to democracy, avoiding the bloodbath that many had predicted. In recognition of their efforts, Mandela and de Klerk were awarded the Nobel Peace Prize in 1993.

In 1998, he married Graça Machel, widow of the late President of Mozambique, Samora Machel and the following year, Nelson Mandela's long life in politics ended when he finally retired, aged eighty-one.

JOHN F. KENNEDY

IT HAS BECOME commonplace to recall where you were when something momentous happened – when John Lennon was shot, the Twin Towers collapsed or Princess Diana met her end. However, the first of those moments probably occurred on 23 November 1963, when the 35th President of the United States, John Fitzgerald Kennedy was assassinated by Lee Harvey Oswald in Dallas. The event was made all the more shocking and memorable because his young wife Jackie was seated next to him in the car when he was shot, his blood soaking into her pink Chanel suit.

They had arrived in the White House full of promise, as if a new generation had picked up the reins. He was the second-youngest person ever to become president, at forty-two – Teddy Roosevelt had been forty-one – and as if to emphasise their youth and the bright future they seemed to embody, they had two young children to run around the corridors of the White House, the first for many years.

John Kennedy had enjoyed a privileged upbringing in one of America's top families. Born in Brookline, Massachusetts in 1917, his two grandfathers had been important Boston politicians and his father was a successful and very wealthy businessman who was a leading light in the Democratic Party and in the American-Irish community. President Roosevelt appointed him as first Chairman of the Securities and Exchange Commission and, at the outbreak of the Second World War, was United States Ambassador to the United Kingdom.

Kennedy graduated from Harvard University and his thesis was published as the book, *Why England Slept*, a discourse on Britain's failure to prevent the Second World War. In spring, 1941, with war looming, he volunteered for the US Army but was rejected because he suffered from a bad back. His influential father pulled some strings, however, and he was accepted by the Navy. When America entered the war, following the Japanese raid on Pearl Harbour, he was assigned for duty in Panama and then sent to the Pacific, given command of a patrol torpedo boat, a small, fast-moving and highly manoeuverable vessel that was used by the Navy to attack large enemy ships.

On 2 August 1943, while Kennedy's boat, *PT-109,* was participating in a night patrol near New Georgia in the Solomon Islands, it was rammed by the Japanese destroyer, *Amagiri.* Kennedy's already troublesome back was further damaged when he was tossed across the boat's deck by the impact. Nonetheless, he still managed to swim, struggling for five hours, while towing a badly-injured member of his crew to an island, later swimming to another island from where he and his men were rescued. He was awarded the Navy and Marine Corps Medal for what his citation described as 'extremely heroic conduct' and would be further decorated for other courageous actions, including the award of the Purple Heart.

By December 1943, his back was too badly injured for him to continue and he was sent home to the United States where he was promoted to lieutenant and became a PT instructor in Florida. He was discharged in 1945, after an operation on his back.

Kennedy worked as a journalist for the next twelve months, writing about a number of events including the 1945 General Election in Britain and the United Nations Conference that was held in San Francisco.

He first entered politics in 1946 when he won a seat in the US House of Representatives and he displayed support for President Truman over the next few years, following the Democratic Party line, championing low-cost housing, progressive taxation and social welfare. In 1951 he toured the world on behalf of the Senate

Committee on Foreign Affairs. In Europe, he visited half a dozen countries, reporting back that the United States should persevere with its policy of helping in the defence of Western Europe but suggesting that, perhaps, European nations could make more of a contribution. He also travelled to the Middle East, Asia and the Far East. He maintained a dislike for colonial empires, arguing that France should get out of Algeria, something that took the French more than a decade to realise was a good idea.

In 1952, he was elected to the Senate and the following year he married Jacqueline Bouvier, daughter of a rich Wall Street stockbroker. The couple, who had moved in the same social circles and met at a dinner party, would have four children, only two of whom would survive.

Meanwhile, Kennedy continued to suffer from back problems and underwent several operations, none of which alleviated his problem. While recovering, however, he turned his hand once more to writing and his book, *Profiles in Courage*, describing acts of bravery and integrity by eight United States Senators taken from throughout Senate history, became his second bestseller, winning the prestigious Pulitzer Prize.

Kennedy's father had spent a great deal of money on making his son one of the best-known Senators in the United States and it paid off in 1960 when he entered the race for the Democratic nomination for that year's Presidential race, winning enough primaries to be nominated on the first ballot at the Democratic Party Convention. He selected Lyndon B. Johnson, a Senator from Texas, as his Vice Presidential running mate. It was a controversial nomination and, if elected, John Kennedy would be the first Roman Catholic ever to become President.

His opponent, Richard Nixon had been President Eisenhower's Vice President for eight years and had vast experience compared to the young Senator from Massachusetts but Kennedy won, albeit in a tight race.

His inauguration on 20 January 1961 was notable for Kennedy's customarily brilliant oratory. He threw out a challenge to the United States which resonates to this day: 'Ask not what your country can do for you, but rather what you can do for your country.' In that famous inauguration speech, he also announced the formation of the Peace Corps, a scheme whereby he hoped to send 10,000 young American volunteers to provide aid in Asia, Africa and Latin America. It seemed a bold and imaginative gesture from a bold and imaginative President.

His very first speech to the American people dealt head-on with the issue that would dog American foreign policy for more than a decade – Vietnam. Kennedy told the people that he would be persevering with the previous president's support for the South Vietnamese against the threat from the Communist North Vietnam. He argued that if South Vietnam were to fall then the region would experience a 'domino effect', nations falling one by one to communism, until the entire world would be under threat. 'No other challenge is more deserving of our effort and energy ...' he said. 'Our security may be lost piece by piece, country by country.' He went on to say that under his leadership, 'America would be willing to pay any price, bear any burden, meet any hardship, support any friend, oppose any foe to assure the survival and success of liberty.'

The other major, and more pressing issue of Kennedy's presidency was Cuba. Under President Eisenhower, a plan had been devised to invade the island that had fallen to Fidel Castro's Communist revolution a few years previously. Although Kennedy had some doubts as to the plan's efficacy, he felt he could not reject it for fear of being seen as soft on communism. He was advised that the invasion would encourage the Cuban people to rise up against Castro and provide support for US invasion forces.

On 14 April 1961, B-26s began to bomb Cuban airfields, destroying the Cuban Air Force. Two days later, 1400 Cuban exiles, trained by the CIA, were landed from five merchant ships in an area known as the Bay of Pigs. Disaster followed as two of the American ships were sunk, two planes were shot down and within seventy-two hours all of the invading troops had been killed, wounded or had surrendered. It was a humiliating embarrassment for Kennedy and his brand-new administration. CIA Director, Allen Dulles and the CIA man who had planned the whole operation, Richard M. Bissell Dr, were forced to resign, although Kennedy said at the time, that if they were operating in a parliamentary democracy it would have been his head on the chopping block.

In September 1962, U-2 spy planes brought back disturbing news for Kennedy. Aerial photos clearly showed that the Soviet Union was building surface-to-air missile (SAM) launch sites on Cuban soil. At the same time, an increase in the number of Soviet ships sailing into Cuban harbours was of concern. Kennedy worried that they were being used to supply the Cubans with Soviet-made weapons.

Kennedy complained to the Soviet premier, Nikita Khruschev, warning him that the United States would not accept offensive missiles on Cuban soil – SAMs were considered to be defensive. However, there was now a danger to American spy planes and Kennedy could not afford to look weak in such a situation. Congressional elections were on the horizon and he needed all the help he could get in Congress to push his policies through. Worse still, opinion polls showed his ratings to have plummeted to their lowest since he had taken office. Naturally, his Republican opponents began to push Cuba up the agenda.

In order to lessen the chances of a plane being shot down, he made a decision to cut the number of U-2 flights over Cuba and pilots were ordered not to fly the whole length of the island. On 15 October, however, he was given the news he had been dreading. The Soviets were installing long-range offensive missiles at San Cristobal.

Kennedy called an emergency meeting of the Executive Committee of the National Security Council where an air attack on the sites was discussed. He decided to wait, however, and at another meeting that night it was decided that such an attack would in all likelihood lead to all-out nuclear war. For the next two days they argued about the most effective course of action until gradually the meeting began to favour a naval blockade to prevent the Soviet ships from landing their cargo.

Nonetheless, Kennedy also instructed the Air Force to make ready for an attack on bases on Cuba while 125,000 troops were assembled in Florida. If the Soviet ships failed to turn back when faced with the US blockade, there would be no option but to launch the attack.

For a short while, as the world held its breath, war seemed inevitable. Angry demonstrations against nuclear war were staged outside the US Embassy in London and people demonstrated in other European capitals.

On 24 October President Kennedy was given the news that the ships had stopped short of the United States vessels maintaining the blockade. Khruschev was incandescent with rage, accusing Kennedy of stage-managing the whole affair in order to win the Congressional elections. It worked – he won twelve extra seats in Congress.

It was not quite over yet, however. Khruschev wrote again to Kennedy telling him he would not remove his missiles until Kennedy had promised to evacuate US nuclear bases in Turkey. When a US spy plane was shot down over Cuba as they discussed how to respond to the Russian premier, American military leaders and the CIA were quick to remind Kennedy of his promise that if a plane were to be shot down, he would launch an airstrike. Kennedy refused and, instead, sent Khruschev a letter accepting his terms. The first and only nuclear crisis between the world's two superpowers was ended and Kennedy's coolly rational handling of the Soviet leader contributed a great deal to ensuring the safety of the world.

Vietnam, of course, would continue to be a thorn in America's side long after President Kennedy's death and he contributed to its escalation when he became convinced that it was necessary to send more military advisers to the country. By the end of 1962, there were more than 12,000 there. He also sent 300 helicopters whose pilots had orders not to become engaged in combat, an order that would prove impossible to carry out in the volatile situation they found themselves in. Some said after he died that he was becoming seriously concerned about the way the conflict was escalating and that if he had won election for a second term he would have withdrawn US troops from Vietnam.

On 22 November, President Kennedy arrived for a visit to Dallas where he intended to do some fund-raising for his next election campaign. At around 12.30 pm as the cavalcade of cars in which he and other dignitaries were travelling entered Elm Street, in the city's business district, shots rang out. John F. Kennedy was hit in the left shoulder and the head. His car rushed him to Parklands Memorial Hospital, but at 1 pm, he was declared dead.

Within a couple of hours, a suspect, Lee Harvey Oswald was arrested and then he, in turn was shot dead two days later by night-club owner, Jack Ruby, as he was being transported from the city to the county jail. Speculation about the reasons behind the assassination of President John F. Kennedy continues even now, almost fifty years later.

MARGARET THATCHER

MARGARET THATCHER WAS one of the world's most charismatic, influential and respected world leaders of her time, a time that saw the spread of democracy, the end of the Cold War and the fall of Communism. The mere mention of her name in Britain even now, some eighteen years after her resignation, however, still stirs up a vigorous debate. Some consider her economic policies to have been socially divisive, that her politics were uncaring and that she displayed a singular lack of care for the welfare state. Her supporters would point to the economic performance of the country during her government and list trade union reform, privatisation, deregulation and control of inflation, tax and spending as her great successes.

What supporters and critics have in common, however, is a belief that the premiership of Margaret Thatcher was a fundamentally important time for Britain. She re-shaped British politics from top to bottom, changing not only her party, but also the Labour Party; its New Labour approach under the leadership of Tony Blair would have been unthinkable without Margaret Thatcher's time in office. She challenged the atmosphere of decline and failure that had become rooted in Britain since the Second World War, throwing her remarkable energy and determination behind a national recovery both at home and in the international arena where she became Britain's best-known politician since Winston Churchill.

Interestingly, a poll conducted by the *Daily Telegraph* newspaper asked who Britons considered the best prime minister since World War II. Thatcher came first with thirty-four per cent of the vote, beating Winston Churchill into second place with a mere fifteen per cent.

Margaret Hilda Roberts was born in the east coast town of Grantham in 1925. Her father, Alfred, owned a grocer's shop and he and his wife, Beatrice, were Methodists who lived over the shop with their two daughters.

In 1943, Margaret won a place at Oxford University where she studied chemistry at Somerville College. She had as a tutor Dorothy Hodgkin, the Nobel Prize-winning pioneer of X-ray crystallography.

At Oxford, however, she became immersed in Conservative politics. Her father had been a Conservative councilor in Grantham and the political issues of the day were never far from their conversations. She was elected president of the Oxford University Conservative Association, a position that brought her to the attention of the leadership of the Tory party which had just been badly beaten by Labour in the 1945 General Election.

She graduated from Oxford in 1950, having gained a BSc degree and a postgraduate degree and began working in Colchester as a research chemist. In January 1949, a friend who worked for the Dartford Conservative Association informed her that they were on the lookout for candidates for election. She put herself forward and was selected. She found a job developing ways to preserve ice cream and moved to Dartford.

It was a largely working class constituency and a strong Labour seat and, inevitably, she lost, both in 1950 and 1951, but gained a great deal of publicity as the youngest woman candidate, at twenty-five years of age, in the election. She also learned a great deal from her experience in Dartford and did succeed in reducing the Labour majority.

It was also in Dartford that she met her future husband, Dennis Thatcher, a divorcee who ran the family business but would later become an executive in the oil industry. They married in 1951 and in 1953 they had twins, Mark and Carol.

Meanwhile, Dennis was funding law studies for her and in the same year as the birth of her children she became a barrister, specialising in taxation.

She continued to look for a safe Tory seat, narrowly losing in a by-election at Orpington in 1955. Finally, in the 1959 General Election, she won Finchley for the Conservatives and she would represent that constituency until 1992. Her maiden speech was in support of a Private Member's Bill she introduced that required local councils to hold their meetings in public. In 1961, she voted against her own party in support of the restoration of the birch.

In 1961, she was appointed to her first junior office in Prime Minister Harold Macmillan's government, as Parliamentary Under-secretary at the Ministry of Pensions and National Insurance, a position she retained until the Conservatives lost the election of 1964.

In the 1965 vote for the new Conservative leader, following the resignation of Sir Alec Douglas-Home, Thatcher voted for the eventual winner, Edward Heath. She became Conservative spokesperson on Housing and Land, first mooting the policy of allowing council house tenants to buy their council houses. In 1966, she moved to the Shadow Treasury team, strongly opposing the Labour government's price and income controls. She was now being viewed as a senior member of the party and when the Conservatives returned to government in 1970, with Edward Heath as Prime Minister, she joined the Cabinet as Secretary of State for Education and Science.

It was not a good time to be Education Secretary. Student radicalism was rife and her speeches were often disrupted by hecklers. Heath had decided to cut public spending and, although she maintained spending on academic needs, she was forced to carry through unpopular policies such as the abolition of free milk for schoolchildren between the ages of seven and eleven. She was vilified in the press and was given the unfortunate epithet 'Thatcher, Thatcher, Milk Snatcher'. As she later wrote, she had succeeded in obtaining the maximum amount of unpopularity for very little political benefit.

Importantly, she fought, during her term of office, to retain as many grammar schools as possible, abandoning the commitment of the previous government to the introduction of comprehensive education.

By the time the Heath government was thrown out by a disaffected electorate in 1974, Britain was in a mire of inflation and industrial strife. Conservatives were ready for change and Margaret Thatcher put herself forward in a leadership run-off with Heath. She defeated him on the first ballot and then, when Heath resigned, won an outright victory over half-a-dozen senior Tories in the second, becoming the first woman ever to lead a western political party and the first female leader of Her Majesty's Opposition in the House of Commons. Edward Heath would never forgive her for what he considered her disloyalty in standing against him.

She appointed many of Heath's supporters to her Shadow Cabinet and then worked carefully to convert the Conservative Party to her monetarist beliefs. Her reputation was growing, however, and following a speech about the threat posed by the Soviet Union, the Soviet Defence Ministry newspaper Krasnaya Zvezda (Red Star) dubbed her the 'Iron Lady'. Her critics, however, gave her a less favourable nickname – 'Attila the Hen'.

The winter of 1978-79 became known as the 'Winter of Discontent' following an extraordinary number of strikes and industrial disputes. Even the Labour government's allies seemed to be deserting it. It was no surprise, therefore, that the Conservatives won a majority of 43 in the 1979 General Election. Margaret Thatcher became the first woman Prime Minister of the United Kingdom.

Her main task was to reverse the economic decline that had gathered momentum in Britain since the war. Although direct taxation was reduced, indirect taxes were increased. Interest rates were increased to fight inflation and halt the recession that was fast approaching. Britain's manufacturing base began to suffer, many companies going out of business, and unemployment stood at a staggering three million. It would take her until 1986 to make any impact upon that figure.

In the early 1980s, the economy began to rally and there was room for optimism. It would be a totally unexpected event that would ensure her government's re-election in 1983, however. Argentina invaded the British-ruled Falkland Islands in the South Atlantic in April 1982, in pursuit of a claim to the islands that had been smoldering since 1810. Margaret Thatcher had her war – the Falklands War.

A British military taskforce sent to the islands swiftly defeated the Argentinians and re-took the islands by June, although with considerable loss of life on both sides. The British public, awash with patriotic enthusiasm, was ecstatic and the way was now open for Thatcher to operate a more independent foreign policy. More importantly, she increased her majority in the General Election to 144 seats.

The immediate challenge she faced in her second term was the Miners' strike of 1984–85, the longest and most violent industrial action in British history.

She had committed her government to reducing the power of the trade unions and had largely succeeded. In 1984, the militant Miners' Union ordered a strike, without a national ballot, in protest at proposals to close a large number of mines with the loss of thousands of jobs. Characteristically, she refused to budge in the face of their demands, famously saying at one point, 'We had to fight the enemy without in the Falklands. We always have to be aware of the enemy within, which is much more difficult to fight and more dangerous to liberty.'

Violence on the picket lines became an everyday item on the television news and controversial police tactics were heavily criticised. After a year, however, the union's leadership surrendered without achieving a deal of any kind. All but fifteen of the country's coal mines were shut down and they were eventually sold off in 1994.

In the middle of the strike, in October 1984, the Irish Republican Army horrifically tried to assassinate Thatcher and her Cabinet when they exploded a bomb in the Grand Hotel in Brighton where she and other Conservatives were staying during their party conference. She survived, although five people were killed. Indomitable as ever, she insisted that the conference began on time that day and delivered a defiant speech that won approval from politicians of all persuasions.

The government now controversially launched a policy of selling state assets – the utilities and the railways, for instance – an initiative that spread across the world to other countries. Shares were offered to the general public and many more people began to save through share ownership. She revived her thinking about the sale of council houses and many became home-owners. People were also encouraged to take out private pension policies.

She was not without crises within her own party. The Westland Affair of January 1986 and the subsequent resignation of Defense Minister, Michael Heseltine, tested her leadership as never before when she was heavily criticised by the left wing of the Conservative party. She then faced criticism for allowing US warplanes to take off on an attack on Libya from British bases.

She responded by winning a third term in office in the 1987 General Election and introducing an ambitious and contentious programme. She put forward measures to introduce a national curriculum to British schools and to introduce an element of competition into the National Health Service for the first time. Controversially, she proposed a new local tax system – the Community Charge, popularly known as the 'poll tax'. What she had not expected was that councils would seize the opportunity to increase taxes and blame it on central government. It was the most unpopular policy she ever championed and as she refused, as ever, to compromise, riots broke out across the country, the most serious in Trafalgar Square in March 1990 when 100,000 people protested and 400 were arrested. Her popularity began to wane.

There were economic problems, too. Interest rates doubled in 1988 and many lost their homes. The Tories attitude towards Europe damaged her standing, too, as she pushed the party increasingly in a Euro-sceptic direction. She was dangerously at odds with her Foreign Secretary, Sir Geoffrey Howe over the European question.

Meanwhile, her standing abroad rose ever higher. She formed a double-act with US President Ronald Reagan, strengthening the Western Alliance and standing up to the Soviets. Then, when Mikhail Gorbachev looked like he was becoming the Soviet leader, she invited him to Britain for talks, pronouncing famously that he was a man she could do business with. She played a major diplomatic part in ensuring that the break-up of the Soviet Empire proceeded smoothly in 1989–91.

The first sign that things were beginning to unravel occurred in November 1990 when Sir Geoffrey Howe resigned from the government, delivering a bitter and hostile resignation speech in the Commons. The divisions in the government over Europe became clear for all to see. Michael Heseltine launched a leadership challenge but although she won a majority of the vote, it was not enough to give her outright victory. Being informed of the result while attending a conference in Paris, she announced her determination to fight on.

At Cabinet next day, however, it became clear that her colleagues, believing that she could not win a fourth general Election, were deserting her. She resigned as Prime Minister on 28 November and was succeeded by John Major.

OSAMA BIN LADEN

BORN IN MARCH 1957, Osama bin Laden, the man behind the 9/11 terrorist outrages in the United States that claimed 2,974 lives, enjoyed a privileged upbringing in Riyadh in Saudi Arabia. His father, Muhammed bin Laden, Hamida al-Attas, a wealthy businessman, was a favourite of the Saudi royal family and Osama's mother was his tenth wife. He was brought up in the Sunni Muslim faith and attended a school for the scions of wealthy Saudi families, the secular Al-Thager school.

At Abdulaziz University, he studied civil engineering, although there are doubts as to what degree he obtained while there, if, indeed, he actually got one. Degree or not, university was a defining time in his life as he became interested in religion while there, interpreting the Qur'an and doing charity work. He also wrote poetry during his time there.

It was during this time, too, that he developed his belief in Sharia Law, the legal system based on Islamic principles of jurisprudence that deals with just about every aspect of daily life. Bin Laden rejected all other ideologies – political and social – as futile. He began to believe that 'Jihad' – holy war – was the only way to achieve his goals and lined up his enemies – the United States, Israel and the West in general – as enemies of Islam. He has berated Americans for their way of life, calling on them to 'reject the immoral acts of fornication, homosexuality, intoxicants, gambling, and usury' and demanded an end to American involvement in the Middle East.

He married for the first time, aged seventeen, and is said to have had four wives by the time he was forty-five, fathering anything between twelve and twenty-six children by these women, according to reports.

Aged twenty-two, he left university and immediately began to put his beliefs into practice, travelling to Afghanistan to fight the invading Russians on the side of the Mujahadeen, led by Abdullah Azzam. In Peshawar, on the Pakistani side of the Afghan border, he formed an organisation, Maktab al-Khadamat, that raised funds for the fighting of 'immoral acts of fornication, homosexuality, intoxicants, gambling, and usury'. He recruited many different nationalities to his cause, Egyptians, Turks, Lebanese and others amongst them. Ironically, given his later activities, he was given a great deal of support from the American government, keen to see the Soviet Union's ambitions in Afghanistan thwarted. He also used his own vast wealth to fund his operation.

By 1988, bin Laden was determined to branch out on his own and actually fight rather than merely provide the infrastructure for the Mujahadeen. He was encouraged in this by Ayman al-Zawahiri, the man who would become his co-conspirator in al-Qaeda in later years. He formed his own army of volunteers and led them in battle against the Soviets.

When the Russians were finally defeated, bin Laden's reputation was assured and he returned to Saudi Arabia a hero of the Afghan War. Thus, when Saddam Hussein's forces invaded Kuwait in 1990, he offered his services to the Saudi ruler, offering to defend his country against the Iraqi threat. He was seriously disappointed, however, when his offer was rejected and berated the Saudi ruling family for their dependence on the United States to protect them. Unpopular at home, he was forced to relocate to Sudan in 1992. Once again, however, his rigid anti-Americanism and criticism of the government created problems for him when the Saudis withdrew his passport and revoked his Saudi citizenship. Worse still, his allowance of around $7 million a year, the money he used to fund his operations, was stopped by his family.

At this time, bin Laden felt far from safe in Sudan and probably with just cause. The Sudanese wanted him out of their country and it is said that they offered to deport him to the United States, reports that have never been substantiated. He also survived an assassination attempt. The only place safe enough for him was Afghanistan where he was welcomed by the leader of the Taliban, Mullah Mohammed Omar. He turned to the sources that had helped him fund Maktab al-Khadamat and began to re-build his organisation. It was 1992 and he decided it was time to spread Jihad across the world using al-Qaeda, a loose network of terrorist cells.

His philosophy controversially justified the killing of innocent people, making no exception for women and children. A fatwa issued solely to members of al-Qaeda by Mamdouh Mahmud Salim stipulated that the killing of a person standing close to an enemy target is justified because the innocent person would enter paradise if they were good Muslims.

His first attack was on a hotel in Aden. On 29 December, his operatives exploded a bomb in the Gold Mihor Hotel, killing two people. He also became involved in struggles in Algeria, Egypt and continued fighting in Afghanistan. Algerian militants were funded by him and encouraged to use violence instead of negotiation to achieve their goals. More than 200,000 Algerians would die in the subsequent war.

He fought with the Taliban against the Northern Alliance in Afghanistan and his men were involved in the horrific massacre of around 6,000 inhabitants of the city of Mazar-e-Sharif.

His next outrage occurred in 1997 when sixty-two tourists were massacred by gunmen at Luxor in Egypt. Instead of encouraging Jihad, however, the callous disregard for innocent lives disgusted Egyptians and turned them against Islamic extremism.

His future course was set in 1998 when he and al-Zawahiri issued a manifesto of terror, a fatwa in the name of the World Islamic Front for Jihad Against Jews and Crusaders. In this statement, he proclaimed that it was the individual duty of every Muslim to kill North Americans and their allies. He demanded the liberation of the al-Aqsa Mosque in Jerusalem and the holy mosque in Mecca. Chillingly, he announced to journalists that North Americans are 'very easy targets . . . You will see the results of this in a very short time.'

He was soon putting his thoughts into practice. Bombings were carried out on American embassies and US president Bill Clinton immediately froze assets that could be linked to bin Laden. He also signed an executive order authorising his arrest or assassination.

Osama bin Laden's responded with a plan to perpetrate the biggest terrorist attack of them all, the horrific 2001 attack on the Twin Towers of the World Trade Center and America's military stronghold, the Pentagon.

The nature of al-Qaeda makes it difficult to place responsibility for attacks at the feet of anyone, but it is clear that bin Laden knew about the projected attack on America in advance. He initially denied any knowledge a few days after 9/11 but has, on several occasions since them, claimed responsibility. US forces found a tape in November 2001 in which he discusses the attacks before they happened with Khaleb al-Haribi, a wheelchair-bound al-Qaeda associate. Doubts have been expressed, however, about the translation of the tape and it has been claimed that it does not actually prove his guilt.

Since then, however, he has reaffirmed his responsibility. Just four days before the 2004 presidential election he released a video – his preferred method of communicating to the world – in which he says that he had personally directed the hijackers of the four planes. He claimed to have been inspired by Israel's destruction of towers in Lebanon in 1982.

Further tapes provided still more confirmation of his involvement. He is pictured with some of the hijackers and says, 'I am the one in charge of the nineteen brothers...I was responsible for entrusting the nineteen brothers . . . with the raids.'

Bin Laden is sought by many countries, although he has become an enigmatic figure in recent years and it is not known whether he is even still alive. The Libyans issued a warrant for his arrest in 1998 following the killing by al-Qaeda of two German citizens there in 1994. The Americans wanted him long before 9/11 for al-Qaeda's bombing of a US-run Saudi Arabian National Guard training centre in Riyadh that killed five Americans and two Indians. They accused him in an indictment of 'conspiracy to attack defense utilities of the United States', and of funding terrorist activity around the world through al-Qaeda. A grand jury in the United States indicted him in November 1998 for the murder of US nationals outside the United States and, following his organisation's attacks on US embassies in Kenya and Tanzania, for attacks on a federal facility resulting in death.

The Americans had been trying to have him extradited for years before 9/11 to face these charges. President Clinton obtained United Nations sanctions against Afghanistan in order to persuade the Taliban to deport bin Laden, but his efforts proved futile. President George W. Bush placed him at number one on a new Most Wanted list – Most Wanted Terrorists. He is the only man to appear on both that list and the FBI's Most Wanted list.

Eventually, American bombing of targets in Afghanistan per-suaded the Taliban that bin Laden was becoming too hot to handle. They offered to hand him over to face justice in a third-party nation in return for an end to the bombing and cast-iron evidence of his involvement in 9/11. President Bush rejected the offer out of hand, saying, 'We know he's guilty.'

As US forces swept through Afghanistan, they had one major objective – to locate Osama bin Laden. They came close to capturing him in late 2001 during the Battle of Tora Bora. Bin Laden was attending a meeting of al-Qaeda operatives in a cave complex along the eastern border between Afghanistan and Pakistan. US forces in the area were informed of his whereabouts, but by the time they arrived, he was long gone.

Since then there have been sporadic reports and the release occasionally of a tape or a video. In recent years, however, he has been silent, leading many to speculate that he is in fact dead. In April 2005 it was reported in an Australian newspaper that he had died of organ failure while the French Secret Service have reported his death of typhoid the same year in Pakistan. Saudi intelligence services also believe he is dead. The response of the US government is, however, 'No knowledge and no comment' and the hunt goes on.

In the unlikely event that Osama bin Laden is ever found, his finders would become very rich. The reward offered for his location is the biggest in history. Originally $25 million, it has now risen to $50 million and to that can be added a further $2 million from the American Airline Pilots Association and the US Air Transport Association, both of whom, of course, were seriously affected by the attacks on the Twin Towers and the Pentagon.

Under a whole range of aliases and nicknames – the Prince, the Sheikh, Al-Amir, Abu Abdallah, Sheikh Al-Mujahid, the Lion Sheik, the Director, Imam Mehdi and Samaritan – he is the most wanted man in the world and probably the most wanted in history. He has used his incredible leadership and organisational skills to turn terrorism into an international phenomenon, a loosely organised network ready to strike anywhere, at any time, that fills people across the world with fear.

BARACK OBAMA

IT IS DOUBTFUL if anyone has changed the world just by being elected. However, when Barack Hussein Obama swore his oath on the west steps of the Capitol building in Washington DC, it did, indeed, seem as if that was what he had done. The world felt entirely different after that moment, but it probably felt that way not just because a new administration had arrived, but also because an old and unloved one had departed the stage. George W. Bush had become one of the most unpopular presidents not only in his own country but also around the world and, the US presidency wielding so much power in the world in every area, whether, economic, political or military, Obama's arrival made it all feel fresher and, dare we hope, safer.

Of course, Obama had campaigned on the idea of change and that was exactly what everyone hoped he would bring. If by change he meant a different type of person occupying the White House, then he had certainly achieved that, compared to recent presidents. Of course, to begin with, he was black, the first black president, elected to the tears of old civil rights workers such as Jesse Jackson who was at Martin Luther King's side when he was shot and who now must have looked on, almost in disbelief as a black man swore the Oath of Office. But Barack Obama was also different by upbringing, born to a man from Nyanza Province in Kenya and a white woman, Ann Durham who grew up in Wichita in Kansas.

It all began in 1959 when twenty-three-year-old Barack Obama Sr, who had grown up herding goats, while his father worked as a domestic servant for the British, won a scholarship to the University of Hawaii. He left behind his first wife, Kezia who was pregnant at the time and their son Roy would be born in 1958.

In February 1961, he married Ann Dunham whose father had worked on oil rigs during the Depression and had fought for Patton in Europe during the Second World War. He and his wife had moved to Hawaii after the war. Ann became pregnant with the future president and left the University of Hawaii to look after her baby who was born on 4 August 1961, while her husband graduated and went to Harvard to further his studies in economics. In July 1964, she obtained an uncontested divorce from Obama Sr.

Obama Sr returned to Kenya where he became a senior economist in the Ministry of Finance. He later lived in poverty, turned to drink and died in a car crash in 1982 at the age of forty-six. President Obama met him only once, when he was ten years old.

Ann Durham returned to the University of Hawaii to complete her interrupted degree and remarried in 1965. Her new husband and the infant Barack's new stepfather was Lolo Soetoro, a fellow student from Indonesia. In 1967, the new president of Indonesia, Suharto, recalled all of his country's students living and studying abroad. Lolo took his young family home with him to Jakarta and there Barack's half-sister Soetoro-Ng, was born.

By this time known as 'Barry', Obama would spend four years in Indonesia, attending a good school there that was paid for by Ann's parents. His mother worked hard at her son's education during this period, enrolling him in English correspondence courses and playing him speeches by Martin Luther King Dr At the age of ten, however, she made the painful decision to send Barry back to Hawaii to be looked after by her grandparents, Madelyn and Stanley Durham. A year later, his mother, too, returned home, remaining there until 1977 when she returned to Indonesia to work as an anthropological field worker but she did not live with her former husband when she returned.

In 1979, Barack Obama enrolled at Occidental College in Los Angeles and from there went to Columbia University in New York where he studied political science, emerging with a BA in 1983.

During his time in New York, he worked for the Business International Corporation, followed by a stint at the New York Public Interest Research Group.

Aged twenty-four, he next moved to Chicago where he found work as Director of a Developing Communities Project on the city's South Side, remaining in that role for three years and growing its staff from one to thirteen and its budget from $70,000 to $400,000. He set up various programmes as well as a tenants' rights initiative.

In 1988, he made his first visit to Europe, followed by five weeks in Kenya when he met many of his extended family for the first time.

Returning to the United States, he enrolled at Harvard University and by the end of his first year there had become editor of the Harvard Law Review, gaining national media attention as the magazine's first black editor. His sudden fame led to a publishing contract for a book about race relations. *Dreams of My Father* would be published in 1995 and when he became president, would become an international bestseller. Meanwhile, he spent his summers working for law firms in Chicago. He graduated *magna cum laudae* in 1991 and went back to Chicago.

He spent April to October 1992 running Illinois's voter registration drive, Project Vote, succeeding in registering more than a third of the state's 400,000 unregistered African Americans. His success made many begin to take notice of him and he was named in a 1993 poll entitled '40 Under Forty' – the forty people under the age of forty most likely to succeed.

He taught law at the University of Chicago Law School for the next ten years, also working during that time for a law firm that specialised in civil rights cases and neighbourhood economic development.

In 1996, Obama was elected to the Illinois Senate as the Democratic Senator for the state's 13th District, enjoying considerable success in legislation that reformed ethics and health care laws. He persuaded the Senate to increase tax credits for the low-paid and worked on welfare and child-related issues. He was re-elected in 1998 and in 2002. That year, however, he was well beaten in an attempt at election to the United States House of Representatives.

In 2004, however, he was elected to the US Senate, having won a landslide in the Democratic primary election – he won fifty-three per cent of the vote while his nearest rival polled twenty-nine per cent behind him. In the general election, he defeated the Republican candidate by seventy per cent to twenty-seven per cent, the greatest winning margin for a statewide election in Illinois's history. Suddenly the Democrats began to look at Barack Obama slightly differently, perhaps even as a presidential hope.

The speech he delivered at the 2004 Democratic Party National Convention that endorsed John Kerry as the Democratic candidate for that year's election, was sensational and propelled him up the ranks of presidential hopefuls should Senator Kerry fail in his bid to oust George W. Bush from the White House. He dealt with the subjects that would ultimately win him the presidency – the withdrawal from Iraq, the partisan quality of American politics – 'There is not a liberal America and a conservative America; there's the United States of America,' he said to massive acclaim.

He was sworn in as a Senator on 4 January 2005, the fifth African American Senator in the history of the institution and only the third to have been elected.

On 10 February 2007 Obama announced his candidacy for President of the United States symbolically in front of the Old State Capitol Building in Springfield, Illinois, the site of President Abraham Lincoln's famous 'House Divided' speech in 1858.

As ever, there were numerous candidates for the Democratic nomination but there was always really only one real rival to Obama and that was the Senator from New York and wife of a former president, Hilary Clinton. It was a tight race throughout the primaries and a decision to give space at the convention to the delegates from Michigan and Florida whose primaries had been disputed, reduced Obama's delegate lead as the convention loomed. In early June, however, Clinton suspended her campaign, and conceded victory in the Democratic race to Obama. At the convention, Obama was acclaimed and named Senator Joe Biden as his vice-presidential running mate. His acceptance speech was watched by millions of people worldwide.

Obama's campaigns both for the nomination and for the presidency itself set phenomenal fund-raising records. There were numerous small donations and it seemed that people wanted him to win to such an extent that they were sending what they could to help him, even if it was only a few dollars. Furthermore, he was the first major presidential candidate to turn down public funding since the system had been reformed more than thirty years previously.

In Presidential elections the televised debates can make or break a candidate and Obama with his skilful oratory and ability to extemporise with confidence and ease was considered to have come out on top on each occasion.

In November 2008, Barack Obama won the United States Presidential Election by 365 electoral votes to 173; he won 52.9 per cent of the popular vote compared to John McCain's 45.7 per cent.

That night, in Chicago's Grant Park, with his wife, Michelle, and two young daughters – Malia and Natasha – by his side, Barack Obama delivered an eloquent and emotional speech to tens of thousands of supporters plus a global audience of hundreds of millions. His only sadness was that his grandmother, Madelyn Dunham had died just two days before he was elected President.

In his first few weeks in office Obama moved swiftly. The world was in economic turmoil, following the credit crunch and the events of autumn 2008 when the world's banking system almost collapsed. The economy was his top priority as he adjusted the pens on his desk in the Oval Office. He busied himself on other matters, too. In his first few days, he overturned President Bush's ban on federal funding to foreign institutions that allow abortions; he improved procedures promoting disclosure under the Freedom of Information Act; he ordered military chiefs to develop plans to withdraw troops from Iraq and issued orders that the Guantanamo Bay detention camp should be closed by January 2010 at the latest. Then, on 17 February, a month after taking office, he signed into law a $787 billion economic stimulus package. The new president was not letting the grass grow under his feet.

It is still very early days for the presidency of Barack Obama, but many things have already changed, not least America's view of the outside world, something that is important to everyone. When he used 'Change we can believe in' as his campaign slogan, it seems as if he just might have meant it.